CW01236865

The Theology of John Smyth
Puritan, Separatist, Baptist, Mennonite

The Theology of John Smyth
Puritan, Separatist, Baptist, Mennonite

by
Jason K. Lee

Mercer University Press
Macon, Georgia USA
2003

ISBN 0-86554-760-2   MUP/H572

The Theology of John Smyth.
Puritan, Separatist, Baptist, Mennonite.
Copyright ©2003
Mercer University Press
All rights reserved
Printed in the United States of America

The paper used in this publication meets the minimum requirements
of American National Standard for Information Sciences—
Permanence of Paper for Printed Library Materials,
ANSI Z39.48-1984.

Library of Congress Cataloging-in-Publication Data

Lee, Jason K.
  The theology of John Smyth :
Puritan, Separatist, Baptist, Mennonite / by Jason K. Lee.
   p. cm.
Includes bibliographical references and index.
   ISBN 0-86554-760-2 (hardcover : alk. paper)
  1. Smyth, John, d. 1612. 2. Theology—History—17th century.
I. Title.
   BX6495.S58L44 2003
   230'.6'092—dc21
                                                      2003006963

Contents

Preface ix

Introduction xi

1. Sixteenth- and Seventeenth-Century Background 1
   English Background . . . 3
   Dutch Background . . . 19

2. Smyth's Life, Debates, and Writings 41
   Puritan Stage . . . 41
   Separatist Stage . . . 46
   Baptist Stage . . . 71
   Mennonite Stage . . . 83

3. Smyth's Use of Typology 97
   Two Uses of Typology . . . 97
   Smyth's Typological Interpretation of Scripture . . . 99
   Smyth's Use of Typology in Defending His Theology . . . 106
   Smyth's Mennonite Typology . . . 119
   Conclusion . . . 126

4. Smyth's View of Covenant 127
   The Covenant of the Separatists . . . 128
   Smyth's Separatist Writings . . . 135
   Smyth's Baptist Writings . . . 145
   Smyth's Mennonite Writings . . . 152
   Modern Views on Smyth's Use of the Covenant . . . 157
   Conclusion . . . 164

5. Smyth's View of General Atonement 167
   Smyth's Reformed Views . . . 167
   Smyth's Rejection of Reformed Views . . . 174
   Source of Smyth's Views . . . 182
   Reason for Smyth's Views . . . 196

Debate with the Separatists . . . 201
Conclusion . . . 207

6. Smyth's View of Christ 209
   Mennonite Christology and the Incarnation . . . 209
   Smyth's Early Christology . . . 214
   Smyth's Christology as a Mennonite . . . 220
   Smyth's Revisions to His Christology . . . 234
   Smyth's Acceptance of Mennonite Christology . . . 238
   Conclusion . . . 242

7. Smyth's View of Church and State 245
   The Background to Smyth's View of Church and State . . . 245
   Smyth's Writings on Church and State . . . 255
   Source of Smyth's Thought . . . 266
   Relationship with Other Aspects of Smyth's Theology . . . 279
   Comparison of Smyth with Thomas Helwys . . . 282
   Conclusion . . . 287

8. Conclusion 289
   Smyth's Pursuit of Truth . . . 289
   Smyth's Mennonite Doctrine . . . 291
   Smyth's Influence on the General Baptists . . . 292

   Bibliography 295

   Index 307

For Kimberly

Preface

One question inevitably surfaces in my Baptist history courses: "Where do Baptists come from?" My response to the inquisitive pedagogue: "That depends on whom you ask." My sarcastic reply eventually leads to a discussion of Baptist origins and three historic positions: Puritan-Separatist roots, Anabaptist connections, and historical succession. A brief synopsis of each position includes John Smyth, an English Baptist pioneer. Smyth provides the first definitive nexus of the three positions, making him a pivotal character in the Baptist tradition.

Similarly, Smyth's theological positions draw attention to the related question of traditional Baptist theology. As the contemporary debate rages—"What have Baptists believed in the past?"—Smyth's theological journey provides valuable insight to this question. Though Smyth's theology underwent many revisions, certain aspects of his thought influence the English Baptist tradition.

In addition to Smyth's importance for Baptist history, his story portrays a struggle typical of seventeenth-century England. Within the English Puritan tradition and the Dutch Mennonite tradition similar questions arose. Which ecclesiological differences demand correction and which ones can be tolerated? How does cultural or theological context affect a person's beliefs or practice? What relationship is appropriate with former associates who hold to a position no longer espoused? Smyth's life and work supply a valuable resource for a case study of these larger questions.

This book and the thesis on which it is based, owes much to the support and encouragement of many friends and family. My supervisor, Professor W. P. Stephens of the University of Aberdeen, provided many helpful insights through his "iron sharpens iron" approach to supervision. I would like to express my thanks to my former colleagues at Southeastern Baptist Theological Seminary and in the postgraduate community in Aberdeen for their willingness to listen to my ideas. I am grateful to the staffs at the Queen Mother Library in Aberdeen and the Angus and Bodleian Libraries in Oxford for their work.

Many churches have supported my work including congregations in Louisville, Mississippi; Mobile, Alabama; and Aberdeen and Stonehaven,

Scotland. H. Gene Wilson, Frank McCorkle, and the deacons at Stonehaven deserve special mention. I give thanks to God for your prayers, encouragement, and financial gifts. The support of my family has been crucial through this project: Ken and Sybil Lee and Ronnie and Debbie McCullough. Most of all, I would like to honor my precious wife, Kimberly. Thank you for your servant's heart.

Introduction

John Smyth is one of the most intriguing figures in Baptist history. Though most renowned as a pioneer of the General Baptists, Smyth was actually a Baptist for less than two years. His pilgrimage of faith included stages as a Puritan, a Separatist, a Baptist, and a Mennonite.[1] These changes took place in a period of about a decade. How could a man of such transition be considered a shaper of any denomination? Was there any coherence to his transitions? Was there a principle or theme in which Smyth was consistent? What were the major tenets of his thought? How did his background and contemporaries influence him? These are just a few of the questions that arise during an examination of Smyth's thought.

Both historical and theological considerations must be addressed to understand Smyth's thought properly. This work will attempt to investigate the theological background that could have influenced Smyth. The second consideration is a description of Smyth's career, including an assessment of his writings and debates. Then, dominant themes in his thought are presented and analyzed. From these discussions, some conclusions can be drawn about Smyth's theology, about the influences on him, and about his impact on his followers and opponents.

The seven chapters of the book offer a contextualized understanding of Smyth's theology. The first two chapters focus on the historical context in which Smyth lived. Chapter 1 gives a brief survey of both the

---

[1] The terms "Puritan," "Separatist," "Baptist," and "Mennonite" are used throughout this book in reference to Smyth. "Puritan" refers to those of a Reformed theology who remained within the Church of England though often in disagreement with its official positions. "Separatists" are those who held a similar theology as the Puritans, but saw the corruption of the Church of England as being irreparable. Therefore, they founded independent congregations outside the authority of the Church of England. "Baptist" is used for those groups or individuals (mainly English) who accept the practice of believers' baptism but maintain a distinct existence from Continental "Anabaptists." "Mennonite" refers to the Anabaptists of the Dutch tradition. Primarily in Smyth's context, Mennonite and Waterlander Mennonite are used interchangeably though a distinction could be made.

English and Dutch backgrounds that influenced Smyth's thought. In the English background, sixteenth-century radicals and Elizabethan Separatists receive the most attention. In the Dutch background, the radical tradition is outlined with special interest in the Mennonite tradition and its immediate predecessors. The inclusion of these backgrounds need not imply theological influence on Smyth. However, an informed discussion of Smyth's theological pilgrimage necessitates at least a working knowledge of the English and Dutch climates.

Chapter 2 introduces Smyth's life, debates, and writings. The four distinct stages of his career are discussed. In each of these stages the debates or writings in which Smyth engaged are highlighted. Smyth's cultural context influences his theological positions or at least his arguments for those positions. Insight into to this context comes in this second chapter. Awareness of the context will prepare the reader to observe its influence on Smyth's theology as it is discussed in the later chapters.

Chapters 3–7 focus on the theology that Smyth presents in his writings. Chapter 3 asserts that typology is a central element in Smyth's interpretation of scripture as well as serving for a structure to defend his theology. His continual use of contrasting pairs to explain his position demonstrates the typological nature of his theology. Revisions in his use of typology are indicative of his theological changes.

Chapter 4 concentrates on Smyth's use of "covenant."[2] As a Separatist, Smyth uses this term to describe the manner of establishing a true church. Later, as a Baptist, the term is important in his discussion of the carnal and spiritual covenants. The carnal covenant features in the Old Testament and is represented by circumcision. The spiritual covenant exists in the Old Testament, but becomes clearer in the New Testament. Smyth links the baptism of the Spirit, which is symbolized by believers' baptism, with the spiritual covenant.[3] Though covenant themes dominate

---

[2]Smyth's use of the term "covenant" has several dimensions. He has both ecclesiological and theological uses of the term. These various uses are discussed in chap. 4.

[3]I prefer "believe*rs'* baptism" over "believe*r's* baptism." The former phrase depicts more of the communal nature of the practice in the eyes of its seventeenth-century participants. See George H. Williams, *Radical Reformation*, 3rd ed. (Kirksville MO: Sixteenth Century Journal Publishers, 1992) 99n.42, for further discussion.

his early writings, they rarely appear in his later writings.

Chapter 5 traces Smyth's early support and then later rejection of Reformed doctrine. The question of which person or group has the most influence on Smyth's later views is discussed. Smyth's reliance on Hans de Ries's "A Short Confession of Faith" is demonstrated.

Chapter 6 examines Smyth's Christology. His views as Puritan, Separatist, and Baptist differ with his views as a Mennonite. Smyth's understanding of the natural and spiritual flesh of Christ features prominently in his Mennonite writings. This chapter questions Smyth's supposed acceptance of the Melchiorite heavenly flesh theory of the incarnation.

Chapter 7 describes Smyth's views on church-state relations. This chapter assesses the influence of Separatist and Mennonite thinking on Smyth as well as his similarities with his successor, Thomas Helwys. Smyth's thought changed from supporting a godly magistracy to questioning the validity of a Christian magistracy. Though Smyth moves to a position of pacifism, he does not rule out the possibility of a Christian serving as a magistrate.

In 1984, in the *Baptist Quarterly*, four historians debated Smyth's theology. Douglas Shantz, James Coggins, Stephen Brachlow, and B. R. White each wrote articles identifying the central theme in Smyth's theology.[4] Shantz concluded that Smyth's central theme was the ruling of the resurrected Christ. He claimed that this thought was the foundation for Smyth's theology and ecclesiology. Coggins claimed that Smyth based his theology on the work of the Spirit. Brachlow was less specific on a central theme of Smyth's theology. However, he stated that Smyth's theology was a natural outgrowth of radical Puritanism and Separatism. White used his article to defend his position that Smyth's central theme was the covenant. He held that Smyth believed that the covenant God made with humans had to be the focus of the church. Therefore, Smyth's

---

[4]Douglas Shantz, "The Place of the Resurrected Christ in the Writings of John Smyth," *Baptist Quarterly* 30 (January 1984): 199-203; James R. Coggins, "The Theological Positions of John Smyth," *Baptist Quarterly* 30 (April 1984): 247-64; Stephen Brachlow, "John Smyth and the Ghost of Anabaptism: A Rejoinder," *Baptist Quarterly* 30 (July 1984): 296-300; B. R. White, "The English Separatists and John Smyth Revisited," *Baptist Quarterly* 30 (October 1984): 344-47.

theology and ecclesiology were driven by the idea of covenant.

Shantz's theory appears to be applicable to all stages of Smyth's career, in that the idea of the ruling Christ appears in each stage. Shantz claims he is attempting to prove this doctrine central to Smyth's thought; however, in his conclusion he says that the ruling Christ is "the dominating factor in Smyth's view of the Church."[5] Even if the ruling Christ is central to Smyth's thinking on the church as a Mennonite, there are other doctrines that are more central to his theology as a whole.

Coggins's theory about the Holy Spirit lacks specificity. He does not clarify the difference in Smyth's understanding of "spiritual" as related to inward compared to "spiritual" pertaining to the Holy Spirit. Coggins is also too inclusive in the topics he says relate to Smyth's understanding of the Holy Spirit. For example, Smyth's view of the "spiritual" flesh of Christ is not synonymous with the Holy Spirit, although Coggins implies that it is.[6]

Brachlow's theory of a continuation of Puritan and Separatist views throughout Smyth's career does not give enough weight to the major transition Smyth makes upon becoming a Mennonite.[7] It could be argued that his move from Puritan to Separatist was a logical progression. A similar case could even be made for his move from Separatist to Baptist. However, Smyth's acceptance of Mennonite views caused major changes in most areas of his thought.

White's theory of covenant as central provides insight into Smyth's Separatist and Baptist stages. However, Smyth's Mennonite writings rarely mention covenant except to say that the covenant is not an adequate defense of infant baptism. Covenant is certainly not a dominant theme in Smyth's Mennonite writings.

The views of these four scholars suggest beginning points in understanding Smyth's theology.[8] They raise questions that can only be answered by a proper study of Smyth's thought and its historical context. It is the intended task of this book to provide such a study.

---

[5]Shantz, "The Place of the Resurrected Christ," 199, 202.
[6]Coggins, "The Theological Positions of John Smyth," 256.
[7]Brachlow, "John Smyth and the Ghost of Anabaptism," 296 and 299.
[8]The views of these four scholars are discussed in greater detail in chap. 4.

Chapter 1
Sixteenth- and Seventeenth-Century Background

Not only was John Smyth responsible for organizing the first group of English Baptists, but his thought also survived among them for several decades. However, several decades prior to Smyth, different groups and persons throughout England and on the continent laid the groundwork for English Baptists. The exact nature of these groups and the amount of influence they had on early Baptists has been a topic of hot debate. Some scholars, such as E. A. Payne, Michael Watts, and James Coggins, would stress the influence of the Mennonites and other continental radical groups on the English Baptists. Others, such as B. R. White, W. T. Whitley, and Champlin Burrage, downplay the importance of these groups, but rather trace the heritage of these Baptists through the English Separatist tradition. It is not the primary purpose of this book to debate these origin theories. Rather, it will examine the theology of John Smyth. However, Smyth's theology has definite affinities to the theologies of both Separatists and Mennonites. Therefore, attention must be given to the religious culture in which Smyth operated.

This study will follow both a *dynamic* and an *organic* approach to historical connections. Martyn Whittock introduces these terms into the study of Baptist history. He believes that research about the relationships between early Baptists, English radicals, continental Anabaptists, Puritans, and Separatists is done according to one of these two models. The organic model centers on continuity found in official doctrinal statements such as confessions. Through these documents "structural continuity by direct propagation" can be seen.[1] This approach allows definitive statements about the connections between diverse movements. For example, Smyth's view on covenant ecclesiology expressed in his works demonstrates an explicit connection with early Separatist covenants.

While such organic connections do exist, the majority of Smyth's theology will be understood through a dynamic approach. This approach sees

---

[1] Martyn Whittock, "Baptist Roots: The Use of Models in Tracing Baptist Origins," *Evangelical Quarterly* 57 (1985): 319.

dependence mainly in the similarity of ideas, even though historical connections may be nebulous. It allows the popular ideas of certain groups to be linked with similar ideas of earlier groups even if direct relationships are difficult to ascertain. Whittock emphasizes the two strengths of the dynamic approach: its stress on "the exchange of 'small packages' of ideas without these being part of a total confessional system" and "laity ideas that may be at variance with official church dogma."[2] E. A. Payne demonstrates this principle by saying, "Ideas have wings as well as legs."[3]

Smyth belonged to a period of fragmentation and fierce competition between religious movements. At different stages of his career, he disparaged Puritans, Separatists, and Anabaptists. Holding derogatory views of other movements was not uncommon in his time. Also, in his quest for a true church, he tried to show that his thoughts were based on scripture not on human tradition. So, Smyth and his contemporaries downplayed many theological influences. In a day when groups were in such animosity and many groups claimed that their theology was a direct result of their study of scripture, establishing organic connections can be difficult. Therefore, a dynamic approach is a necessary complement to an organic approach.

Much of Smyth's theology shares common characteristics with the teachings of contemporary groups or individuals. Many thoughts evidenced in his writings had been expressed earlier by groups or individuals who may have influenced him. These influences could have come through direct promulgation, through the ideas of different groups being mixed together by the interaction of lay people, or through the influence of the printed page. The numerous influences on Smyth may not be evident through historical data alone, but they may become more clear through noticing common thought. Once common thought between him and his predecessors is recognized, then the historical data can be evaluated to see if there is support for probable influence.

Smyth's intellectual debt to his Separatist predecessors is easy to

---

[2]Whittock, "Baptist Roots," 321.
[3]Ernest A. Payne, "The Anabaptist Impact on Western Christendom," in *The Recovery of the Anabaptist Vision*, ed. Guy F. Hershberger (Scottdale PA: Herald Press, 1957) 313.

establish. What is not quite as clear is the exact nature of this influence. By the early seventeenth century, several groups of Separatists had been established in England and the Netherlands. Many of their ministers had attended Cambridge University with several completing their Master's degrees there. They had also benefitted from holding a theology similar to the Puritans who were gaining in influence in England. However, in the sixteenth century, the Separatists and other radicals were not so well established.

English Background

In the middle and late sixteenth century there were numerous religious groups in England that opposed elements of the established church. Among such groups, the English radicals and the English Separatists had at least an indirect influence on John Smyth.

English Radicals. During the sixteenth century, southeastern England had a reputation for having several groups of religious radicals. These groups shared an intense desire to return to scriptural authority and to base Christian practices on biblical patterns. Because of limited source documents, it is difficult to determine the precise nature of some of the groups. Some scholars hold that they form the beginnings of the Puritan and Separatist movements. Irvin Horst indicates that these groups must have had connections with continental radicals.[4] Michael Watts concurs with Horst's claims by saying that these radicals were Anabaptists from the continent as well as Englishmen who had been converted to Anabaptist thinking. However, he also recognizes that their history is elusive.[5] Therefore, it is difficult to comprehend what type of groups they were and the extent of their influence on later Separatists.

B. R. White agrees that these radical groups existed, though he doubts there is any significant continental Anabaptist influence through them to the Separatist tradition, which many connect to them. White makes a clear stance on the connection between these groups and the later Separatists. He says of the seventeenth-century Separatists that it is

---

[4]Irvin Horst, *The Radical Brethren: Anabaptism and the English Reformation to 1558* (Nieuwkoop: B. DeGraaf, 1972) 170-76.

[5]Michael R. Watts, *The Dissenters*, vol. 1, *From the Reformation to the French Revolution* (Oxford: Clarendon Press, 1978) 7.

"rather difficult to demonstrate any direct debt to the continental Anabaptists."[6] Even if scholars such as White are correct that there is no direct continental influence of these early radicals on the later Separatists, some people in this region exhibited a willingness to resist the established church.

The Protestant reforms that took place during the reign of Edward VI came to an abrupt end when Queen Mary I ascended the throne. Her notorious persecution of Protestants, however, did not squelch the many radicals who held private religious meetings.[7] During her reign, there was an independent congregation meeting in London that would have historical influence. This "Marian congregation" was considered a pioneering group by many Separatist groups who succeeded it. The Pilgrim father, William Bradford, many years later referred to this group as being one that, when it came to Separatism, "professed and practised that cause before Mr. Browne wrote for it."[8] This group is substantial because it seemed to have a succession of leaders that added to its consistency. B. R. White lists five ministers of this congregation, including a certain John Rough.[9] Rough came to London from exile in November 1557 and became the pastor of this underground congregation. However, shortly after his coming, on 12 December, he was arrested with some more members for trying to meet under the pretense of seeing a play.[10]

An expression of this congregation's presumed independency came on the Friday before Rough's arrest. Apparently his congregation, thinking they had the power to do so, excommunicated Margaret Mearing

---

[6]B. R. White, *The English Separatist Tradition* (London: Oxford University Press, 1971) xii.

[7]Kenneth Hylson-Smith, *The Churches in England from Elizabeth I to Elizabeth II*, vol. 1, *1558–1688* (London: SCM Press, 1996) 25.

[8]*Plymouth Church Records 1620–1859*, vol. 22 (Boston: Publications of the Colonial Society of Massachusetts, 1920) 132.

[9]White, *The English Separatist Tradition*, 10-11, lists Edward Scambler, later bishop of Norwich; Thomas Fowle, a fellow of St. John's College, Cambridge; Augustine Bernhere; John Rough; Thomas Bentham, later bishop of Lichfield.

[10]John Foxe, *Acts and Monuments*, vol. 8 (London: Seeley, Burnside, and Seeley, 1849) 444-47. (Subsequent editions and versions of Foxe's *Acts and Monuments* are popularly known as *The Book of Martyrs* and then as *Foxe's Book of Martyrs*.)

for subverting their church. Obviously, this act was done without any consultation of the established church, which gives some indication of the depth of their separation. This episode ends ironically because later Margaret Mearing was condemned to die along with John Rough for being a part of his group.[11]

Their separation was also expressed by the fact that they received an offering for the prisoners from their congregation. The offering was received and administered by Cuthbert Simson. Obviously, this action violated parish polity. Therefore, Mr. Simson was a target for the authorities.[12] The group received some attention from John Foxe in his *Acts and Monuments*. The increasing popularity of Foxe's work expanded the reputation of this congregation to the point where later arguments for and against Separatism referred to them. The defenders of the Church of England pointed out that members of the group were martyred in their attempt to retain the Anglican Church. The Separatists pointed out that this congregation had sought the truest form of the church that they knew. Later Separatists argued that if Rough's church had been exposed to the truer forms of the Separatists, then they would have pursued these practices.

Robert Browne was among the later Separatists who would laud this congregation. He claimed that the established church of his day would have persecuted the Marian martyrs because of their unwillingness to accept "pollution."[13] Henry Barrow explained that the group had been faithful to the light that had been revealed to them. He held that the Marian congregation did not push for further reforms because they had not been removed from the "popish church" long enough to see the possibilities of a church established on the scriptural pattern.[14] Francis Johnson indicated a closer relationship between the Marians and the Separatists when he claimed that the Marian congregation "joined in covenant by voluntary profession" just as the later Separatists did.[15] John Smyth also

---

[11]Foxe, *Acts and Monuments*, 450-51.

[12]Foxe, *Acts and Monuments*, 458-59.

[13]Robert Browne, *The Writings of Robert Harrison and Robert Browne*, ed. Albert Peel and Leland H. Carlson (London: Allen & Unwin, 1953) 413.

[14]*The Writings of Henry Barrow, 1590-1591*, ed. Leland H. Carlson (London: George Allen & Unwin, 1966) 323.

[15]Francis Johnson, *An Answer to Maister H. Jacob His Defence of the*

showed his awareness of the group by claiming that it was a true church because its intent was to separate from a false church and to establish a true church.[16]

English Separatists. Separatists heralded the Marian congregation under John Rough as true witnesses, but it was under Elizabeth I that the Separatist movement began to take the form for which it was to be known over the next century. Many Protestants were hopeful when Elizabeth took the throne in 1558. They were eager to see if she was going to be aggressive in enacting Protestant reforms within the Church of England. However, early in her reign, Elizabeth demonstrated that she was not going to be the catalyst for reform. Elizabeth had come to power when England was threatened from inside and outside. While there was unrest with Spain and France, the tension between the traditionalists and the Puritans was just as much a concern. Elizabeth needed to take a mediating position to solidify her power.[17]

While the Puritans remained within the Church of England, they desperately desired to reform its practices. When Elizabeth presented her *Prayer Book,* she had bowed to some of the Protestant pressures. However, the Puritans were not satisfied and pushed for more reforms.[18] Some people remained outside the church hoping to see further reform, and it is possible that the "Marian congregation" was still meeting privately at this time.[19] One offense that became a rallying point for the Puritans was the eucharistic vestments that the ministers were to wear. For most Puritans, the vestments constituted a return to the Roman church and its practices.[20] Aspiring to duplicate the reforms in Geneva and Zurich, many Puritan leaders pushed for changes in the Anglican liturgy.

In March 1566, Archbishop Matthew Parker wrote his *Advertisements,* which would enforce conformity to many of the rituals that were

---

Churches and Ministery of England (Middelburgh, Holland: n.p., 1600) 29.

[16]*The Works of John Smyth, Fellow of Christ's College, 1594–1598,* 2 vols., ed. William Thomas Whitley (London: Cambridge University Press, 1915) 2:386.

[17]Patrick Collinson, *The Elizabethan Puritan Movement* (London: Jonathan Cape, 1967) 30.

[18]Collinson, *The Elizabethan Puritan Movement,* 33-36; Hylson-Smith, *The Churches in England* 1:36.

[19]White, *The English Separatist Tradition,* 20.

[20]Collinson, *The Elizabethan Puritan Movement,* 34.

unpopular among the Puritan ministers such as the wearing of the eucharistic vestments.[21] Any disobedience was to be punished and the minister's license was to be revoked. This event along with other mounting frustrations strengthened the resolve of many dissenters against the Church. As a result, more groups who resisted the established church began to form and gain popularity.

Two such congregations were the Plumbers' Hall congregation and Richard Fitz's "Privy church." On 19 June 1567, local authorities discovered the Plumbers' Hall congregation holding a meeting under the guise of a wedding. Bishop Edmund Grindal wrote to Henry Bullinger about this group that they had "openly separated from us; and sometimes in private houses, sometimes in the fields, and occasionally even in ships, they have held their meetings and administered the sacraments."[22] Even though this group achieved some degree of separation, it lacked many of the characteristics of the later Separatists. The Plumbers' Hall congregation was similar to the later independent congregations of the seventeenth century. It was not fully separated from the Church of England, but rather had removed itself from the papist practices that had been continued in the church. Its members considered their separation as both partial and temporary.[23]

There were a few of the members of the Plumbers' Hall group who advanced to the point of full Separatism. Thomas Bowland and Randall Partridge were two of these. They were later mentioned as being members of Richard Fitz's church, a Separatist congregation.[24] There are at least three factors that distinguish this church as Separatist. The first is that they described themselves as a separate congregation. In their petition to Queen Elizabeth they claim:

---

[21]Hylson-Smith, *The Churches in England* 1:54.

[22]Champlin Burrage, *The Early English Dissenters in the Light of Recent Research*, 2 vols. (Cambridge: Cambridge University Press, 1912) 1:80.

[23]Burrage, *The Early English Dissenters* 1:82-87.

[24]Bowland and Partridge are mentioned in the list of prisoners taken from the Plumbers' Hall congregation (Burrage, *The Early English Dissenters* 2:10). They are also mentioned in Fitz's congregation's petition to Queen Elizabeth (2:17). A third connection between the two groups could be Elizabeth Leonard (2:17), if she was indeed the wife of John Leonard of the Plumbers' Hall group (2:10).

8 / The Theology of John Smyth

> We are a poore congregation whom god hath seperated from the churches of englande and from the mingled and faulse worshipping therin used, out of the which assemblies the lord our onely saviour hath called us, and still calleth, saying cume out from among them, and seperate your selves from them.[25]

Some other dissenting groups had been labeled as separate by others, but this congregation makes the claim for itself.

The second factor is that they desired to establish a separate church that exhibited the true marks of a church. The three marks Richard Fitz identified as being necessary were biblical preaching, proper sacraments, and church discipline.[26] They tried to establish biblical preaching by meeting together twice a week for teaching, prayer, and presumably to administer the sacraments. They also met on a weekly basis to exercise church discipline according to Matthew 18.[27]

The third factor that demonstrates their separation is that they had a primitive form of a church covenant. While the document does not use the term "covenant," it does mention a voluntary agreement by the members to join the group. Fitz writes, "I have joyned in prayer, and hearyng Gods worde, with those that have not yelded to this idolatrouse trash."[28] He also adds that the nature of their agreement is to "come not backe agayne to the preachynges. &c, of them that have these markes of the Romysh beast."[29]

Included with this covenant is a document that stated nine reasons why they were separating from the established church. The prevailing theme of the reasons is that these early Separatists believed that they were not to have any communion with the corruption of the church. The eighth reason mentions specifically their disagreement with the eucharistic

---

[25]Burrage, "Letter from Fitz's Congregation to Queen Elizabeth," *The Early English Dissenters* 2:16-17.

[26]Burrage, "A Printed Paper by Richard Fitz, Minister," *The Early English Dissenters* 2:13.

[27]Burrage, "Letter from Fitz's Congregation to Queen Elizabeth," *The Early English Dissenters* 2:17.

[28]Burrage, "The Separatist Covenant of Richard Fitz's Congregation," *The Early English Dissenters* 2:14.

[29]Burrage, "The Separatist Covenant," *The Early English Dissenters* 2:14.

vestments, "These Popish garments. &c, are now become very Idolles in deede, because they are exalted aboue the worde of the almightie."[30]

Fitz's group drew on biblical covenant imagery. They understood that if they would separate from the wickedness of the established church, then they would be entering into God's covenant blessing. They wrote, "touche no unclean thing, then will I receyue you, and I wilbe your god and you shalbe my sonnes and doughters sayth the lord."[31] The depth of this group's separation provides some explanation for the church's continuing to meet for several years after Fitz and their deacon, Thomas Bowland, died in prison.

Unfortunately, these early English radicals and Separatists left very few documents that indicate their doctrine, especially their ecclesiology with much detail. It is difficult to determine how much influence these early groups had on their Separatist successors such as John Smyth and his contemporaries. However, the next Separatist leader to emerge, Robert Browne, left many more writings which express his thought and practice. He would become the father of the English Separatist movement.

1. *Robert Browne.* By the 1580s the climate was perfect for a radical to suggest that the established church was a false church and that the only hope for a true church was among a separated, covenanted community of believers. Robert Browne, nicknamed "Troublechurch Browne" by his contemporaries, was that radical.[32] Browne expressed his Separatist views by claiming that God's church had to be reestablished by "the worthie."[33] In 1582, he published *A Treatise of Reformation without Tarrying for Anie*, creating controversy for both him and his movement. The work encouraged the ministers and church members who wanted reform not to delay it by waiting for the magistrates' lead.

Browne had come from a Puritan background. From his days at

---

[30]Burrage, "The Separatist Covenant," *The Early English Dissenters* 2:15.

[31]Burrage, "Letter from Fitz's Congregation to Queen Elizabeth," *The Early English Dissenters* 2:17.

[32]White, *The English Separatist Tradition*, 44.

[33]Browne, *The Writings of Robert Harrison and Robert Browne*, 402. Browne's publications include several combinations of lettering to represent the letter "w" (e.g. vv, vu, Vv). These have been emended for the reader. For example, here "vvorthie" has been emended to "worthie." Each quotation that is emended in this way is noted. See also chap. 2, n. 20, below.

10 / The Theology of John Smyth

Cambridge, he had been a presbyterian Puritan, possibly as a result of the influence of Thomas Cartwright.[34] Cartwright created quite a disruption with his lectures on the book of *Acts*, in which he declared that the presbyterian type of government was the only kind upheld in scripture. These lectures were delivered in the 1570s, when Robert Browne and his future associate, Robert Harrison, were undergraduates at Cambridge.[35] Perhaps his time at Cambridge caused Browne to question the position of the bishops. He went on to hold that the congregation had been given the authority in the church and that groups could handle decisions better than a single person.[36]

One of Browne's arguments was that episcopalian government handed authority down from one bishop to another. However, he believed that the congregation under the leadership of the elders was the recipient of Christ's power, which allowed authority to be handed down from Christ to many.[37] Albert Peel's *Seconde Parte of a Register* includes segments of a letter that Browne and Harrison and others sent to Queen Elizabeth requesting that she reform the Anglican church by setting up a church government system of elders chosen by the local churches. This request also included a plea to allow local congregations to choose their own ministers. They requested that the Queen would reform the church

> by removing the dumb ministrie . . . and by placing those ministers which have wherwith to feede Christs flocke . . . which maie not be chosen by corrupt patrones which have nothing to doe therwith, but by the flock whose soules pertaine to the ministers charge.[38]

---

[34]Michael Haykin, *Kiffin, Knollys, and Keach* (Leeds: Reformation Today Trust, 1996) 19.

[35]John Venn and J. A. Venn, *Alumni Cantabrigienses*, pt. 1, vol. 1 (Cambridge: University Press, 1927) 237; John Venn and J. A. Venn, *The Book of Matriculations and Degrees* (Cambridge: University Press, 1913) 106; Watts, *The Dissenters* 1:28.

[36]Browne, *The Writings of Robert Harrison and Robert Browne*, 270-71.

[37]Browne, *The Writings of Robert Harrison and Robert Browne*, 399-400.

[38]Albert Peel, *The seconde parte of a register: being a calendar of manuscripts under that title intended for publication by the Puritans about 1593, and now in Dr. Williams' Library, London*, 2 vols. (Cambridge: Cambridge University Press, 1915) 1:158.

In 1581, Robert Browne led a group of about forty people in Norwich to covenant together to form a church.[39] He reported that "a covenant was made and their mutual consent was given to hold together."[40] This covenant states that it is a voluntary commitment to the Lord. The congregation's submission was to Christ's rule in the church. The covenant also points to the necessity of their separation to avoid corruption. They agreed to a basic structure for their meetings, which were to include "prayer, thanksgiving, reading of the scriptures, for exhortation and edifying, either by all men which had the gift, or by those which had a special charge before others."[41]

The group was the object of some persecution. Still, Browne originally resisted the congregation's idea of fleeing to Scotland. He did not want to diminish their witness in England.[42] However, many of the leaders of the congregation were being put in prison; so he agreed to go to Middelburg in the Netherlands. While the congregation was in Middelburg, Browne published several works including *A treatise of reformation* and *A treatise upon the 23 of Matthew*. Another book he produced, *A book which sheweth the life and manners of all true Christians*, was to serve as the congregation's instruction manual for matters of theology and ecclesiology. It was divided into four columns for the different levels of readers. The first two columns were for the unlearned who needed plainness and the second two columns were for the more mature who "seeke deepnes."[43]

In Middelburg, a conflict arose between Browne and Robert Harrison. There were personal charges leveled by both men, including those against the other's wife.[44] Harrison called meetings to denounce Browne on several occasions. At these meetings, Browne accused Harrison of slander because he had made the charges without two or three witnesses. While these personal charges were troublesome, the ultimate matter of disagreement was on separation from the established church. Often the two had

---

[39] Burrage, *The Early English Dissenters*, 97.
[40] Browne, *The Writings of Robert Harrison and Robert Browne*, 422.
[41] Browne, *The Writings of Robert Harrison and Robert Browne*, 422.
[42] Browne, *The Writings of Robert Harrison and Robert Browne*, 423-24.
[43] Browne, *The Writings of Robert Harrison and Robert Browne*, 222-23.
[44] Browne, *The Writings of Robert Harrison and Robert Browne*, 425-27.

debated the position of the preachers who refused to leave the established church. Browne held that Harrison was trying to hold on to the Church of England by continuing to support these preachers. Harrison perceived that Browne had gone too far in separating completely from these men.[45]

The conflict led to Browne's excommunication from his own congregation and then his departure for Scotland in 1583. However, his reception in Scotland was no better than his treatment in Middelburg; he was imprisoned shortly after his arrival. He was released from prison in Scotland and returned to Middelburg for a brief period. There he wrote a defense of the Separatist position against a letter written by the Puritan, Thomas Cartwright. He then returned to England, but was imprisoned again for his radical views on church polity. During this imprisonment, he recanted many of his views and agreed to a statement accepting the Archbishop of Canterbury's authority and recognizing the Church of England as a true church.[46]

Upon Browne's submission, he was released and allowed to return to England, but it seems that he was involved in further Separatist activity until 1589. Shortly thereafter, a weary Browne turned his back on Separatism and returned completely to the Church of England. However, he had launched a movement that would continue to strengthen under new leadership. Collinson calls the schism led by Browne and Harrison, "the most extensive and serious movement of separation yet experienced."[47]

While most Separatists decried any association with Browne, many made a similar exodus from the Church of England. Perhaps John Smyth had more in common with Robert Browne than any of the other second-generation Separatists. B. R. White suggests that the local church covenant was emphasized more by Smyth and Browne than by any other Separatist.[48] Smyth and John Robinson debated the level of separation necessary from the Church of England. In their debate, Smyth takes the same stance of strict separation as Browne had against Harrison. Also, Smyth's vigor reflects more of the radical spirit of the young Robert

---

[45]Browne, *The Writings of Robert Harrison and Robert Browne*, 412, 428.
[46]Marshall M. Knappen, *Tudor Puritanism* (Gloucester MA: Peter Smith, 1963) 308.
[47]Collinson, *The Elizabethan Puritan Movement*, 204.
[48]White, *The English Separatist Tradition*, 125.

Browne than his Separatist contemporaries.

2. *Henry Barrow and John Greenwood.* Henry Barrow and John Greenwood formed a vital part of the new leadership for the Separatist movement. Barrow was a graduate of Clare College, Cambridge, and Greenwood was at Corpus Christi College, Cambridge from 1578 to 1581.[49] Other details of their lives before 1585 are unknown. Greenwood was a preacher from Norfolk and had been deprived of his benefice in the autumn of 1585.[50] At some point, he entered into a covenant with others in London. This congregation may have included the remnants of earlier Separatist congregations.[51] On 8 October 1587, John Greenwood was among twenty-one "Brownists" taken from Henry Martin's house, where they were meeting. Six weeks later, on 19 November, Henry Barrow was arrested while visiting Greenwood in prison.[52] From this time until 1593, these two men were the leaders of the Separatist movement from their prison cells.

Barrow wrote more extensively than did Greenwood. He pushed for the congregation to become completely separate from the established church. He cited four basic reasons that the Church of England was apostate and beyond reform. In his reply to George Gifford, *A Plaine Refutation*, Barrow gives these reasons in the form of four charges. The first charge was that the Church of England had replaced the scriptural pattern of worship with the liturgy of *The Book of Common Prayer*. He writes "That they worship God after a false maner; their worship being made of the invention of man, even of that man of sinne, erroneous, and imposed upon them."[53]

Barrow's second charge dealt with the church's membership. He

---

[49]Watts, *The Dissenters* 1:35; White, *The English Separatist Tradition*, 70; Venn and Venn, *The Book of Matriculations*, 45.

[50]Burrage, *The Early English Dissenters* 2:20.

[51]Nicholas Crane is listed with Greenwood in the arrests of this congregation. Crane had been a member of the Plumbers' Hall congregation. It is possible that other members of the earlier congregation also joined with Greenwood. Burrage, *The Early English Dissenters* 1:121-23; Watts, *The Dissenters* 1:35.

[52]*The Writings of Henry Barrow, 1587–1590*, ed. Leland H. Carlson (London: George Allen & Unwin, 1962) 91; Burrage, *The Early English Dissenters*, 121-29, includes a discussion of his arrival at these precise dates.

[53]Barrow, *The Writings of Henry Barrow, 1590–1591*, 60.

laments "That the prophane ungodlie multitudes without the exception of anie one person, are with them received into, and retayned in the bozome and bodie of their church."[54] Barrow argued that there was no repentance required to be a member of the established church, so the membership was profane. Instead he stated that "at the beginning of ouer Queene Elisabethe's reigne, were all at one instant receyved as members into this church."[55]

The third charge reprimands the Church of England for maintaining the episcopalian government of the Roman Church. According to Barrow, the members of the Church of England "have a false antichristian ministrie imposed upon them, retained with them, and maintained by them."[56] He states that the New Testament taught that a minister or officer should not be over more than one church at a time and that the local church should be responsible for choosing its officers.[57]

The fourth charge declared the lack of discipline found in the Anglican church. Barrow states that "their churches are ruled by and wilfully remaine in subjection unto an antichristian and ungodly government, contrarie to the institution of our Saviour Christ."[58] He also discussed the "monstrous" negligence to follow the pattern of discipline set out by Christ in the scriptures.[59] These four charges would be the basis of the Separatist movement and their opposition to the Church of England throughout the next few decades.

One factor that makes organic connections hard to establish is that many of the radicals did not want to admit any debt to tradition. They claimed to have erected the true church exclusively on the teachings of scripture. Separatists especially avoided connections with Robert Browne, because he had seen the light and yet had gone back to the established church. Both Barrow and Greenwood specifically denied any influence from Robert Browne.[60] Barrow claimed that he was not even aware of the

---

[54]Barrow, *The Writings of Henry Barrow, 1590–1591*, 102.
[55]Barrow, *The Writings of Henry Barrow, 1590–1591*, 109.
[56]Barrow, *The Writings of Henry Barrow, 1590–1591*, 183.
[57]Barrow, *The Writings of Henry Barrow, 1590–1591*, 199.
[58]Barrow, *The Writings of Henry Barrow, 1590–1591*, 302.
[59]Barrow, *The Writings of Henry Barrow, 1590–1591*, 306.
[60]*The Writings of John Greenwood, 1587–1590*, ed. Leland H. Carlson (London: George Allen & Unwin, 1962) 58, 218, 240.

Brownist opinions concerning the Church of England.[61] These men should be taken at their word, that they had never accepted any doctrinal statements from Browne. Their similarities could be through dynamic connections rather than organic. While it is possible that these men never read Browne's works, their similarities indicate that they were not immune to his influence through other channels.

Much like Browne, many Separatists were bedeviled by their teaching on civil authorities. The Separatists taught that if a civil ruler commands something against the will of God, then the churches should obey God rather than man.[62] This belief along with the fact they continued to produce "seditious books" caused Barrow and Greenwood to be convicted of treason for subverting the authority of the queen. They were hanged on 6 April 1593.[63]

The brand of Separatism that Barrow and Greenwood promoted was different in several ways from the ideas of John Smyth. Two of the more obvious differences with Barrow and Greenwood were Smyth's emphases on more congregational authority and less rigid worship services. After the deaths of these two men, the leadership of the Separatist movement was then passed on to Francis Johnson.

3. *Francis Johnson and Henry Ainsworth.* Francis Johnson (1562–1618) was perhaps the most influential figure in the early years of Separatism. He attended Christ's College, Cambridge, and received his B.A. in 1582 and his M.A. in 1585.[64] While at Cambridge, he caused trouble for himself by disagreeing with the authorities. He was jailed in January 1589 for preaching a sermon at Great St. Mary's that advocated presbyterian government and spoke of the corruption within the Church of England.[65] Released from prison in December 1589, Johnson was shocked at the inability of the heads of Cambridge colleges to recognize and to submit to the truth that he was preaching.[66] He was then forced to

---

[61]Barrow, *The Writings of Henry Barrow, 1590–1591*, 325.
[62]Greenwood, *The Writings of John Greenwood, 1587–1590*, 28.
[63]Hylson-Smith, *The Churches in England* 1:67; Watts, *The Dissenters* 1:37.
[64]Venn and Venn, *The Book of Matriculations*, 387.
[65]Peter Lake, "Dilemma of the Establishment Puritan: The Case of Francis Johnson," *Journal of Ecclesiastical History* 29 (January 1978): 29. Lake gives a detailed account of Johnson's trial, his sermon, and his refusal to take an oath.
[66]Lake, "Dilemma of the Establishment Puritan," 34.

resign his fellowship at Christ's College. Afterwards, he moved to Middelburg in the Netherlands, where he served as a minister. While he was there, Johnson's frustration with the Church of England advanced to the point where he accepted Separatist views.[67]

In October 1591, he failed to get his congregation to sign a covenant that was similar to a Separatist covenant. Shortly thereafter, he left for London and by the autumn of 1592 became the pastor of the Separatist congregation there. On 5 December 1592, Johnson was arrested and imprisoned again. However, this time he remained in prison for four years. In prison, Johnson worked along with Henry Ainsworth to write "A True Confession." This confession was presented in 1596 as a general defence of the Separatist cause. The purpose of the confession, as stated in the preface, was to instruct those who are interested and "published for the cleering of our selves from those unchristian slanders of heresie, schisme, pryde, obstinacie, disloyaltie, sedicion, &c. which by our adversaries are in all places given out against us."[68]

The forty-five articles of the confession express both Separatist doctrine and church polity. The theology is Reformed in nature with predestination, election, and original sin all being defended in the first five articles. The Christology of the confession also demonstrates the Puritan roots of the Separatists. The major portion of the Christological material is dedicated to a description of Christ in his roles of "Prophet, Priest, and King of the Church."[69] The confession also gives guidelines for the ministry. Ministers are to have influence only within the congregation by whom they have been elected and may be removed from the ministry, if necessary. The episcopalian government of the Church of England is denounced as being foreign to the New Testament.[70] The confession describes the true church as a church of the faithful, along with their children. Its members,

> are willingly to joyne together in christian communion and orderly covenant, and by confession of Faith and obedience of Christ, to unite

---

[67]Lake, "Dilemma of the Establishment Puritan," 34.

[68]"A True Confession," in *Baptist Confessions of Faith*, rev. ed., ed. William L. Lumpkin (Valley Forge PA: Judson Press, 1969) 82.

[69]"A True Confession," 85.

[70]"A True Confession," 91.

themselves into peculiar Congregations; wherin, as members of one body wherof Christ is the only head, they are to worship and serve God according to his word, remembring to keep holy the Lords day.[71]

In the confession's articles on government, the magistrates are encouraged "to suppress and root out by their authoritie all false ministeries, voluntarie Relligions and counterfeyt worship of God."[72] Also, within their responsibility is to protect true religion by making laws that protect them. Though most of the articles indicate Separatist support for the magistracy, article 42 adds:

> That if God withold the Magistrates allowance and furtherance heerin, they yet proceed together in christian covenant & communion thus to walke in the obedience of Christ even through the middest of all tryalls and aflictions, not accompting their goods, Lands Wyves, Children, Fathers, Mothers, brethren, Sisters, no nor their own lyves dear unto them, so as they may finish their course with joy, remembering alwayes that wee ought to obey God rather then man.[73]

This thought of the Separatists was being tested even before it was included in this confession.

In 1593, Parliament had passed a statute that forbade any "Brownist" activity. By this statute Barrow and Greenwood were executed. However, the executions brought some sympathy for their cause, so afterwards the authorities encouraged emigration instead. As a result of this statute, many people in Johnson's Separatist congregation agreed to emigrate from England to Amsterdam. When Johnson was released from prison in 1597, he rejoined the church there as pastor.[74]

Johnson's pastorate in Amsterdam was successful, but not peaceful. For, once he was in Amsterdam, a quarrel broke out in the church over his wife's apparel. She had a been a wealthy widow when Johnson married her while he was still in prison. Francis's brother, George, led the opposition to her trendy apparel. This disagreement expanded to include other issues and ended with Francis excommunicating his brother as well

---

[71]"A True Confession," 92.
[72]"A True Confession," 94.
[73]"A True Confession," 95-96.
[74]Knappen, *Tudor Puritanism*, 313-14.

18 / The Theology of John Smyth

as his father who had come from England to settle the dispute.[75] These excommunications did not end the disputes in the "Ancient Church," which was the popular name among the Separatists for Johnson's church.

Henry Ainsworth (1570–1623) was the teaching elder in Johnson's church. He had entered St. John's College, Cambridge, while Johnson was a fellow at Christ's College.[76] The church elected him teaching elder while Johnson was still in prison.[77] He served as teacher from about 1595 until 1610. He was more temperate than the dogmatic Johnson, but he was also a capable scholar. He defended Johnson aptly in the series of disruptions that befell the Ancient Church in the first decade of the seventeenth century including the disputes with Richard Bernard, George Johnson, and John Smyth.[78]

In 1610, a dispute broke out in the Ancient Church that would separate even Johnson and Ainsworth. In December that year, Ainsworth ended a long dispute with Johnson by seceding from the church. William Bradford said that the tensions between the two factions were present even as early as 1608. This tension was one of the factors for John Robinson's church moving to Leyden in the spring of 1609.[79] The grievances centered on the belief that Johnson and the ruling elder, Daniel Studley, had assumed too much authority. Ainsworth's group, probably a majority of the congregation, left because they were convinced that more of the power ought to be with the congregation as a whole.[80] Ainsworth argued that the authority in the church belongs to Christ and he then empowers everyone who submits to him in a covenant. Ainsworth held that this was a basic principle of Separatism that Johnson was abandoning.[81]

---

[75]Knappen, *Tudor Puritanism*, 314-15.

[76]Venn and Venn, *The Book of Matriculations*, 5.

[77]White, *The English Separatist Tradition*, 98.

[78]Fred J. Powicke, *Henry Barrow, Separatist, and the Exiled Church of Amsterdam* (London: James Clarke & Co., 1900) 238-54.

[79]Bradford, *Of Plymouth Plantation*, 16-17.

[80]Powicke, *Henry Barrow, Separatist*, 256; White, *The English Separatist Tradition*, 114.

[81]Powicke, *Henry Barrow, Separatist*, 268-71. Ironically, in Johnson's later defense of the presbytery, he uses the testimony of the Puritans, Thomas Cartwright and Douglas Fenner, to support his arguments. See Francis Johnson, *A Christian Plea Conteyning three Treatises: The first, touching the Anabaptists,*

In 1617, Johnson published his last book, *A Christian Plea*, and made his final public remarks on this controversy. In this work, he called for an independent congregation with a presbyterian government. Johnson argues that the phrase, "tell the church" in Matthew 18:15-18 refers to the elders, not the whole congregation. Johnson even criticizes Ainsworth for abandoning this position that the latter had once defended against Smyth.[82] Johnson died in January 1618, less than a year later. He served as the Amsterdam congregation's pastor for twenty-five years. Under his leadership, the congregation at one time grew to have as many as 300 members. Tragically, most of the remaining members of his congregation died on a voyage to Virginia in 1619.

Both Johnson and Ainsworth had extensive contact with John Smyth. Johnson especially had a heavy influence on Smyth in his days at Cambridge. However, later in their careers, Johnson and Ainsworth would become chief adversaries for John Smyth. In the early seventeenth century, both men published tracts against Smyth and his followers. These documents and Smyth's contributions to the debates will be discussed in the next chapter.

Dutch Background

The Anabaptist connection with the early Baptists has been a subject of great debate. Many scholars, such as B. R. White, hold that the Baptists developed from the English Separatist tradition with little influence by the Anabaptists. Others, such as James Coggins, hold that while Baptists had origins in Separatism, the influence of the Anabaptists, especially the Mennonites, had a dramatic impact on their development. Still others, such as Irvin Horst, hold that both Separatists and Baptists were influenced by Anabaptists in England and that this influence was solidified by their immigration to the Netherlands. He argues that many Anabaptist doctrines can be shown to be present in the same areas where the English Separatists were strongest. The peculiar Christology held by

---

& others mainteyning some like errours with them. The second, touching such Christians, as now are here, commonly called Remonstrants or Arminians. The third, touching the Reformed Churches, with whom my self agree in the faith of the Gospel of our Lord Jesus Christ (Amsterdam: n.p., 1617) 312.

[82]Johnson, *A Christian Plea Conteyning three Treatises*, 308.

many of the Dutch Anabaptists was among these doctrines.[83] Although he agrees with Horst, when George Williams speaks of Robert Browne, the Separatist pioneer, he admits that

> a comparison of names and publications of the English Anabaptists with Browne's known contacts and sources reveals no trace of any connection between this Separatist and the English Mennonites. Browne, in fact, disclaimed any relationship to Anabaptism.[84]

E. A. Payne also agrees with the continental connection of Smyth and his Separatist predecessors. He states:

> The contacts of John Smyth with the Mennonites are well known. But the early English Baptists provided only one of many bridges by which the ideas of the continental radicals passed over into Britain and the new lands across the Atlantic.[85]

All of these theories have some application to John Smyth. He seems to be a microcosm of the Baptist tradition as a whole. While this thesis does not attempt to answer the question of origins for all Baptists, it does hypothesize about the possible sources of Smyth's theology.

In his *Development of Dutch Anabaptist Thought and Practice*, William Keeney mentions three aspects of theology that were fairly common to the Dutch Anabaptists. He observes that they held that the Old Testament was fulfilled in the New Testament, that a true church is made up of believers only, and that many Dutch Anabaptists held troublesome incarnational beliefs.[86] Robert Friedmann adds another aspect of Anabaptist thought: their strong sense that the best way to relate to

---

[83]Horst, *The Radical Brethren*, 51-52, 92. Williams makes many of the same observations: George H. Williams, *The Radical Reformation*, 3rd ed. (Kirksville MO: Sixteenth Century Journal Publishers, 1992) 1207.

[84]Williams, *The Radical Reformation*, 1208. The social and possible political ramifications of being connected to the continental Anabaptists would almost necessitate Browne's disclaimer.

[85]E. A. Payne, *The Anabaptists of the Sixteenth Century and Their Influence in the Modern World* (London: Carey Kingsgate Press, 1949) 19.

[86]William E. Keeney, *The Development of Dutch Anabaptist Thought and Practice from 1539 to 1564* (Nieuwkoop: B. De Graaf, 1968) 192-96.

God is through the community of believers.[87] All four of these characteristics find their place in Smyth's theology. His belief that the New Testament is the fulfillment of the Old Testament and that the church is for believers only are major aspects in his theology. Smyth was also charged with holding many of the same troublesome incarnational beliefs such as the Melchiorite "heavenly flesh" theory of the incarnation.

The fourth characteristic would seem to have less similarity with Smyth's views until one takes into account his views on the local church covenant. Throughout much of his career Smyth believed that the local church covenant was the appropriate response to God's offer of the covenant of grace. In other words, the proper way to relate to God is through the covenanted community of believers. From this perspective, Smyth held much in common with the Anabaptists' belief that the best way to relate to God was through the community of believers.

C. A. Snyder notes one additional characteristic of Anabaptists that has an obvious similarity with Smyth. Along with realizing that the Old Testament found fulfillment in the New Testament, Snyder says that many Anabaptists interpreted the Old Testament as a "figure" for the New Testament church.[88] This figurative approach found many adherents among the Anabaptists and was the dominant approach for Smyth. These thoughts, along with Smyth's rejection of Calvinism and the Christian magistracy, suggest possible evidence for Mennonite influence.

It seems that many of Smyth's basic beliefs have similarities with a significant number of Anabaptist teachings. However, before any analysis can be done of Smyth's relation to Anabaptist thought, the people who were the possible sources for these common beliefs need introduction. These men can be shown to be a part of a doctrinal relationship that ties the early Dutch Anabaptists to the Waterlander Mennonites, who were contemporary with Smyth. Calvin Pater's work demonstrates the historical connections between these early Anabaptists and Smyth. The focus of this section will not be to recycle the historical evidence that is adequately developed by Pater, instead it will be to note a few of the radical

---

[87]Robert Friedmann, *The Theology of Anabaptism: An Interpretation* (Scottdale PA: Herald Press, 1973) 81.

[88]C. A. Snyder, *Anabaptist History and Theology* (Kitchener ON: Pandora Press, 1995) 369.

22 / The Theology of John Smyth

reformers who have doctrinal similarities with Smyth.[89]

Spiritualists and Anabaptists. Two representatives from the early continental radicals, Caspar Schwenckfeld, a Spiritualist, and Melchior Hofmann (alternatively, Hoffmann), an Anabaptist, left a lasting impression on the radical movement in Holland with which Smyth had contact.

1. *Caspar Schwenckfeld (1489–1561).* While it is true that Schwenckfeld was not an Anabaptist in the purest sense of the term, his thoughts were a definite influence on Anabaptist theology.[90] He was a lay preacher throughout Silesia from as early as 1522 to 1527. In this role, he encouraged many to join the new reforms that were being instituted throughout Europe. In 1525, he had a debate with Martin Luther concerning the Lord's Supper. This debate resulted in Luther sending him a harsh reply. It was at this point that Schwenckfeld broke away from Luther's leadership and moved more to Spiritualist views.[91]

His Spiritualist tendencies were first evidenced in his views on the Lord's Supper. He attempted to show that his views were different from those of the other reformers. He demonstrated his differences from the Lutheran view, and then focused on the other reformers by saying,

> Although the Zwinglians and Calvinists (who are the third party), together with us seek Christ in heaven above, they do not discern His body and blood spiritually according to divine truth, but physically, according to the order of earthly things. Thus circumscribed, he cannot be a true food of our souls. Hence we cannot participate with them.[92]

Schwenckfeld arrived in Strassburg (Strasbourg) in May 1529. There

---

[89]Calvin A. Pater, *Karlstadt as the Father of the Baptist Movements* (Toronto, Buffalo, London: Universtiy of Toronto Press, 1984) 236-69.

[90]Schwenckfeld did not hold to the exclusive validity of believers' baptism. He was not overly concerned with the outward ordinances and their various forms. He did not accept believers' baptism personally, so he is not considered an Anabaptist proper.

[91]Selina Gerhard Schultz, *Caspar Schwenckfeld von Ossig* (Norriston PA: Board of Publication of the Schwenckfelder Church, 1947) 102-104.

[92]Schultz, *Caspar Schwenckfeld von Ossig*, 114; Caspar Schwenckfeld, *Corpus Schwenckfeldianorum*, 19 vols., ed. Chester David Hartranft et al. (Leipzig: Breitkopf & Hartel, 1907–1965) vol. 16, doc. 1,161.

he was a leader for reform from 1529 to 1533.[93] While in Strassburg, he expounded Spiritualist views on topics beyond the Lord's Supper. In each of these, he stressed the inner over the outer. This is apparent in his views of the Old and New Testaments. He sees the external being emphasized in the Old Testament, whereas the spirit is emphasized in the New. When he speaks of the Old and New Testaments, he says:

> The Old Covenant consisted entirely in external, perishable services. . . . In short all that pertained to it was external, temporal, typical and figurative. The other is called the New Covenant. . . . It is called new because it rests on better promises than the old, consists of Spiritual, abiding riches and promises.[94]

Schwenckfeld's views go beyond simple typology comparing the Old and the New Testament. He also argues for the spiritualization of New Testament texts. He argues from 2 Corinthians 3:2-3 that there is a need to find the inward instructions of the Lord in any epistle. He also includes numerous references to a spiritual interpretation of the New Testament's writings on the Lord's Supper.[95]

His spiritualizing also affected his Christology, including his incarnational views. He believed that Christ had received His flesh from Mary, but the flesh underwent a process of deification.[96] On 6 December 1543, Martin Luther responded to a letter Schwenckfeld had written to him. Luther's response was hostile, calling for the Lord's judgment on Schwenckfeld. One of the charges Luther makes is that the Silesian reformer is a Eutychian, who denies the humanity of Christ. Schwenckfeld answers Luther's charges in his work, *An Answer to Luther's Malediction*. In this work he states:

> I recognize nothing of creation or creatureliness in Christ but rather a new divine birth and natural Sonship (*kindtschafft*) of God. Wherefore

---

[93]Horst Weigelt, "Caspar von Schwenckfeld: Proclaimer of the Middle Way," in *Profiles of Radical Reformers*, ed. Hans-Jürgen Goertz (Scottdale PA: Herald Press, 1982) 217-20.
[94]Schultz, *Caspar Schwenckfeld von Ossig*, 190; *Corpus Schwenckfeldianorum* 4:419-25.
[95]Schultz, *Caspar Schwenckfeld von Ossig*, 379-84.
[96]Weigelt, "Caspar von Schwenckfeld," 221.

I cannot consider the Man Christ with his body and blood to be a creation or a creature. Rather, I believe and confess with Scripture that he is wholly God's only begotten Son and that Christ, the Son of God, his Heavenly Father, the whole Person indivisibly (*unzertailig*) God and Man, was born in time of the Virgin Mary.[97]

While Schwenckfeld believed that Christ's humanity was unique, he did not see this as denying the humanity of Christ. He replies to Luther that he has no intent to diminish Christ's humanity. He writes, "This has never in my whole life come into my mind, that is, that I should not hold and confess Christ as a hero (*heldt*) with two natures to be true God and true man."[98] His Christology seems to have influenced Melchior Hofmann, though Hofmann and Schwenckfeld disagreed on the nature of Christ's incarnation.[99]

2. *Melchior Hofmann (ca. 1495–1543)*. Melchior Hofmann was a radical thinker who was in Strassburg at the same time as Schwenckfeld. He was originally from Schwäbisch-Hall. He held Lutheran views before his acceptance of Anabaptist views, possibly through the influence of Andreas Karlstadt.[100] He converted to Anabaptism probably on his first visit to Strassburg. His second visit was from June 1529 to April 1530.[101] While in Strassburg the second time, Hofmann's debate with Schwenckfeld helped develop his Christology, which was similar to Schwenckfeld's in that he said that Christ did not receive His flesh from Mary in the natural manner.[102] His beliefs were slightly different from Schwenckfeld because he said that Christ brought His flesh from heaven.[103] His incarnational view was accepted by many of the Dutch Anabaptists,

---

[97]Caspar Schwenckfeld, *An Answer to Luther's Malediction*, trans. George H. Williams and Selina Gerhard Schultz, in *Spiritual and Anabaptist Writers*, ed. Williams et al. (London: SCM Press, 1957) 180.

[98]Schwenckfeld, *An Answer to Luther's Malediction*, 179-80.

[99]Snyder, *Anabaptist History and Theology*, 145.

[100]Pater, *Karlstadt as the Father of the Baptist Movements*, 175-76.

[101]*The Mennonite Encyclopedia*, vol. 5, ed. Cornelius J. Dyck and Dennis D. Martin (Scottdale PA: Herald Press, 1990) 384.

[102]Klaus Deppermann, "Melchior Hofman: Contradictions between Lutheran Loyalty to Government and Apocalyptic Dreams," in *Profiles of Radical Reformers*, ed. Hans-Jürgen Goertz (Scottdale PA: Herald Press, 1982) 186.

[103]Snyder, *Anabaptist History and Theology*, 357-63.

including Menno Simons and Dirk Philips.

Hofmann's approach to interpreting scripture and his emphasis on the church as a covenanted community also influenced the Mennonites who followed him. His approach to scripture was figurative, a mixture of allegory and typology. Hofmann held that the important aspects of salvation had types that symbolized them before they came into existence. This applied to the Old Testament prefiguring the New Testament, but also to both Testaments pointing to present and future events.[104] Klaus Deppermann attempts to differentiate between Hofmann's typology and his allegory. He states:

> Typological interpretation brings together actual figures and characters by "figuration," the linking of concrete persons or events to form pairs (e.g., Melchizedek and Christ). But the allegorical method aims at revealing the hidden spiritual meaning of a past external event (e.g., the exodus of the Israelites' the progress of the human soul).[105]

Even though these two may be different, for Hofmann they are both involved in his figurative exegesis. It is possible that this spiritualizing of certain aspects of scripture could also have been an influence of Schwenckfeld.

Hofmann's figurative approach to scripture can be seen in *The Ordinance of God*. In this work, he stated that a special gift was necessary to unravel the figures of the Bible. He believed that to be a proper minister one must have this gift of figurative interpretation. It was only through this approach that the Bible could be understood clearly. Hofmann called his approach the cloven claw. The Old Testament and the New Testament were the two clefts of one cloven-footed beast. Because of this, he says, "Scripture is not a matter for everybody—to unravel all such involved snarls and cables, to untie such knots—but only for those to whom God has given the power."[106]

In *The Ordinance*, Hofmann also emphasizes his view that the church

---

[104]Klaus Deppermann, *Melchior Hofmann*, trans. Malcolm Wren, ed. Benjamin Drewery (Edinburgh: T. & T. Clark, 1987) 241.

[105]Deppermann, *Melchior Hofmann*, 242.

[106]Melchior Hofmann, *The Ordinance of God*, trans. George H. Williams, in *Spiritual and Anabaptist Writers*, 203.

is a covenanted community. He writes that the members of the church, "wed and bind themselves to the Lord Jesus Christ, publicly, through that true sign of the Covenant, the water bath and baptism."[107] Hofmann refers to the "covenant of baptism" as what the church does to commit itself to Christ.[108] He continues by saying that Jesus covenanted himself to the Father through his baptism.[109] This served as a "figurative" example to his followers. Therefore all believers need to "covenant and betroth themselves to the Lord Jesus Christ, under the covenant of God."[110] They would then be prepared to follow Christ in obedience as a covenanted body.

Many of Hofmann's radical views left full opportunity for his followers to go on to some extreme measures. The more revolutionary segment of his followers fell into disrepute. It was through the work of a more stable group led by Menno Simons that Hofmann's views survived into later Dutch Anabaptist thought.[111] It was through the Mennonites that the ideas of Schwenckfeld and Hofmann came into direct contact with John Smyth. Hofmann's figurative approach to scripture and his incarnational theory were major aspects of the debate within the Mennonites during Smyth's interaction with them. Schwenckfeld's spiritualism resurfaced in some of the ideas of Hans de Ries, who helped facilitate the communications between Smyth's congregation and the Amsterdam Waterlanders.

Mennonites. The Waterlander congregation with which Smyth interacted in Amsterdam was part of a wider Mennonite tradition. This tradition had several leaders who shaped its theology and church practices. Some of the main leaders from the mid-sixteenth century until the early seventeenth century were Menno Simons, Dirk Philips, Lubbert Gerrits, and Hans de Ries.

1. *Menno Simons (1496–1561).* Menno Simons was born in Witmarsum, Friesland, in 1496. In 1524, he was ordained as a priest in

---

[107]Hofmann, *The Ordinance of God*, 186-87; Cornelius Krahn, *Dutch Anabaptism: Origin, Spread, Life, and Thought (1450–1600)* (The Hague: Martinus Nijhoff, 1968) 191.

[108]Hofmann, *The Ordinance of God*, 187.

[109]Hofmann, *The Ordinance of God*, 189-90.

[110]Hofmann, *The Ordinance of God*, 190.

[111]*Mennonite Encyclopedia* 5:385.

Utrecht.[112] However, early in his career, Simons accepted sacramentarian views as a result of his study of the Bible.[113] He remained a priest, but began to study baptism as well. He came to the conclusion that infant baptism was wrong, but continued as an evangelical preacher.[114] Then, in 1531, after the execution in Leeuwarden of Sicke Freerks Snijder who had been baptized in Emden as an adult, a dismayed Simons publicly rejected infant baptism.[115] It is unclear how much the Anabaptists influenced the change in his views of the Lord's Supper and baptism. Certainly, his study of scripture played a significant role.[116] He was baptized in 1536 or 1537 in Groningen by Obbe Philips, and in 1537 he was ordained by Philips.[117] He became a stabilizing factor for the Dutch Anabaptists. Because of his immense influence in this region, these Dutch Anabaptists became known as Mennonites.[118]

Simons's Christology implies possible influence from Schwenckfeld and Hofmann. His incarnational view is similar to Hofmann's.[119] From 1544 to 1554, Simons debated with Jan à Lasco, a Zwinglian reformer, on the subject of the incarnation.[120] In an attempt to clarify his view of this debate, Simons wrote an explanation of his incarnational views that was published as a *Brief and Clear Confession* (1544). Lasco then wrote his *Defensio* (1545) to which Simons replied with *The Incarnation of Our Lord* (1554).[121] In both of his works, Simons defended his Melchiorite Christology.[122] Simons took Hofmann's view of the incarnation and modi-

---

[112]Krahn, *Dutch Anabaptism*, 171.

[113]Krahn, *Dutch Anabaptism*, 170-71.

[114]Krahn, *Dutch Anabaptism*, 172.

[115]Irvin B. Horst, "Menno Simons: The New Man in Community," in *Profiles of Radical Reformers*, ed. Hans-Jürgen Goertz (Scottdale PA: Herald Press, 1982) 208.

[116]Horst, "Menno Simons," 209-10.

[117]Krahn, *Dutch Anabaptism*, 173.

[118]Franklin H. Littell, *The Origins of Sectarian Protestantism* (New York: Macmillan, 1964) 40.

[119]Pater, *Karlstadt as the Father of the Baptist Movements*, 252.

[120]*The Complete Writings of Menno Simons*, ed. John Wenger (Scottdale PA: Herald Press, 1956) 335.

[121]Simons, *Complete Writings*, 784.

[122]Krahn, *Dutch Anabaptism*, 179-80.

fied it slightly. He held that Christ had drawn nourishment from Mary while in the womb. However, in agreement with Hofmann, Simons believed that the Word became flesh, but did not take His flesh from Mary.[123]

Christ's flesh, Simons believed, was a heavenly one that he brought with him from heaven. Simons remarks: "Reader, consider the Word of your Lord. Christ says that His flesh came from heaven, and the learned ones say that it came of Adam's flesh."[124] Simons believed the incarnation had vital connections with salvation. He said that if Christ was flesh in the natural manner then that meant His sacrifice would not have been perfect because of original sin. Simons understood that Christ's being the *only begotten of God* meant that Christ came solely from God, not God *and* Mary.[125]

Simons interpreted the Old Testament typologically in contrast to the literal interpretation held by many of Melchior Hofmann's more radical followers such as John of Leiden.[126] He understood the history of God's revelation as two time periods. The Old Testament was a "dispensation of imperfectness"; the New Testament was a "dispensation of perfectness."[127] In his work *Blasphemy of John of Leiden*, Simons argues that Christians should not use literal swords as the people of God in the Old Testament did, but they should use "the Word of God which is a two-edged sword."[128] During this discussion, Simons gives a brief description of his typological view of scripture. He states, "Now we should not imagine that the figure of the Old Testament is so applied to the truth of the New Testament that flesh is understood as referring to flesh; for the figure must reflect the reality; the image, the being, and the letter, the Spirit."[129] He insists that errors in interpretation will occur if types of the Old Testament are wrongly brought over into the New Testament church. Simons submits that this is the nature of the error of those who have

---

[123]Simons, *Complete Writings*, 431.
[124]Simons, *Complete Writings*, 796.
[125]Simons, *Complete Writings*, 825.
[126]Keeney, *Development of Dutch Anabaptist Thought and Practice*, 37.
[127]Hans-Jürgen Goertz, *The Anabaptists*, trans. Trevor Johnson (London and New York: Routledge, 1996) 57.
[128]Simons, *Complete Writings*, 42-43.
[129]Simons, *Complete Writings*, 42.

mistakenly held to infant baptism because it relates to the figure of external circumcision. In *Foundation of Christian Doctrine*, he says that Paul "does not teach that external circumcision is a figure of baptism, but of inward circumcision."[130] The proper understanding of this concept depends on one's use of typology.

Baptism is not the only aspect of the church that Simons uses typology to explain. In his work *A Clear Account of Excommunication*, Simons dedicated considerable material to showing the Old Testament figures of excommunication. As rebellious people were removed from Israel, so unfaithful church members were to be isolated from the people of God unless they repented. Simons used several other aspects of the Old Testament figuratively to illustrate an aspect of the New Testament church.[131] Simons indicates that the Old Testament contains figurative representatives of Christ. He says that Christ is portrayed in the Mosaic Bronze Serpent, the Mercy Seat of the Ark, and the Tree of Life.[132]

Like most Dutch Anabaptists, Simons thought the church was to be a community of believers. In one discussion of the church, he says, "It must be said that the community of God, or the church of Christ, is an assembly of the pious, and a community of the saints."[133] In his books *Instruction on Excommunication* and *The New Birth*, Simons describes the church as an "assembly of the righteous" and a community of saints, which he says is an orthodox description.[134] An important aspect of being a righteous assembly is obedience to the Lord and his commands. Therefore, obedience is an essential aspect of membership in the church. It is a natural result of a person being a Christian and belonging to the church. In the *True Christian Faith* he says:

> The church of Christ is God's elect, His saints and beloved, who have washed their clothes in the blood of the Lamb; who are born of God and driven by the Spirit of Christ; who are in Christ and He in them; who hear and believe His Word; who in their weakness obey His commandments, follow in His footsteps with all patience and humility;

---

[130]Simons, *Complete Writings*, 133.
[131]Snyder, *Anabaptist History and Theology*, 370-71.
[132]Simons, *Complete Writings*, 820-21.
[133]Simons, *Complete Writings*, 734.
[134]Simons, *Complete Writings*, 99, 967.

who hate evil and love the good; who earnestly desire to apprehend Christ as they are apprehended of Him.[135]

A church made up of believers only is central to Simons's thought. This belief relates to another essential doctrine, dealing with an ordinance of the church: the rejection of infant baptism. He argued that infants were not a part of the church because they could not express repentance. Therefore, they should not be baptized; baptism follows repentance and the inner washing. In *Foundation of Christian Doctrine*, Simons gives eight false arguments for infant baptism. His response to these arguments can be summarized in two statements. First, infants should not be baptized because only the work of Christ, not baptism, can take away sin. Second, infants should not be baptized because baptism should follow repentance as the scriptures teach.[136]

Simons argues for believers' baptism because of what baptism symbolizes. In his *Reply to Gellius Faber*, Simons argues that, while only males were circumcised, both males and females were in the covenant of God, and members of the Old Testament church. He then says, "Similarly in the New Testament. The Gospel is preached, and all who believe it and are baptized, shall be saved; be they men or women. They are members of the church of Christ, in God's covenant and grace."[137] Outward baptism demonstrates that a person has experienced the inner baptism and belongs to the church. The inner baptism is what brings salvation and outward baptism comes as an aspect of obedience to Christ in this new relationship.[138]

2. *Dirk Philips (1504–1568)*. Dirk Philips was born in 1504, probably in Leeuwarden.[139] He was a contemporary and an associate of Menno Simons, though perhaps more of a theologian. Pieter Houtsagher baptized him sometime between 25 December 1533 and 2 January 1534 in Leeuwarden. Shortly thereafter, he was ordained by his brother, Obbe

---

[135]Simons, *Complete Writings*, 402.

[136]Simons, *Complete Writings*, 130-38.

[137]Simons, *Complete Writings*, 706.

[138]Simons, *Complete Writings*, 247.

[139]William E. Keeney, "Dirk Philips, a Biography," in *The Writings of Dirk Philips*, ed. William E. Keeney et al. (Scottdale PA: Herald Press, 1992) 19.

Philips.[140] Dirk Philips, along with Menno Simons, was responsible for stabilizing the Dutch Anabaptists after the disaster at Münster.[141] Philips agreed with Simons in many beliefs and even sided with him in various debates. In one particular instance Philips helped Simons debate Adam Pastor. After the debate failed to persuade Pastor to renounce his unitarianism and to support Melchiorite Christology, Philips agreed with Simons to excommunicate him.[142]

After Simons's death, Philips became the unofficial leader of the Mennonites. It was in this capacity that he tried to serve as the arbitrator in a dispute between the two Mennonite groups, the Frisians and the Flemish. Lubbert Gerrits had been unsuccessful in striking an agreement between the two sides. Philips was called to solve the problem. This episode ended in Gerrits being suspended from the office of minister and without a permanent resolution for the opposing sides.[143] In this dispute, Philips denounced the harsh judges along with the Frisian Covenant of Four Cities and the compromise agreed to by the Flemish and Frisians.[144]

Philips was similar to Simons in much of his theology. In relating the Testaments, Philips believed the Old Testament was to be understood as a shadow of the New Testament.[145] The Old Testament contains many figures and types that are removed in the New Testament. Philips contends that this is an important distinction in interpreting the two. He says that numerous Old Testament figures are to cease because of their ceremonial nature. However, the "essential significance" or meanings behind the figures remain and are in harmony with the New Testament. So, while the natures of the Testaments are different, they share the same

---

[140]Obbe Philips, *A Confession*, trans. Christiaan T. Lievestro, in *Spiritual and Anabaptist Writers*, 204; Krahn, *Dutch Anabaptism*, 174.

[141]Keeney, "Dirk Philips, a Biography," 25. On 25 June 1535 several hundred Anabaptists who had participated in the revolt at Münster were killed by the bishop of Münster's forces. This slaughter brought the inevitably bloody end to the apocalyptic "New Jerusalem" movement at Münster. Meic Pearse, *The Great Restoration* (Carlisle UK: Paternoster Press, 1998) 92-93.

[142]Williams et al., *Spiritual and Anabaptist Writers*, 490-91.

[143]*The Writings of Dirk Philips*, ed. William E. Keeney et al. (Scottdale PA: Herald Press, 1992) 499-509; Keeney, "Dirk Philips, a Biography," 34-36.

[144]Philips, *The Writings of Dirk Philips*, 471.

[145]Keeney, "Dirk Philips, a Biography," 36.

basic message. The Old Testament reveals aspects of God's nature and so it can be used to support the teachings of the New Testament.[146] Therefore, while Philips often used the New Testament directly to explain his doctrines, he mainly used the Old Testament for supporting texts. He often quoted New Testament verses, but he listed in the margins of his writings only the references for the Old Testament texts.[147]

Philips used this typological approach to scripture in his work, *The Ban*. Like Simons, he used figures of the Old Testament as examples of the ban. He interpreted the demands of the Old Testament for a holy community as prefiguring the purity that the ban would help obtain for the church.[148] Along with his views on the ban, Philips uses typology in discussing the proper attributes of a minister. He says, "Again, how the ministers of God are ordained and must be sent, that is certainly to be learned and noticed out of the figures of Aaron and his children of the Old Testament . . . there these figures of Aaron and his children certainly may be understood rightly according to the spirit."[149] The example of the Old Testament not only gives direction for the selection of ministers, but it also gives ministers a description of their task. Philips gives his understanding of the ministers' task when he says that they are to separate correctly "the Old and New Testaments, Matt. 13:52, between the letter and the Spirit and with a pure understanding of the divine secrets, Eph. 6:19; 2 Tim. 4:8."[150]

The spiritual leaders of a congregation must be able to discern the differences in the Testaments because the church should not maintain the types of the Old Testament. Philips explains: "For, in principle, we are not to be guided by the figures, images, and incompleteness of the Old Testament, but by the true and perfect being and spirit of the New Testament, Heb. 7:11."[151] The reason for not being guided by the Old Testament images is that the New Testament church should not follow the letter of the Old Testament but instead should follow the "new nature of

---

[146]Philips, *The Writings of Dirk Philips*, 264, 268.
[147]Keeney, "Dirk Philips, a Biography," 38.
[148]Snyder, *Anabaptist History and Theology*, 371.
[149]Philips, *The Writings of Dirk Philips*, 364.
[150]Philips, *The Writings of Dirk Philips*, 365.
[151]Philips, *The Writings of Dirk Philips*, 108.

the Spirit."[152]

Dirk Philips held to a Melchiorite Christology. Much like Menno Simons, he emphasized a connection between the incarnation and salvation. It was important that Christ was a perfect sacrifice for sins. This could happen only if he had untainted flesh. Philips saw the Melchiorite incarnational view as providing the way for Christ's flesh to be perfect. Only if his flesh was a heavenly flesh, not generated by Mary, could Christ avoid being tainted by original sin. Philips asks, "How should the body of Christ remain pure if it were of a human seed, which is, after all, impure, Job 14:4?"[153] It is through this celestial flesh that believers are able to partake of the divine nature. This happens as believers become obedient to Christ, which is partaking in his flesh.[154]

While John Smyth was never in direct contact with Caspar Schwenckfeld, Melchior Hofmann, Menno Simons, or Dirk Philips, their influence lived on in the Mennonites with whom Smyth did interact. After Philips's death, two leaders of Waterlander congregations, Lubbert Gerrits and Hans de Ries, sought to bring unity to the fragmented Mennonites. These two men had a great impact on the Mennonites' relationship with John Smyth and his congregation.

3. *Lubbert Gerrits (1534–1612).* Lubbert Gerrits was pastor of the Mennonite congregation in Amsterdam. His congregation was a mixture of Frisians and Waterlanders with the latter being the more dominant. The Waterlanders began as a splinter group of Mennonites in 1556. They formed originally among groups that had been banned by Leonard Bouwens for their moderate stance on the church ban and their opposition to the Wismar Articles.[155]

These Waterlander churches became a little more accepting toward other groups than the other Mennonites tended to be. Some of the Waterlander churches even allowed their members to hold lesser magisterial positions that would not require the use of the sword. They preferred the name *Doopsgezinden* ("baptism-favorers") over "Mennonite," partly

---

[152]Philips, *The Writings of Dirk Philips*, 108.
[153]Philips, *The Writings of Dirk Philips*, 137.
[154]Philips, *The Writings of Dirk Philips*, 138-39; Williams et al., *Spiritual and Anabaptist Writers*, 750-52.
[155]Williams et al., *Spiritual and Anabaptist Writers*, 737, 743-44.

because Menno Simons had supported the opposition in their debate over the ban. Their openness led them to recognize as Christians all who had experienced regeneration of the inner man through Jesus Christ.[156] This openness earned them the nickname *drekwagen* ("garbage wagon") by those whose position on the ban was more rigorist. Their acceptance of various views and backgrounds would be important in their discussions with Smyth's congregation.

In 1559, Gerrits came to Hoorn from Amersfoort. Later that year, he was ordained by Dirk Philips. Gerrits found himself in controversy in the 1560s. In 1567, he served in Hoorn and was chosen as one of the arbitrators in the Flemish-Frisian debate.[157] This debate ended in a split between the two groups. Dirk Philips was called in to help rectify the situation. He summoned Gerrits and his fellow arbitrator, John Willems, to appear before him. Both men refused to appear before Philips. Accordingly, they were suspended by Philips for their poor judgment as arbitrators and for not appearing before him when summoned.

In spite of this episode, Gerrits was known for his tolerance and had along with Hans de Ries led the unification of the Mennonite groups, the Young Frisians, the High Germans, and the Waterlanders into the *Bevredigde Broederschap* ("Reconciled or Pacified Brotherhood") in 1601.[158] The discussions took almost ten years with each group producing a series of publications. These served to demonstrate the similarities of the groups, thereby allowing the union to be established. It was not a binding union, but did serve as method of communication for the groups.

Gerrits was a preacher and an elder in his congregation, with the latter giving him authority in other Waterlander congregations.[159] He encouraged the acceptance of Smyth's congregation and helped Ries with

---

[156] Williams et al., *Spiritual and Anabaptist Writers*, 745.

[157] Williams et al., *Spiritual and Anabaptist Writers*, 1181.

[158] *Mennonite Encyclopedia*, vols. 1–4, ed. Harold S. Bender and C. Henry Smith (Scottdale PA: Mennonite Publishing House; Hillsboro KS: Mennonite Brethren Publishing House; Newton KS: Mennonite Publishing Office, 1955–1959) 2:505; Cornelius J. Dyck, "Hans de Ries: Theologian and Churchman: A Study in Second Generation Dutch Anabaptism" (Ph.D diss., University of Chicago Divinity School, 1962) 141-43.

[159] James R. Coggins, *John Smyth's Congregation: English Separatism, Mennonite Influence, and the Elect Nation* (Scottdale PA: Herald Press, 1991) 82.

the confession they were to sign.[160] He wrote a letter to the Waterlander congregations outside Amsterdam to solicit their approval to the union with Smyth's group. He defended the baptism and theology of Smyth's group to these other congregations. He writes:

> There, first of all, we ministers have, according to the desire of our brethren, summoned these English before us, and again most perfectly examined them as regards the doctrine of salvation and the government of the church, and also inquired for the foundation and form of their baptism, and we have not found that there was any difference at all, neither in the one nor the other thing, between them and us.[161]

In 1612, on his deathbed, Gerrits encouraged the leaders of his congregation to pursue the merger of Smyth's group. He said that he "earnestly desired that the cause of the English should not be forgotten, and that it be attended to as soon as possible."[162]

4. *Hans de Ries (1553–1638).* Hans de Ries was born in Antwerp, Belgium. After a personal struggle with Roman Catholic dogma, he considered Reformed doctrine for a period before accepting an Anabaptist position. He was drawn to the toleration of the Waterlander Mennonites and was baptized by Simon Michels in 1575 or 1576.[163] Soon after his baptism, Ries became involved in trying to bring unity to the fragmented Mennonites. His irenic spirit would allow him to coordinate unions between Mennonite groups for the next half-century. Cornelius Dyck says that Ries preferred to "exhort the faithful to obedience and love rather than to parry subtle questions."[164] Although peace was important to Ries, he did not see the necessity of sacrificing essential doctrine to achieve unity.

Ries's systematic mind was put to service with the Waterlanders early

---

[160]Sjouke Voolstra, "The Path to Conversion," in *Anabaptism Revisited*, ed. Walter Klaassen (Scottdale PA: Herald Press, 1992) 105.

[161]Benjamin Evans, *The Early English Baptists*, vol. 1 (London: J. Heaton & Son, 1862; facsimile repr.: Greenwood SC: Attic Press, 1977) 212.

[162]Burrage, *The Early English Dissenters* 2:214; translated in Pater, *Karlstadt as the Father of the Baptist Movements*, 264. The story of Smyth's group and their negotiations with the Waterlanders is continued in chap. 2.

[163]*Mennonite Encyclopedia* 4:330.

[164]Dyck, "Hans de Ries," 89.

in his career. Along with four other ministers, Ries worked to compose the "First Waterlandian Confession" in 1577. It is a testimony to his skills and maturity that he had such an important role when he was only twenty-four.[165] This confession was used to explain the Waterlander doctrine to the other Mennonite groups: the Flemish, the Frisians, and the High Germans. The confession includes a statement on the Trinity that emphasizes the unity of the Father, Son, and Holy Spirit. It is not clear from this confession if the Waterlanders were yet dealing with the threat of anti-Trinitarianism that would surface among them in the next few decades. The confession's statement on the incarnation is not in the Melchiorite "heavenly flesh" tradition. However, this incarnational view is not ruled out completely. Predestination is rejected in favor of the foreknowledge of God. The confession reads:

> We believe with Holy Scripture that God has known from all eternity all things that happen, have happened, and will happen, both good and bad. [Nevertheless] this foreknowledge compels no one to sin. We confess also that though He foreknows all things, that which happens is not all His will or work.[166]

Original sin and limited atonement are also rejected. On the sacraments, the confession supports believers' baptism and a memorial view of the Lord's Supper. The confession supports the use of the ban, but it is liberal in its statement on avoiding those under the ban.[167]

Ries was imprisoned in Middelburg in April 1578, under the charge by a Reformed minister that he had performed a wedding ceremony without parental permission.[168] When Reformed opposition to the Mennonite cause surfaced as the actual reason for his imprisonment, he wrote a personal confession to explain his position to the magistrates.[169]

---

[165]Dyck, "Hans de Ries," 89; Hans de Ries, "The First Waterlandian Confession of Faith," trans. Cornelius J. Dyck, *Mennonite Quarterly Review* 36 (January 1962): 7.

[166]Ries, "First Waterlandian Confession," 9.

[167]Ries, "First Waterlandian Confession," 12.

[168]Dyck, "Hans de Ries," 89.

[169]Coggins, *John Smyth's Congregation*, 85; See Dyck's introduction to Hans de Ries, "The Middelburg Confession of Hans de Ries," trans. Cornelius J. Dyck, *Mennonite Quarterly Review* 36 (April 1962): 147.

Its style and doctrine were similar to the earlier Waterlander confession. As with the earlier confession, his rejection of predestination and original sin is apparent. In comparison, there is a fuller statement on the incarnation. He states that Christ originated in God and "in the fulness of time" became man from the seed of Mary. The most striking aspect of his incarnational statement is when he says, "that the Scriptures do not tie salvation to a knowledge of the origin of the flesh of Christ. Therefore we do not reject or condemn to hell those who are weak in confessing this."[170] So, while Ries does not support the heavenly flesh theory of Hofmann and Menno Simons, he does not reject those that do. This indicates his desire for peace in an issue that continually troubled the Mennonites. He also states that the magistrates should not be involved in the matters of the church, but should have full authority in civil matters. Also, in the confession, a pacifist view of war is defended.[171]

Over a decade after his release from the Middelburg prison, Ries worked with Lubbert Gerrits in bringing unity to the Waterlanders, the Young Frisians, and the High Germans. This partnership would be important in the negotiations in 1610 with John Smyth's congregation. When Smyth's congregation petitioned to join the Amsterdam Waterlanders, Lubbert Gerrits and Reynier Wybrands, the two ministers of the Mennonite congregation, consulted with Ries. Ries's reputation as a catalyst for unity, combined with the fact that Ries and Gerrits had worked together in forming the Bevredigde Broederschap, made him a natural selection as mediator.[172] Ries's leadership was respected throughout the Waterlander community, and as an elder in the Waterlander congregation in Alkmaar he would have some authority in interchurch matters.[173]

Together with Gerrits, Ries authored the confession that Smyth's congregation was to sign as a testimony to their agreement with Mennonite doctrine.[174] This confession was the "Short Confession" and was probably written in early 1610 as the basis of a conference set for 23

---

[170]Ries, "Middelburg Confession," 152.

[171]Ries, "Middelburg Confession," 153.

[172]Voolstra, "The Path to Conversion," 104-105.

[173]Coggins, *John Smyth's Congregation*, 82. Coggins suggests that it is also possible that Ries spoke English, although Dyck doubts this.

[174]Voolstra, "The Path to Conversion," 105.

May, concerning the acceptance of Smyth's congregation by the Mennonites. Besides a means of union with Smyth's group, the confession became widely used by the Amsterdam Waterlanders to explain their beliefs to their critics, including other Mennonite groups.

The confession includes a precise statement on the Trinity, which could have been intended to combat the anti-trinitarian influence that Ries and others were facing. Original sin, total depravity, and predestination are rejected.[175] Christ is described as filling the roles of Prophet, Priest, and King. The spiritual knowledge of Christ is extolled as essential to the Christian. The internal meaning of the sacraments and other church ordinances is stressed.[176] The idea of a Christian magistracy is rejected. The confession states, "He [Christ] has not called his disciples to be secular kings, princes, dukes, or authorities, nor instructed them to seek and assume such office, nor to rule the world in a worldly manner."[177] This confession was consented to by Smyth's group and then sent to the surrounding Mennonite groups for their scrutiny.[178]

One criticism of the confession by an anonymous Reformed critic was that it contained Schwenckfeldian ideas.[179] Schwenckfeld's influence on Ries is evident in his writings, even though he rarely mentions him.[180] Ries exhibits the same dualistic worldview that Schwenckfeld had. He defends an external and internal Word, external and internal sacraments, and an external (historic) and internal (spiritual) Christ.[181] Although he emphasizes the latter in each of these, he did not accept the spiritualist

---

[175] Hans de Ries, "A Short Confession of Faith by Hans de Ries," trans. Cornelius J. Dyck, *Mennonite Quarterly Review* 38 (January 1964): 11-12.

[176] Ries, "A Short Confession of Faith," 16-18.

[177] Ries, "A Short Confession of Faith," 18. There is more discussion of this confession and its impact on Smyth in several chapters of this book.

[178] Coggins proposes that the publication of the "A Short Confession of Faith" along with the acceptance of Smyth's group by the Waterlanders led to the breakup of the Bevredigde Broederschap in 1613. James Coggins, "A Short Confession of Hans de Ries: Union and Separation in Early Seventeenth-Century Holland," *Mennonite Quarterly Review* 60 (1986): 135-38.

[179] Smyth did not deny this charge in his defense of Ries, Smyth, *Works* 2:697.

[180] Dyck, "Hans de Ries," 196.

[181] Dyck, "Hans de Ries," 196.

position of denying the value of the externals. So, while he defended the preeminence of the inner, he did not neglect the Mennonite emphasis on proper church ordinances.

The Word of God is one area of thought that demonstrates Ries's emphasis on retaining both the external and the internal.[182] In his debate with Nittert Obbesz, he says:

> Our dispute is over the Word of God. We teach that there are two senses of the Word of God, the Word that was in the beginning with God and is God, through whom all things were created, and the scriptures, the written Word of God. We say, teach, and confess therefore, that there are two senses of the Word of God.[183]

This thought is one in which Ries admits Schwenckfeld's influence. He responds to Obbesz:

> It may well be that I said at that time, as you claim, that Caspar Schwenckfeldt has written right and well concerning the Word of God, but in saying this I most certainly did not condone and accept everything he has said and written.[184]

Ries affirmed the importance of the scriptures as the written Word of God. He wrote to Obbesz, "Surely, all men can see that we hold firmly to the written Word, not seeking to be wise beyond its teaching, as you seem to suspect."[185] The reason that Ries's allegiance to the scriptures was in question was that he stressed the importance of the eternal Word of God (Christ and His Spirit) over the written Word. Cornelius Dyck recapitulates Ries's view by saying that for the Dutch radical the eternal Word is "not merely a second revelation parallel to the written Word but a culminating, higher source of knowledge."[186] Ries writes, "God teaches and speaks to man not alone through the written Word, but primarily

---

[182] Voolstra, "The Path to Conversion," 109.

[183] Hans de Ries, *Ontdeckinghe der dwalingen*, 2; quoted in Dyck, "Hans de Ries," 201-202. Obbesz was a Mennonite pastor who opposed the spiritualist tendencies of Ries and others.

[184] Ries, *Ontdeckinghe der dwalingen*, 20-21; in Dyck, "Hans de Ries," 203.

[185] Ries, *Ontdeckinghe der dwalingen*, 263; in Dyck, "Hans de Ries," 200.

[186] Dyck, "Hans de Ries," 205.

through His eternal Word in cooperation with the Holy Spirit."[187] This is just one aspect of Ries's emphases on the inward or spiritual. Many in the Waterlander brotherhood accepted Ries's views because they supported a spiritual view of scripture, which led to a search for the inner meaning of passages.[188] After Gerrits's death, Ries's spiritualist views gained ground among the Waterlanders. Because of this vast influence, Ries's opponents often referred to him as the "pope of Waterlanders."[189]

It is perhaps through Gerrits and Ries that much of the Mennonite thought was passed on to Smyth and therefore the early Baptists. The tolerance of Gerrits and Ries as well as Ries's spiritual views seem to have found fertile ground in the mind of John Smyth. Smyth's interactions with the Separatist tradition perhaps prepared him for his eventual move into the Mennonites. Smyth's relationships with the English Puritans and Separatists and the Dutch Mennonites will be discussed in the next chapter.

---

[187]Ries, *Ontdeckinghe der dwalingen*, 165; in Dyck, "Hans de Ries," 203.
[188]*Mennonite Encyclopedia* 4:330; H. E. Dosker, *The Dutch Anabaptists* (Philadelphia: Judson Press, 1921) 152-53.
[189]Voolstra, "The Path to Conversion," 101.

Chapter 2

Smyth's Life, Debates, and Writings

Changes and debates marked John Smyth's life and career. Smyth's writings or theology cannot be assessed properly without recognizing these events. Rather than simply relaying a full biographical sketch of Smyth's life, the purpose of this chapter is to concentrate on the controversies that plagued him and became a driving force for his publications. For it is in the context of these debates that Smyth expounds his theology.

Smyth's works portray the substance of his debates and indicate some of the contemporary influences on him. The events of his life affect his theology and vice versa. Often Smyth alienated his associates by some action driven by his acceptance of a new thought. Noticing this characteristic in Smyth, Michael Watts declares that "John Smyth was a man of original mind, an enthusiast for new ideas who once having seized a notion would pursue it ruthlessly to its logical conclusion. For Smyth the consistency which indicated a closed mind was no virtue."[1]

Puritan Stage

Born in approximately 1570, Smyth's early days are unknown. He is thought to have been the son of John Smyth, a yeoman of Sturton-le-Steeple, Nottinghamshire.[2]

Smyth's time at Cambridge. Smyth entered as a sizar in Christ's College, Cambridge in the Easter term of 1586. He received his Bachelor of Arts in 1590, Master of Arts in 1593, and served as a fellow at the college from 1594 to 1598.[3] He was most likely ordained in Lincoln in 1594, but had definitely been ordained by 1595 because his fellowship required that ordination be done within a year of election. Smyth does not

---

[1]Michael R. Watts, *The Dissenters*, vol. 1, *From the Reformation to the French Revolution* (Oxford: Clarendon Press, 1978) 43.

[2]B. R. White, "John Smyth," *Biographical Dictionary of Seventeenth-Century Radicals*, ed. Richard L. Greaves and Robert Zaller (Brighton: Harvester Press, 1984) 3:186; Coggins, "The Theological Positions of John Smyth," 247.

[3]Venn and Venn, *Alumni Cantabrigienses*, 4:101.

give an exact date, but he does indicate that his ordination was performed by Bishop William Wickham upon his election as fellow.[4]

During Smyth's days there, Christ's College was a haven of Puritan beliefs. Other Cambridge colleges had their Puritan influences, but Christ's was the center. Out of Christ's ranks came those of a Puritan mind-set, such as William Ames, Richard Bernard, Arthur Hildersham, Francis and George Johnson, and William Perkins.[5] While Cambridge was a stronghold of Puritan Reformed views, it was not isolated from the views that would later be known as Arminianism. A professor of divinity, Peter Baro, challenged Reformed views such as predestination.[6] This background of challenging Reformed views would resurface during Smyth's days in Amsterdam.

Perhaps Francis Johnson and William Perkins introduced Smyth to Puritan ideas. They both preceded Smyth as fellows at Christ's before they became pastors.[7] Johnson had an excellent opportunity to influence Smyth, serving as his tutor at Cambridge.[8] While Smyth does not mention Johnson directly, he does admit receiving a portion of his Cambridge education from contemporary Separatists.[9] As a Bachelor of Arts, Smyth studied Hebrew under Hugh Broughton and had Richard Bernard as a

---

[4]Smyth, *Works* 2:493; W. T. Whitley, "Biography," in *The Works of John Smyth*, xxxv-vi; Walter H. Burgess, *John Smyth, the Se-Baptist, Thomas Helwys and the First Baptist Church in England* (London: James Clarke, 1911) 42-43; White, "John Smyth," *Biographical Dictionary* 3:186.

[5]Venn and Venn, *The Book of Matriculations and Degrees*, 13, 42, 345, 387, 388, 524.

[6]Carl Bangs, *Arminius: A Study in the Dutch Reformation* (Nashville and New York: Abingdon Press, 1971) 207. The extent of Baro's influence on Smyth's later rejection of Reformed views will be a topic of discussion in chap. 7.

[7]Keith L. Sprunger, *The Learned Doctor William Ames* (Urbana, Chicago, London: University of Illinois Press, 1972) 13.

[8]Richard Bernard, *Christian Advertisements and Counsels of Peace: Also Dissuasions from the Separatists Schisme, Commonly Called Brownisme* (London: Felix Kyngston, 1608) 37; A. C. Underwood, *A History of the English Baptists* (London: Baptist Union Publication Department, 1947) 34; Whitley, "Biography," xxv.

[9]Smyth, *Works* 1:71.

sizar.[10] John Smyth joined a succession of Christ's College graduates who were reprimanded for their preaching. His criticism of the surplice, the Anglican burial service, and the churching of women caused him the most trouble.[11] In this period, although there is no known official record of the event, it seems that he married his wife, Mary, in 1598. Accordingly, Smyth then left his fellowship due to his marriage.[12] There is no record of his activities between leaving his fellowship in 1598 and his appointment as city lecturer of Lincoln in 1600.

Smyth's time in Lincoln. On 27 September 1600, Smyth became the city lecturer for Lincoln.[13] Mayor Edward Dynnys proposed Smyth for the position, and he was elected by eight votes to seven over Thomas Luddington, the current lecturer.[14] Two years later, on 2 September 1602, Smyth was appointed as city lecturer for life by the mayor. Unfortunately, the opposition party struck out against the mayor and abolished all of his appointments including Smyth's. On 13 October, the opposition party returned their candidate, Luddington, back to the post. After a series of court battles and compromises, both Luddington and Smyth were removed. However, as a part of the settlement, Smyth did receive some financial compensation.[15] Though accused of preaching against the Lord's Prayer, most likely Smyth was a victim of a political struggle in Lincoln where he was identified with the losing faction.[16] Smyth relays his version of his removal from the lectureship, "being then Lecturer in the Citie of Lincolne: but partly the motion of some friends, partly and chiefly the satisfying of some sinister spirits have in a manner wrested from me that [lectureship]."[17] After leaving the well-paid lectureship,

---

[10]Whitley, "Biography," xxxi.

[11]White, *The English Separatist Tradition*, 116; Sprunger, *The Learned Doctor William Ames*, 16.

[12]Whitley, "Biography," xxxvi-xxxvii; Underwood, *A History of the English Baptists*, 34.

[13]White, "John Smyth," *Biographical Dictionary*, 3:186.

[14]Whitley, "Biography," xli; Burgess, *John Smyth, the Se-Baptist*, 46.

[15]Whitley, "Biography," xlv-xlvii; Burgess, *John Smyth, the Se-Baptist*, 51-53.

[16]Smyth, *Works* 1:68-69 and 1:71-72; William R. Estep, *The Anabaptist Story*, 3rd ed. (Grand Rapids MI and Cambridge: Eerdmans, 1996) 286.

[17]Smyth, *Works* 1:68.

Smyth probably supported himself as a physician.[18]

While in Lincoln, he preached the sermons that were later published as *The Bright Morning Starre* (1603) and *A Paterne of True Prayer* (1605).[19] In *The Bright Morning Starre*, Smyth intended to contradict false teachings that were being published and to help with "the understanding of the simple."[20] *The Bright Morning Starre* was originally preached as four sermons, as an exposition of Psalm 22. Smyth uses these sermons to explain the work of Christ. His overall description of Christ's work is Puritan in nature with an emphasis on Christ's sufferings. In this publication, Smyth upholds belief in original sin, total depravity, predestination, and the perseverance of the saints.[21] Smyth affirms the five church officers of bishop, teacher, ruling elder, deacon, and widow, also the swearing of oaths, and encourages the magistrates to aid religion.[22]

Two years later, Smyth published *A Paterne of True Prayer* as his defense against accusations concerning his teachings, especially those on prayer. Smyth dedicated this work to the earl of Sheffield who acted as his arbitrator in the legal struggle at Lincoln. In "The Epistle Dedicatorie," Smyth states the purpose of *A Paterne of True Prayer*: "For the cleering of the truth I am bold to publish this present Treatise."[23] In both of his first books, Smyth shows himself to be a Puritan who is loyal to the Church of England. In *A Paterne of True Prayer*, he states, "I doe iudge that there is no one doctrine or opinion contrarie to the doctrine of this Church in all this tractate."[24] *A Paterne of True Prayer* is an exposition of the Lord's Prayer. Smyth admits that he is probably not adding anything new on the subject. His friends had requested that he publish these sermons to defend himself by clarifying his views on prayer.

Smyth says that his reason for publishing is "onely the cleering of my

---

[18]Underwood, *A History of the English Baptists*, 34.
[19]Smyth, *Works* 1:1 and 1:68.
[20]Smyth, *Works* 1:2. Smyth occasionally placed a mark over vowels to denote the letter "n" or "m." This quotation, and others to which this practice applies, have been emended for the reader. For example, here "understâding" has been emended to "understanding." Each quotation that has been changed is noted.
[21]Smyth, *Works* 1:181, 1:62 and 1:108, 1:134, 1:220, respectively.
[22]Smyth, *Works* 1:158 (all five church offices), 1:140, 1:166, respectively.
[23]Smyth, *Works* 1:69.
[24]Smyth, *Works* 1:71.

selfe from vniust accusations."[25] He denies the charge of rejecting set prayers as the Separatists had done by saying, "I am far from the opinion of them which separate from our Church, concerning the set forme of prayer."[26] The Separatists had ruled out set prayers, but Smyth said that set prayers were acceptable, adding though that he wished "all the people of God could conceiue prayer."[27] Throughout this work Smyth reaffirms the Lord's Prayer and the practice of set prayers. He attempts to suppress all his detractors by making these closing remarks in *A Paterne of True Prayer*, "The Lords prayer is the best forme of prayer that euer was deuised. The Lords prayer is the best prayer that euer was deuised. He that prayeth the Lords prayer in words and matter, prayeth well."[28] Apparently Smyth had not yet accepted Separatist views. He attempts to make this point clear by emphasizing how "far" he is from their opinion.[29] He identifies himself with the Church of England, not the Separatists in stating "there are some (whom we wil account brethren, though they doe not so reckon of vs, seeing they haue separated from vs)."[30]

After his removal from Lincoln, Smyth continued to draw criticism for "personal preaching." However, on 23 March 1603, the archbishop gave Smyth permission to preach in the province of Canterbury. This included Lincoln, where Smyth was still a controversial figure. Therefore, Bishop Chaderton of Lincoln complained about Smyth's appointment to Archbishop Whitgift. Four months later, on 26 July 1603, Whitgift revoked Smyth's licence and requested that this revocation be widely published. The revocation did not silence Smyth. On 26 March 1606, in St. Benedict's Church, Smyth was charged with preaching in Gainsborough against the bishop's orders.

Jerome Phillips was the minister responsible for the parish that included Gainsborough. The congregation had invited Smyth to teach after Phillips's continued absence from his pulpit.[31] Instead of gratitude for his willingness to help, Smyth was reprimanded. Two letters were

---

[25]Smyth, *Works* 1:71.
[26]Smyth, *Works* 1:71.
[27]Smyth, *Works* 1:71.
[28]Smyth, *Works* 1:247.
[29]Smyth, *Works* 1:71.
[30]Smyth, *Works* 1:81.
[31]Whitley, "Biography," lvi-lvii.

written to defend Smyth's actions, and apparently at this time Smyth still held to his Puritan views. However, this reprimand possibly pushed Smyth toward a Separatist position.[32]

Other ministers in the Gainsborough area who were in trouble for advancing Puritanism included Richard Clyfton and William Brewster. When Smyth later met with others who were interested in reform in the Coventry home of Sir William Bowes, they discussed the arguments of the Separatist position. After nine months of deliberating, Smyth and others decided to follow the example of other Separatists and form a covenanted congregation.[33]

Separatist Stage

In 1606, Smyth, Richard Bernard, William Bradford, William Brewster, Hugh Bromhead, Richard Clyfton, Thomas Helwys, John Robinson, and others agreed to resist the established church.[34] They probably held meetings at Gainsborough as an independent congregation or conventicle before they formally established a Separatist church.[35] By the autumn of 1607, they covenanted together into a Separatist church in Gainsborough in the lower Trent valley.[36]

Smyth's congregation at Gainsborough. Although Smyth indicates that his study of scripture had brought him to the act of covenanting, his awareness of Francis Johnson and other Separatists must have had some influence.[37] In his work, *Principles and Inferences concerning the Visible Church*, Smyth's description of the church closely resembles the model of Johnson and Henry Barrow. Smyth's church covenant was similar to

---

[32]Estep, *The Anabaptist Story*, 287; White, *The English Separatist Tradition Separatist*, 120-21.

[33]Smyth, *Works* 2:331-37.

[34]Whitley, "Biography," lx; Underwood, *A History of the English Baptists*, 34; Watts, *The Dissenters* 1:41-42.

[35]Leon McBeth, *The Baptist Heritage* (Nashville: Broadman Press, 1987) 33.

[36]Haykin, *Kiffin, Knollys, and Keach*, 22; William Bradford, *Of Plymouth Plantation*, new edition, ed. Samuel Eliot Morison (New York: Alfred A. Knopf, 1952) 9. Burgess gives the date of the formation of this congregation as 1606; Burgess, *John Smyth, the Se-Baptist*, 81.

[37]Whitley, "Biography," lxi-lxii.

a covenant Johnson had drawn up in Middelburg in 1591.[38]

In 1607, Smyth wrote *Principles and Inferences* "to manifest the true constitution of the Church."[39] In it he also describes "the ordinances of Christ for the dispensing of the covenant since his death." He asks his readers to compare the Church of England or "the assemblies of the land" with his description of the church.[40] In this work, Smyth shows his acceptance of Separatist doctrine. His definition of the church involves the Separatist idea of a local church covenant. He applies the concept of covenant to the visible church as well as the invisible church, or the elect. He describes a visible church in these words:

> A visible communion of Sainctes is of two, three, or more Sainctes joyned together by covenant with God & themselves, freely to vse al the holy things of God, according to the word, for their mutual edification, & Gods glory.[41]

He continues by saying that a true visible church requires three things: true matter, true form, true properties. The true matter is the saints, or the faithful. The true form has both an inward and an outward part. The inward part is made up of three things: "1. the Spirit. 2. Faith. 3. love."[42] The outward part is the covenant that is agreed to by all members. The true properties of the church are "communion in al the holy things of God" and "the power of our Lord Iesus Christ."[43] This description of the church indicates that when the faithful join together in a covenant, then they become a true church. This church is empowered by Christ and has full authority to appoint ministers, administer the sacraments, preach, and exercise discipline.

In *Principles and Inferences*, Smyth supports the church offices of pastor, teacher, ruling elder, deacons, and widows. One of the responsibil-

---

[38]Burrage, *The Early English Dissenters* 1:138, 230; Coggins, "The Theological Positions of John Smyth," 249; White, *The English Separatist Tradition Separatist*, 124.

[39]Smyth, *Works* 1:270. This shortened title will be used for *Principles and Inferences concerning the Visible Church* in the remainder of the book.

[40]Smyth, *Works* 1:250.
[41]Smyth, *Works* 1:252.
[42]Smyth, *Works* 1:253.
[43]Smyth, *Works* 1:254.

ities of the deacons is to tend to the church treasury, which should not contain any gifts from outside the membership.[44] Smyth also gives some detailed instructions on how the true church should administer church discipline, including the admonition that the discipline should be redemptive.[45]

Soon after its formation, Smyth's church began to meet in two locations. The group in Gainsborough was under Smyth's leadership; the other group met in Scrooby in Nottinghamshire and was led by Richard Clyfton and John Robinson.[46] William Bradford gives the following description of Smyth's group:

> These people became 2. distincte bodys or churches, & in regarde of distance of place did congregate severally; for they were of sundrie towns & villages, some in Nottinghamshire, some of Lincollinshire, and some of Yorkshire, wher they border nearest togeather. In one of these churches (besids others of note) was Mr. John Smith, a man of able gifts, & a good preacher, who afterwards was chosen their pastor. But these afterwards falling into some errours in the Low Countries, ther (for the most part) buried them selves, & their names.[47]

Bradford says that the two groups met separately in England because of the distance between them. The separation was not as permanent as would happen in Amsterdam.[48] The churches maintained a close fellowship. For example, Richard Clyfton indicated that he belonged to the congregation that had covenanted with Smyth, even though he was a leader in the Scrooby group.[49] Bradford also records that sometime after they had covenanted together, Smyth was chosen as pastor of the Gainsborough group.

Although John Robinson does not mention these two groups specifically, he does write that a church should be small enough to meet in one location to promote unity within the body. He also expressed concern that if a church was too large or covered too great an area, then

---

[44]Smyth, *Works* 1:259.
[45]Smyth, *Works* 1:266.
[46]Bradford, *Of Plymouth Plantation*, 9-10; Estep, *The Anabaptist Story*, 287.
[47]Bradford, *Of Plymouth Plantation*, 9.
[48]Whitley, "Biography," lxviii.
[49]Smyth, *Works* 2:575.

the minister could not meet the needs of the parishioners sufficiently.[50] Perhaps these reasons played a part in the decision of the congregations to meet separately and choose ministers for both groups.

Smyth's departure for Amsterdam. In July 1607, Joan Helwys (wife of Thomas Helwys) and others were arrested and confined in York Castle. These arrests were the culmination of the prolonged persecution endured by Smyth's group. They served as the final blow that encouraged Smyth and company to leave England for the tolerance of the Netherlands.[51] William Bradford describes the conditions that plagued the fledgling Separatist congregations:

> But after these things they could not long continue in any peaceable condition, but were hunted & persecuted on every side, so as their former afflictions were but as flea-bitings in comparison of these which now came upon them. For some were taken & clapped up in prison, others had their houses beset & watched night and day, & hardly escaped their hands; and the most were fain to flee & leave their houses & habitations, and the means of their livelihood.[52]

Bradford's account provides a few details of the persecution that caused both congregations to leave their homeland. This trip was supported financially by the more affluent members of the congregations such as William Brewster of the Scrooby group and Thomas Helwys of the Gainsborough group. Incidentally, both of these men would eventually serve as pastors and would lead portions of these groups out of the Netherlands to the New World and back to England, respectively.[53] The emigration of Smyth's congregation took place in 1607 or 1608.[54]

---

[50]*The Works of John Robinson, Pastor of the Pilgrim Fathers*, 3 vols., ed. Robert Ashton (London: J. Snow, 1851) 3:12-14.

[51]Whitley, "Biography," lxxii; Estep, *The Anabaptist Story*, 287; Burgess, *John Smyth, the Se-Baptist*, 94; Henry C. Vedder, *A Short History of the Baptists*, rev. ed. (Philadelphia: American Baptist Publication Society, 1907) 202.

[52]Bradford, *Of Plymouth Plantation*, 10.

[53]White, *The English Separatist Tradition*, 125; Whitley, "Biography," lxxiv; William H. Brackney, *The Baptists* (New York: Greenwood Press, 1988) 5.

[54]Murray Tolmie, *The Triumph of the Saints: The Separate Churches of London 1616–1649* (Cambridge: Cambridge University Press, 1977) 69; Burgess, *John Smyth, the Se-Baptist*, 95; Estep, *The Anabaptist Story*, 287; Keith L.

William Bradford writing years later gives this account of their move:

> Yet seeing themselves thus molested, and that there was no hope of their continuance there, by a jointe consent they resolved to go in the Low Countries, where they heard was freedom of religion for all men; as also how sundry from London and other parts of the land had been exiled and persecuted for the same cause, and were gone thither, and lived at Amsterdam and in other places of the land. So after they had continued together about a year, and kept their meetings every Sabbath in one place or other, exercising the worship of God amongst themselves, notwistanding all the diligence and malice of their adversaries, they seeing they could no longer continue in that condition, they resolved to get over into Holland as they could. Which was in the year 1607 and 1608.[55]

So, according to Bradford, the move spanned a period that included parts of 1607 and 1608. This dating can be evidenced further by looking at the dates of Smyth's publications. His work, *Principles and Inferences*, was published in 1607.[56] It appears that at this time Smyth was still in England, because in his note to the reader he mentions that he wants them to "compare the truth here expressed with the frame ministerie and government of the assemblies of the land."[57] The land with which he compares his understanding of the church is England.

There is a short time lapse between Smyth's publishing of *Principles and Inferences* and his writing of *The Differences of the Churches of the Separation*. In his introduction to the latter work, Smyth says that it was "Not long since I published a litle methode intituled principles & inferences concerning the visible Church."[58] *The Differences of the Churches* was published in 1608 in Amsterdam.[59] There is just a short time between publishing *Principles and Inferences* in England and writing *The Differ-*

Sprunger, *Dutch Puritanism* (Leiden: E. J. Brill, 1982) 66.
[55] Bradford, *Of Plymouth Plantation*, 10.
[56] Smyth, *Works* 1:249.
[57] Smyth, *Works* 1:250. This quotation does not indicate Smyth's whereabouts, but it could imply that he is still in England.
[58] Smyth, *Works* 1:270.
[59] Smyth, *Works* 1:269. This shortened title for *The Differences of the Churches of the Seperation* will be used henceforth.

ences of the Churches in Amsterdam, and Smyth would have had to be in Amsterdam long enough to have observed some of the differences between his congregation and Johnson's. Hence, Smyth's congregation emigrated to Amsterdam probably in 1607, but certainly by early 1608. If the moving of the whole congregation required numerous trips, then Bradford could be correct in saying that the church moved in 1607 and 1608.

Before and after their migration to Amsterdam, Smyth and Robinson were developing reputations as Separatist leaders. This becomes apparent from the correspondence of one of their adversaries. Bishop Joseph Hall wrote at some length against Separatism. In one letter he focused his criticism on John Smyth and John Robinson whom he referred to as the "Ring-leaders" of the Separation.[60] Later, when Smyth became a Baptist, Hall says that Smyth was the real leader of the Separation with Robinson as "his Shadow."[61] In his letter to Smyth and Robinson, Hall declares that all Separatists were guilty of taking part in a schism. He says that the Separatists have turned their back on their mother, the Church of England, who had raised and trained them. Hall's attack on Smyth and Robinson was especially sharp as he writes, "This unnaturalness is shameful; and more heinous in you, who are reported not parties in this evil, but authors."[62]

Hall declares that they have been misguided in their pursuit of truth. He says that their wrongdoing is compounded by the fact that they also lead others into their errors. He also states that if the Separatists would have been more humble and peaceful, then the schism could have been avoided. He describes their arrogance by saying:

> Your zeal of truth hath mis-led you, and you others: a zeal, if honest, yet blind-folded, and led by self-will. Oh, that you loved peace, but half

---

[60]Joseph Hall, "To Mr. Smith, and Mr. Rob., Ringleaders of the Late Separation; at Amsterdam," in *The Works of the Right Reverend Father in God, Joseph Hall*, 10 vols., ed. Josiah Pratt (London: C. Whittingham, 1808) 7:171.

[61]Joseph Hall, *A Common Apology of the Church of England, against the Unjust Challenges of the Over-Just Sect, Commonly Called Brownists*, in *The Works of . . . Joseph Hall* 9:401. This may not be an accurate description of the relationship between Robinson and Smyth. Hall was attempting to ridicule the Separatists and Robinson by saying their leader had fallen into Anabaptism.

[62]Hall, "To Mr. Smith and Mr. Rob," *The Works of . . . Joseph Hall* 7:171.

so well as truth: then, this breach had never been; and you, that are yet brethren, had been still companions.[63]

The errors that the Separatists alleged to be in the Church of England were not serious offences according to Hall. He is incredulous that they would leave the Church over such insignificant points. Hall indicates that he may agree with their dislike for certain church practices. However, these practices do not merit dividing the church. He pleads for Smyth and others to repent and come back to the Church of England, and adds that

> Otherwise, your souls shall find too late, that it had been a thousand times better to swallow a Ceremony, than to rend a Church; yea, that even whoredoms and murders shall abide an easier answer, than separation.[64]

Smyth was one of many Puritan-minded people who either had moved or would eventually move to Amsterdam. Others include John Robinson, John Paget, Henry Jacob, Henry Ainsworth, Francis and George Johnson, John Canne, Thomas Hooker, and John Forbes.[65] Though many people of similar inclination came to Amsterdam, they did not become a unified church. Although not all of these men became Separatists, their division does indicate the fragmentation that plagued Separatism. A good indication of this intrinsic individualism is Smyth's relationship with the Ancient Church of Amsterdam.

Smyth's disagreements with other Separatists. As Smyth's congregation arrived in Amsterdam in 1607 or 1608, they encountered Francis Johnson's church.[66] Their fellowship was strained from an early stage as Smyth disagreed with the Ancient Church in many of its practices. The conflict led Smyth to publish *The Differences of the Churches*, which he describes as "a correction and svpplement" to *Principles and Inferences*.[67]

Smyth says he has three purposes in writing *The Differences of the*

---

[63]Hall, "To Mr. Smith and Mr. Rob," *The Works of . . . Joseph Hall* 7:171.
[64]Hall, "To Mr. Smith and Mr. Rob," *The Works of . . . Joseph Hall* 7:173.
[65]Sprunger, *The Learned Doctor William Ames*, 28, 212.
[66]Sprunger, *Dutch Puritanism*, 80. Underwood incorrectly states that this was also Smyth's first contact with Robinson's church in Amsterdam; Underwood, *A History of the English Baptists*, 35.
[67]Smyth, *Works* 1:269.

Churches. His first purpose is "For the satisfaction of every true lover of the truth especially the Brethren of the Seperation that are doubtfull."[68] This shows his attempt to encourage the immigrant Separatists. His second purpose is "for the removing of an Vnjust calumnie" that had been cast upon his church.[69] Apparently, Smyth's group had been reproved for not joining with Johnson's church. He wanted to make clear his reasons for this decision. His third purpose is that he is trying to explain the proper manner of worship and governing in the church. He writes: "Finally for the cleering of the truth: & the discovering of the mysterie of iniquitie yet further in the worship & offices of the Church."[70]

Some scholars debate whether Smyth's congregation ever became a part of Johnson's or if they remained two distinct congregations. Michael Watts agrees with many older historians who suggest that Smyth's group joined Johnson's church.[71] However, the majority of modern scholars hold that Smyth's group interacted with Johnson's church, but never joined them.[72] The confusion results from the statements similar to that of Henry Ainsworth, teacher in Johnson's church, who says about Smyth that "He with his followers breaking off communion with us charged us with sin for using our English Bibles in the worship of God."[73] In this statement,

---

[68]Smyth, *Works* 1:269.
[69]Smyth, *Works* 1:269.
[70]Smyth, *Works* 1:269.
[71]Watts, *The Dissenters* 1:83; J. M. Cramp, *Baptist History* (London: E. Stock, 1871) 254; Thomas Armitage, *A History of the Baptists*, rev. ed. (New York: Bryan, Taylor & Co., 1886) 453; David Bogue and James Bennett, *History of Dissenters*, 4 vols. (London: printed for the authors, 1808–1812) 1:149; Crosby says that Smyth joined the ancient church but refers to Ainsworth as the pastor of the congregation: Thomas Crosby, *The History of the English Baptists*, vol. 1 (London: printed by the editor, 1738; photoreprint: Lafayette TN: Church History Research & Archives, 1979) 91.
[72]Whitley, "Biography," lxxxi-lxxxii; Coggins, *John Smyth's Congregation*, 48-49; Haykin, *Kiffin, Knollys, and Keach*, 22; Estep, *The Anabaptist Story*, 288; Underwood, *A History of the English Baptists*, 35; Pater, *Karlstadt as the Father of the Baptist Movements*, 253; Sprunger, *Dutch Puritanism*, 66; White, *The English Separatist Tradition Separatist*, 126; Burgess, *John Smyth, the Se-Baptist*, 98; Vedder, *A Short History of the Baptists*, 202; Robert G. Torbet, *A History of the Baptists*, rev. ed. (Valley Forge PA: Judson Press, 1963) 34-35.
[73]Henry Ainsworth, *A defense of the Holy Scriptures* (Amsterdam: Giles

Ainsworth does not mean that Smyth and his followers were within the membership of the Ancient Church. Instead, he is indicating the reason Smyth's congregation refused to join in worship with the Ancient Church.

As has been stated, Smyth came to Amsterdam in 1607 or early 1608. He wrote *The Differences of the Churches* at approximately the same time, for it was published in 1608. On the title page of this publication, Smyth refers to his congregation as the "second English Church at Amsterdam."[74] Therefore, shortly after Smyth's group arrived in Amsterdam, Smyth was explaining the differences between the two churches. So, this short time lapse between his arrival and his publication of *The Differences of the Churches* suggests that Smyth's group had differences with Johnson's church from early in their stay and probably never officially joined it.

Smyth's *The Differences of the Churches* contains two areas of conflict: the liturgy of the church and the ministry of the church.[75] In each area, Smyth makes three points. Concerning the liturgy of the church, Smyth says that books should not be used in worship, prophesying, or singing in a time of spiritual worship. Concerning the ministry of the church, Smyth holds that there is only one type of elder and that is a pastor. Second, he argues that there can be many pastors within a congregation. Third, he states that financial support for the ministry of the church should come only from the membership.[76] Smyth's most inflammatory arguments relate to his congregation's removal of the Bible and other books from worship proper. Additionally, Smyth's disagreed with Johnson over the elders' role in the church.

Smyth's first concern with Johnson's church was the limitation of the Spirit during worship. He believed that the Spirit was quenched when a human invention such as a translation of scripture was used. Smyth explains, "A translation being the worke of a mans witt . . . & therefore not to be brought into the worship of God to be read."[77] Smyth's opposition is not just to translations. One of the chapters of *The*

Thorp, 1609) 3.
   [74]Smyth, *Works* 1:269.
   [75]Smyth, *Works* 1:269.
   [76]Smyth, *Works* 1:273.
   [77]Smyth, *Works* 1:291-92.

Differences of the Churches is entitled "Reasons proving the Originals not to be given as helps before the eye in worship."[78] Acheson says that Smyth argues "that continued use of the Scriptures in translation from the Greek or Hebrew was suggestive of the excessive formality of ritual."[79] Pearse makes similar comments by indicating that Smyth was reacting against the prayer books of the Church of England and was insisting on worship that was ordered by the Spirit.[80]

Watts claims that Smyth's break with Johnson's church was mainly over formalism in worship and differences in church government. While these two reasons are both discussed, the limiting of the Spirit in worship seems to be the main concern.[81] A great deal of material in *The Differences of the Churches* indicates the necessity of removing any hindrance to spiritual worship. Smyth says, "In performing spirituall worship wee must take heed of quenching the spirit."[82] He challenged the Separatists by saying that they had removed books from their prayers, but they also needed to remove books from "prophesying & singing of Psalmes."[83]

Another area of conflict was that Francis Johnson had tried to calm strife that had become commonplace in his church by putting the authority into the hands of the elders.[84] This was not acceptable to Smyth who held that the congregation maintained its authority.[85] Smyth's choice of congregational government was not a move away from Separatism. Robert Browne believed that church authority was given to the entire

---

[78] Smyth, *Works* 1:282.

[79] R. J. Acheson, *Radical Puritans in England, 1550–1660* (London and New York: Longman Group, 1990) 20.

[80] Meic Pearse, *The Great Restoration*, 189-91.

[81] Watts, *The Dissenters* 1:43; Burgess, *John Smyth, the Se-Baptist*, 125-26. Although Smyth does not mention size as a reason for not joining Johnson's church, Meic Pearse suggests that this could have made any amalgamation impractical and unnecessary. The Smyth/Robinson congregation would have numbered around 150. Pearse, *The Great Restoration*, 189.

[82] Smyth, *Works* 1:277.

[83] Smyth, *Works* 1:283.

[84] Watts, *The Dissenters* 1:43.

[85] Watts, *The Dissenters* 1:43-44. This issue would divide the Johnson's church itself in 1610, with Henry Ainsworth leading those who supported congregational government.

church, but they would select elders to administer that authority.[86] Also, Browne put the role of the elders in these terms: "Therefore is the church called the pillar & ground of trueth. 1. Tim. 3. 15. & the voice of the whole people, guided bie the elders and forwardest, is saied to be the voice of God."[87] The elders were to provide leadership for the church, which was the seat of authority.

It was under Henry Barrow's leadership that the Separatists became predominantly of a presbyterian mind-set. Barrow held that the authority in a church was given to the elders.[88] Johnson had followed in Barrow's thought. Smyth himself had been more sympathetic to this view earlier in his *Principles and Inferences*. This work was published in Gainsborough, and it gave authority to the elders through the church.[89] However, after encountering Johnson in Amsterdam, Smyth realized that the church should retain its authority, even though it has elders for leadership. Smyth says, "The presbytery hath no powre, but what the Church hath & giveth vnto it: which the Church vppon just cause can take away: Colos 4. 17. Gal. 1. 9. Revel. 2. 2. 1. Cor. 16. 22."[90] These beliefs on church government combined with Smyth's views on worship caused Smyth's group to remain separate from Johnson's church.

The views that Smyth expressed in *The Differences of the Churches* angered many of his fellow Separatists. Clyfton, Johnson, and Ainsworth all responded to his views in their various works. In his *A Christian Plea*, Francis Johnson defended the practices of his church against Smyth's arguments. In *The Differences of the Churches*, Smyth had called for each church to have several pastors or elders who have similar responsibilities in the church. He said that all elders have been given spiritual gifts for the work of a pastor. He concludes, "Therfor all the Elders have the same office of the pastor: & so are all of one sort."[91] Johnson disagreed with this and said that there may be many elders, but there should be only one

---

[86]Browne, *The Writings of Robert Harrison and Robert Browne*, 335.

[87]Browne, *The Writings of Robert Harrison and Robert Browne*, 399. "Whole" has been emended.

[88]Barrow, *The Writings of Henry Barrow, 1590-1591*, 303.

[89]Smyth, *Works* 1:256-59.

[90]Smyth, *Works* 1:315.

[91]Smyth, *Works* 1:309.

Smyth's Life, Debates, and Writings \ 57

pastor for each church.[92] Henry Ainsworth agreed with Johnson that there should be only one pastor for each church. Discounting Smyth's view that there is only one type of elder, Ainsworth maintained three types of elders: pastor, teacher, and ruling elders.[93]

Francis Johnson also challenged Smyth about receiving gifts from outside the church. His stance was that where the church is poor, the minister can receive financial help from outside the church.[94] Smyth had argued that there must be a separation of the treasury along with a separation of communion. Money given to the church from outside should be set aside for common use and not be placed in the treasury.[95]

Additionally, Johnson opposed Smyth's practice of allowing the Lord's Supper and baptism to be administered by someone within the congregation if the church was without a minister. He states, "And the ministration of the Sacraments, and blessing of the bread and wine, is a work of the ministerie."[96] Smyth agreed that it was proper for a pastor to administer the sacraments. However, he argued that the congregation maintained all authority. So, if there was no minister available the church could administer "the seales of the covenant."[97]

Smyth's arguments in *The Differences of the Churches* about the church's authority being given by Christ to the congregation were refuted by Johnson. Henry Ainsworth also defended Johnson's position. However, some of Smyth's arguments may have influenced Ainsworth, for later he led a split from the Ancient Church that centered on a disagreement on where authority lay in the church. Johnson says that the phrase "tell the church" in Matthew 18 means the elders, not the congregation. He says that by accepting congregational rule, Ainsworth had fallen into the error that he earlier had exposed in Smyth.[98] Johnson cites Thomas Cartwright and Dudley Fenner as witnesses to the fact that power is with the elders, contradicting the views of Smyth, Ainsworth, John Robinson, and Henry

---

[92]Johnson, *A Christian Plea*, 262.
[93]Ainsworth, *A defense of the Holy Scriptures*, 90-91.
[94]Johnson, *A Christian Plea*, 317.
[95]Smyth, *Works* 1:318.
[96]Johnson, *A Christian Plea*, 287.
[97]Smyth, *Works* 1:315.
[98]Johnson, *A Christian Plea*, 308.

Jacob.[99]

Johnson was not the only Separatist to oppose Smyth's comments made in *The Differences of the Churches*. Henry Ainsworth and Richard Clyfton also wrote against Smyth's positions. Ainsworth focuses on Smyth's opposition to using scripture translations in a time of worship. He points out that Smyth calls the word of God the matter of worship, but excludes it from worship.[100] Smyth explains that the scriptures should be taught, but not in a time of worship. Books and "writings" are images or ceremonies. As ceremonies they have no place in spiritual worship.[101] Ainsworth disagrees with Smyth's view of the scripture and books being only an image. He says that a book gives instruction where an image does not. Sarcastically, he adds that if Smyth sees no difference between books and images, then his next publication should be pictures only. Ainsworth says this would keep Smyth from misleading so many.[102]

Ainsworth challenges Smyth's arguments for excluding scripture translations from worship. Smyth had argued that using a book was ceremonial and restricted the work of the Spirit.[103] Ainsworth defends the practice of using translations with several arguments. First, he attacks Smyth's argument that the reading of the Old Testament is a ceremony. Ainsworth says that even if the Old Testament is conceded as ceremonial, this would not apply to the New Testament. The New Testament has been given to the church and should be read in worship.[104] Ainsworth continued by saying that Smyth contradicts himself in *The Differences of the Churches*. In one place he says the Old Testament worship began in the book, and in another he says that the book had no place in Jewish worship.[105] Ainsworth urges his readers to recognize Smyth's error in saying that the entire Bible is a ceremony. He writes, "If M. Smyth. make the substance of the scripture a ceremonie, that is a shadow to be ended and abolished at Christs coming, it is a wicked error."[106]

---

[99] Johnson, *A Christian Plea*, 312-14.
[100] Ainsworth, *A defense of the Holy Scriptures*, 7.
[101] Smyth, *Works* 1:279-82.
[102] Ainsworth, *A defense of the Holy Scriptures*, 23.
[103] Smyth, *Works* 1:302.
[104] Ainsworth, *A defense of the Holy Scriptures*, 25.
[105] Ainsworth, *A defense of the Holy Scriptures*, 40.
[106] Ainsworth, *A defense of the Holy Scriptures*, 53.

Smyth also had dismissed scripture translations from worship because he said that they were made by man, not by God.[107] However, Ainsworth affirms translations as being useful tools of ministry that have been given by God. He writes, "The holy scriptures faithfully expressed in English or any language, is the work of Gods wisdome & unserchable knowledge: and cannot without injury to his majestie, be said to be the work of mans wit & learning; though man have used his skil in writing or translating it according to the original copie given of God."[108]

Ainsworth also assails Smyth's view that the Spirit is quenched if the Bible is used in worship. He argues that if a minister or any Christian can be inspired to speak God's message during a time of worship, then surely the scriptures are equally trustworthy. It is the scriptures themselves that are to be the guide for Christian belief. They are inspired by the Spirit, so they will not restrict His work. Ainsworth asserts:

> Neyther is it against the nature of spiritual worship, to read Gods book in the eares of the Church: for if it be worship in them to heare the spirit speak out of the Ministers hart; it is worship also in them to hear the spirit speak, out of the holy book. And it cannot be deneyed but Gods spirit speaketh there; and that which commeth out of the hart of man, must be tried by that book; and accordingly, accepted or refused.[109]

During the time Ainsworth and others were responding to Smyth's attacks on his fellow Separatists, Smyth continued his debate with the Puritans who had remained within the Church of England.

Smyth's debate with Richard Bernard. In 1609, Smyth published *Paralleles, Censures, Observations* as a compilation of his debate with Richard Bernard, a Puritan. Richard Bernard had followed Smyth's example and formed a covenanted group at Worksop. However, he later renounced this covenant, returned to the Church of England, and was restored as vicar of Worksop.[110] Smyth's book also includes his remarks on Henry Ainsworth's *Counterpoyson*, which was his response to Bernard's work. There are three sections to *Paralleles, Censures,*

---

[107]Smyth, *Works* 1:291.
[108]Ainsworth, *A defense of the Holy Scriptures*, 48.
[109]Ainsworth, *A defense of the Holy Scriptures*, 37.
[110]Smyth, *Works* 2:331-37.

Observations. The first and largest section is a letter written to Richard Bernard by John Smyth. This letter was included in Bernard's answer in June 1608, which was entitled *Christian Advertisements and Counsels of Peace. Also disswasions from the Separatists schisme, etc.*, but became known as *The Separatists Schisme*.[111] Smyth says that he did not intend his letter to Bernard to be published. However, since Bernard had published it as a part of his book, Smyth felt it necessary to publish the letter and add comments where necessary. Smyth puts it this way:

> [B]icause of Mr. Bernards misaledging & misconstruing divers parts of my letter written vnto him, I have thought meet, not barely to publish this lettre, but parallele-wise to compare Mr. Bernards book, Mr. Ainsworths answer, & this my lettre together, as also to annexe a few animadversions & observations aperteyning therevnto, that by this meanes the agrement & difference being discovered, the truth may appeare where it is.[112]

The second section of *Paralleles, Censures, Observations* is a letter written by Smyth to a "Mr. A. S.," a minister of the Church of England. The identity of "A. S." is unknown. He had written to a "Mr. H." in Smyth's congregation, which was presumably Thomas Helwys. Apparently, Helwys misplaced the letter. "Mr. A. S." wrote a second letter criticizing the Separatists and their inability to answer his arguments. Smyth wrote to him to demonstrate otherwise. Smyth asked "Mr. A. S." whom he knew from Cambridge to pass this letter to their mutual friend, "Mr. B." who was most likely Richard Bernard.[113]

The third section of *Paralleles, Censures, Observations* is a letter written to "certayne Brethren of the Seperation."[114] This third letter was possibly written in Amsterdam, because Smyth mentions the problem of getting a messenger to take his response to them. He was writing to encourage his fellow Separatists in "S." who were being challenged by a "Mr. K." of the Church of England. Coggins suggests that these Separatists were in Suffolk and that "Mr. K." was John Knewstubs.[115] The

---

[111] Whitley, "Biography," lxvii.
[112] Smyth, *Works* 2:329. "Animadversions" has been emended.
[113] Smyth, *Works* 2:547.
[114] Smyth, *Works* 2:327.
[115] Coggins, *John Smyth's Congregation*, 39. Burgess suggests Suffolk, but

location could also be Scrooby, meaning that the letter was used to encourage the church members that were unable to emigrate to the Netherlands.

In *Paralleles, Censures, Observations*, Smyth concurs with other Separatists in many beliefs. This does not mean Smyth was in full agreement with other Separatists as late as 1609. Smyth is publishing this work to deal with the personal accusations made by Bernard in his book and to consider Ainsworth's work, which were both written after Smyth's original letter to Bernard. So, most of this work was written by Smyth much earlier when he agreed with other Separatists.

Smyth and Ainsworth had defended the Separatist cause against the attacks of a former adherent, Richard Bernard. Bernard's work, which, as mentioned above, became known as *The Separatists Schisme*, is a polemic against the Separatist movement and many of its leaders. Bernard discounts the writings of Barrow and Greenwood as the work of discontent schismatics.[116] He was also aware of the strife between George and Francis Johnson. He says that this disagreement between these leaders shows how volatile the Separatists were.[117] Bernard contends that the Separatist movement was not necessary, but was begun because of "passionate impatiencie."[118] The Church of England was making the necessary reforms, but the Separatists would rather split from the Church than to be patient concerning reform.

Bernard asserted that the Separatists' greatest contempt was reserved for the Church of England. He said that the Separatists had their beginning in the Church and ought to be grateful for the education that the Church had provided to most of them. Instead Bernard claims that the Separatists had such animosity to the Church of England that they would rather return to the Catholic Church than "to returne to us againe, so great hatred is bred in them, against our way and standing even in the best

---

also says that it could have been written to the Scrooby group while Smyth was at Gainsborough because they still looked to him for guidance. Burgess, *John Smyth, the Se-Baptist*, 93.

[116] Bernard, *Christian Advertisements and Counsels of Peace*, 163. Bernard also cites other Puritans such as William Perkins who concur about the contentious nature of the Separatists, 31-32.

[117] Bernard, *Christian Advertisements and Counsels of Peace*, 35-36.

[118] Bernard, *Christian Advertisements and Counsels of Peace*, 58.

things, which are all one as the worst."[119] One of the results of this hatred was the common Separatist practice of not allowing their members to hear Puritan preachers. Bernard challenged this practice by saying that hearing the Word of God is advantageous, so no one should be prohibited from hearing it expounded.[120]

According to Bernard, the Separatists' view of the true church was flawed. They held to the misconception that the church consisted of the faithful only. Bernard says that they have confused the invisible church with the visible church, because "the visible Church, as I have said, is a mixt companie."[121] So, a true visible church is not based on a local church covenant as Smyth and other Separatists maintained. Bernard holds that if the true Word of God is preached and the true sacraments are administered, then there is a true church.[122] He contradicts the Separatists by saying that discipline is not an essential property of the church. There are more important elements of the church that the Separatists have excluded. Bernard holds that their strict discipline prevents them from ministering to the needs of their church members. He also disapproves of their separation from the unfaithful, which he believes prevents teaching them.[123]

Bernard does not agree with the Separatist definition of the true matter of the church. Smyth, like other Separatists, had declared that saints were the true matter of the church.[124] However, Bernard argues that the church's true matter is all people who "professe Christ." He describes them as true matter, but allows that they may be "good matter" or "bad matter."[125] Bernard uses the illustration of a wife to demonstrate his

---

[119]Bernard, *Christian Advertisements and Counsels of Peace*, 55.

[120]Bernard, *Christian Advertisements and Counsels of Peace*, 152-54. Not all Separatists observed this practice. This is one of the early differences between Smyth and John Robinson. Robinson allowed his congregation to listen to Puritan preachers.

[121]Bernard, *Christian Advertisements and Counsels of Peace*, 87. On p. 83, Bernard also discusses the Separatists' mistake of confusing the visible church and invisible church.

[122]Bernard, *Christian Advertisements and Counsels of Peace*, 118-24.

[123]Bernard, *Christian Advertisements and Counsels of Peace*, 124-27.

[124]Smyth, *Works* 1:253.

[125]Bernard, *Christian Advertisements and Counsels of Peace*, 113-14.

principle. When a woman makes her wedding vow to a man, then she becomes his true wife. If she is a faithful wife, then she is a good wife. If she is unfaithful, then she is a bad wife. Either way she remains a true wife. Members of the church may be faithful (good matter) or unfaithful (bad matter), but they are all the true matter of the church.[126] Smyth countered by saying that the scriptures teach that the church is made up of saints. He declares, "if the Church be framed of those that are not Saynts, it is framed of another matter then the Scripture appointeth."[127]

A common challenge against the Separatists was that their congregational government was an error. Joseph Hall writes, "Nothing, say we, can be more disorderly, than the confusion of your Democracy; or popular state; if not Anarchy: where all, in a sort, ordain and excommunicate."[128] Bernard echoes this charge against Smyth and the other Separatists. He contends that they believe that the act of covenanting gives Christ's power to all members.[129] So, he says that they believe anyone could preach, administer the sacraments, and censure members. They choose certain men to fill the pastoral roles, only because of order, not because of calling. However, if a minister is not found, anyone could replace him.[130] Bernard says that Smyth was mistaken in these beliefs. He insists that only God calls and equips ministers, and so the church must find the ones that God has called.[131] Smyth answers Bernard by affirming that the congregation has authority because of Christ's power. While God does gift certain men for ministry, the church has been given the authority to place these men into service. He says:

> Wherfor I say vnto you that the gifts of preaching, administration of the Sacraments & Governing, are given vnto some men, but the office & officers indued with these gifts are given vnto the Church, who have powre to appoint them to their office, & who do receave both their office & powre to administer in their office from the Church, vnto

---

[126] Bernard, *Christian Advertisements and Counsels of Peace*, 115.
[127] Smyth, *Works* 2:380.
[128] Hall, *A Common Apology*, in *The Works of . . . Joseph Hall* 9:395.
[129] Bernard, "To the Christian Reader," in *Christian Advertisements and Counsels of Peace*, unpaged.
[130] Bernard, *Christian Advertisements and Counsels of Peace*, 89-90.
[131] Bernard, *Christian Advertisements and Counsels of Peace*, 132-34.

whome the office & powre of Christ is given primarily, being the next Lord therof vnder Christ the Monarch.[132]

The brand of Separatism that Bernard attacked was more Brownist than Barrowist in its polity. Robert Browne had been an advocate of congregational government. Barrow and Greenwood had put the authority within the hands of the elders. This is one of the issues that caused controversy within the Separatist movement. Francis Johnson, Richard Clyfton, and the early Henry Ainsworth supported presbyterian government. John Smyth, John Robinson, and the later Henry Ainsworth practiced congregational polity.[133]

Ainsworth's response to Bernard's comments represents his early position, which is that he does not support congregational government, but encourages the presbytery.[134] He says that the New Testament establishes that the elders were to govern the church, including disciplining and decision making. Ainsworth argues that it is God's plan for the elders to rule the church and for the members to submit to their authority. He writes:

> And if the holy Ghost have set Elders and shepherds over the whole flock: can any man doubt, but they must teach rule and direct the whol? & if they must doe this by authoritie from God: is not the whole flock bound to be taught ruled & directed by them in the Lord?[135]

He denies Bernard's charge that Separatists hold that all members can preach, administer sacraments, or execute censures. He said that this would be chaos.[136]

Smyth presents a third view. He does encourage the use of elders to provide leadership for the church. However, this leadership cannot overrule the body of the church. The church has delegated its authority to the elder, but this does not mean that the body must follow passively.

---

[132]Smyth, *Works* 2:423. "Men" has been emended.

[133]Before 1610, Ainsworth opposed congregational government. After that date, he supported congregational authority because of abuses that could occur in rule by elders.

[134]Ainsworth, *A defense of the Holy Scriptures*, 124-27.

[135]Ainsworth, *A defense of the Holy Scriptures*, 128-29.

[136]Ainsworth, *A defense of the Holy Scriptures*, 131.

Smyth writes:

> [Y]et we say the Elders are to lead & governe al persons & causes of the Church, but to lead & governe contrary to the definition & voice of the body that we deny, & that we say is Antichristian.[137]

The power given to the elders is a "leading powre" not a "ruling powre."[138]

In addition to differing over church offices, Bernard attacks Smyth's view on the necessity of separation. Bernard holds that the scriptures do not allow for a schism such as the Separatists to exist as a true church. He writes:

> But that such a companie should be a Church of God truly constituted, who so breake foorth from Churches and will not joyne to any other, but wil be a Church of themselves, such a gathering together to be a lawfull assemblie gathered in the name (that is, in the power, authoritie & good pleasure) of Christ, from amongst us with condemnation, his will in his Testament sheweth not.[139]

In fact, the very separation from the unfaithful that Smyth lauds as a basis for the Separatist movement is what Bernard declares as one of its major mistakes.

Bernard's comments are similar to Bishop Hall's statements. They both agreed that the errors that the Separatists held against the Church of England did not warrant separation. Hall was as harsh as Bernard on the Separatists when he described them as "enemies to the Sceptre of Christ, and Rebels against his Church and Anointed."[140] Hall agrees in principle with the Separatists that there must be separation from evil. However, the Separatists have misunderstood the proper type of separation. He holds that the Church of England is sufficiently separate from evil. He says that they have separated from pagans and papists. No further separation is necessary.[141]

---

[137] Smyth, *Works* 2:417.
[138] Smyth, *Works* 2:439.
[139] Bernard, *Christian Advertisements and Counsels of Peace*, 101-102.
[140] Hall, *A Common Apology*, in *The Works of . . . Joseph Hall* 9:480.
[141] Hall, *A Common Apology*, in *The Works of . . . Joseph Hall* 9:393.

In *The Separatists Schisme*, Bernard also makes some personal attacks on Smyth. He chastises Smyth for first publishing a defense of the Lord's Prayer in *A Paterne of True Prayer* but then later turning his back on this position. Bernard questions whether someone like Smyth can be trusted.[142] He evens contends that God has tried several times to keep Smyth out of the Separatist errors, but that Smyth has continously rejected God's guidance. Bernard writes a skewed portrayal of Smyth's pilgrimage from Puritan to Separatist. He gives this account:

> And it may seeme that God would not have had M. Smith to have gone that way, by so often thwarting his judgement. I. To publish in print on the Lords Prayer, against that way, and for as much. II. In falling into it after, againe under his hand to renounce the principles of that way called Brownisme. III. Brought againe to like it, but not wholly, for he held some true Church, some true Pastors here, and did dislike the distinction of true and false Church in respect of us: then went hee, and conferred with certaine godly and learned men, whereby he became so satisfied, as he kneeled downe, and in prayer praised God, that he was not misled farther, and was so resolved, as hee purposed to disswade his Tutor M. Johnson, from the same, saying, he would goe to Amsterdam for that end. This will be, and is confidently avouched by divers then there present. Besides these crosses in judgement, the Lord did chastise him with sicknesse nigh unto death, to consider better with himselfe yet of his course.[143]

Smyth's publishing of *Paralleles, Censures, Observations* as an answer to Bernard's challenges is not surprising. However, the timing of Smyth's publication raises questions. Why would Smyth publish these Separatist views written years earlier in England when he is in Amsterdam having already become a Baptist? There are two answers to this question.

First, Smyth's main reason for publishing *Paralleles, Censures, Observations* was to answer Bernard's accusations of Smyth's bitterness. Smyth felt he must reproduce the letter accurately to show his actual comments to Bernard. Smyth says:

---

[142]Bernard, *Christian Advertisements and Counsels of Peace*, 73.

[143]Bernard, *Christian Advertisements and Counsels of Peace*, 36-37.

> I cannot nor may not with fidelity alter one sentence or word of it, but as Mr. Bernard hath it copyed in his hands, so have I published it word for word without any the least chandg to my knowledg, least Mr. Bernard should say it is not the lettre he had from mee.[144]

So, even if Smyth believed differently in some points than he did when he wrote the letter, he felt obliged not to change the letter.

John Robinson saw the warrant of Smyth's defense against Bernard's charges. He said that the main reason that Bernard led his congregation to form a covenant was to keep them from joining Smyth after they had been persuaded by his arguments.[145] Robinson also claimed that Bernard had wrongfully slandered Smyth. He says that Smyth's *Paralleles, Censures, Observations* answered Bernard's arguments and corrected Bernard's "evil dealing with him in this case."[146]

Smyth's second reason for publishing a Separatist work after becoming a Baptist was that he believed that accepting baptism was just a development of Separatist principles. This is evident from at least two sources. In his debate with Richard Clyfton, Smyth said that it was only through rejecting the baptism of the Church of England that he had become truly separate from them.[147] So, in that case, a true Separatist would reject infant baptism. Also, in *The Last Booke*, which he wrote as a Mennonite, Smyth refers to both Henry Ainsworth, a Separatist, and Thomas Helwys, a Baptist, as being members of the "seperation."[148] Therefore when *Paralleles, Censures, Observations* is published, Smyth, a Baptist, would still have seen himself within the Separatist tradition, and he would have been willing to publish his earlier Separatist arguments.

Smyth's relationship with John Robinson. Richard Bernard responds to Smyth in his *Plaine Evidences*, published in 1610. This publication creates an opportunity for John Robinson to enter the debate with his extensive work, *A Justification of Separation*. Robinson had already

---

[144]Smyth, *Works* 2:328-29.
[145]Robinson, *The Works of John Robinson* 2:101.
[146]Robinson, *The Works of John Robinson*, 2:459.
[147]Smyth, *Works* 2:566.
[148]Smyth, *Works* 2:752.

written the work when Bernard's *Plaine Evidences* came into his hands. Therefore, Robinson's work mainly centers on Bernard's earlier work and the responses given by Ainsworth and Smyth. His interactions with Smyth give modern readers some contemporary insight into the relationship between them.

In his *A Justification of Separation*, Robinson mentions Smyth on numerous occasions. These references indicate that Robinson and many other Separatists held Smyth in high esteem before his acceptance of believers' baptism. Robinson supports Smyth's defense of Henry Barrow's writings, which Bernard had criticized too harshly. He agrees with Smyth's views on the gross evil of maintaining a false church, the true properties of the church, and the error of successionism.[149] Robinson even seems to sympathize with Smyth's oppositon to using scripture in a time of worship. Although he does not agree with Smyth on this point, he does not misrepresent the nature of Smyth's comments.[150] Not all of Robinson's references to Smyth are positive. He speaks of Smyth's "instability" and corrects him on his use of scripture in several instances.[151]

While Smyth was still in England, his congregation had met in two groups, one of which was led by Robinson. The two groups had originally covenanted together to form one church, though they developed apart from each other. Some scholars hold that Robinson's congregation was seen as separate from Smyth's even from their arrival in the Netherlands.[152] However, it seems that at least for a short while, the two groups joined forces in Amsterdam. This may have been out of necessity for survival, for convenience of fellowship, or for the simple reason that they had once been one congregation and now geographical separation was not a problem.

Whatever the reasons for their consolidation, the fellowship did not last long. It seems that around the early part of 1609, Robinson led his group to break from Smyth and move their fellowship to Leiden. William

---

[149]Robinson, *The Works of John Robinson*, 2:90, 100-101, 359, 432-33.
[150]Robinson, *The Works of John Robinson*, 2:455.
[151]Robinson, *The Works of John Robinson*, 2:62, 387, 111. One area of disagreement between Robinson and Smyth on the interpretation of scripture is in their respective views of the covenant. This will be a topic of discussion in chap. 4.
[152]Sprunger, *Dutch Puritanism*, 66.

Bradford records these events with these words:

> And when they had lived at Amsterdam about a year, Mr. Robinson their pastor and some others of best discerning, seeing how Mr. John Smith and his company was already fallen into contention with the church that was there before them, and no means they could use would do any good to cure the same, and also that the flames of contention were like to break out in that anciente church itself. . . . For these and some other reasons they removed to Leyden.[153]

The contention Smyth had with Johnson's church has been noted. The Ancient Church itself had its own problems, with Henry Ainsworth leading a group which broke away around 1610. So, while contention is the main issue that Bradford cites for the split, it is the "other reasons" that are intriguing. Acheson claims that Smyth and Robinson split over a series of radical beliefs held by Smyth. He lists the necessity of complete spiritual and social separatism, the use of the untranslated Bible in worship, the rejection of infant baptism, and the validity of congregational democracy.[154]

Acheson's suggestions are not all correct. Smyth's view was not that the Bible should be untranslated, but that any book, including the Bible, would hinder the Spirit if it was used during a time of worship. Robinson understood the nature of Smyth's argument and was sympathetic to it.[155] If Smyth's rejection of infant baptism and his group's rebaptism were major factors in Robinson's decision to move to Leiden, surely Bradford would have mentioned these major differences. Robinson's description of Smyth's baptism indicates that the separation had already occurred. Surely, if Robinson's group were in fellowship with Smyth up to that time, then his depiction would have mentioned Smyth's baptism as what wrecked their fellowship.

Robinson would not have separated from Smyth because of differences over congregational democracy because their beliefs were similar. Robinson states that there are three types of government: monarchy,

---

[153] Bradford, *Of Plymouth Plantation*, 16-17.

[154] Acheson, *Radical Puritans in England*, 20. Pearse argues that Smyth's rebaptism was the final blow which led to the separation of the Smyth/Robinson congregation. Pearse, *The Great Restoration*, 193.

[155] Robinson, *The Works of John Robinson* 2:455.

aristocracy, and democracy. He says that the church is all three. Christ is the monarch, the elders serve as aristocrats, and the members serve in a democracy. The members have been given authority by the king who is Christ. They, in turn, empower the elders to lead them.[156] This analogy of church government is similar to the one in Smyth's work, *Paralleles, Censures, Observations*. In this work, Smyth writes:

> [Y]ou are to remember that Christs church in several respects is a Monarchie, an Aristocraty, a Democratie. In respect of Christ the King it is a Monarchy, of the Eldership an Aristocratie, of the brethren joyntly a Democratie or Popular government.[157]

Both men hold that Christ gives his authority to the covenanted congregation to be the church. The elders are to be respected leaders, but they are to be held accountable by the congregation who are empowered by Christ.

The issue of complete separatism seems to be the best suggestion by Acheson as to the reason for Smyth and Robinson's split. While they were in England, Robinson and Smyth had been in constant debate over this issue. Private communion with nonseparating Puritans was a definite area of disagreement between Smyth and Robinson. Robinson argues that the Separatist movement involved separating from the church practices of the established church, but not from all the people belonging to it. He says that this view did not contradict the Separatist Confession of 1596, which spoke of separation from the parish assemblies. Robinson indicates that he and Smyth had written to each other several times on the subject with Smyth urging complete separation. Robinson mentions this specifically as a reason that Smyth and his followers would not accept him fully. He writes about Smyth, "with whom I also refused to join, because I would use my liberty in this point: and for which I was, by some of the people with him, excepted against, when I was chosen into

---

[156]Robinson, *The Works of John Robinson* 2:140.

[157]Smyth, *Works* 2:416. "Remember" has been emended. See Richard A. Rankin, "The Use of Aristotelian Logic and Metaphysical Principles in the Ecclesiology of John Smyth" (Ph.D. diss., Southwestern Baptist Theological Seminary, 1994) on Smyth's use of Aristotelian terms in his ecclesiology.

office in this church."[158]

Robinson's move to Leiden was caused by several factors. The contentions within the Ancient Church, the contentions between Smyth and the Ancient Church, and the longstanding differences between Smyth and Robinson on separation, all played a part in Robinson's decision. An additional factor could have been finance: the growing number of English refugees vying for the limited number of low-paying jobs that were available to them could have put a strain on the community. The university town of Leiden would provide fresh opportunities for Robinson's congregation.

It appears that Robinson took approximately one hundred people with him to Leiden. Haykin notes that after Robinson left with one hundred members, Smyth was left with around fifty.[159] Whitley dates Robinson's break in late 1608 or early 1609. Also, he indicates that Morton Dexter has shown that Robinson's Leiden group was not simply the former Scrooby group. Most of them had come from Norfolk where Robinson had been a minister before his move to Scrooby.[160]

Baptist Stage

While Smyth was a Separatist, his relationships with other Separatists were often strained. This division would be solidified through his acceptance of Baptist views.

Smyth's act of baptism. In late 1608 or early 1609, Smyth shocked his fellow Separatists by rejecting infant baptism and reestablishing his church through believers' baptism.[161] The fact that, according to early accounts, Smyth had baptized himself added to their bewilderment. Most early Baptist historians discredited these reports.[162] Ivimey says that in

---

[158]Robinson, *The Works of John Robinson* 3:103.
[159]Haykin, *Kiffin, Knollys, and Keach*, 23.
[160]Whitley, "Biography," lxxxii-lxxxiii.
[161]Coggins, "The Theological Positions of John Smyth," 252; Burgess, *John Smyth, the Se-Baptist*, 149; Underwood, *A History of the English Baptists*, 37.
[162]Cramp, *Baptist History*, 255; Evans, *The Early English Baptists* 1:205-208; Crosby, *The History of the English Baptists* 1:98-99; John T. Christian, *A History of the Baptists* (Nashville: Sunday School Board of the Southern Baptist Convention, 1922) 225-26.

Hall's charges against Smyth, he does not mention self-baptism. Therefore Ivimey concludes, "There is no doubt but this silly charge was fabricated by his enemies."[163] He also concludes that the mode of Smyth's baptism was immersion. He holds that Smyth's process was that first he rejected the baptism of the Church of England, then rejected all infant baptism, and finally accepted believers' baptism by immersion.[164] While the self-baptism of Smyth is doubted by early Baptist historians, later Baptists were more willing to accept the evidence. Whitley and Burgess note that it is most likely that Smyth baptized himself and the others out of a basin, not by immersion.[165]

There are several contemporary testimonies that indicate that Smyth did baptize himself and that he did it probably by affusion. Henry Ainsworth, who was in Amsterdam, knew Smyth and possibly some members of his congregation. Ainsworth declares that "Mr. Sm. anabaptised himseelf with water."[166] His statements also give some indication of the mode of baptism. When he mocks Smyth's reasoning that only believers can experience his baptism, Ainsworth says that a child "could cast water on himself."[167]

Smyth's own statements indicate that the congregation did not seek any other group for their baptism. In a later debate with Thomas Helwys, Smyth says that it is wrong for a group "being as yet vnbaptized [to] baptize themselues (as we did) and proceed to build churches of themselues." He explains his actions by saying that "onlie this is It which I held, that seeing ther was no church to whome wee could Joyne with a Good conscience to haue baptisme from them, therfor wee might

---

[163]Joseph Ivimey, *History of the English Baptists*, 4 vols. (London: 1811–1830) 1:115.

[164]Ivimey, *History of the English Baptists* 1:114; Armitage and others suggested that Smyth's baptism was by immersion; Armitage, *A History of the Baptists*, 457-58; Christian, *A History of the Baptists*, 226-29.

[165]Whitley, "Biography," xciii-xcv; Burgess, *John Smyth, the Se-Baptist*, 161; Vedder, *A Short History of the Baptists*, 203-204; Torbet, *A History of the Baptists*, 35.

[166]Ainsworth, *A defense of the Holy Scriptures*, 69.

[167]Ainsworth, *A defense of the Holy Scriptures*, 69. His statement seems to indicate affusion as the mode of baptism. If the mode was immersion, then he would probably have said that a child "could cast himself in water."

baptize our selues."[168] John Robinson provides the clearest contemporary account. He writes:

> I have heard from themselves, on this manner: Mr. Smyth, Mr. Helwisse, and the rest, having utterly dissolved and disclaimed their former church state and ministry, came together to erect a new church by baptism. . . . And after some straining of courtesy who should begin . . . Mr. Smyth baptized first himself, and next Mr. Helwisse, and so the rest, making their particular confessions. . . . These things thus being, all wise men will think that he had small cause either to be so much enamoured of his own baptism, or so highly to despise other men's for the unorderly or otherwise unlawful administration of it.[169]

Smyth suggested that Helwys baptize the group, but Helwys deferred to him. Smyth baptized himself, Helwys, and then the rest of the congregation.[170] Smyth answered Robinson, Richard Clyfton and his other accusers about his self-baptism by saying that one could administer the Lord's Supper to himself, and baptism should be no different. Smyth indicates that Abraham had administered circumcision to himself and the priests of the Old Testament would wash themselves before entering the tabernacle. Smyth said if two people want to covenant with the Lord and each other, then they become a church. In this agreement, Christ grants them the power of a church. Smyth understood that most Separatists would agree to this method of forming a church. He argues that if two people who are unchurched can make themselves a church, then they can baptize themselves as well. He explains himself: "[A] man cannot baptise others into the Church, himself being out of the Church: Therefore it is Lawfull for

---

[168]Smyth, *Works* 2:757.
[169]Robinson, *The Works of John Robinson* 3:168-69. This secondhand account lends itself to the argument that Robinson and Smyth had already ended fellowship. If the act of re-baptism had wrecked their fellowship, Robinson would have added this to arrogance and disorder as his reasons for disapproval.
[170]Smyth, *Works* 2:757; Watts, *The Dissenters* 1:45; Acheson, *Radical Puritans in England*, 20; Tolmie, *The Triumph of the Saints*, 70; Underwood, *A History of the English Baptists*, 37-38; Haykin, *Kiffin, Knollys, and Keach*, 24; Sprunger, *Dutch Puritanism*, 81; Estep, *The Anabaptist Story*, 288; White, *The English Separatist Tradition Separatist*, 138.

a man to baptize himself together with others in communion."[171]

Smyth's rejection of the baptism of the Church of England. Smyth's baptism stirred up a debate within Separatism that had simmered for a long time. The Separatists had defended the legitimacy of their baptism which was received in the Church of England. Smyth maintained that a false church such as the Church of England could not retain a true ordinance. He states:

> [T]ruly for my part I hold it as lawful to retaine the Church & Ministery of England, as to retaine the baptisme: & when I shal yeeld to the truth of the baptisme of England I wil yeeld to the truth of the Church & ministery of England: & I wil confesse I have been a Schismatique, & returne & acknowledg my error: but bicause I know the ministery & Church of England is false, therfor it must needes be that the baptisme which is the forme of the Church is false essentially: & therefore having Seperated justly from the Church & Ministery of England for the falsehood of them, I must needes also Seperate from the baptisme which is false, for the Church is false bicause baptisme the forme of the Church is false: & if baptisme the forme of the Church of England be true, the Church of England is true also.[172]

Many of the Separatists responded by saying that although the Church of England was false, their baptism was true. Bishop Joseph Hall attacked this apparent duplicity. He echoes Smyth's argument:

> To shut up your Constitution, then, there is no remedy: either you must go forward to Anabaptism, or come back to us. All your Rabbis cannot answer that charge of your rebaptized brother: If we be a True Church, you must return: if we be not (as a False Church is no Church of God) you must rebaptize. If our Baptism be good, than is our Constitution good.[173]

Francis Johnson attempts to answer Smyth's charge on one side and Hall's charge on the other. He argues that the Separatists received their baptism from the same place as the Church of England did, through the Church of Rome. Even though this church was a false church, they had

---

[171]Smyth, *Works* 2:660.
[172]Smyth, *Works* 2:664-65.
[173]Hall, *A Common Apology*, in *The Works of . . . Joseph Hall* 9:400.

maintained true baptism. The Church of Rome had the essentials of the faith, so their baptism could be retained.[174] Johnson chastises other Separatists such as Ainsworth and Clyfton who had rejected the baptism of Rome. He says that if the former baptism was false, then it should not be retained which would force the Separatists to rebaptize as Smyth had done.[175]

Ainsworth counters by saying that baptism from Rome was indeed corrupt, for it added many symbols to baptism that were unnecessary. The Church of England made the same mistake by adding other symbols such as the sign of the cross to the baptismal ceremony. He concludes:

> Therefore in their sinful estate, & abuse of baptisme, it is not unto them Gods ordinance, but an Idol, not true baptisme, but false; not a true sacrament, but a false, and a lying signe, as circumcision also in Israels apostacie was unto them: &c.[176]

While Ainsworth held that the Church of England did not have a true baptism, he did not see any reason for Separatists to be rebaptized. Their baptism is made true by their separation from the false church and by becoming the true church.

A state of apostasy does not affect the validity of the sacrament according to Johnson. He argues that abuses within the church or in the baptismal ceremony itself, do not cause a false baptism. Baptism is protected from corruption because it belongs in the covenant of God. The covenant is an eternal covenant that is preserved by God. Johnson states, "And the Covenant of God is an everlasting covenant; which God continueth and respecteth, even in the times of apostacie."[177] So, the baptism of Rome or England is not false, though the churches are.

Smyth's charges against the Separatists were common knowledge even to those outside the debate. Bishop Hall disagrees with Smyth's acceptance of believers' baptism. However, he also notices that Smyth's move has caused him to have a common opponent with Hall, that is, his

---

[174] Johnson, *A Christian Plea*, 28-29.

[175] Johnson, *A Christian Plea*, 30-33.

[176] Henry Ainsworth, *An animadversion to Mr Clyftons advertisement* (Amsterdam: Giles Thorp, 1613) 68.

[177] Johnson, *A Christian Plea*, 35; see also 133-34.

former Separatist brethren. Hall writes:

> Woe is me! he hath renounced our Christendom with our Church: and hath washed off his former water, with new; and now condemns you all, for not separating further, no less than we condemn you for separating so far.[178]

Ainsworth's response to Smyth's move to Baptist practices was unsurprisingly negative. He said that the quarrel between Smyth and the other Separatists had gone too far. Not only did Ainsworth indicate that Smyth's Baptist work, *The Character of the Beast*, was too extreme, but he also said that his last Separatist work, *Paralleles, Censures, Observations*, was problematic. Ainsworth reminds Smyth that when his quarrel with the other Separatists began it was over the use of scripture translations in worship.[179] Now, Smyth had become even more radical. Ainsworth points out to him that even in *The Differences of the Churches* he had praised the Separatists for their discovery of the true church. However, in *The Character of the Beast*, Smyth claims that the Separatists have a false church. Smyth's attacks on the Separatists and his new views on covenant are lamented by Ainsworth. He says that Smyth has done violence against the covenant of God.[180]

Though it would isolate him from his fellow Separatists, Smyth moved swiftly in implementing his new views.

B. R. White holds that there were three possible factors in Smyth's acceptance of believers' baptism. First, there was the Separatists' uneasiness about the baptism they had received from the Church of England. Smyth just took this uneasiness and pursued it to its conclusion. He did not understand how a corrupt church could pass on a pure baptism. Second, Smyth was continuing to study the Bible because of trying to establish a church on the New Testament model. The study of the New Testament led him to believe that the apostolic example was believers' baptism. Third, Smyth became aware of the practice of the

---

[178]Hall, *A Common Apology*, in *The Works of . . . Joseph Hall* 9:384-85.
[179]Ainsworth, *A defense of the Holy Scriptures*, 1.
[180]Ainsworth, *A defense of the Holy Scriptures*, 3. See chap. 4 for the discussion of Smyth's view of covenant as a Baptist.

Mennonites.[181] His knowledge of their teaching caused him to reject the practice of infant baptism. William Estep argues that Smyth accepted the theology of believers' baptism as a direct result of the teaching of the Mennonites.[182] Smyth's debate with Richard Clyfton provides some assistance in dating Mennonite influence on Smyth's baptism.

Smyth's debate with Richard Clyfton. In 1609, Smyth published *The Character of the Beast* as a compilation of his debate with Richard Clyfton. The dispute started after Smyth had become convinced of the error of infant baptism. Clyfton says that two members of Smyth's congregation, Edward Southworth and Hugh Bromhead, came to him and tried to persuade him to reject infant baptism. He said that these two men had assumed that he would be open to their beliefs. He states that he had rejected them at once and had refused to allow them to explain their argument fully. When they insisted that he make some concession to hear their ideas, he agreed to read Smyth's arguments if they were sent to him personally.[183]

Smyth used this occasion to write two propositions to Clyfton. These two propositions are: "1. That infants are not to bee baptized. 2. That Antichristians converted are to be admitted into the true Church by Baptisme."[184] Clyfton responded to those propositions on 24 March 1609.[185] Smyth then divided Clyfton's response into sections and answered it point by point. Smyth's reply is dated 3 April 1609.[186] Later that year Smyth attached his "Epistle to the Reader" and published his propositions, Clyfton's response, and his answer as *The Character of the Beast*. The publication of the work and the inclusion of Clyfton's response help establish an approximate date for Smyth's baptism. His baptism must have taken place sometime between late 1608, after the publishing of *The*

---

[181]B. R. White, *The English Baptists of the Seventeenth Century*, rev. ed. (Didcot: Baptist Historical Society, 1996) 19. The influence of the Mennonites on Smyth's baptism is discussed later in this chapter.

[182]Estep, *The Anabaptist Story*, 289-91.

[183]Richard Clyfton, *The Plea for Infants and Elder People, concerning Their Baptisme* (Amsterdam: Gyles Thorp, 1610) 4.

[184]Smyth, *Works* 2:574.

[185]Clyfton, *The Plea for Infants and Elder People*, 213; Smyth, *Works* 2:674. Clifton lists 14 March 1608 (old style).

[186]Smyth, *Works* 2:679. Smyth lists 24 March 1608 (old style).

Differences of the Churches, and early 1609, in time for Clyfton to respond to Smyth's propositions by March. Early 1609 appears the most logical, for Smyth's reply to Clyfton's response in ten days implies that the baptism was a hot issue.

Clyfton says that Smyth published their private correspondence without his knowledge, just as Smyth had complained about Richard Bernard.[187] So, Clyfton published *The Plea for Infants* to clarify his arguments and to defend the truth against Smyth's writings. Clyfton was under the impression that Smyth's work was being circulated widely in England. About *The Character of the Beast* he writes: "And seing the same book is sent over into our own country, and is spread abroad into the hands of many; I have thought good also, to give warning to all that love the Lord Jesus and are carefull of their own salvation, to take heed therof."[188] It is impossible to ascertain where Clyfton got his information on Smyth's audience, but he did see Smyth's influence as a threat.

Richard Clyfton echoes Ainsworth's sentiments on the nature of Smyth's errors. He said that Smyth began to stray when he sought to remove the translated scripture from worship. Smyth's error had become more severe, because he now sought "to distroy the covenant of grace."[189] Smyth never responded to *The Plea for Infants* because by 1610 he had moved into communion with the Mennonites and into other debates.[190]

The Character of the Beast includes Smyth's view on an issue that had plagued the Separatists for years: baptism. Henry Barrow had been unclear when dealing with the baptism of the Church of England. Smyth's challenges forced Francis Johnson and John Robinson to adopt the awkward position of holding that, while the Church of England was a false church, they had maintained a true baptism. Smyth was not satisfied with this mediating position. He rejected the idea that the false church could preserve a true ordinance. He argues, "but bicause I know the ministery & Church of England is false, therfor it must needes be that

---

[187]Clyfton, "The Preface," in *The Plea for Infants and Elder People*, unpaged.
[188]Clyfton, "The Preface," in *The Plea for Infants and Elder People*, unpaged.
[189]Clyfton, "The Preface," in *The Plea for Infants and Elder People*, unpaged.
[190]White, *The English Separatist Tradition Separatist*, 132.

the baptisme which is the forme of the Church is false essentially."[191]

Smyth argues that the baptism of the Church of England is also false because it has a false matter. He states, "So that the true matter of baptisme is a new creature: one regenerate: a confessor."[192] He also denied that baptism was to be linked to Old Testament circumcision. Therefore, he rejected infant baptism as a continuation of an Old Testament ceremony. Infants are not to be baptized because they cannot experience repentance. Smyth argued that repentance preceded the baptism of the Spirit that was symbolized in water baptism.[193] In his debate with Clyfton, Smyth relies heavily on a typological interpretation of the Old Testament and his understanding of a carnal and spiritual covenant to propagate his baptismal views.

The last part of *The Character of the Beast* to be written was the "Epistle to the Reader." It serves as a preface to the work. In this preface, Smyth addresses four points. First, he admits that the position he is publishing is different from his previous publications. He expresses his sorrow over being a party to false teaching. He says, "If wee therfor being formerly deceaved in the way of Pedobaptistry, now doe embrace the truth in the true Christian Apostolique baptisme: Then let no man impute this as a fault vnto vs."[194]

Second, Smyth makes it very clear that he no longer believes that Separatists have established a true New Testament church. He says, "[W]e do challendg al the Seperation in special to the combat. Be it knowne therfor to all the Seperation that we account them in respect of their constitution to bee as very an harlot as either her Mother England, or her grandmother Rome is, out of whose loynes she came."[195] Any church that baptized infants had a false constitution. Smyth defines the true constitution of the church as "a new creature baptized into the Father, the Sonne, & the holy Ghost."[196]

Third, Smyth charges all Separatists to move forward into the truth that he has accepted. He says that if they retain the baptism of the Church

---

[191]Smyth, *Works* 2:664.
[192]Smyth, *Works* 2:654.
[193]Smyth, *Works* 2:567-68.
[194]Smyth, *Works* 2:564. "Man" has been emended.
[195]Smyth, *Works* 2:565.
[196]Smyth, *Works* 2:565.

of England, then they cannot claim that the Church of England is false. Smyth states that Separatists claim that the Church of England is false, but that the baptism received from it is true.[197] Smyth insists that there cannot be such a mixture of true and false elements. He challenges the Separatists to make their separation complete. He writes that

> they that do Seperate from England as from a false Chu. must of necessity Seperate from the baptisme of England, & account the baptisme of England false, & so account the baptisme of infants false baptisme: Therefor the Separation must either goe back to England, or go forward to true baptisme.[198]

Fourth, Smyth answers the charges made by his opponents who accuse him of some popular errors of the Anabaptists. He says that his congregation is being accused of "denying the old Testament & the Lords day." Smyth says that he holds the Old Testament to be inspired and that it should be studied.[199] Second, concerning the Lord's day, Smyth says that saints should come together on Sunday for prayer, teaching, communion, and worship. Also, Christians should not work on Sunday, so that they may focus on the matters of the church.[200] A third charge was that Smyth's group denied the magistracy. Smyth replies that the magistrates are an "ordinance of the L[ord]." He thinks that there are some questions about the expedience of a magistrate being a Christian, so he refuses to make any definitive statement on the issue.[201] The fourth charge was that Smyth's group denied the humanity of Christ. This charge was that Smyth had accepted the Mennonite heavenly flesh theory of the incarnation. Smyth responds that he believes that Christ was the human seed of David and that he was made of the substance of his mother, Mary.[202]

An additional item that is discovered in the "Epistle to the Reader" is the mention of a possible lost work of Smyth. Smyth notes that he used a proper understanding of covenant in *The Character of the Beast*, but

---

[197]Smyth, *Works* 2:566.
[198]Smyth, *Works* 2:567.
[199]Smyth, *Works* 2:571.
[200]Smyth, *Works* 2:571-72.
[201]Smyth, *Works* 2:572.
[202]Smyth, *Works* 2:572. This statement will be discussed in chap. 5.

then he says:

> I have thought good to referre these particulars to a more ful discourse intertained vpon occasion with another of the Mrs. of the seperation, not doubting but very shortly through Gods goodnesse that treatise also shalbe published, wherin the reader shal find larger instruction & satisfaction concerning the forsaid particulars of the covenants or Test. & other matters therto aperteyning.[203]

It has been suggested that this reference could be to *Paralleles, Censures, Observations* that was published in quick succession to *The Character of the Beast*. This work dealt with the covenant but was mainly against Richard Bernard whom Smyth probably would not refer to as being "of the seperation." If *Paralleles, Censures, Observations* is not the work to which Smyth referred, then it is possible that this intended publication was referred to by Ainsworth. In his work, *A defense of the Holy Scriptures*, Ainsworth says that Smyth had printed against Clyfton (*The Character of the Beast*) and was threatening to do the same against Robinson.[204] If both Smyth's reference and Ainsworth's reference are about the same work, then it appears that Smyth intended a further defense of his views of the covenant from his Baptist perspective. This defense would have addressed John Robinson specifically. Apparently, this work was never published.

When Clyfton published *The Plea for Infants*, he included "An answer to M. Smyths Epistle to the Reader." In this response Clyfton addresses the early development of Smyth's group after receiving baptism. He shows that by this time Smyth had begun to deal with his hastiness in his self-baptism. Smyth had also begun negotiations with the Mennonites, because Clyfton mentions Helwys's group as a separate body. He remarks that Smyth's group had divided into three congregations since rejecting infant baptism. One held to the Mennonite incarnational theory. The second group was the one led by Helwys. The third group was Smyth's group that doubted the validity of their baptism.[205]

---

[203]Smyth, *Works* 2:570.
[204]Ainsworth, *A defense of the Holy Scriptures*, 4.
[205]Clyfton, "An Answer to M. Smyths Epistle to the Reader," in *The Plea for Infants and Elder People*, unpaged.

Clyfton says that the development of these three divisions so soon after their baptism proves their inconsistency. He writes, "Wherby it is manifest, that these men can not cleare themsleves of instabilitie & changeablenes in Religion, but are guilty of that inconstancie that is worthy [of] reproof and damnable."[206]

Clyfton comments on Smyth's "Epistle to the Reader" and his responses to the charges against him. First, concerning the charge that Smyth denies the Old Testament, Clyfton says that Smyth denies God's eternal covenant by calling it a carnal covenant in the Old Testament. This coupled with his rejection of infant baptism makes him guilty of denying the Old and New Testament.[207] Concerning the Lord's day, Clyfton, as Smyth, does not give much information. Clyfton says that he does not know much about this issue except that "it is reported that some of their company, makes question therof."[208]

When Clyfton addresses Smyth's response about a Christian magistrate, he demands that Smyth clarify his statements. He says that Smyth's option of remaining silent on the issue is unacceptable. Because he refuses to answer the question with certainty, Smyth is guilty of one of two things. Either he denies that the New Testament teaches all things necessary for the church, or he denies the possibility of a Christian magistrate but will not admit it.

Clyfton's response to Smyth's comments about the incarnation also involves another charge against Smyth. Clyfton recognizes that it is well known that a group left Smyth's congregation because they held to the Mennonite incarnational theory. He says that Smyth may not be guilty of holding to the doctrine of the heavenly flesh. However, the reports that Clyfton has heard about Smyth's view of the first and second flesh of Christ cause suspicion. Clyfton wonders, once again, if Smyth has accepted Mennonite doctrine but has failed to admit it. Clyfton says that even if Smyth is not guilty of this error, he cannot deny holding to the errors of general redemption and free will. He says that this has been

---

[206]Clyfton, "An Answer to M. Smyths Epistle to the Reader," in *The Plea for Infants and Elder People*, unpaged.

[207]Clyfton, "An Answer to M. Smyths Epistle to the Reader," in *The Plea for Infants and Elder People*, unpaged.

[208]Clyfton, "An Answer to M. Smyths Epistle to the Reader," in *The Plea for Infants and Elder People*, unpaged.

made clear by Smyth's presentation of two propositions: "1. Christs Redemption strecheth to all men. 2. Man hath not lost the faculie of willing any good thing that is shewed him. And with all added thereunto his Reasons in defence thereof."[209]

Mennonite Stage

What was the extent of Mennonite influence on Smyth's view of baptism? When did Smyth first become influenced by the Mennonites? Why did he not seek them for his baptism? These are some of the questions that arise about Smyth's relationship with the Mennonites.

Smyth's contact with the Mennonites. Early contact came when Smyth's group moved into the former East India Company Bakehouse, belonging to the Mennonite, Jan Munter. James Coggins suggests that Smyth's group did not move into the Mennonite bakehouse until after the break with Robinson in February 1609.[210] This timing seems likely. Smyth opened communications with the Mennonites because critics asked him why he had not sought baptism from them.[211] John Hetherington's book, *A Description of the Church of Christ with her peculiar privileges* challenged Smyth's rejection of infant baptism. In Hetherington's attacks on the Separatist movement, he addressed Smyth as if he was still within the Separatists. He mocks Smyth's frequent changes in thought by saying:

> And if every man should publish bookes so often as they change their mind, how many Religions then should spring from one man, and he perhaps be author of so many sects, what heapes of bookes are there at this day of severall opinions?[212]

---

[209]Clyfton, "An Answer to M. Smyths Epistle to the Reader," in *The Plea for Infants and Elder People*, unpaged. These propositions of Smyth have not been recovered, so Clyfton's record of them stands as the evidence to their existence.

[210]Coggins, *John Smyth's Congregation*, 60-61; Pearse states that Smyth's move to the bakehouse was after accepting believers' baptism. Pearse, *The Great Restoration*, 195.

[211]Underwood, *A History of the English Baptists*, 39; Haykin, *Kiffin, Knollys, and Keach*, 24.

[212]John Hetherington, "To M. John Smith," in *A description of the Church of Christ, with her peculiar priuiledges* . . . (London: for Nathaniel Fosbrooke, 1610) n.p.

Hetherington also questioned the apparent lack of concern that Smyth had for proper order. He saw no scriptural precedent for Smyth's self-baptism. He asks, "By what rule baptised you your selfe? what worde or example had you for that in all the Scriptures?"[213] His concern for order prompted him to ask Smyth why he did not seek baptism from the Mennonites since they also practiced believers' baptism. He believed Smyth's pride had caused him to slander all other groups as unfaithful. He remarks: "It was wonder you wold not receive your baptisme first, from some one of the Elders of the Dutch Anabaptists; but you will be holyer then all, and see how you have marred all."[214]

Hetherington held that Smyth's acceptance of believers' baptism was a grievous error. He had broken God's laws and violated "the word and waies of Christ."[215] He held that Smyth's changes were due to his rebellious spirit that was common to Separatism. This antagonistic nature would lead him to ruin. Hetherington says that this divisiveness was apparent in Smyth's fledgling Baptist congregation. He remarks, "And for you Master Smith and your company: here is newes come to England already, that you are devided."[216]

It seems likely that Smyth's group accepted believers' baptism and initiated fellowship with the Mennonites based on that similarity. Other scholars hold that Smyth and his group went immediately to the bakehouse when they moved to Amsterdam and that Smyth had been in contact with the Mennonites for about a year.[217] These scholars believe Smyth approached the Waterlander church for help on infant baptism, and that they convinced him of the errors of infant baptism.[218] His reasons for not getting them to baptize him were that it was unnecessary and because they differed in Christology.[219] This view fails to take into account the

---

[213]Hetherington, *A Description of the Church of Christ*, 23.

[214]Hetherington, *A Description of the Church of Christ*, 23.

[215]Hetherington, *A Description of the Church of Christ*, 21.

[216]Hetherington, *A Description of the Church of Christ*, 94.

[217]Underwood, *A History of the English Baptists*, 35; Pater, *Karlstadt as the Father of the Baptist Movements*, 261; Estep, *The Anabaptist Story*, 290.

[218]Tolmie, *The Triumph of the Saints*, 69-70; Estep, *The Anabaptist Story*, 290.

[219]Estep, *The Anabaptist Story*, 290; White, *The English Baptists of the*

rigid separatism of Smyth's group. He would not worship with his fellow English Separatists mainly because of their use of scripture translations. Therefore, it is unlikely that they would overlook their significant differences from the Mennonites when they first arrived in Amsterdam.

The question of when Smyth encountered the Mennonites or moved into the bakehouse is difficult to answer. Clearly, Smyth does not promote Mennonite views in *The Character of the Beast*, which was his defense of his views on believers' baptism. Smyth indicates that the Mennonites were insignificant in his decision to accept believers' baptism. He acknowledges that when he baptized himself and the others, they did not see the Mennonites as a true church. Smyth says "seeing ther was no church to whome wee could Joyne with a Good conscience to haue baptisme from them, therfor wee might baptize our selues."[220]

It was only after their acceptance of believers' baptism that Smyth's group sought the fellowship of the Mennonites. Months after initiating this fellowship, Smyth penned his "Epistle" and appended it to *The Character of the Beast* when he published it. James Coggins presents a great deal of evidence to prove that the Mennonite influence on Smyth first occured between his writing of *The Character of the Beast* and his "Epistle."[221] Coggins points out that there is no Mennonite influence evident in *The Character of the Beast*, but obviously Smyth was dealing with charges of accepting Anabaptist theology by the time of writing the "Epistle."

Reinforcing the idea of Mennonite influence coming after Smyth's baptism and *The Character of the Beast*, but before the "Epistle," is Smyth's use of the church fathers. During his debate with Clyfton, Smyth quotes witnesses from the church fathers who opposed infant baptism. He includes quotations from several sources including Eusebius.[222] These quotations are his main argument against Clyfton's supposition that infant baptism reflected the position of the Fathers. However, later when Smyth writes his "Epistle" he refers to only two "pregnant" or excellent testimonies. These two testimonies are his best examples for the Fathers'

Seventeenth Century, 19.
[220] Smyth, *Works* 2:757.
[221] Coggins, *John Smyth's Congregation*, 63-65, 73-75.
[222] Smyth, *Works* 2:616-19.

opposition to infant baptism. One of the testimonies is Eusebius and the other is Tertullian.[223] If these are two of his best examples, then why did he refer to Tertullian here, but not before? Perhaps the most logical explanation is that he did not know of that testimony.

In Menno Simons's *Foundation*, which was well known to the Mennonites, Menno uses testimonies of the Church Fathers to oppose infant baptism. He includes Eusebius and Tertullian in his testimonies.[224] So, conceivably it was through learning the arguments of the Mennonites that Smyth learned of a new testimony from the Fathers. Once Smyth learned of Tertullian's testimony, it became one of his favorite defenses. This is shown later in his Mennonite work, *Argumenta Contra Baptismum Infantum*, when Smyth uses the testimonies of the fathers. In his arguments at that point, he again refers to his two favorite testimonies, Tertullian and Eusebius.[225] So, it seems that its absence from *The Character of the Beast* shows that Smyth probably was not aware of the Mennonite argument drawn from Tertullian before he wrote that work. However, he became aware of it a short time later before its use in the "Epistle."

After months of fellowship with the Mennonites, Smyth realized their theology was more acceptable to him than he had anticipated. He began to reconsider his decision to baptize himself.[226] During this time, Smyth rejected many aspects of his Reformed thought, making him more comfortable with the Mennonites, who held beliefs similar to Arminianism. Most scholars also state that at this point Smyth changed his position on his major reason for opposing the Mennonites, their Christology. However, it is possible that Smyth had not accepted Mennonite Christology, but no longer saw it as a reason to withhold fellowship. Either way, once he had overcome these differences, he sought union for the sake of order.[227] Unfortunately, this proposed union did not bring order. Instead, further division was caused by Smyth's leading the congregation to join with the Dutch Waterlanders. As Smyth moved closer to the Mennonites,

---

[223] Smyth, *Works* 2:568-69.
[224] Simons, *Complete Writings*, 137-38.
[225] Smyth, *Works* 2:731.
[226] Smyth, *Works* 2:757.
[227] Smyth, *Works* 2:757; Estep, *The Anabaptist Story*, 291; Tolmie, *The Triumph of the Saints*, 70. Smyth's acceptance of Mennonite Christology will be discussed in a later chapter.

Thomas Helwys and a small group pulled away because of successionism and Mennonite Christology.[228]

Smyth's negotiations with the Mennonites. In February 1610, Smyth and others sought union with the Mennonites. They presented a petition to the Waterlander Mennonite congregation to be accepted as members expeditiously. The petition states that they "now desire, on this account, to be brought back to the true church of Christ as quickly as may be suffered."[229] Smyth's insistence on this union prompted Helwys and ten members to secede. Helwys and some others wrote two letters to discourage the Mennonites from accepting them. In his second letter to the Mennonites urging them not to accept Smyth, Helwys refers to successionism as "Antichrists cheife hold."[230] He says that holding to succession is Smyth's main reason for seeking the union with the Mennonites. Helwys's first letter to the Mennonite church is undated, but the second can be dated 22 March 1610.[231]

After receiving the application of membership from Smyth's congregation, the Mennonites offered the "Short Confession" of Hans de Ries to the Englishmen. This confession had been written by Ries with some assistance by Lubbert Gerrits. The thirty-eight articles of the confession outlined the basic teachings of the Waterlanders. To show their desire to unite with them, Smyth and his group signed the confession.[232]

As a part of Smyth's continued negotiations with the Mennonites, he wrote a Latin confession of twenty articles, known as *Corde Credimus*, to submit to the Mennonites. As Smyth and his group produced this confession, the Helwys's group responded with their confession, *Synopsis Fidei*.[233] Whitley dates *Corde Credimus* no later than April 1610, which

---

[228]Smyth, *Works* 2:758-59; Burrage, *The Early English Dissenters* 2:185; Acheson, *Radical Puritans in England*, 20.

[229]Translation by Evans, *The Early English Baptists* 1:209. *quique jam cupiunt hinc veræ Christi ecclesiæ veniri, ea quâ feri possit expeditione.* Evans, *The Early English Baptists* 1:244; Burrage, *The Early English Dissenters* 2:178.

[230]Burrage, *The Early English Dissenters* 2:185; Sprunger, *Dutch Puritanism*, 81.

[231]Burrage, *The Early English Dissenters* 2:181-87. The letter is dated 12 March 1609 (old style).

[232]Sprunger, *Dutch Puritanism*, 82.

[233]Sprunger, *Dutch Puritanism*, 82.

would put it at the beginning of the union negotations with the Mennonites.[234] Smyth's *Corde Credimus* was used to demonstrate to the Mennonites what the beliefs of his group were. Therefore, the confession was written in Latin, so that the Mennonite congregation could refer to it.

In this confession, Smyth's group indicates their acceptance of a Mennonite position. The renouncing of Reformed views is the most conspicuous factor. Articles 2, 3, and 5 are straightforward in rejecting predestination and original sin.[235] Also, some aspects of Smyth's earlier thought are reiterated in *Corde Credimus*. In article 16, Smyth's group justifies only two church officers: bishops and deacons.[236] In explaining his stance on church government, Smyth demonstrates that authority in the church remains with the congregation by saying:

> That the church of Christ has power delegated to themselves of announcing the word, administering the sacraments, appointing ministers, disclaiming them, and also excommunicating; but the last appeal is to the brethren or body of the church.[237]

In Smyth's *Corde Credimus*, he shows agreement with the Mennonites on believers' baptism, and he rejects his former Reformed beliefs. There are three possible influences in Smyth's rejection of Reformed views: Peter Baro at Cambridge, Mennonite rejection of Reformed views, and the contemporary debate throughout the Netherlands on Arminianism.[238] Watts notes that the timing of Smyth's writings on the subject indicate that the Mennonites were a deciding factor in his break with Reformed views. This had not been a point of contention in his earlier

---

[234]Whitley, "Biography," cvi. Since the confession was not published officially, it bears no title. I have used the first two words of the confession as a title. Whitley refers to it as "The First Baptist Confession," Smyth, *Works* 2:682.

[235]Smyth, *Works* 2:682.

[236]Smyth, *Works* 2:683.

[237]Translation by Evans, *The Early English Baptists* 1:254. *Ecclesiam Christi habere potestatem sibi delegatam, verbum anuntiandi, sacramenta administrandi, ministros constituendi et abdicendi, denique excommunicandi: ultimam autem provocationem esse ad fratres, sive corpus ecclesiae.* Smyth, *Works* 2:683.

[238]White, *The English Baptists of the Seventeenth Century*, 19; Watts, *The Dissenters* 1:45-46.

debates with Puritans or Separatists who were Reformed.[239] So, it does appear that Smyth rejected Reformed views at the beginning of his negotiations with the Mennonites. However, Brachlow has pointed out that the mutual covenant of Separatism made Smyth's transition from Reformed views a logical outcome of his Separatist background, making Mennonite influence an unnecessary conclusion.[240]

The "Short Confession" of Hans de Ries was published later in 1610 with the addition of two new articles. The document was criticized by an anonymous Reformed opponent. Later, Smyth wrote his *Defence of Ries's Confession* against the arguments of the unnamed critic. This critic could have been either someone of the Dutch Reformed Church or the English Reformed Church in Amsterdam.[241] The only information Smyth gives about the critic is to say that he is of the Reformed tradition.[242]

Smyth's authorship of *Defence of Ries's Confession* is questioned by Whitley in his collection of Smyth's works. Coggins, however, presents a convincing case for Smyth's authorship.[243] Coggins points out that the style and the terminology of the work are Smyth's. He also indicates that the language of the manuscripts suggests Smyth's authorship. There are two manuscript copies of this work in the Mennonite archives. The first is a Latin copy in Smyth's handwriting. The other is a Dutch copy in the handwriting of Reymier Wybrands. A logical explanation of this is that Smyth wrote the work in Latin so that the Dutch could refer to it. Wybrands then translated it into Dutch for more common use. Smyth did not know Dutch, so he could not have translated Wybrands's copy. If his copy was the translation then surely it would have been in English, so that his congregation could use it more readily. This work's presence in the Mennonite archives also suggests that Smyth wrote it, then sent it to the Mennonites who translated it into Dutch.[244]

---

[239]Watts, *The Dissenters* 1:46.
[240]Stephen Brachlow, "Puritan Theology and General Baptist Origins," *Baptist Quarterly* 31 (October 1985): 179. Smyth's rejection of Reformed views will be examined in chap. 5.
[241]Alice Clare Carter, *The English Reformed Church in Amsterdam in the Seventeenth Century* (Amsterdam: Scheltema & Holkema NV, 1964) 55-56.
[242]Coggins, *John Smyth's Congregation*, 175, 178, 180, 186, 189, 192.
[243]Coggins, *John Smyth's Congregation*, 89-93.
[244]Coggins, *John Smyth's Congregation*, 89-90.

If Smyth's authorship is accepted, then there are still some questions about why Smyth wrote *Defence of Ries's Confession*. It is possible that the "Short Confession" was being attacked as an official Waterlander Confession and Smyth wanted to show his allegiance to this group.[245] A second suggestion is more personal in that Smyth's signature on the original document and his detailed defense in his own work demonstrate that Smyth had come to accept much of the Mennonite doctrine. Because of his acceptance of this doctrine, his purpose in writing would include a personal apology for his beliefs.

About this time, Smyth also published another defense of believers' baptism. *Argumenta Contra Baptismum Infantum* contains nineteen syllogisms against the practice of baptising infants. This work was written in Latin, which suggests that Smyth's intended audience included the Dutch. Was it simply used to give the Mennonites more information about his stance on baptism? Perhaps it was Smyth's contribution to a contemporary debate on the Mennonites' behalf.

It is almost certainly not the lost work that Smyth mentions in his "Epistle." That work is described as being a debate with someone within the Separatist tradition. As previously mentioned, the audience of *Argumenta Contra Baptismum Infantum* was mainly Dutch, not English. The lost work is also described as expanding his arguments on the covenant of Abraham.[246] *Argumenta Contra Baptismum Infantum* contains some mention of the covenant. However, in comparison with the detailed analysis given in *The Character of the Beast*, its cameo appearances in *Argumenta Contra Baptismum Infantum* could hardly constitute the "more ful discourse" which Smyth describes in his "Epistle."[247]

While it is difficult to ascertain Smyth's intended audience or purpose in *Argumenta Contra Baptismum Infantum*, the arguments are straightforward. Smyth debates infant baptism using logic that is similar to that which he uses in *The Character of the Beast*. He uses his familiar argument that circumcision was a figure that was used in the Old Testament to point to the spiritual circumcision of the New Testament.[248]

---

[245]Coggins, *John Smyth's Congregation*, 91.
[246]Smyth, *Works* 2:570.
[247]Smyth, *Works* 2:570.
[248]Smyth, *Works* 2:718-19.

Smyth affirms that through Moses and the Old Testament much of Christ is revealed, but that the ceremonies of Moses should not continue now that Christ has been revealed fully in the New Testament.[249] One new argument that Smyth adds to his defense is that John the Baptist had introduced baptism after repentance. This baptism supersedes circumcision for believers. This is shown by Christ's remarks about John the Baptist being the greatest of the prophets.[250]

Smyth's posthumous publications. Smyth died of consumption in August 1612. An English confession of one hundred articles by Smyth was published after his death, in 1612 or 1613, under the title of *Propositions and Conclusions Concerning True Christian Religion.*[251] This posthumously published "confession" showed aspects of his Mennonite position.[252] While *Propositions and Conclusions* shows similarities to the twenty Latin articles of *Corde Credimus*, the later confession is much more than an expansion of the earlier confession. It is in the later confession that Smyth's "Arminian" beliefs are described in detail. Underwood holds that Smyth's rejection of Reformed views is the most significant aspect of this confession.[253] It seems that in a great deal of the confession Smyth tries to state his theology in terms that would be familiar to a Reformed audience. There are various Reformed beliefs that are opposed by Smyth. In articles 28 and 35, he opposes limited atonement. In at least ten articles, Smyth makes statements that contradict predestination or original sin.[254] Similar to his statement in *Corde Credimus*, in article 76, Smyth rejects the Reformed system of church officers by naming only two officers: pastors and deacons.

There are other important aspects to this confession besides Smyth's rejection of Reformed views. Underwood claims that *Propositions and Conclusions* is the "first full claim for full religious liberty ever penned in the English language."[255] Underwood has in mind article 84 which states:

---

[249]Smyth, *Works* 2:722.
[250]Smyth, *Works* 2:726.
[251]Henceforth, the shortened title *Propositions and Conclusions* will be used.
[252]Sprunger, *Dutch Puritanism*, 82.
[253]Underwood, *A History of the English Baptists*, 42.
[254]Smyth, *Works* 2:734-43; articles 10, 14, 17, 18, 19, 25, 26, 27, 58, and 59.
[255]Underwood, *A History of the English Baptists*, 42.

> That the magistrate is not by vertue of his office to meddle with religion, or matters of conscience, to force and compell men to this or that form of religion, or doctrine: but to leaue Christian religion free, to euery mans conscience, and to handle onely ciuil transgressions Rom. 13. iniuries and wronges of men against man, in murther, Adulterie, theft etc. for Christ onelie is the king, and lawgiuer of the church and conscience Jas 4. 12.[256]

Keith Sprunger notes that another trait of this confession is that Smyth remained vague on Melchiorite Christology.[257] In this confession, Smyth deals with his Christology in several articles. However, only in a few articles is the incarnation given any attention. Like the articles on church-state relations, these articles on Christology will be discussed in chapter 6, below.

Smyth's approach to explaining his theology is interesting considering his audience. Smyth could be attempting to demonstrate his beliefs to his fellow Englishmen. This would include both Puritans and Separatists, who were of a Reformed mind-set. Possibly, this is the reason for his taking time to present his thoughts in a Reformed context. It is also noteworthy that Smyth does not dwell on ecclesiology, interpreting Scripture, covenant, or baptism. However, we can see from his *The Last Booke* that Smyth was still answering accusations in these areas. So, why did Smyth not approach these subjects? The answer is simple. It lies in the nature of the work. It is strictly a confession, not an apology or polemic like most of Smyth's works. It seems Smyth was trying to state his beliefs with very little argument. Because of the confessional character of the work, it has a vital role in determining what was the focus of Smyth's theology. Smyth did not structure this confession as a debate, but instead he structured it in the way that he believes will best depict his theology.

In Smyth's *The Last Booke of John Smyth Called the Retractation of His Errours, and the Confirmation of the Truth,* the reader can see a difference in Smyth's tone. His words are much softer and less divisive.

---

[256]Smyth, *Works* 2:748. Smyth deals with church-state relations in articles 83 through 85 of this confession. These articles are discussed in greater detail in chap. 7.
[257]Sprunger, *Dutch Puritanism*, 82-83.

He asks forgiveness for all "hard phrases" he had written in the past.[258] More than likely, this work was not complete by his death but was finished by one of his followers, probably Thomas Pygott.[259]

The purpose of *The Last Booke* is different from his other works. It is not a collection of sermons. Neither is it a confession in the strict sense of the word, though Smyth does describe a few of his beliefs. He does not want to engage in debate, although he is being attacked by Ainsworth and Helwys. When he is giving his purpose for writing, he mentions Ainsworth and Helwys:

> [O]f which sort are those of our English nation, who publish in print ther proclamation against all churches, except those of their owne societie and fellowshipp: I mean the double seperation maister Hainsworth, and maister Helwys. although the one more neare the truth, then the other: neither is my purpose in this my writinge, to accuse and condemne, other men, but to censure and reforme my selfe.[260]

Smyth's approach to this book is to retract his harshness, but to affirm his earlier beliefs. Clearly, Smyth does not see significant differences from his former arguments, but he dislikes the manner in which he expressed himself. An example of this reproof of his harshness, while affirming his position, is his comment on *Paralleles, Censures, Observations*. He says:

> Particularly that booke against maister Bernard. wherin Maister Marbury, Maister White, and others are mentioned, and cruelly taxed: I retract not for that it is wholly false, but for that it is wholly censorious and criticall: and for that therin the contention for outward matters, which are of inferiour note, hath broken the rules of loue and charitie, which is the superiour law.[261]

Once Smyth has apologized for his earlier comments, he moves on to answer charges levelled against him by Thomas Helwys. There seem

---

[258]Smyth, *Works* 2:753. The shortened title *The Last Booke* is used elsewhere in the book.
[259]Underwood, *A History of the English Baptists*, 43.
[260]Smyth, *Works* 2:752; Acensure" has been amended: see n. 20.
[261]Smyth, *Works* 2:754. See Smyth, *Works* 2:545 and 2:335 for his comments on Marbury and White, respectively.

to be four charges: successionism, blaspheming the Holy Ghost, denying the flesh of Christ, and the misuse of money. Even in answering these charges, Smyth has a gracious tone that is lacking in his earlier works. In his response to denying the flesh of Christ, Smyth gives a brief summary of his views on the first and second flesh of Christ.[262] Smyth answers Helwys's charge of successionism by saying that he retains his former view that succession was broken by the infidelity of the Roman Church. However, if true churches exist, who administer the sacraments properly, then they should be sought for baptism for the sake of order.[263] Smyth also admonishes Helwys for his harsh charge of blasphemy. Smyth argues that he has not turned his back on any truth. However, even if he had, that would not constitute blasphemy.[264]

Concerning the misuse of money, Smyth makes it clear how little financial support he had received from Helwys. He says that the only debt he had to Helwys was that while he was sick in England, Helwys helped him financially. Since that time he had offered to repay him, but Helwys had refused.[265] Smyth also says that he had helped the poor every bit as much as Helwys. This brings up some questions about the sponsorship of the group's trip to Amsterdam. If Helwys had sponsored it alone, then he certainly was not responsible for Smyth's trip or he would have mentioned it at this point. Also, if Smyth's comments about helping the poor just as much as Helwys are taken seriously, then it is possible that Smyth had helped to underwrite the trip. Perhaps his medical career was prosperous, though it is even more likely that the settlement from his city lectureship allowed him to assist other members of the congregation with the journey. Unfortunately, Smyth was unable to complete *The Last Booke*. His followers reproduce faithfully his last lines, for the work ends abruptly with "concerning the."[266] Apparently, the mind of the man had more energy than his body.

Even though Helwys made harsh charges against Smyth, he obviously had once had a strong affection for Smyth. Just months before Smyth's death, Helwys wrote about him:

---

[262] See chap. 6 for more discussion.
[263] Smyth, *Works* 2:756-57.
[264] Smyth, *Works* 2:757-58.
[265] Smyth, *Works* 2:759.
[266] Smyth, *Works* 2:760.

Yea, what would we not have endured or done? Would we not have lost all we had? Yea, would we not have plucked out our eyes? Would we not have laid down our lives? Doth not GOD know this? Do not men know it? Doth not he know it? Have we not neglected ourselves, our wives, our children and all we had and respected him? And we confess we had good cause so to do in respect of those most excellent gifts and graces of GOD that then did abound in him. And all our love was too little for him and not worthy of him.[267]

After Smyth's death, his group continued to use the bakehouse of Jan Munter as a meeting hall and a dwelling place.[268] His church of about thirty members was admitted into the Waterlander Church on 21 January 1615.[269] The group met separately from 1615 to 1640 under Thomas Pygott, but was a part of the Dutch congregation. After Pygott's death, the English group faded into the other church. After 1640, there were no visible marks of two congregations. The amalgamation was complete.[270]

---

[267]Thomas Helwys in the preface to *A Declaration of Faith of People Remaining at Amsterdam in Holland* (Amsterdam: n.p., 1611) reprinted in Walter H. Burgess, *John Smyth, the Se-Baptist, Thomas Helwys and the First Baptist Church in England* (London: James Clarke & Co., 1911) 208. Hereafter, the shortened title, *A Declaration of Faith*, will be used.

[268]Sprunger, *Dutch Puritanism*, 83.

[269]Underwood, *A History of the English Baptists*, 43-44; White, "John Smyth," *Biographical Dictionary* 3:187; Sprunger, *Dutch Puritanism*, 83; Burgess, *John Smyth, the Se-Baptist*, 270-72; Pater, *Karlstadt as the Father of the Baptist Movements*, 264; Evans, *The Early English Baptists* 1:220-21. According to a Dutch document in *The Early English Dissenters*, Smyth's group had not been accepted as late as 17 January 1612; Burrage, *The Early English Dissenters* 2:213-15. Torbet, *A History of the Baptists*, 37, says January 20.

[270]Sprunger, *Dutch Puritanism*, 84.

Chapter 3
Smyth's Use of Typology

John Smyth often used contrasts when explaining his thought. These contrasts were couched in typological terms. Like many of the Reformers, he had a typological approach to interpreting scripture. He understood the Old Testament as containing types of spiritual truths that were more clearly revealed in the New Testament. The use of typology to interpret scripture is characteristic of Smyth's theology throughout his career. Moreover, he uses typological arguments to defend his theology even when he is not contrasting the Old and New Testaments.

Two Uses of Typology

Certain characteristics of the term "typology" must be discussed before the term is applied to the thought of John Smyth. A workable definition of typology is important. Typology is used in two ways in this chapter. First, it refers to a method of interpreting scripture. Second, it refers to a method of argument that is used for a theological defense.

Typology of scripture. R. T. France describes typology as "the recognition of a correspondence between New and Old Testament events, based on a conviction of the unchanging character of the principles of God's working."[1] Bernard Ramm defines typological interpretation of scripture as "specifically the interpretation of the Old Testament based on the fundamental theological unity of the two testaments whereby something in the Old shadows, prefigures, adumbrates something in the New."[2] These definitions describe how typology is used to relate the Old Testament and the New Testament.

While a typological understanding of scripture may contain several different nuances, there is a basic premise that remains consistent. The Old Testament texts find their proper understanding in the light of the New Testament. The proper relationship between the two testaments is

---

[1]Richard T. France, *The Gospel according to Matthew*, TNTC (Grand Rapids MI: Eerdmans, 1985) 40.

[2]Bernard Ramm, *Protestant Biblical Interpretation*, 3rd rev. ed. (Grand Rapids MI: Baker, 1970) 223.

one of continuity. Therefore, the ceremonies and commandments of the Old Testament were meant to prepare people for the fuller revelation of the New Testament. The elements of the Old Testament foreshadow the elements of the New Testament. To use typological terms: Old Testament types point to New Testament truths.

A typological interpretation of scripture attempts to show how God has a continuing purpose of liberating his people and that Christ is the ultimate means of fulfilling God's purpose. So, all biblical concepts are a part of God's ultimate purpose and can be fully understood only through Christ's work. The Old Testament events have a literal meaning and purpose historically, yet they find their ultimate fulfilment in being understood as a foreshadowing of Christ and his work.[3]

Typological defense of theology. The use of the term "typology" in reference to a method of interpreting scripture is normative. However, this chapter will describe John Smyth's thought as employing a typological defense. When used in this manner, typology can go beyond the relationship of the Old and New Testament. It involves a type as a shadow, symbol, or illustration of a truth. Knowledge of the type gives a person a starting point in perceiving the truth. Often when the truth is presented, then the type has completed its task and must not continue, because the truth is now in existence. Occasionally, the type can exist at the same time as the truth, but it serves as a constant reminder of the truth. Using a typological defense for theology allows a person to compare one concept that may be limited or dated with a concept that gives a fuller revelation.

James Coggins refers to Smyth's thought as resembling a type of dualism. However, dualism carries the notion of two opposing ideas. The two ideas are seen as polar opposites that are in conflict with each other. Coggins describes Smyth's thinking as being different from classical dualism because it does not have this conflict between two parts. He says that for Smyth "the two parts should be considered as two steps in a progression."[4] While Coggins captures the essence of Smyth's theology

---

[3]Leonhard Goppelt, *Typos. The Typological Interpretation of the Old Testament in the New*, trans. Donald H. Madvig (Grand Rapids MI: Eerdmans, 1982) 18.
[4]Coggins, *John Smyth's Congregation*, 121.

with his description, his use of the term "dualism" could be improved. Dualism does not indicate that the type or outward aspect of a matter sheds light on the truth or inward aspect of a matter. If Smyth's theological defense is described as typological, then the idea is clearer. This would encompass Smyth's use of typology to interpret scripture and his typological defense of his thought. These two kinds of typology are often intertwined in Smyth's writings.

Smyth's various uses of typology in defending his theology also suggest that typology is the best description of his method. In a typological defense of theology the type can contrast with the truth. Yet, this is not true in every case. The type and truth can have the same basic purpose. The type is seen as a complement to the truth, with the truth fulfilling the promises of the type. Instead of opposing ideas, the type and the truth are seen as means to the same end. Therefore typology has much more flexibility. It can point out opposition between the type and the truth, but it can also emphasize their similarities.

Although he may indicate some contrast between the two, Smyth also points out that the type is used to understand the truth or to help prepare the way for the truth. Smyth uses a typological structure to his arguments in many of his debates including those on the church, the covenant, Christology, and the magistrates. Because of Smyth's use of type and truth in these vital aspects of his theology, Smyth should be understood as having a typological defense of his theology as well as using typology to interpret scripture.

Smyth's Typological Interpretation of Scripture

In his earliest work, *The Bright Morning Starre*, Smyth uses a typological interpretation of Psalm 22. His exposition begins with the comment, "The Prophet Dauid is here to be considered. 1. in his owne person. 2. sustaining the person of a godly man. 3. as a type of Christ."[5] A typological understanding of scripture is the norm for Smyth throughout his theological career, although his theological shifts do bring some revision to his typological defense of certain ideas.

---

[5]Smyth, *Works* 1:15.

Smyth's underlying perception in relating the testaments is that the Old Testament's purpose is to reveal God's nature. However, the Old Testament is chiefly ceremonial, and therefore it does not reveal God's nature as clearly as the New Testament. As the truth of God has become clearer, the tools that had been used to teach about Him are no longer needed. Because the New Testament and its practices have greater clarity, the Old Testament practices have been superseded. However, Smyth argues that this did not mean that the Old Testament is to be done away with.

Smyth holds that believers are commanded to obey the principles of both testaments. He maintains that both the Old and New Testaments are inspired.[6] However, his typological understanding of scripture and his acceptance of believers' baptism led Richard Clyfton to charge him with the Anabaptist view of denying the Old Testament.[7] Smyth answers this charge by reaffirming the inspiration of the Old Testament, "we deny not the Scriptures of the Old Testament, but with the Apostles acknowledg them to bee inspired of God."[8]

Smyth argues for typology. During his debates, it becomes clear that Smyth's view is that the Old Testament should be understood typologically. In his work, *Paralleles, Censures, Observations*, he states:

> I answer: First to that of the old Testament objected by you, I say you bewray therein great ignorance of the true nature & constitution of the Church of the Old Testament, as also of the ministery, worship, & government thereof, which were al typical & ceremonial: Know you therfor Mr. Bern. that ther is as much difference betwixt the Old Testament with the ordinances thereof, & the new Testament with the ordinances therof, as ther is betwixt the signe & the thing signified: betwixt the ceremony & the substance: the type & the truth: the shadow & the body: Literal & Spiritual: the lettre & the Spirit.[9]

Here, Smyth uses several terms in an attempt to demonstrate the differences between the Old and New Testaments. These terms are dis-

---

[6] Smyth, *Works* 1:281-82.

[7] Denying the Old Testament was a common charge against all Anabaptists regardless of their actual beliefs.

[8] Smyth, *Works* 2:571. "Apostles" has been emended.

[9] Smyth, *Works* 2:375.

cussed more fully later in this chapter. His plea with Richard Bernard is that he should recognize the ceremonial nature of the Old Testament practices and not base his church practices on these typical ordinances.

Throughout his debate with Bernard over the nature of the true church, Smyth relies heavily on his typological understanding of the testaments. As he argues that saints are the true matter of the church, Smyth says:

> This was a Type figure shadow, ceremony, signe, literal ordinance in the old Testament, therefor we must not have that type, figure, shadow, ceremony, signe, literal ordinance in the new Testament, but we must have the thing typed, figured, shadowed out, signified thereby.[10]

He sees the Old Testament as containing types or signs which point to a higher truth or principle. So, the types are not to be maintained, but the principles behind them are. Smyth believes that God was not trying to instruct his people about the importance of a ceremony, but was trying to teach them about himself. While the Old Testament has a ceremony that points to the truth, the New Testament reveals the truth in its clearest form. Once the truth has been discovered, the truth is to be extolled, and the type is to be eliminated.

Later in *Parallels, Censures, Observations*, Smyth wants Bernard to realize that he must relate the testaments typologically if he is going to understand the church properly. Smyth states:

> The ground of this argument is the Analogie and proportion which ther is betwixt the type and the truth, the shadow and the substance, the lettre and the Spirit, the Old Testament with the ordinances therof, & the new Testament with the ordinances thereof: For seing the old Testament was a type of the new.[11]

This statement depicts two of Smyth's fundamental beliefs about the testaments. The Old Testament contains the type of the truth and the New Testament contains the truth. This view is the basis of Smyth's arguments indicated by his use of the phrase, "The ground of this argument." His typological interpretation of scripture is the basis from which Smyth

---

[10]Smyth, *Works* 2:376.
[11]Smyth, *Works* 2:497.

defends much of his theology. In another debate, he charges his opponent, Richard Clyfton, with bringing the type from the Old Testament into the New Testament to the detriment of the latter.[12]

Smyth's view of the New Testament as a further revelation is also evident in the statement, "the L. taught no such thing in the old Testament & in the typical communion therof: but now in the new Testament we having the truth that was then signified by the old Testament & the ordinances therof."[13] The practices of the church are to derive from the truth of the New Testament, not the type of the Old Testament. Smyth's contrasts between the Old Testament ordinances and the New Testament practices appear throughout his ecclesiastical debates.

Two expressions of Smyth's typological interpretation of scripture. Whether Smyth is debating with someone within the Church of England or with one of the Separatists, his writings depict the Old Testament as typing the New Testament. There are two basic ways Smyth expresses the differences in the Old and New Testament.

1. *The ceremonial nature of the Old Testament.* The first expression is that the Old Testament is predominantly ceremonial in nature. Smyth believes the Old Testament contains many rituals, and these rituals are to point the Hebrews to God. They are just rituals and not the complete revelation of God, which causes the need for further revelation. When Christ came, he established a new testament or covenant. As he did this, he removed the necessity of the rituals to understand God. Since they are no longer needed to understand God, they are discontinued. Smyth makes this point clear in his Separatist work, *The Differences of the Churches*, by stating, "The writings of the old Testament being ceremonial are therfor abolished by Christ only so far forth as they are ceremonial."[14]

Later in his Mennonite work, *Defence of Ries's Confession*, he argues that the Old Testament ceremony of circumcision has been discontinued. Infant baptism is improper because it is the church's adaptation of the Old Testament practice of circumcision. Smyth defends his position against a Reformed critic by saying that because of a typological understanding of the Old Testament, many of its ceremonies had been dis-

---

[12]Smyth, *Works* 2:623.
[13]Smyth, *Works* 2:454.
[14]Smyth, *Works* 1:281.

continued in deference to the truths which they typed. He says that his Reformed opponent as well as others accepted that many ceremonies of the Old Testament needed to be discontinued. Smyth argues that those who continued infant baptism were holding to a ceremony that he and the Mennonites believed that Christ had not established. He writes, "Do you shatter the honor of the Old Testament when you want the entire ceremonial law and most of the judicial [law] lifted from Christian people? You lift much, we in fact most, of the entire Old Testament from the community because Christ fastened it to His cross and abolished it."[15]

Smyth contends that while the principles the Old Testament teaches are intact and the Old Testament scriptures are useful, the outward ceremonies are to be eliminated. In describing the church of the Old Testament, he says, "For to the constitution of the typical Church ther was not required true holynes, but ceremonial cleanenes."[16] This ceremonial cleanliness is to give way to the true holiness of the New Testament. Smyth maintains that the Old Testament's ordinances are not to be carried over to the New Testament. He contends that Christ brought in the New Testament and cancelled the Old Testament ceremonies.[17]

One example of Smyth's understanding of the ceremonial nature of the Old Testament occurs in *The Differences of the Churches*. Smyth debates the practices of Francis Johnson's church by saying that translations of scripture should not be used in a time of worship. Smyth relies on his typology to defend his belief. He claims that not only are the practices of the Old Testament ceremonial, but also the Hebrew letters and alphabet are ceremonial. He says, "Hence it followeth that the holy originals the Hebrue scriptures of the old Testament are ceremonyes."[18] Smyth contends that the Septuagint was not a proper translation for many reasons. One of his reasons is that, "Bicause the Hebrue characters & writings were Ceremonyes & so ought not to have been profaned among

---

[15]Translation by Coggins, *John Smyth's Congregation*, 189. *num vos honorem veteris testamenti diminuitis, cum totam legem ceremonialem et paene judicialem sublatam vultis e populo christiano: ea lege qua vos multum, nos plurimum immo totum vetus testamentum e medio tollimus cum Christus idem cruci suae affixit et abolevit.* Smyth, *Works* 2:704.

[16]Smyth, *Works* 2:377.

[17]Smyth, *Works* 2:522.

[18]Smyth, *Works* 1:281.

the Grecians by their writings."[19] He holds that the Old Testament should not have been translated out of the Hebrew before the New Testament was established. Because the truth had not yet been established, the type or ceremony of the Hebrew scripture should not have been usurped.

2. *The New Testament clarifies the Old Testament.* The second expression of how Smyth uses typology is that he sees the New Testament as bringing clarity to the Old. The Old Testament becomes a way of preparing people for the New. When Smyth refers to the Jews of the Old Testament, he says, "they were trayned vp, or Schooled to Christ, being by all the ceremonial law & old Testament, or carnal commaundement, as it were by so many meanes consecrated or dedicated to that holy end & purpose, which was tiped & shadowed by those figures & similitudes of heavenly things."[20] The apparent purpose of the Old Testament was to teach the people about Christ, as indicated by Smyth's statement "The law or old Testament was a Schoolmr. only to teach Chr."[21] If the Old Testament teaches Christ, then its teachings prepare the people for Christ. For Smyth, aspects of the spiritual nature or "heavenly things" are taught in the Old Testament, but are not apparent until the New Testament. So, the best way of interpreting the Old Testament is through the light of the New Testament.

God reveals Himself through scripture. In the Old Testament, however, God's revelation is a shadow of the fuller revelation that comes with the New Testament. The New Testament, referred to as "the Gospel," is open for everyone to see clearly. However, the Old Testament, or "the Law," has a veil that prevents a clear view or understanding of the nature of God. Smyth indicates the heightened clarity of the New Testament by saying, "For seing the new Testament is more manifest then the old, the Gospel being with open face, the Law being hid vnder the vele."[22]

In relating the Old and New Testaments as a Mennonite, Smyth draws on comparisons between Moses and Christ. Moses is presented as the deliverer of the Law. The Law's revelation is limited in comparison

---

[19]Smyth, *Works* 1:289.
[20]Smyth, *Works* 2:599.
[21]Smyth, *Works* 2:598.
[22]Smyth, *Works* 2:622.

with the truth that is revealed by Christ. Smyth says, "The Law has been given through Moses. The truth comes through Christ."[23] The Old Testament needs Christ to come to bring clarity to its revelation. Until Christ comes, the Old Testament's types are not properly understood. Smyth asserts, "Christ in the New Testament revealed to us the hidden mysteries of the Old Testament."[24]

The Old Testament contains the truths of the New Testament, but they cannot be drawn out clearly. Smyth says that going to the Old Testament to find truths for the New Testament church is like someone who might

> put aside the light of the sunne at noone, & set vp a candle as the Papists do in their funerals: for although it be meet that we attend vnto the Prophets as unto a light shining in a dark place, yet seing the day star is come, & the sunne of righteousnes is risen vppon vs, let vs walk in this cleer light.[25]

The reason for the dim light of the Old Testament is that Christ cannot be perceived clearly there. Again, Smyth uses the image of the veil to describe the revelation of Christ in the Old Testament. He states, "wherby Chr. in that vele of the old Testament was preached vnto the Iewes, it being ther Schoolmr. to teach them Christ."[26] The Old Testament's revelation is inferior because it does not depict Christ fully.

Smyth reasons that the Old Testament teaches about Christ, just not with the same exactness the New Testament does. He states that Christ uses the Old Testament to testify of himself.[27] The fact that Christ can be found in the Old Testament leads Smyth to affirm its importance. In referring to scriptures from the Old Testament, Smyth states, "in them wee may find everlasting life, & that they do testifie of Christ."[28]

Another dimension of the New Testament's superior clarity is that Smyth sees the New Testament as a clearer picture of God's covenant.

---

[23]*Per Mosen lex data est: veritas per Christum accidit.* Smyth, *Works* 2:721.
[24]*Christus in novo testamento revelavit nobis occulta mijsteria veteris testamenti.* Smyth, *Works* 2:730.
[25]Smyth, *Works* 2:623.
[26]Smyth, *Works* 2:631.
[27]Smyth, *Works* 2:571.
[28]Smyth, *Works* 2:571.

The carnal covenant and the spiritual covenant are both present in the Old Testament, but in the New Testament only the spiritual covenant remains. The carnal covenant is more evident in the Old Testament and the spiritual covenant only becomes manifest in the New Testament. Smyth also holds that the coming of Christ causes definite changes in the administration of the covenant. He expresses this thought in this way:

> Remember that there be alwaies a difference put betwixt the covenant of grace; and the manner of dispensing it, which is twofold: the forme of administring the covenant before the death of Christ, which is called the old testament; and the forme of administring the covenant since the death of Christ which is called the new Testament or the kingdome of heaven.[29]

Smyth states that there is a difference between the covenant practices of the Old Testament and the covenant practices of the New Testament. The covenant that is represented by the Old Testament and its ordinances is a carnal covenant that types the spiritual covenant. Smyth says, "the matter & forme of the Church of the old Testament, (that is the members, & covenant) is not the truth: that is the members are not truly holy, but ceremonialy holy, the covenant is not the everlasting covenant, but the typical carnal covenant or commaundement."[30] Smyth refers to the carnal covenant or old testament being the "type" and the spiritual covenant or new testament being the "truth."[31] Although the spiritual covenant is present in the Old Testament, it is not fully realized until the New Testament.

Smyth's Use of Typology in Defending His Theology

Smyth's use of typology is not limited to his interpretation of scripture. Typology is a dominant characteristic of many aspects of his theology. In his typological understanding of scripture, Smyth observes that God uses carnal things to teach spiritual truths. Smyth argues that the Old Testament uses ceremonies to point to the spiritual truths of the New Testament. His emphasis on the spiritual dynamic of truth correlates with Smyth's typological explanation of truth. He believes that there is an

---

[29]Smyth, *Works* 1:250.
[30]Smyth, *Works* 2:597.
[31]Smyth, *Works* 2:606.

outward dimension to certain aspects of truth that point to a fuller, spiritual, inward dimension. Similar to the relationship between the testaments, in Smyth's theological defense the type is limited while the truth has a deeper, fuller meaning.

To understand many of Smyth's arguments the type and the truth must be located. The relationship between the type and truth needs to be discerned in context, because Smyth relates the two in different ways. Occasionally, he says that once the truth has come then the type must be abandoned. Two examples of types that are to be discontinued are the carnal covenant and Old Testament ceremonial worship. In other instances Smyth argues that the type and truth exist simultaneously because the type is a constant reminder of the truth. For example, the outward communion of the church points to the inward communion, which is actual believers. Another example is the natural flesh of Christ which symbolizes the deeper, spiritual flesh. Both aspects of His flesh have inherent value. One way to understand Smyth's use of typology better is to be familiar with the typological terms that Smyth employs.

Contrasting terms that Smyth employs. Smyth uses many terms to indicate the typological nature of a certain practice or teaching. Often, Smyth uses terms in contrasting pairs. Smyth lists most of these pairs in two sections of his writings.[32] The identifiable pairs are as follows: literal and spiritual, sign and thing signified, ceremony and substance, shadow and substance or body, figure and thing figured, letter and spirit, outward and inward, carnal and spiritual, type and truth. The first term in each pair is essentially synonymous with the other first terms, and the second term of each pair with the other second terms. This becomes obvious when we notice that Smyth will occasionally interchange the terms by importing one half of a pair and linking it with the other half of another pair. Three of these pairs are used frequently by Smyth. He uses outward and inward, carnal and spiritual, and type and truth in many sections of his writings. Smyth's use of these three pairs is significant because they become central terms in his typological defense. These three major pairs are discussed more fully later in this chapter.

1. *The minor pairs.* A brief description of the minor pairs will help in introducing Smyth's use of typological pairs. Smyth uses the contrast

---

[32]Smyth, *Works* 2:375, 497.

of literal and spiritual on several occasions. In each case, Smyth is using these terms to compare worship that is formal with worship that is less restricted. Four uses of the comparison of literal and spiritual appear in Smyth's Separatist stage in his work *The Differences of the Churches*.[33] In these instances, Smyth uses the word literal to refer to the worship of the Old Testament. He refers to the sacrificial system as literal ordinances that point to the spiritual worship to come. Two additional uses of this contrast appear in his Separatist work *Paralleles, Censures, Observations*.[34] Both of these uses are also a comparison of the literal ordinances and worship of the Old Testament with the spiritual worship to follow. Smyth's desire in each of these instances is to move away from the literal ordinance and to seek the spiritual worship.

The next two pairs appear together in a few instances. Sign and thing signified appear along with ceremony and substance. While discussing Old and New Testament ordinances, Smyth says, "Ther is as much difference betwixt the Old Testament with the ordinances thereof, & the new Testament with the ordinances therof, as ther is betwixt the signe & the thing signified: betwixt the ceremony & the substance: the type & the truth."[35] In one section of *The Differences of the Churches*, Smyth takes a term from each pair to make his contrast. Smyth is showing that the ceremonial nature of the Old Testament is cancelled, but that these ceremonies signify something greater to come. The "law of God" and the "new testament" are things signified by the ceremony. He states, "The writings of the old Testament being ceremonial are therfor abolished by Christ only so far forth as they are ceremonial. . . . The thing signified by the book viz: the law of God & the new testament remayneth."[36]

Smyth uses the term "shadow" to contrast with both "substance" and "body."[37] Most of the appearances of these terms are in a list of other typological contrasts. Therefore, it is difficult to determine any significant difference in these terms and the other pairs. Smyth refers to calling, profession, and baptism as outward images that shadow sanctification

---

[33]Smyth, *Works* 1:275, 303-304, 2:323.
[34]Smyth, *Works* 2:375, 497.
[35]Smyth, *Works* 2:375.
[36]Smyth, *Works* 1:281.
[37]Smyth, *Works* 2:321, 375, 383, 497, 597, 721.

superficially.[38] A similar comparison is used in Smyth's Mennonite work, *Argumenta Contra Baptismum Infantum*, where he says that faith, repentance, and conversion are the "body and substance" whereas the Old Testament ceremonies are "mere shadows."[39] Smyth uses the term shadow to denote something that represents another concept that has a higher meaning.

The terms "letter" and "spirit" appear in the two sections listing typological contrasts, and in at least one additional instance.[40] Smyth holds that the letter prepares the way for the spirit. He writes that the ministry of the Old Testament is the "ministery of the lettre, seing it dispenced the ceremonial & literal ordinances & beganne in the lettre."[41] He contrasts this with the New Testament in saying, "The ministration of the New Testament is called the ministery of the Spirit: seing it dispenced the true & spiritual ordinances typed by the foresaid literal ordinances, & beginneth in the spirit originally, though prepared by the lettre."[42] Since the New Testament is the ministry of the Spirit, Smyth says that the worship of the New Testament church should not be confined to the letter of books, read prayers, or even the scripture.

One other minor term Smyth utilizes is "figure." This term is used on at least two occasions, but on one of them it does not have a directly related contrasting term.[43] While it is difficult to comprehend what term is in comparison with figure, it is not difficult to understand how Smyth uses this term with his other typological terms. He uses the term "figure" as a synonym for his other terms meaning "type." Smyth writes, "The type, shadow, figure, similitude of a thing is not the truth, the substance, the thing it self."[44] In his Mennonite work, *Argumenta Contra Baptismum Infantum*, Smyth refers to the Old Testament ceremonies as "superficial figures" that point to the truth that is coming in Christ.[45]

---

[38]Smyth, *Works* 2:383.
[39]*corpus . . . et substantiam, umbrae merae*, Smyth, *Works* 2:721.
[40]Smyth, *Works* 1:302-303, 2:375, 497.
[41]Smyth, *Works* 1:303.
[42]Smyth, *Works* 1:303.
[43]Smyth, *Works* 2:376, 597, 599, 715-16, 721.
[44]Smyth, *Works* 2:597.
[45]*figurae superficiariae*, Smyth, *Works* 2:721.

Smyth uses all of these minor pairs predominantly in his discussions of the church. More specifically, he uses them most often to show that formal worship is a type for the truth of a more free worship. Smyth's uses these minor typological pairs frequently in his Separatist stage, where his debates focus on his understanding of the church.

2. *The three major pairs.* While Smyth uses many terms in his typological arguments, there are three pairs that appear most often: outward and inward, carnal and spiritual, type and truth. The minor pairs appear most often in Smyth's Separatist stage, but these major pairs are employed frequently throughout Smyth's career. Therefore, an understanding of Smyth's use of these main pairs aids in a comprehension of Smyth's entire theological system. Smyth uses the pairs with a great deal of similarity. However, there are slight variations of thought for each pair, or at least different subject areas where Smyth seems to prefer the use of one pair over the others. The terms "type" and "truth," and "carnal" and "spiritual" are used in relating the Old Testament to the New Testament, as well as in other areas of his theology. The terms "outward" and "inward" are used in interpreting scripture, but more often they are used in other aspects of Smyth's typological defense of his theology.

a. *Outward and inward.* The terms "outward" and "inward" are used by Smyth in three different ways. The first way is that Smyth attempts to show that the outward indicates the presence of the inward. In his Separatist work, *Paralleles, Censures, Observations*, he discusses the issue of outward confession of faith. He states:

> That although an outward calling, profession, and baptisme to the faith be part of the signes of Saynts: Namely, visible markes outwardly: yet they must be thus qualified, els they are nothing but pictures, or images, resembling & shadowing Sanctification superficialy: For they must be true & inward also: True calling, profession & baptisme: & inward calling, profession, & baptisme, are the infallible tokens of Sanctification and Saynts: The inward must be discerned by the outward . . . so he by reason of his outward true calling, true profession of the true faith, and true baptisme is discerned & judged to be inwardly called, inwardly to have faith, to be inwardly baptized, & that truly.[46]

---

[46]Smyth, *Works* 2:383.

The outward signs can be counterfeited, but the inward marks are genuine. However, because inward marks are impossible to discern, Smyth argues that only through the proper expression of outward signs can the inward be considered present. The inward is "discerned" by the outward, so, the outward signs are important because they indicate the presence of the inward. The outward signs do not have a value of their own.

Smyth's second way of using these terms is to teach that the outward precedes the inward. It is easier to understand and accept the inward because of the presence of the outward. This is evident in Smyth's discussion of Old Testament worship. He says, "Bicause as all the worship which Moses taught began in the letter outwardly, & so proceeded inwardly to the spirit of the faithfull: so contrariwise all the worship of the new testament signified by that typicall worship of Moses must beginne at the Spirit, & not at the letter originally."[47] His point in this statement is to show that Moses uses a ritual during worship in which everyone could participate outwardly. However, only the faithful experience the spiritual aspect of worship. In this scenario, the outward ceremonies precede the inward, spiritual worship. For the faithful, the outward rituals help prepare them to enter into true, inward worship.

Smyth believes that this is a proper pattern for Old Testament worship, but it should not be the pattern for the New Testament. In New Testament worship, the outward beginning in rituals is to be done away with, and for the individual, worship should begin in the spirit. According to Smyth, this was assisted by removing books or ordered services, and proceeding directly to a time of prophecy.[48]

Another discussion in which Smyth shows that the outward precedes the inward is in his discussion of the theology of the covenant. In a section of *The Character of the Beast*, Smyth explains how the Apostle Paul taught that the Israelites had been under an outward covenant of the Law, but were offered an inward, spiritual covenant. Smyth refers to the outward covenant as "preaching the other, the law being a scholemr. to Christ."[49] This statement illustrates Smyth's understanding that the

---

[47]Smyth, *Works* 1:283.
[48]Smyth, *Works* 1:283-84.
[49]Smyth, *Works* 2:592.

outward covenant prepares the way for the inward or spiritual covenant of Christ that was to come.

A third example of this relationship between outward and inward is found in his work, *Defence of Ries's Confession*. Smyth says that the inward miracles that Christ performed and still performs are greater than the outward, natural ones. Smyth says that the outward are a prelude (*preludia*) to what is to come in the inward miracles. The preceding outward miracles prepare the people to receive the inward miracles. The inward work that Christ does in the hearts of believers surpasses any of his outward, physical miracles.[50]

The third way that Smyth uses this contrasting pair is to show that the outward does not have the depth of the inward. Occasionally, Smyth holds that both the outward and the inward must continue to exist. In these cases Smyth believes that the outward has a legitimate, separate purpose other than leading to or symbolizing the inward. His main concern in these cases is to make sure that the inward exists along with the outward. While the outward does have a significant purpose, the inward remains the core of the matter or thought. This conception of the inward being the more important aspect of the church can be seen in the writings of the Separatist, Robert Browne. He emphasizes that "inwarde obedience" to preaching should be the focus of the church.[51] Smyth places the same emphasis on the importance of the inward nature of the church.

Smyth says the church consists of an outward and inward communion. The inward communion is known only to God. The outward communion can be discerned by humans. According to Smyth, a person must be judged by men to be a member of both the outward and the inward communion if that person manifests "an outward visible faith."[52] Although the church consists of those of outward and inward communion, those who are members of the outward communion only are "hypocrites."[53] There is value in being a member outwardly, but it must be connected with the deeper reality of being a member inwardly.

---

[50]Smyth, *Works* 2:698; Coggins, *John Smyth's Congregation*, 184.
[51]Browne, *The Writings of Robert Harrison and Robert Browne*, 156-57.
[52]Smyth, *Works* 2:372-73.
[53]Smyth, *Works* 2:373.

As Smyth discusses worship, he describes worship as having both outward and inward helps. The inward helps are "the word & the spirit." The outward helps are "the manifestation of the Spirit: & the seales of the covenant . . . with the instruments creatures & actions apperteyning therto."[54] These outward helps are the practical aspects that assist in worship such as speaking, breaking bread, and washing with water. Though outward helps are necessary aspects of worship, they should not exist without the inward helps.

The fact that the outward does not have the depth of the inward is depicted again in Smyth's work, *Defence of Ries's Confession* when he writes, "For that first outward sacrifice was a certain figure and shadow of this later and inward one, containing, nevertheless, its power and truth and yet inferior to the later one."[55] Smyth refers to Christ's outward sacrifice on the cross as being an shadow (*umbra*) of the inward sacrifice where the sins and desires of the heart are daily crucified. The outward sacrifice contains truth, but is less than or inferior to the inward, later one. The ongoing inward sacrifices, like the inward miracles, take precedence over the outward works.

Probably the most intriguing use of outward and inward by Smyth to show the superior depth of the inward is in his discussion of the local church covenant. Smyth discusses the "true form of a true visible Church" as having two parts: one inward and one outward. Smyth states, "The inward part of the forme consisteth in 3. Things 1. the Spirit 2. Faith. 3. love."[56] He also states, "The outward part of the true forme of the true visible church is a vowe, promise, oath, or covenant betwixt God and the Saints: by proportion from the inward forme."[57] Smyth refers to the church covenant as being the outward part of the true form of a church. It is obvious from Smyth's Separatist writings that he believed the covenant to be essential for a church. However, even this crucial element is seen as being the outward part of the true form. It comes from

---

[54]Smyth, *Works* 1:277.
[55]Translation by Coggins, *John Smyth's Congregation*, 184. *nam illa prima externa victima hujus posterioris et internae figura quaedam et umbra fuit, suam in se tamen continens vim et veritatem etsi posteriori minorem.* Smyth, *Works* 2:699.
[56]Smyth, *Works* 1:253. "Consisteth" has been emended.
[57]Smyth, *Works* 1:254.

the inward part, "by proportion." The Spirit, faith, and love must accompany the covenant. The outward part, or covenant, derives from the inward part. This serves as the best example of Smyth's third usage of outward and inward. While the covenant is crucial and serves a distinct purpose, it still does not contain the depth of the truth that the inward parts of the Spirit, faith, and love do.

b. *Carnal and spiritual.* The second major pair of typological terms that Smyth uses is "carnal" and "spiritual." He uses this pair most frequently during his Separatist and Baptist stages. His use of these terms can be separated into two categories. As a Separatist, he contrasts various carnal aspects of the Old Testament with various spiritual aspects of the New Testament. However in his Baptist stage, he uses these terms almost exclusively to refer to the covenant.

In his Separatist work, *Paralleles, Censures, Observations*, Smyth debates with Richard Bernard about ministerial authority. Smyth argues that a succession of ordination is not necessary to pass on spiritual authority in the church. After arguing for the whole body of the church to have the authority passed to them, not just the church officers, Smyth compares an extensive list of elements of the Old Testament with those of the New Testament. In the list Smyth employs the contrast of carnal and spiritual. He writes:

> In the old Testament they had carnal parents a carnal seed, carnal children, carnal circumcision, carnal commaundements, a carnal temple, a carnal cittie, a carnal preisthood, a carnal Kingdom: in the new Testament we have spiritual parents, a spiritual seed which is the word, spiritual children, viz: the faithful, circumcision made without hands, spiritual commaundements, a spiritual temple, an heavenly cittie, spiritual Preists & Kings, & a spiritual kingdom & preisthood.[58]

Each carnal element of the Old Testament contrasts with a spiritual element of the New Testament. In this use of these terms, "carnal" does not carry an evil connotation. Smyth's main contrast between the two is that the carnal elements of the Old Testament are more limited than the spiritual elements of the New Testament. Smyth pleads with Bernard to leave the carnal elements behind in favor of the spiritual elements.

---

[58]Smyth, *Works* 2:415-16. "Commaundements" has been emended.

In his book, *The Differences of the Churches*, Smyth employs a similar comparison of carnal and spiritual in comparing the priests of the "old Testament" with the saints as priests of the "new Testament." He states, "Spirituall sacrifices are such as originally proceed from the spirit: & they are called spirituall in opposition to the carnall or literall sacrifices performed by the sacrificing Preists of the old Testament: which originally proceeded from the lettre."[59] Smyth contrasts the carnal sacrifices of the Old Testament church with the spiritual sacrifices that the New Testament church should offer. His disagreement with Johnson's church revolved around the idea of limiting the spirit by requiring the letter. Smyth desires spiritual worship instead of the carnal worship that would conform to a written liturgy or book.

Another interesting comparison that Smyth uses in *The Differences of the Churches* refers to the power of the church. He holds that each local church has the power to reform itself. He says this power "is spir[i]tuall as is Christs kingdome not worldly, bodily, nor carnal."[60] The two terms linked with carnal give some indication of Smyth's use of the term. The terms "worldly" and "bodily" imply a close connection with human results or understanding. So, it does not appear that he uses the term "carnal" to denote something inherently evil. Instead, Smyth agrees with seventeenth- century common usage by using the term to indicate the finite or temporary nature of something.

While these preceding examples show various areas where Smyth contrasts carnal and spiritual, his main use is in the area of the covenant. A fuller discussion of Smyth's contrast of a carnal and spiritual covenant will appear in the chapter on the theology of the covenant. However, there is an additional comment that can be made presently. A noteworthy aspect of his use of this comparison is his importation of other terms during a discussion. While asserting that God made a carnal and a spiritual covenant with Abraham, Smyth replaces "carnal" with "temporary" or "external."[61] On at least two more occasions, he replaces the term "carnal" with "external."[62] Again, his shift in the use of terms gives some

---

[59]Smyth, *Works* 1:275.
[60]Smyth, *Works* 1:267.
[61]Smyth, *Works* 2:585.
[62]Smyth, *Works* 2:599-600, 650.

indication of his understanding of "carnal." His emphasis is on the limited nature of carnal things. "Temporary" states this limit in terms of time. "External" expresses this limit in terms of depth. Smyth does not use "carnal" to indicate something evil, evidenced by his replacing of "carnal" with "temporary" or "external" instead of with a term such as "sinful." Carnal is not more evil than spiritual, but it is more limited. Moreover, on a few occasions "spiritual" is replaced with the term "everlasting," reinforcing the idea that the main contrast between carnal and spiritual is not one of morality, but one of scope.[63]

c. *Type and truth*. The third major pair that Smyth uses is "type" and "truth." These terms are utilized by Smyth in his typological defense of his theology and his method of interpreting scripture. They are used most frequently during his Separatist and Baptist stages. Later, Smyth seems to have favored the use of "outward" and "inward."

Smyth uses "type" and "truth" for two basic purposes. While these do not take into account every usage of these terms, they do seem to be the main focus for these terms. First, Smyth employs "type" and "truth" in comparing the elements of the Old Testament church and the elements of the New Testament church. He refers to the Old Testament church as a type of the New Testament churches.[64] Smyth mentions specific aspects of the church as well as making general comments about the nature of the church. In his work, *Paralleles, Censures, Observations*, he refers to the typical saints and the typical communion of the Old Testament church.[65] He even mentions that members of the Old Testament church could be typically clean without repentance, where New Testament saints required repentance to be truly clean.[66]

Also in his discussion with Bernard, Smyth makes a general statement concerning the typical nature of the Old Testament church. He states, "I say you bewray therein great ignorance of the true nature & constitution of the Church of the Old Testament, as also of the ministery, worship, & government thereof, which were al typical & ceremonial."[67] Smyth

---

[63]Smyth, *Works* 2:588, 599.
[64]Smyth, *Works* 2:367.
[65]Smyth, *Works* 2:380, 385.
[66]Smyth, *Works* 2:448.
[67]Smyth, *Works* 2:375.

addresses the theme of "typical" worship in his earlier Separatist writing, *Principles and Inferences*. There he states, "The ceremoniall worship performed in the holy place did type most properly the worship of the Church of the new Testament."[68] Smyth often uses type and truth to argue for a worship that leaves behind the typical worship of the Old Testament.

When Smyth moves into his Baptist stage, he continues the comparison of the Old Testament church being the type and the New Testament church being the truth. In his debate with Richard Clyfton, Smyth argues that infants cannot be a part of the New Testament church even though they were a part of the Old Testament church. The central theme of his argument is his typological view characterized by his use of type and truth. He states, "The constitution, viz: the matter & forme of the Church of the old Testament is the type. The constitution or the matter & forme of the church of the new Testament is the truth."[69] The constitution of the Old Testament church is a carnal one that is passed on from generation to generation and includes infants. Smyth believes, however, that the Old Testament church types the true church in the New Testament, which would include only those who have met the requirement of "Faith & repentance."[70]

Smyth's second purpose in applying these terms is as categories to point out his typological argument.[71] Occasionally, he will even capitalize "type" and "truth" to set them apart as titles of categories instead of specific items. Often, when he includes a list of typological terms, he places "type" and "truth" at the beginning of the list.[72] This use at the forefront of other terms reinforces the idea that in these cases "type" and "truth" designate categories for Smyth.

Smyth uses typology to defend his theology, which has been shown thus far mainly by citing examples of typological terms used in his writings. However, there is an even stronger case for Smyth's use of typology as the basis of his defense. As a Separatist, Smyth argues against

---

[68]Smyth, *Works* 1:304.
[69]Smyth, *Works* 2:597.
[70]Smyth, *Works* 2:597.
[71]Smyth, *Works* 2:375-77, 424-26, 585, 609, 665-66.
[72]Smyth, *Works* 2:376.

Richard Bernard that the church is made up of saints only. Smyth says that the reason that Bernard does not understand this point or the other Separatist arguments is that he misunderstands typology. In the following quotation, the fundamental nature of typology to Smyth's defense becomes evident. Smyth claims that one must have a proper approach to theology, and this would include using typology correctly. He states:

> Therfor if you wil reason aright as you ought to doe, you must frame your reason from the Type to the Truth after this manner. This was a Type figure shadow, ceremony, signe, literal ordinance in the old Testament, therefor we must not have that type, figure, shadow, ceremony, signe, literal ordinance in the new Testament, but we must have the thing typed, figured, shadowed out, signified thereby.[73]

Once someone understands typology correctly, then they will be able to remove the types, having only the truth remaining. This quotation demonstrates Smyth's use of "type" and "truth" as categories. He gives several other terms that come under these categories. Smyth's style could have been more consistent had he used the term "Truth" instead of the "thing typed" in the second half of the quotation.

There is another occasion in his debate with Bernard, where Smyth uses "type" and "truth" to designate his typological categories. He argues that all saints are responsible for "Government Ecclesiasticall." As he makes his argument, he says that he will "answer breefly from the Type to the truth concerning matters of the Old Testament."[74] As before, Smyth appeals to Bernard to interpret the Old Testament in the light of typology. Smyth makes typology a basis for his argument that the church as a whole is a group of kings and priests that are foreshadowed by the kings and priests of the Old Testament.

Later, as a Baptist, in at least three instances in his debate with Richard Clyfton, Smyth refers to the proper use of the categories of type and truth. Smyth disagrees with Clyfton's view that circumcision was a seal of the eternal covenant, and therefore should be linked with infant baptism in the New Testament. Instead, he says that the carnal infants of the Old Testament type the "Spiritual infants of the new Testament, that

---

[73]Smyth, *Works* 2:376.
[74]Smyth, *Works* 2:424.

is, men regenerate baptized."[75] Similar to his charge against Bernard, Smyth charges Clyfton with not demonstrating a proper use of a typological argument. Smyth writes, "But if you wil make true consequents you must reason from the type to the truth proportionably, & not from the type to the type as this argument importeth."[76]

Two other instances of Smyth using "type" and "truth" as categories in his debate with Clyfton are related to infant baptism also. He argues that there should be "a proportion betwixt the Type & the truth."[77] Smyth insists that if Clyfton will interpret typology properly, then he will accept Smyth's position. He declares, "Thus if you would compare the Type & the Truth together, you should easily discerne the sandy Fondation of your false Church ruinated & your false baptisme quite abandoned."[78]

The characteristics of these three major pairs show elements of Smyth's typology. Smyth's frequent use of typology in his theological defense indicates its fundamental nature to his thought. Attempting to answer the charges against him, he relies often on typology to challenge his opponents. As the subject matter of the debates changes throughout Smyth's career, one thing remains consistent: his use of a typological argument. Smyth uses typology as the framework of his argument in many situations throughout his career. He uses it as a Separatist in defending an aspect of his ecclesiology. In his days as a Baptist, he uses it to argue against infant baptism. As a Mennonite, he uses typology to assert the more important spiritual nature of Christ.

Smyth's Mennonite Typology

There are two main reasons why it is important to understand the typological structure to Smyth's theology. First, most of his arguments are framed in typological language. His arguments become clearer once the typological framework is recognized. Smyth's typology is an aspect of his writings in all four of his theological stages—as a Puritan, Separatist, Baptist, and Mennonite. This is important because of his

---

[75]Smyth, *Works* 2:585. "Infants" has been emended.
[76]Smyth, *Works* 2:585. "From" has been emended.
[77]Smyth, *Works* 2:609.
[78]Smyth, *Works* 2:666.

frequent shifts in thought. While his view on a certain topic may change, he still often uses typology in the defense of his position.

The second reason for understanding Smyth's typology also relates to its centrality for his thought. Because typology is so important to Smyth, a significant change in his use of typology would denote a significant change in his thought and possibly the influences on him. In Smyth's Mennonite stage, there is a considerable shift in his typological understanding, reflecting the magnitude of the shift in his theology.

Smyth moves away from Puritanism when he accepts the Separatist ideal of a covenanted community being a church. Smyth moves away from the other Separatists when he accepts believers' baptism as the method of forming a church. Although many of Smyth's contemporaries and modern scholars indicate the magnitude of these changes, these shifts do not affect Smyth's thought as much as his becoming a Mennonite. In his transitions from Puritan to Separatist to Baptist, his typology remains relatively unchanged. However, as a Mennonite, even this fundamental characteristic of Smyth's theology changes.

Significant changes in Smyth's typology. In the Mennonite stage of his career, Smyth's typology experiences three significant changes. The first change has to do with the relationship he sees between Christ and the truth. Earlier in Smyth's career, his interpretation of scripture sees the Old Testament as providing the type for the New Testament truth. Although this manner of relating the testaments remains, Smyth adds another idea. In his Mennonite work, *Defence of Ries's Confession*, he writes:

> For, as all the figures and ceremonies of the Old Testament foreshadow the person of Christ and His attributes, so the same person of Christ, His actions and His sufferings borne in humility were a certain shadow of His own self already exalted in glory at the right hand of the Father.[79]

---

[79]Translation by Coggins, *John Smyth's Congregation*, 183. *Quemadmodum enim omnes figurae et ceremonia veteris testamenti Christi personam ejusque accidentia adumbrarunt: sic ipsa Christi persona, actiones et perpessiones in humilitate gesta, umbra quaedam fuerunt suiipsius jam gloria exaltati ad dextram dei pa[tris].* Smyth, *Works* 2:698.

The person of Christ is not only the truth who fulfils types. The person of Christ is also a type of the glorified Christ. Christ's actions such as his healing miracles are outward and point to the greater inward miracles such as forgiveness. Christ still fulfilled the types of the Old Testament, but his natural life points to a higher spiritual one.[80] A major aspect of Smyth's early typology is that Christ is the fulfillment of Old Testament types. In his Mennonite works, Smyth points to the higher truth of Christ's glorified status.

The second change in Smyth's typology is that he has become a proponent of spiritualist thought. Although Smyth spoke of the contrast between the spiritual and carnal throughout his career, only when he becomes a Mennonite does he devalue outward ordinances. In his Separatist work, *Paralleles, Censures, Observations*, Smyth argues for the precedence of the spiritual over the literal and the truth over the type. However, in his discussion he maintains the value of church ordinances. As he compares Old Testament worship to New Testament worship he says, "Their worship began outwardly in the lettre, & proceded inwardly to the Spirit, so did their constitution, ministery & al: our worship beginneth inwardly in the Spirit, & proceedeth outwardly to the lettre."[81] While Smyth's concern is that worship would originate with Spirit, not with any liturgy, he does declare that worship will include the outward aspects or "lettre."

There is another quotation from *Paralleles, Censures, Observations* that demonstrates Smyth's argument for the existence of outward ordinances. As he continues the debate with Bernard, he says that Bernard needs to know how to compare "the type and the truth, the shadow and the substance, the lettre and the Spirit, the Old Testament with the ordinances therof, & the new Testament with the ordinances thereof."[82] In this quotation, Smyth equates the New Testament ordinances with the truth. The rest of his argument continues with him extolling the value of outward aspects of the church which originate in the Spirit. This discussion is typical to many of Smyth's Puritan, Separatist, or Baptist writings. In those early works, he may make statements that have

---

[80]Smyth, *Works* 2:698, 704.
[81]Smyth, *Works* 2:378. "Constitution" has been emended.
[82]Smyth, *Works* 2:497.

spiritualist overtones. However, usually as Smyth makes these statements it is in defense of some ecclesiastical practice. His concern with the proper outward forms for the church in these early stages indicates that he had not become a spiritualist.

As Smyth becomes more inclined toward spiritualism in his Mennonite stage, he reproves any emphasis on outward aspects of the church. The Christian no longer needs the "outwoard scriptures . . . or ordinances of the church."[83] These outward things are not needed because of the presence of God within the person. According to Smyth, the spiritual ministry of Christ is the truth, the outward expressions of ministry only represent this true ministry. He affirms, "That the preaching of the word, and ministerie of the sacraments, representeth the ministery of Christ in the spirit: who teacheth baptiseth, and feedeth the regenerate, by the holie spirit inwardlie and invisiblie."[84]

Once Smyth's typology is characterized by this spiritualism, the ecclesiology that he had debated so fiercely becomes unimportant. Emphasizing the spiritual aspect of his thought causes him to see the "outward church and ordinances" as mere "shadowes."[85] The reason these ordinances are not central is that they are of the physical nature. In *Argumenta Contra Baptismum Infantum*, he says, "Therefore all the outward things of the outward church are mysteries, because they are administered under Christ, who is revealed in the flesh."[86] These ordinances of the New Testament church had once been referred to by Smyth as the truths that the Old Testament ordinances had typed. Now these New Testament ordinances serve as types as well.

The third change in Smyth's typology as a Mennonite is his tendency to use "outward" and "inward" instead of the other two major pairs. As a Separatist and a Baptist, Smyth often uses "carnal" and "spiritual" and "type" and "truth" to compare aspects of the Old Testament with the New Testament. Although Smyth does not restrict his use of these terms to this purpose, this is his predominant pattern. Also in those stages of his life,

---

[83]Smyth, *Works* 2:743-44.
[84]Smyth, *Works* 2:746.
[85]Smyth, *Works* 2:747.
[86]*Omnia ergo externa ecclesiae externae mysteria, quia sub Christo administrantur in carne exhibito.* Smyth, *Works* 2:721.

Smyth's use of outward and inward is not as frequent as the other two major pairs. Once he becomes a Mennonite, the opposite is true. Outward and inward take on the preferred role in Smyth's typological terms.

Reasons for using outward and inward. One reason for this change could be that the Anabaptists had debated for years the relationship between outward and inward.[87] So, when Smyth is in their fold, he adapts to using their terms. Another possible reason is that Smyth now emphasizes the spiritual aspect of even New Testament concepts. Smyth no longer limits his typological interpretation of scripture to the Old Testament typing the New Testament. New Testament concepts serve as types themselves for higher spiritual truths.

Often when Smyth uses carnal and spiritual and type and truth, he contends that the carnal or the type is to be discontinued because of the presence of the spiritual or the truth. However, for him as a Mennonite the New Testament concepts are not to be discontinued, but are not to be as central as the spiritual truths they represent. This could be a reason for Smyth's use of outward and inward. As a Separatist and Baptist, he uses these terms in cases where the two are to coexist such as the outward covenant of the local church and the inward covenant between the church and God.

In *Argumenta Contra Baptismum Infantum*, Smyth uses outward and inward to debate infant baptism. He says that inward baptism is the priority, not the outward, water baptism. Since infants cannot experience the inward baptism of the Spirit, they should not experience the outward baptism which points to the inward baptism.[88] As he continues his discussion of the sacraments, Smyth says that the sacraments do not get their importance from the outward display. The real power of the sacraments lies in the inward experience they represent. He writes, "Therefore the excellence and dignity of the New Testament sacraments

---

[87]Anabaptists, in general, and Mennonites, in particular, had a continuing debate during the sixteenth and early seventeenth centuries between the spiritualists and literalists. Most Mennonites rejected the spiritualist idea of the nonnecessity of the sacraments. However, the spiritualist emphasis on the inward meaning of the sacraments and the spiritual nature of Christ as primary were retained by many, such as Hans de Ries. Snyder, *Anabaptist History and Theology*, 300-301, 319-24, 357-63.

[88]Smyth, *Works* 2:720.

do not consist in the outward sign, but in the person who partakes in the sacrament."[89]

Smyth applies his typology to things such as the physical miracles of Christ. He writes, "He accepted our weaknesses, and bore our diseases, for the cure which Christ accomplished in the bodies of the sick, was a figure of the healing he accomplishes in the souls of sinners, for sins are diseases of the soul."[90] He says that these miracles are outward signs of the inward miracles that Christ does in the believer. They are both to continue, but the inward miracles are superior. The relationship between the outward and the inward is typical of Smyth's Mennonite writings. So, Smyth's shift in his use of typology could account for his change of preferred typological terms.

Perhaps the most likely reason for Smyth's preference for the terms outward and inward as a Mennonite is the influence of Hans de Ries. Ries is an elder in the Mennonite church and assists in the negotiations between Smyth and the Waterlander Mennonites of Amsterdam. He does not use contrasting or typological language as often as Smyth. However, when he does use contrasts, he seems to prefer the terms "outward" and "inward." Ries expresses some of the same contrasts between the outward aspects of worship and the inward aspects that Smyth does. In his "Short Confession," Ries refers to the outward act of baptism as a reminder of the inward baptism that the believer experiences through the Holy Spirit. The outward act is important mainly because of its admonishment for believers to seek the inward gifts of Christ.[91]

Ries also holds that the Lord's Supper is an example of an outward observance which is to remind believers of the inward dimension of their relationship with Christ. He says:

---

[89]*Ideoque excellentia et dignitas sacramentorum testamenti novi non consistit in externo signo, sed in persona sacramentum participante.* Smyth, Works 2:720.

[90]*Ipse infirmitates nostras accepit, et morbos portavit, nam curatio quam perfecit Christus in corporibus aegrorum, figurabat sanationem quam ipse complet in animis peccatorum: Peccata enim animi morbi sunt.* Smyth, Works 2:729.

[91]Ries, "A Short Confession of Faith," 17. Dyck uses the word *external* in his translation, but Smyth's translation of the confession has the term *outward*. See Burrage, *The Early English Dissenters* 2:196-97.

The external Supper brings to our mind the office and function of Christ in glory, his institution of the spiritual Supper with believing souls, feeding them with truly spiritual food. Likewise the external Supper teaches us to rise above the external in holy prayer, longing for the reality of the gift of Christ.[92]

A third illustration of an outward practice which has a higher meaning is the ban. Ries says that the outward ban on erring church members serves as a reminder of the eternal separation awaiting the unrepentant.[93]

Smyth's tendency to emphasize the spiritual is similar to Ries's emphasis. Ries's influence on Smyth can be seen in his thought on the spiritual nature of Christ's work.[94] Smyth's comments on the physical miracles of Christ as indicating the spiritual miracles that he accomplishes in believers, are similar to Ries's comments. Ries says, "The miracles he performed in the flesh may be worked in us according to the Spirit, healing us of the sickness of the soul, deafness, blindness, leprosy, uncleanness, sin, and death."[95]

Ries declares that the knowing about the physical life of Christ and the events of his ministry is only a beginning, "Rather we must rise higher and confess Christ also according to the Spirit, in his exaltation and glory, according to his glorious office and, as the Scriptures teach, receive this knowledge with a believing heart."[96] Smyth's spiritualist tendencies on the sacraments also have precedent in Ries's work. Ries states, "We must know Christ according to the Spirit that he may baptize us with the Holy Spirit and with fire, feed us with heavenly food and drink, making us partakers of the divine nature."[97]

Smyth's typology adapts to the spiritualist tendencies of Hans de Ries. His typological language is affected in that he favors the terms "outward" and "inward" during the Mennonite stage of his career. He continues to describe the Old Testament as a type of the New Testament.

---

[92]Ries, "A Short Confession of Faith," 18.
[93]Ries, "A Short Confession of Faith," 18.
[94]More discussion of Ries's influence on Smyth can be found in chaps. 5–7.
[95]Ries, "A Short Confession of Faith," 15.
[96]Ries, "A Short Confession of Faith," 14.
[97]Ries, "A Short Confession of Faith," 15.

However, he also looks for the spiritual meaning behind New Testament concepts.

Conclusion

Understanding Smyth's use of typology is important for a proper interpretation of his theology, because he uses typological language throughout his career. Also, the revisions to his typology as a Mennonite demonstrate Smyth's similarities with the spiritualist tendencies of Hans de Ries. The major areas of his thought such as his views on covenant, Christology, atonement, and church-state relations are defended with typological arguments.

Smyth argues for a typological relationship between the carnal and spiritual covenants. The same is true for the outward covenant (local church) and inward covenant (eternal). He contends that there is a typological relationship between Christ's physical flesh and His spiritual flesh. While typology in the atonement is not as explicit as the others, it could be argued that Smyth sees a typological relationship between God's grace of creation and His grace of redemption. Smyth uses a typological contrast between the civil matters of the state and the spiritual matters of the church. Once Smyth's typological framework is noted, his writings on these topics can be interpreted with greater clarity.

Chapter 4

Smyth's View of Covenant

At various stages of his career, the concept of covenant dominates John Smyth's writings. His definition of covenant varies according to the context and stage of his thinking. As a Separatist, he uses the covenant to designate the agreement of the faithful to become a church. However, as a Baptist, he debates with Richard Clyfton about the "carnal" and "spiritual" covenants that were offered to Abraham. In both of these stages of his career, Smyth uses typological language to describe the covenant. As a Separatist, he compares the outward covenant which is a local church covenant with the inward covenant which is the covenant offered by God. As a Baptist, Smyth attempts to differentiate between the carnal covenant that was expressed in the writings of the Old Testament and the spiritual covenant that became more clearly expressed in the New Testament.

Smyth is just one of many who debated the nature of the covenant in the late sixteenth and early seventeenth centuries. Within the Separatist tradition, there is a movement to reject the national covenant of the Church of England for a local church covenant. James Maclear says, "Thus, the covenant answered the need for some instrument which could bring into existence an artificial society to replace the larger natural community now rejected as a legitimate basis for ecclesiastical organization."[1] In the English context, the nature of the covenant is a topic of frequent discussion among Puritans and Separatists during the time of Smyth's writings. Smyth frequently uses the idea of covenant in discussions on the church. There are some conclusions that can be made about Smyth's use of the covenant during his Separatist, Baptist, and Mennonites stages. However, before Smyth's understanding of the covenant can be comprehended, his Separatist predecessors should be examined.

---

[1] James F. Maclear, "The Birth of the Free Church Tradition," *Church History* 26 (June 1957): 105.

The Covenant of the Separatists

A significant influence on the Separatist movement's use of covenant was Robert Browne. After Browne, came the leadership of Henry Barrow, who also emphasized the local church covenant. Barrow's influence spread over to the Separatists who composed the Separatist confession of 1596. The covenant remained a constant theme in Separatist theology in the decades from Browne's leadership to the time of Smyth's Separatist contemporaries in Amsterdam.

Robert Browne. The Separatists emphasized that the church was to be founded on a covenant. The idea was that God's faithful are called to be separate from the unfaithful. This separation is evident in the membership of the local church. Separatists argued that the only way to form a true church was by believers agreeing together on a covenant. The covenant is then requisite for membership in the church. Through their agreement the people submit to the authority of Christ, becoming a true local church. Robert Browne refers to the members' agreement to covenant together under Christ's authority as the foundation of the church. He challenges the Church of England by saying that they have not

> planted the church by layinge the foundacion thereof, for here by is the foundacion laied, when we make & hould the couenant with the Lord to be vnder his gouernment, when we haue the power of the Lord, as it is written Cor. 1. 5. amongst vs, & the septer of Christ Iesus amongst vs.[2]

---

[2]Robert Browne, *The Writings of Robert Harrison and Robert Browne*, ed. Albert Peel and Leland H. Carlson (London: Allen & Unwin, 1953) 421. Although Peel and Carlson suggest either 1 Cor. 2:5 or 1 Cor. 5:4 as corrections for the scripture reference, Browne must have meant to refer to 1 Cor. 5:4. This is apparent when this section is compared with sections elsewhere in Browne's writings where he consistently refers to 1 Cor. 5 when he discusses the power of the Lord among the churches. See Browne, *The Writings of Robert Harrison and Robert Browne*, 443, 446, 456, 461, 505, 525-26 for these references. Several words that contain the letter "w" have been emended: see above, chap. 1, n. 33.

Browne's definition of a church in *A Book Which Sheweth the Life and Manners*, indicates the central role of the covenant:

> The Church planted or gathered, is a companie or number of Christians or beleeuers, which by a willing couenant made with their God, are vnder the gouernment of god and Christ, and kepe his lawes in one holie communion.[3]

The church is a true church because it has joined in a pledge of obedience to God. Browne also demonstrates the close relationship that the Separatists understood between church membership and salvation. In this same work, Browne defines a Christian in a very similar way: "Christians are a companie or number of beleeuers, which by a willing couenuant made with their God, are vnder the gouernment of God and Christ, and keepe his Lawes in one holie communion."[4] The osmosis of the concepts of a true church and a Christian is striking. A Christian's duty is to form a true church through covenanting with other believers to be faithful to God. The covenant then not only becomes central to church membership, but is an essential mark of being a Christian.

The idea of covenant is central to Robert Browne's argument for reform being led by the church and not the magistracy. He states that even in the Old Testament period, the people had first to belong to the covenant before they could be punished for forsaking it.[5] He uses this to argue against a magistrate forcing someone who is not of the faithful to come into the church. He says that, similar to the Old Testament, people must desire the covenant with God. Only when the people respond individually to the covenant will they not forsake it. If people are coerced into the covenant, then they are less likely to be faithful to it. Browne asserts, "For it is the conscience and not the power of man that will driue vs to seeke the Lordes kingdome."[6]

Browne linked church discipline to the covenant. He says that "Separation of the open wilfull, or greeuous offenders, is a dutifulnes of the church in withholding from them the christian communion and

---

[3]Browne, *The Writings of Robert Harrison and Robert Browne*, 253.
[4]Browne, *The Writings of Robert Harrison and Robert Browne*, 227.
[5]Browne, *The Writings of Robert Harrison and Robert Browne*, 161.
[6]Browne, *The Writings of Robert Harrison and Robert Browne*, 162.

fellowship, by pronouncing and shewing the couenaunt of christian communion to be broken by their greeuous wickednes."[7] He adds that one of the purposes of church discipline is to keep the covenant "vnpolluted."[8]

Separation of the faithful from the wicked is essential. The faithful must repent from their own wickedness and refuse to fellowship with wicked people. Browne says, "For this is it that is most & first of all needfull: because God wil receaue none to communion & couenant with him, which as yet are at one with the wicked, or do openlie them selues transgresse his commaundementes."[9] It is unclear if Browne is thinking of the covenant of salvation or the local church covenant. This quotation could also suggest that he sees a close link between proper ecclesiology and salvation. For if he is indeed referring to the covenant of salvation, then he is saying that those who do not deny ungodliness by refusing to fellowship with wicked persons will not be saved. This would indicate why Browne and the other Separatists stress forming a church with a covenant made by the faithful only. The idea of obedience or faithfulness to the covenant was essential to Browne.

Browne understands the covenant as conditional. God takes the obedient for his people, if they "couenaunt to be vnder his gouernement in the Church, and by obeying thereto."[10] The Church of England could no longer claim to be under God's covenant, because it had not been faithful to obeying God. It no longer practiced the discipline necessary to keep the church under Christ's authority.[11] He gives authority to the church through the act of covenanting, so that they could fulfil the condition of obedience. B. R. White suggests that "The reason . . . the power and the practice of discipline was an essential mark of the true Church, according to Browne, was because it made possible the keeping

---

[7]Browne, *The Writings of Robert Harrison and Robert Browne*, 269. "Separation," "offenders," and "communion" have been emended: see chap. 2, n. 20, referring to Smyth.

[8]Browne, *The Writings of Robert Harrison and Robert Browne*, 464.

[9]Browne, *The Writings of Robert Harrison and Robert Browne*, 412. "Will," "with," "which," and "wicked" have been emended.

[10]Browne, *The Writings of Robert Harrison and Robert Browne*, 257.

[11]Browne, *The Writings of Robert Harrison and Robert Browne*, 459-65.

of the conditions of the covenant relationship."[12] The purity of the covenant is maintained through the condition of obedience, which is encouraged through discipline.

Henry Barrow. After Robert Browne returned to the Church of England, the movement that he pioneered continued without him. Most Separatists repudiated any connection with the traitorous Browne. Therefore, many of their opponents called the Separatists "Brownists" as a source of irritation. While the Separatists did not appreciate the title, nevertheless they did continue some of the thoughts of Browne. Separatists such as Henry Barrow continued Browne's emphasis on the local church covenant.

1. *Description of local church.* As Barrow led the Separatists from his prison cell, his allegiance to the idea of covenant becomes apparent. He describes one of the Separatists' emphases with the words, "We seeke the fellowship and communion of his faithfull and obedient servants, and together with them to enter covenant with the Lord."[13] The local church is a communion of saints who are joined by covenant. Barrow again echoes Browne in relating different uses of the term covenant.

In *A True Description out of the Worde of God of the Visible Church,* Barrow links the local church with the eternal covenant. In this work, he says that the universal church is the elect of God, but the local church is a "companie and fellowship of faithful." A local church is entrusted with the promises of God, including his covenant of grace.[14] Therefore, the church protects and shares God's covenant as one of its primary purposes. Barrow argues that the protection of the covenant of grace is fulfilled by the obedience of the local church. Similar to Browne's position, Barrow sees a direct connection between church discipline and the covenant. The relationship of discipline and obedience to the covenant becomes more clear in seeing Barrow's understanding of the conditional nature of the covenant.

2. *Conditional covenant.* Barrow argues with the Puritan, George Gifford, about the conditional nature of the covenant. Barrow says that the covenant belongs only to the faithful and their seed. He says the Old

---

[12]White, *The English Separatist Tradition,* 57.
[13]Barrow, *The Writings of Henry Barrow, 1587-1590,* 84.
[14]Barrow, *The Writings of Henry Barrow, 1587-1590,* 214-15.

Testament teaches the conditional nature of the covenant. If the covenant does not require obedience, then all sorts of evil can exist in the church.[15] Barrow also states that the covenanted community or local church has as much responsibility to be faithful to the covenant of grace as the individual believer has. In *A Brief Discoverie of the False Church*, Barrow states:

> God have made one and the same covenant from the beginning of the world with the whole church, that he hath with everie particular private member therof, and hath given no more libertie to the whole church, than to any private man, to breake the least of his lawes.[16]

The positive side of Barrow's view is that the faithful who are obedient to God can experience the blessing of God's covenant. The negative side is that the people or churches that are not obedient are excluded from the covenant. Barrow stated that "howe we may forfeite this covenant, namelie, by breaking and contemning the lawe of God, in whose love we cannot remaine, except we remaine in his obedience."[17] Barrow added to this concept of obedience to the covenant by saying:

> Now then whilest the whole congregation or anie member therof shall remaine hardened in sinne, deniing to obey Christe's voyce, refusing to repent, who can say that this church or man in this estate, can by us . . . be affirmed and held the true church of Christ within the outward covenant, when Christ himself commandeth us to deliver them up to Sathan in his name, to have no fellowship with them?[18]

Barrow does not claim that the faithful will never sin. He realizes the faithful will sin, but that they must be obedient and repent, for it is "obstinate and presumptuous" sin that breaks God's covenant.[19] Once a church is guilty of remaining in obstinate sin, then it "breaketh the covenant with God, and maketh it cease to be a church, or to be in God's favor, untill they repent."[20]

---

[15]Barrow, *The Writings of Henry Barrow, 1590-1591*, 114-27.
[16]Barrow, *The Writings of Henry Barrow, 1587-1590*, 309.
[17]Barrow, *The Writings of Henry Barrow, 1590-1591*, 117.
[18]Barrow, *The Writings of Henry Barrow, 1590-1591*, 164.
[19]Barrow, *The Writings of Henry Barrow, 1587-1590*, 310.
[20]Barrow, *The Writings of Henry Barrow, 1587-1590*, 318. "Howsoever we

Barrow warns churches that have broken the covenant by their unfaithfulness that "God plighteth not his favour and protection unto us, longer than we vowe our obedience, and keep our faith unto him."[21] He argues that all churches which refuse to separate from the ungodly and commit themselves to obedience have lost the claim to be a church. He declares, "I then denie these assemblies to be the true churches of Christ; seing they have broken the covenant, cast off Christe's yoke, etc."[22] These churches have not fulfilled the condition of obedience, so they are no longer within the covenant.

Difference between eternal covenant and outward covenant. Some Puritans criticized the Separatists' emphasis on a conditional covenant. The Puritans charged that a conditional covenant would make the covenant dependent on human works instead of God's grace. George Gifford had charged Barrow in this manner. Barrow counters that the conditional covenant was not the covenant of grace. God's election determines the covenant of grace.[23] Barrow says that the outward or local church covenant is conditional. He says that he believes "that the Lord our God his covenant was made, established, and preserved unto us in his Christ only without any worckes or merite in us."[24] However, while Christ is the merit for salvation and God's grace is the stability of the eternal covenant, the local church covenant is maintained through obedience. Barrow states that

> Because God requireth obedience of al his servants that enter into or remaine in his house, and commandeth them to have no fellowship with anie, longer than they contynue in the same fayth and obedience,

---

justifie not or tollerate the least sinne that God condemneth in his worde, yet we make not anie sinne, until impenitencie and obstinacie be joyned therunto, to disanul and breake the covenant with God." Barrow, *The Writings of Henry Barrow, 1590-1591*, 294.

[21]Barrow, *The Writings of Henry Barrow, 1587-1590*, 305-306.
[22]Barrow, *The Writings of Henry Barrow, 1587–1590*, 308.
[23]Barrow, *The Writings of John Greenwood and Henry Barrow, 1591–1593*, ed. Leland H. Carlson (London: George Allen & Unwin, 1970) 116.
[24]Barrow, *The Writings of Henry Barrow, 1590-1591*, 163.

therfore we make the stablenes of Gode's covenant to depende upon our worcks.[25]

Barrow holds that Gifford and others who do not understand that the conditional nature applies only to the local church covenant "cannot discerne betwixt the secret election of God and Christe's visible church."[26]

As this debate continues between Gifford and Barrow, Gifford again charges the latter with making the stability of God's covenant rely on human effort. Barrow says that Gifford will never understand his reasoning, because Gifford does not see that he is discussing the outward covenant, not the eternal covenant.[27] However, Barrow tries to make a clear distinction between the covenant of grace and the local church covenant. He writes:

> The covenant and election of God remaineth firme to the endz of the world, neither can the sinns of the parents divert or frustrate his mercies to the children. But we reason not of God's secret election whom he may or will call, but of the outward covenant wherin he hath called, and who may be judged within that outward covenant of us. . . . Because I hould that only such as have made profession of the faith and continue in the same faith and obedience are of us to be esteamed within the outward covenant. Therfore doo I heareupon make the stablenes of God's covenant to depend upon our righteousnes.[28]

Barrow claims that the Separatists have no intention of determining who is within God's eternal covenant. Their concern is that if a person wants to be a part of the visible church of Christ, then he must covenant to be obedient. If a person does not obey God's commands, then he cannot be considered a part of the local church covenant.

Separatist Confession of 1596. Of the four passages of the Separatists' "A True Confession" that mention the covenant, three refer to God's covenant of salvation. Two references are to the fact that the church has

---

[25]Barrow, *The Writings of Henry Barrow, 1590–1591*, 164-65.

[26]Barrow, *The Writings of Henry Barrow, 1590–1591*, 165.

[27]Barrow, *The Writings of John Greenwood and Henry Barrow, 1591–1593*, 166-67.

[28]Barrow, *The Writings of John Greenwood and Henry Barrow, 1591–1593*, 165-66.

been given the signs or seals of the covenant which would include baptism.[29] The third reference to the "euerlasting Couenant of grace between God & man" mentions that Christ is the mediator of this covenant and therefore is head of the church.[30] Only the fourth passage refers specifically to the local church covenant. Here the Separatists describe the true church by saying that

> they are willingly to ioyne together in christian communion and orderly couenant, and by confession of Faith and obedience of Christ, to unite themselues into peculiar Congregations; wherein, as members of one body wherof Christ is the only head, they are to worship and serue God according to his word.[31]

The "confession of Faith" that is mentioned does not exclude infants. The confession is made by the adults or those "of yeeres." Children of these adults are included in the covenant because they are the "seed" of the faithful.[32] The Separatist Confession resembles Browne and Barrow's views on the Covenant as a commitment of obedience to Christ.

Smyth's Separatist Writings

The writings of Browne and Barrow helped establish the Separatism from which John Smyth emerges. As a Separatist, Smyth agrees with much of Browne's and Barrow's views on covenant. Smyth continues the Separatist distinction between the outward or local church covenant and the eternal covenant of grace. While these concepts are distinct in Smyth's thought, they are also inextricably linked.

Smyth makes the same emphasis as Browne and Barrow that the faithful join with each other in the outward covenant. They covenant together in order to be faithful to the eternal covenant that God has offered them. Their agreement to be obedient to God as a group allows

---

[29]"A True Confession," in Lumpkin, *Baptist Confessions of Faith*, 85, 87, 93. The distinction between the uses of the covenant is made easier by the fact that the term is capitalized when referring to the eternal covenant, but not capitalized when referring to the local church covenant.

[30]Lumpkin, *Baptist Confessions of Faith*, 85.

[31]Lumpkin, *Baptist Confessions of Faith*, 92.

[32]Lumpkin, *Baptist Confessions of Faith*, 93.

them to continue as the covenanted community of God. The idea of a covenanted community is important to Smyth because he sees the covenant as the basis for God granting His power to a church. The church has the power to enact reform because it is the covenanted community.

When John Smyth became a Separatist, the covenant became a central aspect of his thinking about the church. He defends the idea that the church is to be formed on a covenant, and then it can be empowered with the authority of Christ.

Local church covenant as entrance to the church. As Smyth became more dissatisfied with the Church of England, he led a group of followers in Gainsborough to form a Separatist congregation. The congregation was formed in the typical Separatist pattern of the members covenanting together to become a church. William Bradford's description of the event includes these pertinent remarks:

> So many, therefore, of these professors as saw the evil of these things in these parts, and whose hearts the Lord had touched with heavenly zeal for His truth, they shook off this yoke of antichristian bondage, and as the Lords free people, joined themselves (by a covenant of the Lord) into a church estate, in the fellowship of the gospel, to walk in all His ways made known, or to be made known unto them, according to their best endeavours, whatsoever it should cost them, the Lord assisting them.[33]

Smyth's Separatist perspective that the true form of the church is a covenanted community resembles the thought of his Separatist predecessors. In his work, *Principles and Inferences*, Smyth alludes to his indebtedness to other Separatists. He refers to them as his "auncient brethren" in the following:

> Therfore especially are those auncient brethren to be honoured, that they have reduced the Church to the true Primitive & Apostolique constitution which consisteth in these three things. 1. The true matter which are sayntes only. 2. The true forme which is the vniting of them together in the covenant. 3. The true propertie which is communion in all the holy things, & the powre of the L. Iesus Christ, for the maintayning of that

---

[33] Bradford, *Of Plymouth Plantation*, 9.

communion. To this blessed work of the L. wherin those auncient brethren have labored I know not what may more be added.[34]

These "ancient brethren" were the Separatists such as Browne, Barrow, and Francis Johnson who had led the faithful out of the Church of England and had formed their true churches on a covenant.

Smyth holds that there are two essential elements in forming a true church. First, believers are needed. Smyth says that true membership of the church consists of "sayntes only." Second, these saints are to coalesce into a church by means of the covenant. The covenant is then the path for membership in the church. Anyone else wishing to join the congregation must agree to the covenant. The covenanted community is then granted the properties of a true church, which are participation in holy things and the authority of Christ.

Smyth's last Separatist publication, which includes "A Lettre written to Mr. A. S.," includes a description of the true church, which is almost identical to his description given in his first Separatist work, *Principles and Inferences*. In this later description, first he affirms saints as the true matter of the church. In the third part of the description, he acknowledges the power of Christ as the true property of the church. Just as in his earlier work, the second part of the description is that the covenant is the true form of the church. However, on this later occasion he also includes the phrase, "the covenant to walke in al Gods wayes," indicating the nature of the local church covenant.[35] At the heart of the covenant is the pledge that the people make to be obedient to God.

The covenant became crucial to Smyth's understanding of the church. In discussing the importance of the covenant of Smyth and his connection with earlier Separatists, B. R. White writes, "In his [Smyth's] thinking about the Church the theology of the covenant was to resume something of the central place it had once held in the thought of Robert Browne."[36] The similarity with Browne is evident in areas such as the necessity of a church covenant. Smyth's statement of the true form being a church united in a covenant is similar to Browne's.

---

[34]Smyth, *Works* 1:270.
[35]Smyth, *Works* 2:555.
[36]White, *The English Separatist Tradition English Separatist*, 125.

With respect to the local church, the term "covenant" is a voluntary agreement to join together to become a local body of believers.[37] This covenanted group then is empowered to become a true church. Smyth says:

> A visible communion of Saincts is of two, three, or moe Saincts joyned together by covenant with God & themselves, freely to vse al the holy things of God, according to the word, for their mutual edification, & Gods glory. This visible communion of Saincts is a visible Church.[38]

For a congregation to be a true church, it must be formed under a covenant. Because the covenant is with God, it can be agreed to by the faithful only. There is no acceptance of the ungodly into the covenant or church. In addition to the agreement with God, there is a second relationship in the covenant. This relationship is among "themselves," the saints. The group of saints that have joined themselves to each other and to God are the "visible" or local church. As people agree to the covenant they are placing themselves under the discipline and authority of that church specifically and Christ ultimately. The covenant here seems to be a combination of a divine covenant and an ecclesiastical covenant. Before the relationship between the two can be understood, a further discussion of the local church covenant is appropriate.

It must be understood why Smyth held the act of covenanting to be of such importance. According to Smyth, once believers have covenanted together, they receive the kingly, priestly, and prophetic authority of Christ. Smyth writes:

> But a true visible church, that is, a communion of Saynts, joyned together in the true covenant, is that only communion of men wherto God hath given his covenant, his promises, his holy things, Christ for King, Preist & Prophet.[39]

In practical terms, this means they can baptize, administer the Lord's Supper, elect elders, and even ordain ministers.[40] It was in the response

---

[37]Smyth, *Works* 2:511-12.
[38]Smyth, *Works* 1:252.
[39]Smyth, *Works* 2:350-51. "Men" has been emended.
[40]Smyth, *Works* 1:315, 2:511-12.

of covenanting that the people were given the authority of Christ to become a true church. Once the covenant had been agreed to, then the people had the authority of a church. Successionism had been ruled out, because authority was passed through the act of covenanting, not through history or tradition.

Smyth believes any church that is formed under a method other than a voluntary covenant of believers is a false church. If the church includes members that have not made any attempt at repentance or coming under the authority of Christ, then it is defiled. The covenant with God made by the local church must be a promise of obedience. In his work, *Paralleles, Censures, Observations*, Smyth confronts Richard Bernard of the Church of England by stating that

> for your assemblie I vse this reason to prove it no true Church: wher the people are not Holy, Elect, & faithful, having not entered covenant to walk in all Gods wayes, standing in confusion with every abhominable liver, subject to al the Antichristian orders & officers set over them, deprived of the powre of Christ for ther mutuall help & edification, ther is no true Church.[41]

Smyth ridicules the covenant that Richard Bernard had made with about one hundred of his parishioners. Smyth says that their covenant had no substance because they had not separated from the ungodly and committed themselves to be obedient.[42] Smyth challenges Bernard to do what he knows is right and form a true covenant by separating from the Church of England.[43] The Church of England had defiled itself by not making repentance and covenanting essential for church membership. Such a church could not have true worship, because it had not entered into a covenant of obedience.

Relationship between the theology of the covenant and covenant ecclesiology. In the English tradition, there were many Reformed theologians who stressed a conditional covenant while holding to predestination.[44] The conditional understanding of the covenant found in

---

[41]Smyth, *Works* 2:462.
[42]Smyth, *Works* 2:335, 344, 518.
[43]Smyth, *Works* 2:515.
[44]John S. Coolidge, *The Pauline Renaissance in England* (Oxford: Clarendon Press, 1970) 99-140, shows the tendency among Puritans, Separatists, and Con-

Fenner, Cartwright, and Perkins influenced the Puritan tradition from which Separatism sprang. The Separatists continued the idea that man was bound in obedience to God. The saints' agreement to obedience was a major element of the local church covenant. Therefore, obedience was central to the idea of the local church being the covenanted community.

Like other Separatists before him, Smyth agrees that obedience is the main aspect of man's acceptance of the covenant. As the church is formed on a covenant, it agrees to be faithful to God. In his work, *Principles and Inferences*, Smyth states that one part of the covenant is that the faithful are "to be Gods people, that is to obey al the commandements of God."[45] The idea of obedience shows some connection between the local church covenant and the eternal covenant. The people of the local church are to be obedient because they belong to the covenanted people of God. They demonstrate their promise to obedience in their outward covenant. Like many of his Separatist predecessors, Smyth stresses the conditional nature of this covenant. If a congregation refuses to be obedient to God and remains obstinately in sin, then they cease to be a true church.[46]

In the writings of John Smyth, there are two aspects of the term "covenant." One has to do with the theology of the covenant. The other is more akin to the Separatist idea of covenant ecclesiology. These two

---

gregationalists to understand the covenant as conditional. Charles S. McCoy and J. Wayne Baker, *Fountainhead of Federalism: Heinrich Bullinger and the Covenantal Tradition* (Louisville: Westminster/John Knox Press, 1991) 29-41, discuss the influence of Bullinger and the conditional covenant on the English covenant tradition, including Tyndale, Fenner, and Perkins. R. T. Kendall, *Calvinism and English Calvinism to 1649*, new ed. (Carlisle UK: Paternoster Press, 1997) 42-43, 58, mentions the conditional covenant understanding of Tyndale and Perkins, respectively. Carl R. Trueman, *Luther's Legacy: Salvation and English Reformers* (Oxford: Clarendon Press, 1994) 109-19, demonstrates Tyndale's view of the conditional nature of the covenant. These scholars have differing views on the effect that predestination had on the Reformed view of the covenant. However, the point in this context is that the understanding that there were some conditions to the covenant was present in the thought of many of the English Reformed theologians during this time period.

[45]Smyth, *Works* 1:254.
[46]Smyth, *Works* 2:451.

aspects are difficult to study in isolation from each other, because there is some connection between the two concepts. Smyth derives his idea of covenant ecclesiology from his theology of the covenant. In Smyth's view, the person who accepts the covenant of grace offered by God should respond by agreeing to covenant with other believers to form a church. Although covenanting with other believers derives from the covenant made with God, the two ideas are not synonymous. Smyth shows the differences between the two by stressing the importance of one or the other at different times.

B. R. White says that after a certain point in Smyth's writings, an ambivalence developed in his use of the term "covenant." Occasionally, it is clear that Smyth was referring to the covenant of grace offered by God to the elect. At other times, it is clear that Smyth used the term to mean the union of the local body of believers. Then on a few occasions, Smyth seems almost to blend the concepts. White says this ambivalence points to Smyth's understanding that man's acceptance of the covenant of grace became actualized in the local congregation's covenant.[47] James Coggins rejects this connection, even to the point of suggesting that Smyth's theology of the covenant had nothing to do with his covenant ecclesiology.[48] However, there is a connection between the two. First, the Separatist background from which Smyth drew related the two concepts. Second, the fact that Smyth used the terms in close relationship and in reference to the same groups shows some connection.

Smyth is not the first in the Separatist tradition to imply that there is a relationship between the local church covenant and the eternal covenant. Robert Browne had stated that a person could respond to the gospel without being a member of the church. However, a person should not be a member of the covenanted community, or local church, without responding first to God's covenant.[49] When the covenant of grace was offered by God, the proper response was to "offer and geue vp our selues to be of the church and people of God."[50]

---

[47]White, *The English Separatist Tradition English Separatist*, 128.
[48]Coggins, "The Theological Positions of John Smyth," 249.
[49]Browne, *The Writings of Robert Harrison and Robert Browne*, 422, 442.
[50]Browne, *The Writings of Robert Harrison and Robert Browne*, 256.

Henry Barrow also made similar connections between the two covenants. In his work *A Plaine Refutation* he gives a lengthy discussion of the obedience that was required in the Old Testament period. His phraseology and scripture references indicate his attention to the theology of the covenant.[51] After this discussion of the conditional covenant, he shifts to a discussion of the outward covenant. His conclusion is that, just as rebellious Israel and Judah were removed from the blessings of the covenant, stubborn sinners should be removed from the outward covenant of the church.[52]

As the previous statements have shown, Smyth remained within the Separatist tradition by implying a relationship between the two concepts of covenant. One passage in Smyth's work, *Paralleles, Censures, Observations* depicts his idea of the relationship between the two concepts. Written during the Separatist stage of Smyth's career, *Paralleles* is a debate with the Puritan, Richard Bernard. During the debate, Smyth argues that certain people who have separated from the Church of England have come together to form a true church. He makes the statement, "I hold & maintayne out of the word that a company of faithful people Seperated from al vncleanenes & joyned together by a covenant of the L. are a true Church."[53] The key here is the phrase, "joyned together by a covenant of the L[ord]." While the covenant is of the Lord, it also contains an aspect of the believers' joining with each other.

The local or visible church is a group that has covenanted with God and with each other. As Smyth continues, he attempts to show the validity of two or three believers joining together to become a church by calling them the people "with whome God maketh his covenant to be ther God, & whome he receaveth to be his people, they are a Temple, that is a Church unto him."[54] Although he is referring to a group that has joined together, the emphasis in this use of "covenant" could be described as theology of the covenant. Smyth continues his idea by referring to the

---

[51]Barrow, *The Writings of Henry Barrow, 1590–1591*, 118-25. Phrases such as "a holy nation," "condicion of the covenant," and "seale of the covenant" appear in this discussion. Barrow's references include Gen. 17, Deut. 29, and others, which are known for their covenant language.

[52]Barrow, *The Writings of Henry Barrow, 1590–1591*, 123-27.

[53]Smyth, *Works* 2:386. "Company" has been emended.

[54]Smyth, *Works* 2:386.

covenant that God makes with His people as the same covenant that is offered to the local body. When Smyth is discussing the power of excommunication in the local church, he again relates the two terms:

> Nay say we, the powre of binding & losing is given to the body of the Church, even to two or thre faithful people joyned together in covenant, & this we prove evidently in this manner. Vnto whome the covenant is given, vnto them the powre of binding & losing is given. The covenant is given to the body of the Church, that is to two or three faithful ones: For God is their God, & they are his people.[55]

In this quotation, the term "covenant" is used to depict the covenanted community and the eternal covenant of grace. The phrase "God is their God, & they are his people" alludes to the covenant of grace. Smyth sees the power of Christ given to rule the church as part of God's covenant with His people. As the church agrees together in a local covenant, then God fulfils His part of the covenant by granting that congregation the power of Christ to govern the church. Smyth says:

> We say the Church or two or three faithful people Seperated from the world & joyned together in a true covenant, have both Christ, the covenant, & promises, & the ministerial powre of Christ given to them, & that they are the body that receave from Christs hand out of heaven, or rather from Christ their head this ministerial powre.[56]

Those who have joined in a covenant (ecclesiology) are given the covenant (theology).

The authority within the church belonged to the members of the body because they were participants in the covenant. Smyth's thinking on church authority connects covenant ecclesiology and the theology of the covenant. First, he says that authority in the church is given to the body, "even to two or thre faithful people joyned together in covenant." He then goes on to add that "the covenant & Christ & al the promises, are given to the body of the church." The authority of Christ which is given to the

---

[55]Smyth, *Works* 2:388-89.
[56]Smyth, *Works* 2:403. "From" has been emended.

whole covenanted community comes through the covenant relationship where "God is their God, & they are his people."[57]

Once again, the covenant that the group has joined in is a covenant of the Lord, but also has implications for its members. These implications are mentioned in the following passage from Smyth's *Principles and Inferences*:

> The outward part of the true forme of the true visible church is a vowe, promise, oath, or covenant betwixt God and the Saints. . . . This covenant hath 2 parts. 1. respecting God and the faithful. 2. respecting the faithful mutually. . . . The first part of the covenant respecting God is either from God to the faithful, or from the faithful to God. . . . The second part of the covenant respecting the faithful mutually conteyneth all the duties of love whatsoever.[58]

He states that the outward part of the true form of the church is a vow or covenant, which the people make with God. However, it is also a covenant that is between the saints mutually. Smyth's understanding of the covenant not only included a binding together with God, but also the local church binding together in love. Smyth saw the importance of both uses of the term "covenant." Also it seems that he saw that covenant ecclesiology is based on the eternal covenant. With these few passages, it can be seen that Smyth had no hesitation in relating the two ideas of covenant. The fact that he uses the terms with such fluidity suggests he may see them as two aspects of the same covenant. The church covenant was a human binding together under the eternal covenant. Therefore, he would agree with many of his Separatist predecessors in saying that for a group of believers the church covenant was the proper response to the eternal covenant.

In discussing the two parts of the local church covenant, Smyth says that the first part is between God and the faithful. Smyth sees this first part of the local church covenant as the acceptance of the eternal covenant of grace. After this is complete, then the Christian can agree to be obedient and demonstrate love to his fellow Christian. So, Smyth saw

---

[57]Smyth, *Works* 2:388-89. In the previous quotation "covenant" and "given" have been emended.

[58]Smyth, *Works* 1:254. "From" has been emended.

the church covenant as applying to the faithful who had responded to God's eternal covenant then bonded together to be obedient to Him and faithful to each other. With his understanding of the church covenant, Smyth was in theory calling for a believers' church. Therefore, Smyth's later rejection of infant baptism did not cause an immediate change to many aspects of his view of covenant.

Smyth sees the covenant as fundamental to the Separatist cause. He challenges Bernard to acknowledge the truth. Smyth claims to have made clear the need for a separation from the unfaithful:

> I have labored to manifest the mayne cause of our Seperation, the first fo[u]ndacion & rock of truth, which is, that Christs ministerial powre is given to two or thre Faithful ones, who are the true seed of Abraham, to whome the promises, the covenant of the New Testament, Christ, & al the holy things are given: For this is the groundwork & Foundacion of the L. truth.[59]

One additional aspect of this quotation is that Smyth uses the covenant, the promises, and Christ in close relationship with each other. In his "A Lettre written to Mr. A. S." he uses these terms in connection with each other on several occasions. Smyth stresses that the covenant, promises, and Christ are given only to the faithful who have separated themselves from the wicked.[60] This is the root of the Separatist covenant. Smyth and the other Separatists saw themselves as partaking in the eternal covenant of God and its benefits because they were willing to separate from the wicked and covenant to be obedient to God. Their local church covenant demonstrates their place in the eternal covenant.

Smyth's Baptist Writings

In his Baptist writings, Smyth turns his attention from the local church covenant to relating his new views on baptism to the eternal covenant. As Smyth engages Richard Clyfton in debate on infant baptism, he discusses the idea of covenant at great length.[61] He realizes that if he is going to

---

[59]Smyth, *Works* 2:529.
[60]Smyth, *Works* 2:548-49, 554-55.
[61]Smyth intended to discuss this topic in even greater detail in a work that was lost or never published. Smyth, *Works* 2:570.

convince the Separatists to follow him in rejecting infant baptism, he must deal with the foundation of their ecclesiology, the covenant. He accuses Clyfton and the Separatists of falling short in three areas. He says that they have confused the carnal and the spiritual covenants; they have not recognized faith and repentance as conditions of the spiritual covenant; and they have not understood the typological nature of the covenant.

Confusing the carnal and spiritual covenants. Clyfton argues that infant baptism is a continuation of the Old Testament practice of circumcision. To him, baptism is the seal of the new covenant in the New Testament just as circumcision was the seal of the covenant of Abraham. God instructed Abraham to pass down through his family the covenant and circumcision as the seal of the covenant. Clyfton holds that the church is to do the same with the New Testament covenant. They are to pass down the covenant of grace to their children and are to carry on the seal of baptism.[62]

Smyth counters that there are two covenants. One is carnal and the other is spiritual. He writes:

> [F]first distinguishing the two covenants or testaments . . . one covenant was made with Abraham & his carnal seed & of that covenant was circumcision a seale: another covenant made with Abraham & his Spiritual seed, & of that covenant the holy Spirit of promise is the seale.[63]

One covenant offered to Abraham was a carnal one. Therefore, the seal of that covenant was carnal, circumcision. It was given to Abraham and his carnal seed concerning possession of Canaan and the Law. The other covenant was a spiritual one, an eternal covenant given to Abraham and the faithful that were to follow him. The Spirit serves as the seal to the spiritual covenant given to Abraham and the Spirit continues as the seal of this covenant even into the New Testament. Smyth denies that baptism is the seal of the spiritual covenant. The purpose of baptism is to depict the sealing of the Holy Spirit in the person. Therefore, only believers are to be baptized, in order to bear witness that the Spirit has sealed them. The church is not a part of the carnal covenant that was

---

[62]Smyth, *Works* 2:578-79.
[63]Smyth, *Works* 2:579. "Abraham" has been emended.

sealed with circumcision, but it does have a part in the eternal, spiritual covenant that passed from Abraham through the "Faithful."[64]

Smyth indicates that the Separatists have made two errors by confusing the carnal covenant and the spiritual covenant. First, they err in linking the sign of circumcision with the spiritual covenant. Smyth says it is clear that God has made a carnal and a spiritual covenant, and also carnal and spiritual seals. Baptism and circumcision are not to be linked, because baptism is not a seal, but circumcision is. The Spirit has always been the seal of the spiritual covenant, but baptism serves as an outward sign of that seal. Smyth holds that circumcision was never linked to the spiritual covenant. He says, "I affirme that circumcision was never a seale of that covenant that God made with Abraham in respect of Christ, for the Holy Spirit of promise is the seale of it: but circumcision only was a seale of the external covenant."[65] Because it is improper to link circumcision with the spiritual covenant, baptism cannot be the New Testament version of circumcision.[66]

Their second error is that the spiritual covenant is passed down through Abraham's flesh. Because of the confusion that the Separatists had about the carnal and spiritual covenants, they were mistaken in thinking that the spiritual covenant is passed on to Abraham's carnal descendants. Once it is understood that the spiritual covenant is not passed through lineage, then it is apparent that the covenant is not passed on to infants. Smyth denies that the spiritual covenant was intended to be "conferred to al Abrahams infants according to the Flesh," so he says that it is not to be "conferred to al our infants."[67]

The Separatists were predominantly Reformed in their understanding of election and predestination. At this point in his career, Smyth is also Reformed and appeals to election as an argument for not confusing the two covenants. Smyth says that in their defense of infant baptism, the

---

[64] Smyth, *Works* 2:580-81.

[65] Smyth, *Works* 2:587.

[66] "Bicause circumcision did not aperteyne to Abraham & his infants as a seale of the everlasting covenant of life & Salvation, but of the external temporary covenant of the land of Canaan . . . it doth not follow that baptisme belongs to the Faythful & their carnal infants as a seale of the Spiritual covenant of the New Testament made in respect of Christ." Smyth, *Works* 2:585.

[67] Smyth, *Works* 2:582.

Separatists were saying that the covenant of grace was to be passed down through the families. They held that the covenant offered to Abraham and his natural descendants was the covenant of grace. Smyth disagrees by saying, "therfor I do confidently deny, & you are never able to prove that the carnal infants are actually possessed of the everlasting covenant God made with Abrah. for their parents sakes."[68] Smyth argues that if the covenant that is passed down through genealogy is the spiritual covenant, then God's election and predestination is passed down by families. Smyth says the elect are determined by God and they are the faithful to whom the covenant of grace is given. The covenant that is passed to Abraham's physical descendants is the carnal covenant.

Faith as a condition of the covenant. Smyth indicates that the Separatists have not recognized that faith and repentance are the conditions for the spiritual covenant. Faith and repentance were not required to qualify for the carnal covenant, but are necessary for the spiritual covenant. The carnal covenant required only ceremony, but the spiritual covenant requires true holiness. Smyth writes, "Faith & repentance is the condition & obedience of the matter or members of the new Testament, Marc. 1. 15."[69] Smyth does not mean to imply that faith was a condition of the spiritual covenant only after Christ came. Faith was essential to the spiritual covenant even back to Abraham. Smyth points out that Abraham expressed faith, and then was circumcised.[70]

The idea of faith and repentance being a condition of the covenant became central to Smyth's arguments against infant baptism. He argues that the Separatists were holding that faith and repentance were the requirements for adults to be admitted into the covenant, but infants were being admitted without this stipulation. Smyth argues that this should not be, because faith is always a condition, not just for some. Because infants cannot express the faith necessary to fulfil the covenant, then they should not be granted baptism. Smyth charges Clyfton by saying, "Seing you cannot declare that they have Faith or justification, seing they cannot have actuall Fayth: Therfor you cannot declare that they are actually

---

[68]Smyth, *Works* 2:677-78.

[69]Smyth, *Works* 2:596. In this context, Smyth uses the term "old Testament" to represent the carnal covenant and the term "new Testament" to represent the spiritual covenant.

[70]Smyth, *Works* 2:628-29.

vnder the covenant, by actuall Faith and holines."[71] Smyth says that infants were a part of the carnal covenant that was offered to Abraham and so they were to be circumcised. However, the spiritual covenant was offered only to those who were Abraham's descendants by "actual Fayth."[72]

Baptism does not correspond with circumcision and should not be given to infants who are not able to express faith. Once Smyth demonstrates that circumcision seals the carnal covenant not the spiritual covenant, he then declares that baptism has nothing to do with conferring the spiritual covenant to infants.[73] Smyth argues, "I answer: that baptisme is not the seale of the covenant of the new Test. as circumcision was the seale of the old Test."[74] So, while infants could be circumcised in the Old Testament because of their parents, baptism could not be performed on them because it "required actual faith & repentance confessed by the mouth, Mat. 3. 6. Act. 4. 37. & 10. 47."[75]

Since infants are denied entrance to the covenant until they can express faith, then they are also to be denied baptism. Entrance to the covenant can only come through faith and repentance. Smyth states his position clearly, "Infants are not actually possessed with the covenant: Seing they performe not the condition, viz: confession of their sinnes & their Fayth actually."[76] If infants cannot enter into the covenant by faith, then they are not to be baptized. Smyth declares that baptizing infants is bringing into the covenant those who cannot consent to it. Faith and repentance serve as the agreement to the covenant on the part of the faithful. Smyth says the Lord does not offer the covenant to infants, nor can infants agree, so it is nullified by both parties.[77]

Typology of the covenant. The theology of the covenant that Smyth defends in *The Character of the Beast* is typological in form. Smyth

---

[71]Smyth, *Works* 2:603.
[72]Smyth, *Works* 2:588.
[73]"If circumcision did not seale vp the everlasting covenant to Abraham & al his carnal infants: then (by your proportion) baptisme doth not seale vp the everlasting covenant to the Faithful & their carnal infants." Smyth, *Works* 2:588.
[74]Smyth, *Works* 2:593.
[75]Smyth, *Works* 2:593.
[76]Smyth, *Works* 2:594.
[77]Smyth, *Works* 2:648-49.

asserts that there are two covenants given by God, carnal and spiritual. His understanding is that the carnal covenant is found in the Old Testament and types the spiritual covenant. The spiritual covenant is present in the Old Testament but is not fully revealed until the New Testament. Smyth's language can be somewhat confusing, however, because he often refers to the carnal covenant as the "old testament" and the spiritual covenant as the "new testament." It would appear from this phrasing that Smyth sees the carnal covenant as being the only covenant of the Old Testament and the spiritual covenant as existing only in the New Testament. However, Smyth does not make this distinction. Smyth attempts to eliminate this confusion by discussing his use of the terms, "covenant" and "testament." He states that "a covenant & testament is al one in the originals though the English words are two."[78] Therefore, Smyth sometimes uses "carnal covenant" and "old testament," one time referring to the carnal covenant and at other times to designate the Hebrew scriptures. However, an awareness of his use of these terms does solve the dilemma of how in one section of his writings he says that the old testament is to be abolished, but also says that the Old Testament is commanded to the Church.

Smyth says that the carnal covenant types the spiritual covenant. He insists that to correlate the carnal seal of circumcision with the spiritual covenant instead of the carnal covenant is "to make a disproportion betwixt the type & the truth."[79] This relationship is expounded in another passage where Smyth discusses the nature of the two covenants. First, he explains that the carnal covenant is made with Abraham and his seed with the promise of Canaan. Second, he says that the spiritual covenant is made with Abraham and the faithful to follow him with the promise of everlasting life. Then he relates the two by saying, "The latter which is the truth being signified by the former which is the type."[80]

The carnal covenant and its aspects were just a shadow of the truth found in the spiritual covenant.[81] So, Smyth argues that the typical, carnal covenant ended with the coming of Christ. It had served its purpose of

---

[78]Smyth, *Works* 2:579.
[79]Smyth, *Works* 2:580.
[80]Smyth, *Works* 2:606.
[81]Smyth, *Works* 2:587-97.

pointing to the spiritual covenant that was made clear in Christ. A carnal seal was no longer needed either because the spiritual covenant carried with it the seal of the Spirit.

Smyth is not the first among those of the Separatist tradition to refer to the covenant in typological terms. Barrow gives a description of the covenant which is similar to Smyth's description of the spiritual covenant. Barrow explains that the covenant of grace has been offered to the Jews and the faithful who have come after them. At first the covenant was tied to the ceremonies of the Old Testament, but that was only until Christ, the substance of the covenant, could come. Once Christ came, the types of the Old Testament were not needed to point to Him.[82]

Smyth holds that the spiritual covenant was present during the Old Testament era. So, the coming of Christ did not introduce a completely new covenant. Instead Smyth explains that the spiritual covenant

> is enlarged now since Christs comming only in respect of the cleerer, & more vniversal publication of it: for then the covenant made with Abraham in respect of Christ was shadowed out darkly in types, now since Christ it is preached plainly.[83]

Although Smyth has Separatist precedence for a typological understanding of the covenant, his use of the contrast between the carnal covenant and the spiritual covenant to reject infant baptism as a seal of the spiritual covenant put him at odds with the Separatists. Smyth's rejection of infant baptism led him to a new position on the local church covenant.

Baptism replaces the local church covenant. Once Smyth accepted believers' baptism, then he no longer regarded the local church covenant as the method for entering the church. A person who desired to enter a true church had to do so by baptism that followed a profession of faith. To Smyth, baptism became the proper response to God's offer of the eternal covenant. While the Separatists agreed that aspects of the Old Testament covenant were to be discontinued, Smyth's application of this idea to rejecting infant baptism and the use of covenant as the entrance to the church was not acceptable.

---

[82]Barrow, *The Writings of Henry Barrow, 1587–1590*, 569-70.
[83]Smyth, *Works* 2:587.

As a Separatist, Smyth referred to the act of covenanting as the true form of the church. As a Baptist, Smyth adjusts his thinking to replace the church covenant with baptism. In *The Character of the Beast*, he states, "the true forme of the Church is a covenant betwixt God & the Faithful made in baptisme in which Christ is visibly put on."[84] This statement marks a considerable shift in Smyth's thinking. While he still upholds the presence of a covenant, it takes on a new form. The idea of covenant is included in Smyth's arguments for believers' baptism. He argues that infants are not to be baptized because they are "vnable to enter into the New Testament by sealing back the covenant vnto the Lord, & consenting vnto the contract."[85] The covenant offered by God must be consented to by the individual. The individual makes his consent visible to fellow believers by the sign of baptism. Baptism replaces the local church covenant for Smyth because he now sees that baptism will demonstrate a person's agreement to the eternal covenant. He says that neither he nor the so-called Anabaptists are bringing a new covenant, but instead are renewing the true form of the covenant, which is baptism.[86]

Smyth's Mennonite Writings

Smyth's view of the covenant experiences significant change in his Mennonite stage. No longer is the covenant central to his arguments on infant baptism or the church.

Decline in Smyth's attention to the covenant. The relationship of the covenant to infant baptism is a point of interest in Smyth's *Argumenta Contra Baptismum Infantum*. However, in this work, the debate about the covenant does not have the place of prominence that it has in *The Character of the Beast*. There is a variety of possible reasons for this. Smyth may believe that he has sufficiently answered the question of the relationship between the covenant and infant baptism in *The Character of the Beast*. Perhaps, Smyth's unknown opponent in *Argumenta Contra Baptismum Infantum* does not stress the covenant as much as the Separatists do in their defense of infant baptism. Finally, it could be that the argument from the covenant is no longer a primary interest of Smyth's.

---

[84]Smyth, *Works* 2:645.
[85]Smyth, *Works* 2:645.
[86]Smyth, *Works* 2:659.

It is probable that a combination of these three factors influenced Smyth to not focus on the covenant argument about infant baptism. Smyth indicates in another of his Mennonite works, *Defence of Ries's Confession*, that the covenant argument is old territory. There he complains that the Reformed critic is using "that same old song concerning the covenant and the covenant people, concerning the holy infant."[87] Smyth believes that this argument has been answered sufficiently. Also, Smyth's arguments in *Argumenta Contra Baptismum Infantum* are probably not directed at a Separatist audience specifically, but the Reformed tradition as a whole. Because of this, Smyth did not see the necessity of dealing with the covenant as fully as he did in his Baptist work, *The Character of the Beast*, which was a debate with the Separatist, Richard Clyfton.

In *Argumenta Contra Baptismum Infantum*, Smyth is more interested in rejecting infant baptism on the basis of his new belief in a general atonement. The atonement of Christ removed the guilt of original sin from infants. Moreover, there is no need for baptism of the faithful's infants because original sin is removed from all. Therefore, no individual should be baptized until they repent from their own sinful acts. This argument about original sin takes precedence in *Argumenta Contra Baptismum Infantum* over Smyth's previous views about the carnal and spiritual covenants.

Even though the covenant is not central to Smyth's arguments, he still makes several references to the covenant in *Argumenta Contra Baptismum Infantum*. In one of these sections, Smyth argues that infants cannot agree to the covenant, and so they should not be baptized into it. The covenant of salvation is a mutual agreement, and infants are not able to consent to it.[88] A similar argument had been used earlier by Smyth in *The Character of the Beast*.

It is not only Smyth's discussion of the eternal covenant that becomes less frequent in the final stage of his career. His understanding of a church as a covenanted community also is not a frequent topic. By the time that Smyth and his congregation composed the confession *Propositions and Conclusions*, he moves away from using the term "covenant"

---

[87]Smyth, *Works* 2:705; Coggins, *John Smyth's Congregation*, 190.
[88]Smyth, *Works* 2:713.

when describing the church. As a Separatist and often as a Baptist, his description of the church includes covenant overtones if not the term "covenant" itself. However, in *Propositions and Conclusions* he does not make any reference to the covenant in any of the articles that describe the church. Instead he states, "That the outward church visible, consists of penitent persons onely, and of such as beleeuing in Christ, bring forth fruites worthie amendment of lyfe."[89] This gives some indication of how far Smyth has moved from his Separatist understanding of the church being formed on a covenant.

Universal covenant. In Smyth's Mennonite work, *Defence of Ries's Confession*, he mentions the covenant on only two occasions. Nevertheless, they are significant in the fact that they show Smyth's new understanding of the eternal covenant. For Smyth as a Separatist and Baptist, the eternal covenant brings salvation to those who are willing to fulfil the condition of faith and repentance. However, for him as a Mennonite, the covenant provides a new promise. The covenant is made with Adam and all his descendants, and it involves the removal of the guilt of original sin. Smyth explains that one benefit of Christ's atonement is that the effect of original sin is cancelled. Smyth says, "Therefore, as Cain was made a participant in the sin of Adam, so [he was] also [made a participant] in the benefit of Christ; for truly this covenant was made with Adam and all his children."[90] Later, God renewed this covenant with Abraham. So, the removal of original sin becomes a promise of the covenant and is made possible with the atonement of Christ.

The second mention of the covenant in *Defence of Ries's Confession* is more brief. In this situation, Smyth says the appeal to the covenant to defend infant baptism used by his Reformed opponent was predictable and ineffective. He adds that all people are given the benefit of the covenant, which is the universal grace of the removal of original sin. Therefore, infants do not need to be baptized to receive this benefit of the covenant.[91]

---

[89]Smyth, *Works* 2:744.
[90]Translation by Coggins, *John Smyth's Congregation*, 172. *ergo quemadmodum Cayn particeps factus est Adae peccati, ita et beneficii christi: etenim hoc foedus factum est cum Adamo ipsiusque liberis omnibus.* Smyth, *Works* 2:685.
[91]Smyth, *Works* 2:705-706, Coggins, *John Smyth's Congregation*, 190-91.

An aspect of Smyth's understanding of the covenant that is unique to his Mennonite stage is the universality of the covenant. The covenant is based on the faithfulness of God and remains with humans despite their unfaithfulness.[92] In *Defence of Ries's Confession*, he indicates the universality of the covenant by stating that it was originally made with Adam (and Cain, etc.) and was renewed with Abraham. In *Argumenta Contra Baptismum Infantum*, he uses the idea of the universal covenant to argue against the infants of the faithful being baptized. He says that either all infants or no infants should be baptized because they are all under the grace of covenant, which he describes as the restoration of innocence from sin. Still he holds that adults must respond to the covenant by fulfilling the condition of the circumcision of the heart. However, concerning infants, he says, "But neither the covenant nor the condition of the covenant, namely the circumcision of the heart pertained to infants, who free of sin still remained established in a position of innocence."[93] The covenant has both universal and conditional benefits. The universal benefit of the removal of the guilt of original sin, is made available to all through Christ's general atonement. The conditional benefit of salvation is given upon the fulfillment of the requirements of faith and repentance.

The universality of the covenant makes a significant addition to Smyth's theology of the covenant. Smyth still holds that the individual must respond to the covenant by faith to obtain salvation. However, the covenant of grace does not just pertain to salvation. The covenant of grace also brings the restoration of innocence to humans. The individual is not guilty of original sin because of the work of Christ. This restoration aspect of the covenant is offered to all humans unconditionally. It is not given only to those who will respond faithfully. Smyth comments, "For the grace of the divine covenant is not rendered ineffective by the infidelity of man, Rom. 3: 3-4."[94] Smyth continues by giving an example of the unconditional nature of this aspect of the covenant by citing that,

---

[92]Smyth, *Works* 2:724.
[93]*verum nec foedus nec conditio foederis nempe circumcisio cordis ad infantes pertinebat, qui peccatis vacui in statu innocentiae adhuc constituti, permanserunt.* Smyth, *Works* 2:713.
[94]*gratia enim foederis divini non irrita est per infidelitatem hominum,* "Rom. 3. 3. 4." Smyth, *Works* 2:724.

although the ten tribes of Israel had rebelled against God, the covenant was maintained by the grace of God.[95]

God's covenant with us instead of our covenant with God. During Smyth's Separatist and Baptist stages, he stresses a person's covenant with God by emphasizing the conditional nature of the covenant. He accentuates the necessity of a person agreeing with the covenant and being faithful to the covenant by obedience. As Smyth comments on the covenant as a Mennonite, his emphasis swings to God's covenant with humans. His accent is on the faithfulness of God in offering the covenant to all people through Christ. Also, another important aspect is that one benefit of Christ's work, the removal of original sin, is available to all regardless of their response, because of God's part in the covenant.

As a Separatist, Smyth indicates that the covenant is both an agreement between God and the people and also among the people themselves. When he discusses the first part of this agreement, Smyth mentions that even this first part is a tandem agreement. He says, "The first part of the covenant respecting God is either from God to the faithful, or from the faithful to God 2 Cor. 6. 16." He then continues to explain: "From God to the faithfull. Mat. 22. 32. the sum whereof is expressed 2 Cor. 6. 16 I wil be their God. To be God to the faithful is 1. to give Christ. 2. with Christ al things els."[96] He also says, "From the faithful to God 2 Cor. 6. 16. the summe whereof is to be Gods people, that is to obey al the commandements of God. Deut 29. 9."[97] While Smyth is aware of both sides of the covenant, in his Separatist and Baptist writings, the faithful's covenant with God is the focus of his discussion. However, as a Mennonite, Smyth emphasizes the cancellation of original sin through the work of Christ given to all through the covenant God makes with humans.

Although his Mennonite writings on the covenant differ from his earlier statements, Smyth does not abandon all of his earlier beliefs about the covenant. He says in his *The Last Booke* that he stands by his stance on the two testaments or covenants in his debate with Richard Clyfton. He is referring to his discussion of the carnal and spiritual covenants. So,

---

[95] Smyth, *Works* 2:724.
[96] Smyth, *Works* 1:254. "From" has been emended.
[97] Smyth, *Works* 1:254. "Summe" has been emended.

he is saying that, as a Mennonite, he stills agrees with his discussion of the idea that God offered two covenants to Abraham. The carnal covenant he would pass down through his children. The spiritual covenant would be passed through the faithful who would be linked to Abraham through their faith in God, not genealogy.[98] Even though all humanity has the privilege of the universal covenant in Christ, which removes original sin, Smyth still agrees that the spiritual covenant of salvation comes through the conditions of faith and repentance.

Modern Views on Smyth's Use of the Covenant

Smyth's frequent use of the covenant in his understanding of the church has prompted various attempts by modern scholars to interpret his views on covenant. In 1984, the *Baptist Quarterly* published a series of articles that present various opinions on Smyth's use of the covenant and its importance for his theology. These articles all assume familiarity with B. R. White's comments in his book, *The English Separatist Tradition*.

B. R. White. In his "The Epistle to the Reader" Smyth claimed the covenant was central to Separatist thinking. He says that if he is going to convince Separatists to reject infant baptism, he must deal with the covenant. He writes, "but ther is one, & indeed but one argument which the separation principaly stand vpon, & that is the covenant which say they if it be answered they must ne[e]ds yeeld vnto the truth."[99] He was so aware of the importance of the covenant to Separatist thinking that he intended to write a book with the sole purpose of relating the covenant to baptism.[100]

B. R. White demonstrates the importance of the idea of covenant in Smyth's Separatist writings. He claims that in Smyth's writing as a Separatist "his understanding of the divine covenant dominated his concept of the Church."[101] Yet White claims that Smyth's idea of a close relationship between theology of the covenant and covenant ecclesiology

---

[98]Smyth, *Works* 2:755. He is affirming his statements made in *The Character of the Beast*.

[99]Smyth, *Works* 2:569. "Covenant" and "answered" have been emended.

[100]Smyth, *Works* 2:570. Unfortunately, this book was never written or has been lost.

[101]White, *The English Separatist Tradition English Separatist*, 125.

does not really become a common "characteristic" of his writings until *Parallels, Censures, Observations*.[102] Contrary to White's view, however, the connection between the two uses of covenant is quite clear from Smyth's earliest Separatist work, *Principles and Inferences*. Smyth describes the visible church as one that has gathered together under a covenant, meaning a local church covenant. When he describes the local church covenant he uses terms that relate to theology of the covenant. He says that the first part of this covenant is between God and the faithful, then gives the scripture reference 2 Corinthians 6:16, which alludes to God's covenant of grace.[103] So, it is apparent that, early in his Separatist stage, Smyth saw a strong connection between God's eternal covenant and the local church covenant.

White suggests in his *English Separatist Tradition* that as a Separatist Smyth sees the covenant as central for his understanding of the church.[104] Later in another publication, White is even more specific when he says that a conditional covenant was central to Smyth. He writes, "So, for John Smyth, it was the covenant which demanded the condition [of obedience] which was fundamental."[105] White's thesis is challenged by Douglas Shantz, who says that the "resurrected Christ, in his character as ruling King" is more central than the covenant.[106] It is not entirely clear in *English Separatist Tradition* if White proposes that the covenant is central to Smyth's thinking beyond his Separatist stage.[107] However, as White responds to Shantz's article, he certainly proposes that conditional covenant thinking was central to Smyth from his Separatist stage onward.[108]

The centrality of Smyth's holding to a conditional covenant as a Baptist will be examined in relationship with Stephen Brachlow who

---

[102]White, *The English Separatist Tradition English Separatist*, 128.

[103]Smyth 1:252-54.

[104]White, *The English Separatist Tradition English Separatist*, 125.

[105]White, "The English Separatists and John Smyth Revisited," 346.

[106]Shantz, "The Place of the Resurrected Christ in the Writings of John Smyth," 202.

[107]James Coggins assumes that White holds that the covenant is central beyond his Separatist stage. Coggins, "The Theological Positions of John Smyth," 249.

[108]White, "The English Separatists and John Smyth Revisited," 346.

discusses the idea more fully. However, it can be seen that the covenant was not central to Smyth's thinking for the church as a Mennonite. His scant use of the term comes only as he is defending his rejection of infant baptism.

A further indication that the church covenant was not central for the local church in Smyth's Mennonite thought is his description of a church. It has been shown in this chapter that, as a Separatist, Smyth often uses the term "covenant" in his description of the church. However, in his description of the church that he gives in his Mennonite work, *Propositions and Conclusions*, the term does not appear. He writes, "That the outward church visible, consists of penitent persons onely, and of such as beleeuing in Christ, bring forth fruites worthie amendment of lyfe."[109] In this article and the surrounding articles that deal with the visible church, there is no mention of the covenant. The idea of obedience is still present, but not because the person is at risk of breaking the covenant. Instead, the new creature is to avoid sin because it is "contrarie to regeneration."[110]

The strength of White's argument lies in his awareness of Smyth's reliance on the local church covenant as a Separatist. Also, the fact that White notices the relationship in Smyth's thought between the theology of the covenant and covenant ecclesiology is a valid insight into Smyth's views. White's main weakness is his failure to acknowledge Smyth's move as a Mennonite away from describing the church in terms of the covenant.

James Coggins. Coggins takes a different view on the question of the centrality of the covenant for Smyth. He sees the covenant as merely the Separatist method of forming a church. He charges White with saying that Smyth had confused the two concepts of covenant.[111] Coggins denies that Separatist covenant ecclesiology has any connection with the theology of the covenant.[112] John Coolidge disagrees with Coggins on this

---

[109] Smyth, *Works* 2:744.

[110] Smyth, *Works* 2:744.

[111] Coggins, "The Theological Positions of John Smyth," 249. White had actually used the term "ambivalence" to describe Smyth's use of the term "covenant." White contends that Smyth deliberately relates the two terms. White, *The English Separatist Tradition English Separatist*, 128.

[112] Coggins, "The Theological Positions of John Smyth," 249.

point. He argues that Robert Browne and other Separatists saw their forming of a church by covenant as renewing the covenant relationship with God.[113] It is clear that Smyth saw some relationship between the two concepts of covenant. As a Separatist, Smyth saw the local church covenant as the proper response by the faithful to God's eternal covenant. The local church covenant was a pact by the members to strive together to be obedient to the covenant of grace.

Coggins presents some contrasting statements about Smyth's later use of the covenant. During his debate with White and others about the centrality of the covenant to the thinking of Smyth, he recognizes the centrality of the covenant for Smyth as a Separatist. However, he says that the covenant does not have any prominence before or after Smyth's Separatist stage.[114] In his book on John Smyth's congregation, Coggins seems to contradict his earlier stance by saying that the formula that Smyth used as a Baptist to describe the true nature of the church was basically the same as his Separatist formula.[115] So, Coggins recognizes that the covenant was still a crucial part of Smyth's understanding of the church as a Baptist. He also mentions that Helwys still made comments relating his church to the Separatist covenant after breaking from Smyth's church. Concerning these later Baptists, Coggins says, "Like Smyth, they seem to have regarded believers (sic!) baptism as only a more purified form of the Separatist covenant."[116] So, it does seem that the covenant did retain some importance in Smyth's Baptist stage.

Coggins also states that in any stage Smyth "hardly ever discussed covenant theology at all."[117] His emphasis must be on the term "discussed." Smyth continually mentions the idea of covenant throughout his Separatist and Baptist stages. Surely, the huge section of material in *The Character of the Beast* that focuses on Smyth's debate with Clyfton over the carnal and spiritual covenants constitutes a discussion. Both the fact that *The Character of the Beast* is the only work of Smyth that comes from his Baptist stage and that approximately one-third of this work is on

---

[113]Coolidge, *The Pauline Renaissance in England*, 96.
[114]Coggins, "The Theological Positions of John Smyth," 249.
[115]Coggins, *John Smyth's Congregation*, 62-63.
[116]Coggins, *John Smyth's Congregation*, 106.
[117]Coggins, "The Theological Positions of John Smyth," 249.

the covenant gives strength to the idea that "covenant theology" was a frequent topic of discussion for Smyth. Perhaps Coggins is bringing to the reader's attention the absence of "covenant theology" from Smyth's Mennonite discussions. So, if Coggins were to limit his comments to Smyth's Mennonite stage and not include Smyth's Separatist or Baptist stages, then his observations would be a good overview of Smyth's practice.

Coggins contends that the concept of the "further light clause" was central to the Separatists' idea of covenant. He describes the covenant as having three important aspects. He says that the Separatist covenant stressed the mutual agreement between God and the faithful, obedience to God, and the pursuit of progressive revelation. In his discussion of the Separatists' covenant, Coggins mentions the first two aspects briefly, but gives the most attention to the third aspect of progressive revelation or the further light. He suggests that this concept of the further light is what caused the Separatists to push forward from Puritanism, condemn all their opponents, and have a tendency for church splits.[118]

The concept of progressive revelation does play an important role in the thinking of the Separatists, especially for Smyth. However, the concept of obedience has a much stronger place in Smyth's understanding of the covenant than the concept of further light. One of many examples that exemplifies this is found in *Paralleles, Censures, Observations*. As he debates with Richard Bernard, he was most concerned with Bernard and others who were not being obedient to the ways of God. Smyth says, "you dare not covenant and practise al that you know, but walk in violating of the whole Kingdom of Christ, are mingled among al the refuse of the Land in your Church, worship, & communion of holy things."[119] Smyth's concern with Bernard is not that he was not pursuing further truth. He implores Bernard to be obedient to the truth that he already knows. So, of the concepts of the covenant that Coggins mentions, obedience actually has a more important role than the further light clause.

Stephen Brachlow. Stephen Brachlow proposes that Smyth is one in a long line of English Puritans and Separatists who insist on a conditional

---

[118]Coggins, *John Smyth's Congregation*, 117-20.

[119]Smyth, *Works* 2:515. Some other passages where obedience is central to the covenant are Smyth, *Works* 1:254, 2:386-89, 462.

covenant. Brachlow traces the idea of a conditional covenant through the Puritan and Separatist tradition.[120] In one sense his work builds on the foundation set by John Coolidge. Coolidge also indicates the tendency among the Puritans, Separatists, and Congregationalists to stress the conditional nature of the covenant.[121] Brachlow's work is helpful because he traces the tendency directly to Smyth. He gives evidence of Smyth's predecessors and their stress on obedience to be faithful to the covenant. He even adds that, as a Baptist, Smyth turned the Separatists' emphasis on a conditional covenant against them in his arguments against infant baptism.[122]

However, Brachlow oversimplifies Smyth's thought in one respect. He submits that Smyth's approach to answering Clyfton is to stress the mutualist or conditional nature of the covenant. While Smyth does have some conditional covenant overtones in his discussion, his emphasis lies more on the difference of the carnal and spiritual covenants, not on the conditional or unconditional nature of the covenant. Indeed, Smyth describes both covenants as having some conditions. Obviously, the spiritual covenant has a greater emphasis on obedience.

The greatest weakness of Brachlow's thesis is that he fails to recognize the unconditional aspect of the covenant that Smyth adopts once he becomes a Mennonite. Smyth does maintain the necessity of repentance for the covenant benefit of salvation. However, obedience is not necessary for a person to gain some benefit from the covenant. There is an aspect of the covenant that is offered to all humans no matter their response. The unconditional aspect of the covenant is the removal of the guilt of original sin and the restoration of innocence, and it is given to all through the atonement of Christ. Unfortunately, neither Brachlow nor White recognizes the unconditional aspect of Smyth's Mennonite view of the covenant.

Douglas Shantz. One area of thought that Coggins, White, Brachlow, and Douglas Shantz all discuss is that the covenant is central to the thought of Smyth and the other Separatists. Shantz's approach is different from the others. His supposition is that the idea of the resurrected Christ

---

[120]Brachlow, "Puritan Theology," 180-86.
[121]Coolidge, *The Pauline Renaissance in England*, 99-140.
[122]Brachlow, "Puritan Theology," 188.

is central to Smyth's ecclesiology. The roles of the resurrected Christ as prophet, priest, and king are fundamental to Smyth's understanding of the church. The rule of Christ makes the covenant applicable to the church. Shantz contends that "While White is undoubtedly correct that the covenant is included in Smyth's definition, the central concern seems to be the One with whom the covenant is made—the risen Christ: the Church is the sphere over which Christ rules."[123]

To point to Christ's centrality instead of the covenant, Shantz indicates two examples where Smyth gives a basic description of the church that does not mention the covenant. Both of these descriptions include the idea of the church being obedient to Christ as Head of the Church.[124] Shantz does not deny the importance of the covenant in Smyth's understanding of the church. However, he insists that Smyth is more concerned with the resurrected Christ as the authority of the covenant. Smyth sees the relationship that Christ has with the church as best being expressed in terms of the covenant. Christ is placed as the Head of the Church as a part of God's covenant. The faithful should respond to Christ by covenanting to be obedient to Him.

Coggins dismisses Shantz by saying, "Shantz argues that the ruling Christ is more central than the idea of the covenant, yet in fact, as far as ecclesiology and Smyth's Separatist stage are concerned, both doctrines come from the same verse."[125] This is hardly an adequate dismissal, because it does not contradict Shantz. In fact, it strengthens his argument, because Shantz agrees that the concepts are related. The relationship is what causes him to conclude that in the relationship, the resurrected Christ is primary.

Brachlow's dismissal of Shantz is equally unsatisfying. Brachlow comments that the tendencies that Shantz points out in Smyth are not unique to him and can be found in several of his Puritan and Separatist contemporaries.[126] While this may answer Shantz's proposition of the

---

[123]Shantz, "The Place of the Resurrected Christ in the Writings of John Smyth, 199-200.
[124]Shantz, "The Place of the Resurrected Christ in the Writings of John Smyth," 200. Smyth says that church is to "obey Christ their king, priest and prophet" and "obey Christ in his kingdome." Smyth, *Works* 1:267.
[125]Coggins, "The Theological Positions of John Smyth," 250.
[126]Brachlow, "John Smyth and the Ghost of Anabaptism," 296.

presence of Anabaptist influence in this area, it does not exclude the value of his findings about the centrality of the resurrected Christ. In fact Brachlow's rebuttal does not seem to address the main part of Shantz's thesis.

Finally, White does not provide an adequate rebuttal to Shantz. His answer to Shantz digresses in that White gives a further explanation of what he intended to say in *The English Separatist Tradition*. After further explaining himself, White adds that Shantz had failed to answer his (White's) arguments.[127] Actually, Shantz could make the same comment for White.

A proper critique of Shantz should focus on his conclusions from his research. He insists that Smyth's focus on Christ's role in the covenant is an indication of continental Anabaptism on Smyth and the Separatists. One of Shantz's main proofs for this supposition is that the Separatists' emphasis on the conditional nature of the covenant is not common within English Puritanism. Recent studies have demonstrated that actually the conditional nature of the covenant is evident in many English Puritans.[128] Another criticism of Shantz's comments is that he does not give much attention to two of Smyth's major works, *Paralleles, Censures, Observations* and *The Character of the Beast*.[129] These two works have much material dedicated to expressing the importance of faithfulness to the covenant. His thesis would have to stand true for these two works. Shantz's thesis can be substantiated by using these these two vital works, but he does not do it adequately.

Conclusion

Smyth's view of the covenant is vital for his understanding of the church in his Separatist and Baptist stages. Smyth's covenant ecclesiology gives further indication of the priority he puts on being faithful to God.

---

[127]White ends his discussion of Shantz with the remark, "To have understood this would, I believe, have helped Dr Shantz. He might still feel it necessary to correct me, but at least would be correcting me for what I actually meant to say." White, "The English Separatists and John Smyth Revisited," 345.

[128]See n. 44, above.

[129]Shantz does not mention *Paralleles, Censures, Observations* and gives only six sentences to *The Character of the Beast*.

Obedience to God is an essential condition to the local church covenant in Smyth's Separatist and Baptist works. In his Baptist work, *The Character of the Beast*, Smyth argues that the carnal covenant of the Old Testament should not be continued in the New Testament church. The spiritual covenant must be maintained through the conditions of faith and repentance.

When he becomes a Mennonite, Smyth's thought on the covenant changes and becomes much less central to his arguments. The local church covenant does not appear in Smyth's Mennonite description of the church. Also, in his theology of the covenant as a Mennonite, he stresses the universal result of Christ's work, the removal of original sin.

Chapter 5

Smyth's View of General Atonement

As the English Baptist tradition that began with Smyth developed, the group who returned to England with Thomas Helwys eventually became known as General Baptists. While Smyth sought closer ties with the Mennonites, Thomas Helwys and others of the congregation broke away and migrated back to English soil. One area of their doctrine that had developed while they were with Smyth was their rejection of many Reformed views. They rejected the doctrines of predestination, total depravity, irresistible grace, and limited atonement. Nevertheless, the aspect of their doctrine for which they became known was their acceptance of a general atonement, hence the name General Baptists. While John Smyth began his career supporting Reformed doctrine, later during his Mennonite days he rejected this thought. Smyth's acceptance of a general atonement caused his rejection of other tenets of Reformed views. Scholars have varied views on the timing and sources of Smyth's acceptance of general atonement. However, a crucial factor in Smyth's change that has been often overlooked is the influence of Hans de Ries.

Smyth's Reformed Views

During the early stages of his career, Smyth supported the Reformed doctrine that dominated his English Puritan background. Smyth's writings as a Puritan, Separatist, and Baptist all reveal his Reformed position.

Smyth's Reformed Views as a Puritan and a Separatist. In his Puritan works, *The Bright Morning Starre* and *A Paterne of True Prayer*, Smyth affirms total depravity, original sin, predestination, and the perseverance of the saints. In *The Bright Morning Starre*, he indicates his belief in total depravity in the statement "[F]or he that wanteth grace can neuer desire it, onely he that hath it."[1] In his second work, *A Paterne of True Prayer*, he expresses another aspect of Reformed doctrine by referring to original sin as "*Adams* transgression imputed."[2] Original sin has led to the total depravity of humans. His statement concerning this depravity is that

---

[1] Smyth, *Works* 1:62.
[2] Smyth, *Works* 1:181.

168 / The Theology of John Smyth

repentance is "altogether impossible to flesh and blood," but that the Lord must reveal to humans the need for repentance.[3]

In *A Paterne of True Prayer* he uses the phrase "the Lords predestination."[4] In this instance he is not affirming the predestination of individual souls, but that God has predestined the history of the world. Later in the work, he does confirm the predestination of an individual. As Smyth is affirming the perseverance of the saints, he says, "[F]or perseuerance followeth grace, and is a necessarie consequent thereof."[5] While arguing for perseverance he shows his support of predestination. He says that it is illogical to think that God could predestine someone to be a part of His elect, allow them to experience redemption, but then let them fall with the people He predestined for punishment. Smyth writes, "Againe, this would follow as absurd as the former, that it might be said, God hath from eternity Elected and Reprobated the same man: Christ hath both redeemed, and not redeemed the same man."[6] The obvious implication here is that God does not do both to anyone, but He does do one or the other.

Smyth followed in the footsteps of the Reformed theologian, William Perkins. Perkins had been a Fellow of Christ's College, Cambridge from 1584 through 1595. He was a leading proponent of English Calvinism during the late sixteenth century, and continued to be a major influence even after his death in 1602.[7] Smyth was at Cambridge during Perkins's tenure and defended much of the same doctrine. Similar to Perkins and other Puritans, Smyth defends the doctrine of a limited atonement. In his first work, *The Bright Morning Starre*, Smyth states:

> Secondly that grace is vniuersall no sort or estate of men excluded from Christs kingdom: ethe [the] poore haue intrest to grace and Christ aswell as the rich, the gentill as- well as the Iewe, women as- well as men: yet wee must knowe that the note of vniversality must not be stretcht to euery particular man, but to euery estate and condition of

---

[3] Smyth, *Works* 1:108.
[4] Smyth, *Works* 1:134.
[5] Smyth, *Works* 1:220.
[6] Smyth, *Works* 1:220.
[7] Kendall, *Calvinism and English Calvinism to 1649*, 51-52; Hylson-Smith, *The Churches in England* 1:127-28.

man.[8]

According to Smyth, when Psalm 22 speaks of all men, its meaning is to show that all classes of people have access to the grace of God. Smyth's support of Reformed doctrine continues into his Separatist stage. In *Principles and Inferences*, he states that part of the communion of the church is praying for the elect, uncalled and called. He says to pray "for them that are vncalled that they may be called Rom 10, 1 for them that are called that they may be confirmed. Col. 1, 9-12."[9] While *The Differences of the Churches* does not include any direct mention of Reformed doctrine, the fact that Smyth does not include this in his list of grievances with Francis Johnson's church implies his continued support of Reformed views. In both of these early Separatist works, Smyth focuses on ecclesiology, and so theological issues such as original sin and limited atonement are never the main topics of discussion.

In *Paralleles, Censures, Observations*, Smyth often makes reference to his belief that God has elected some to salvation. He says that even though Richard Bernard and other Puritans are in a false church, God probably has predestined many people within the Church of England to salvation. Smyth argues that because they do not separate from people who are unrepentant, then they are not the true visible church. While they are not in Christ's visible kingdom, they could still be in Christ's invisible kingdom of his elect. He writes:

> But al this is nothing to that which I affirme, for I say thus: that he which is not of a true visible Church, is no subject of Chr. Kingdom, that is he is not under the visible dominion & Lordship of Chr. in his church which is his Kingdom: I do not say that he is invisiblie none of the L. people: for a man may be one of the L. people in election & grace invisiblie, & yet not in the true visible church which is Ch. visible Kingdom.[10]

This quotation should not be misinterpreted as Smyth's seeming to take the visible church lightly. The bulk of his work is dedicated to convincing Bernard and other Puritans to come out of the Church of

---

[8]Smyth, *Works* 1:63.
[9]Smyth, *Works* 1:251-52.
[10]Smyth, *Works* 2:357.

England. Smyth is trying to defuse Bernard's charge that Smyth claimed that all people within the Church of England were heading for damnation. Smyth insisted that the "comprehension of al the el[e]ct in al ages & places: whose persons are vnknowne to vs, & such secreat things the L. hath reserved to himself, & concealed from our knowledg, & therfor we are not to search after them."[11] The doctrine of the invisible and secret elect being known only to the Lord is a consistent theme throughout his work.[12]

Smyth also continues to differentiate between the "visible subjects of Ch. visible church which is his Kingd. & invisible ones known only to the L. certaynly & particularly."[13] On several occasions, Smyth even mentions that he believes that there are thousands in the Church of England that are a "remnant according to the Election of grace."[14] He rejects Bernard's argument that the Church of England is true because souls are converted in it. Smyth declares that the secret work of the Lord is not contained by any church, but that "the Lord hath his thousands even in the depth of popery."[15] He insists that Bernard should recognize that the work of the Lord in election is a separate issue from the correct form of a visible church. The salvation of the elect cannot be used as a stamp of the Lord's approval. Smyth indicates that the Lord's elect are spread throughout many churches. It is impossible for all that "apertayne to the Lords Election" to have visible communion with one another. He writes:

> I may not have visible communion with one that is Elect in the Lords invisible Election, bicause he is not visibly faithful to me, as namely with thousands of you in the assemblies, bicause I cannot possibly know them certainly, & particularly.[16]

Smyth's Reformed Views as a Baptist. Smyth continued his support of divine election and original sin in his Baptist writings. Much like his references in *Paralleles, Censurers, Observations*, in his Baptist work,

---

[11]Smyth, *Works* 2:354.
[12]Smyth, *Works* 2:363, 372-3, 375, 385, 482, 484-85, 506, 518.
[13]Smyth, *Works* 2:358.
[14]Smyth, *Works* 2:459, 469, 485, 503, 546, 473. In the last reference, Smyth uses the term "millions among you."
[15]Smyth, *Works* 2:485.
[16]Smyth, *Works* 2:506; "Election" has been emended.

The Charater of the Beast, Smyth addressed election only in passing because he and Richard Clyfton, his Separatist opponent, shared similar views on this topic. In his Separatist works, Smyth emphasized the invisibility or secret nature of election. This theme continues in The Character of the Beast. Smyth confirms that the scriptures teach that some things pertain to "Gods secreat election, & not of mans knowledg" and that some people are "invisibly elect & beloved of God."[17] Smyth also confirms that although some people demonstrate trues faith, they could belong to God "invisibly as aperteyning to the L. election."[18]

Smyth gives special attention in *The Character of the Beast* to how infants relate to election and how they are affected by original sin. These subjects were of particular concern as he tried to defend his conviction that infants should not be baptized. Smyth exhibited some uncertainty when he related his view of infants and election. When he attempts to argue against infants being baptized because they have a special type of faith granted, Smyth reverts to his argument that only God can know certain things. He writes, "if it be said that infants have a kind of Faith wrought in them invisibly, & after an hidden manner: I say what God worketh invisibly, & secreatly we dispute not nor regard."[19] Smyth concludes that since this invisible faith cannot be validated, infants must be refused baptism, because they cannot prove their invisible faith or demonstrate visible faith. His dubiety is evidenced by his statement about the position of infants, "for infants I say that either they are al saved, though they cannot come to faith by hearing, or that they are one of the L. secrets, & so not to be searched into: & that the Scripture doth speak only to & of them that have eares to heare, & of things visible & known, & not of things invisible & secreat."[20] In this statement, Smyth raises the question of a universal redemption for infants. Nevertheless, he prefers the alternative, which is that only God understands the redemption of infants.

While Smyth demonstrates some uncertainty of how infants belong in divine election, he had no hesitation in relating infants and original sin.

---

[17]Smyth, *Works* 2:596 and 677, respectively.
[18]Smyth, *Works* 2:677.
[19]Smyth, *Works* 2:603. "Hidden" has been emended.
[20]Smyth, *Works* 2:634. "Them" has been emended.

He instructs Clyfton that to baptize infants is to baptize the carnal not the spiritual seed. He reasons, "for al infants are carnal, being conceaved & borne in sinne, being the Children of wrath, vntill the Lord work his work in them, which when he doth I know not."[21] Smyth continues this line of debate by making a statement that attests his uncertainty about infants and election and his certainty of their contamination by original sin. He states,

> [A]lthough I will not say that Children are damned, yet I dare say that they are borne & dead in trespasses & sinnes, & that they doe not nor cannot shew any sparke of grace to mee, & therfor although I dare not say this or that infant is not vnder the election of God, yet I dare say that never an infant in the Earth is actually seased [seized] of the New Testament which is onely atteyned by confession of sinne & Faith.[22]

Clyfton says that Smyth's view of infants being a secret of the Lord is wrong. Just as God cared for the infants of Abraham's day, so He cares for the infants of the New Testament. God was clear in His instructions to include the infants of the faithful in the Old Testament seal of the covenant. God is also clear that the covenant is an eternal covenant. So, the New Testament seal of the covenant, baptism, is to include the infants of the faithful.[23] Clyfton also disputes Smyth's claim that infants should not be baptized because they cannot demonstrate repentance. Clyfton affirms that infants do experience the benefits of repentance because they "are partakers of remission of synns and regeneration: seing they are in the covenant."[24] Their participation in the remission of sins and the covenant makes them eligible for baptism.

In his closing arguments to Clyfton on the first of his two positions defended in *The Character of the Beast*, Smyth again clarifies his belief on infants and original sin. Smyth charges Clyfton with holding an argument that would require him to affirm the universal redemption of infants. Smyth knows that he and Clyfton would reject this view, so he uses it to conclude that no persons, including infants, are to be baptized

---

[21]Smyth, *Works* 2:638.
[22]Smyth, *Works* 2:640.
[23]Clyfton, *The Plea for Infants and Elder People*, 83.
[24]Clyfton, *The Plea for Infants and Elder People*, 159.

until they can demonstrate faithfulness to the covenant. Smyth declares,

> [I]nfants being borne in sinne, cannot nor doe not declare their regeneration at al to vs: & so with them wee have nothing to doe: & whereas you say natural corruption is not imputed to infants no more then to men beleeving, let it bee so, & yet you cannot defend that without the opinion of vniversal redemption, & then I say, that if the infants of the Faithful being delivered from their natural corruption may have therfore bee baptized, then al infants shal be baptized who are pertakers of the same benefit, even the infants of Turkes.[25]

Smyth will later accept the exact position that he requires of Clyfton. Once Smyth moved from his Reformed roots, he came to believe that all infants are indeed innocent, and have avoided the contamination of original sin.[26]

Clyfton answers Smyth's charge of having to hold universal redemption to defend the theory that the infants of the faithful are part of the covenant. He responds:

> As concerning that opinion of general redemption, I reject as an error: but as touching the imputing of natural corruption to infants; thus I mean, that as the children of the faithful are to us within Gods covenant, as wel as their parents, because of the promise made to the faithful and their seed: so of us they are to be esteemed of, as pertakers of the promise, whereof the not imputing of sinne is one.[27]

The infants of the faithful are corrupted by original sin, but because of their parents' inclusion in the covenant the infants are included as well. This benefit does not apply to the children of pagans, so not all infants should be baptized.

An interesting point at this stage of Smyth's life is that even though he has accepted a believers' baptism, this does not require a rejection of Reformed views. Once Smyth had rejected Reformed views, his case for rejecting infant baptism took on a new dimension. In *The Character of the Beast*, he argues that infants should not be baptized because they

---

[25]Smyth, *Works* 2:642. "Even" has been emended.
[26]Smyth, *Works* 2:682, 728, 735.
[27]Clyfton, *The Plea for Infants and Elder People*, 146.

cannot believe.[28] In his Mennonite work, *Argumenta Contra Baptismum Infantum*, he adds that since infants are born without sin, they have no need for baptism.[29] Had Smyth rejected the doctrine of original sin before publishing *The Character of the Beast*, he would have surely included this idea in his reasons for rejecting infant baptism. Instead it is clear from Smyth's statements in the work that during his Baptist stage he saw no necessity for rejecting Reformed views. Only when Smyth began to accept Mennonite views did this change take place.

Smyth's Rejection of Reformed Views

After Smyth petitioned the Waterlander Mennonites to accept his congregation, he presented to them his confession, *Corde Credimus*. The confession accentuates his group's similarity with Mennonites beliefs. A main similarity between the two groups is their agreement on the rejection of Reformed doctrine. This confession is the first extant work that Smyth produces that exhibits his rejection of Reformed views. So, apparently he rejected his Reformed views between the publishing of *The Character of the Beast* in 1609 and his submission of *Corde Credimus* to the Mennonites in 1610.

In article 2 of *Corde Credimus*, Smyth rejects the predestination of humans to condemnation in stating, "That God has created and redeemed the human race to his own image, and has ordained all men (no one being reprobated) to life."[30] The goodness of God in creation and redemption are consistent themes in Smyth's arguments against predestination. He also spurns the Reformed position of original sin. Article 5 says, "That there is no original sin (lit., no sin of origin or descent), but all sin is actual and voluntary, viz., a word, a deed, or a design against the law of God; and therefore, infants are without sin."[31] Even though

---

[28]Smyth, *Works* 2:589.
[29]Smyth, *Works* 2:728.
[30]Translation by Evans, *The Early English Baptists* 1:253. *Deum creasse et redemisse genus humanum ad imaginem suam, omnesque homines (nemine reprobato) ad vitam predestinasse.* Smyth, *Works* 2:682.
[31]Translation by Evans, *The Early English Baptists* 1:253. *Nullum esse peccatum originis, verum omne peccatum esse actuale et voluntarium viz: dictum factum aut concupitum contra legem dei: ideoque infantes esse sine peccato.*

Adam sinned, his sin would have no effect on the free will of humans. God through His grace protected this aspect of His creation. The way in which God protected this free will was through the redemption of Christ. It was through Christ's atonement that God restored to humans the free will that was lost in the Fall. Smyth writes in article 9 of *Corde Credimus*:

> That men, of the grace of God through the redemption of Christ, are able (the Holy Spirit, by grace, being before unto them grace prevenient) to repent, to believe, to turn to God, and to attain to eternal life; so on the other hand, they are able themselves to resist the Holy Spirit, to depart from God, and to perish for ever.[32]

From article 5, it can be seen that it is humans' prerogative to choose or reject sin. Because there is no necessity imposed by the guilt of original sin, each person is responsible for his actions. This is true for everyone except for infants, who remain in a state of innocence. In article 9, Smyth makes it clear that humans are allowed to resist grace. He says that this choice is preserved by grace through the work of Christ. Basically, these two articles demonstrate that Smyth did not believe that Adam's sin corrupted the whole human race. God protected, by grace, humans' innocence and free will, therefore saving grace is not irresistible but humans can freely choose or reject it.

In Smyth's Mennonite work, *Argumenta Contra Baptismum Infantum*, his purpose is to challenge the practice of infant baptism. His rejection of a Reformed position is especially clear in his discussion of original sin. Smyth gives strong arguments against the continuance of original sin. The absence of original sin becomes one of his main arguments against the necessity of baptizing infants. His basic point is that since baptism is to mark the remission of sin, then innocent infants are not to be included. Original sin is not transferred from the parents, so remission of sin becomes necessary only when sins are committed out of acts of volition.

Smyth, *Works* 2:682.

[32]Translation by Evans, *The Early English Baptists* 1:253. *Homines ex dei gratia per Christi redemptionem posse (spiritu sancto per gratiam ipsos preveniente) resipiscere, credere, ad deum convertere, et vitam eternam adipisci: sicut e contrâ, posse ipsos spiritui sancto resistere, á deo deficere, et in eternum perire.* Smyth, *Works* 2:683.

Smyth specifies that through the work of Christ original sin has been cancelled. In this sense, the death of Christ benefits everyone. No one is born with the guilt of original sin, because of the death of Christ. So, Christ's general atonement overcomes the power of original sin. Smyth argues:

> If therefore anybody affirms that Adam's posterity is polluted by original sin, I answer it cannot be, that Christ's redemption was more limited in scope than Adam's transgression. And since Christ the Lamb was slain from the beginning of the world, Christ's death prevented original sin so it was not passed on to Adam's posterity.[33]

After rejecting the effect of original sin, Smyth continues by stating that infant baptism is unnecessary. He says that because infants have no need for forgiveness, there is no need for infant baptism. Also, as infants cannot comprehend sin or repentance, they should not be baptized. Baptism symbolizes that a person has repented from his acts of sin, which infants cannot do. Smyth states, "Finally if we affirm infants to have original sin (which we deny) . . . it does not therefore follow that they must be baptised, which is a sign of remission of sins and not of one sin and that an involuntary sin, consider Romans 5:26, Luke 3:3."[34] As in his earlier work, *The Character of the Beast*, Smyth insists that baptism should come only when a person has realized responsibility for his sins and finds the forgiveness of Christ. He laments infant baptism, because he declares that the infants remain in a state of innocence and cannot possibly comprehend responsibility for sin.

Smyth links the idea of personal responsibility with the idea that sin is not inherited, but chosen by each individual. In *Argumenta Contra*

---

[33]*Si ergo quispiam affirmaret posteritatem Adae per peccatum originale commaculatam esse, respondeo fieri non potest ut Christi redemptio angustior esset quam Adae transgressio: Ideoque cum Christus agnus occisus sit ab initio mundi, mors Christi prevenit peccatum originale ne transiret per traducem ad posteros Adae.* Smyth, *Works* 2:715.

[34]*denique si fateremur infantes peccatum originale habere (quod negamus) . . . non ex inde sequitur debere baptisari, quod baptismus est signum remissionis peccatorum non peccati unius ejusque involuntarij. vide Rom. 5. 26. Luc. 3. 3.* Smyth, *Works* 2:718-19. In this quotation, Smyth gives the reference, Romans 5:26. Since 5:26 does not exist, he likely intends 5:16.

Baptismum Infantum, he uses Ezekiel 18 to argue that original sin does not have any effect on successive generations. He explains, "The Lord indeed testifies openly that the one who sins will die, no son dies on account of his parents' sins. Ezech. 18."[35] Smyth claims that for God to punish one for the sins of another would contradict His divine justice and mercy. Each person is responsible for his own sins.

Smyth declares that the death of Christ breaks any grip of original sin, so infants remain in innocence. They are not guilty of sin until they make their own sinful choices. Smyth writes:

> Infants do not have sins which can be purged away, they still remain in their innocence, for the passage and flow of original sin is cut off by Christ's death, who is the Lamb slain from the beginning of the world . . . Christ does not save infants from their own sins, but impedes and restrains from infants the sin of someone else . . . therefore infants ought not to receive water baptism in their own person, since water baptism should be dispensed only to those, who have a need of the blood of Christ for their sins to be cleansed.[36]

The idea of the universal efficacy of Christ's atonement that halts the passage of original sin is the central aspect of Smyth's rejection of Reformed doctrine in *Argumenta Contra Baptismum Infantum*. The reason that he concentrates on rejecting original sin in this work is its relevance to infant baptism. If his opponents would recognize the innocence of infants, then they would not insist on continuing infant baptism. Since infants do not have sins to cleanse, repentance is impossible making baptism inappropriate.

In his *Defence of Ries's Confession*, Smyth gives several arguments against the Reformed position. In his defense of article 4 he challenges

---

[35] *testatur enim dominus apertissime animam quae peccat morituram, non filium moriturum ob peccata parentum. Ezech. 18.* Smyth, *Works* 2:725.

[36] *Infantes non habent peccata quae possunt expurgari, in innocentia sua adhuc permanent, cursus enim atque fluxus peccati originalis intercipitur per Christi mortem, qui agnus occisus est ab initio mundi . . . Christus non servat infantes a peccatis suis, sed impedit et prohibet ab infantibus peccatum unum alterius . . . infantes ergo non debe[n]t in corpore suo baptismum aquae suscipere, cum aquae baptismus ijs solis dispensum debet, qui sanguine Christi opus habent ad peccata sua propria abluenda.* Smyth, *Works* 2:728.

limited atonement:

> [T]he Holy Spirit wishes [to say] that the benefit of Christ surpasses the disobedience of Adam in dignity and extent. If Christ redeems only certain men, He does not bruise the head of the serpent but the tail, for most of its power remains until now, which Christ neither wishes to nor can repress; and, therefore, Christ's grace is inferior to Adam's sin because the latter ruined all men, [but] the former delivered no more than a very few from destruction.[37]

Another argument that Smyth uses is the comparison of creation and redemption. He states that in the "grace of creation" God formed all men to salvation, but if atonement affects only a few then His "grace of redemption" is less than the former "grace."[38] Because of general atonement, Smyth limits the scope of human depravity. He compares his thinking with the thinking of his "Reformed" critic by saying, "Therefore, I say this in respect to the understanding or seeking of grace: We say that the natural power is weakened and broken and, without divine help, empty and powerless; you argue in respect of grace [that it is] completely destroyed."[39]

General atonement also does away with the idea of irresistible grace. Smyth argues that since the power of choosing good or evil was not destroyed with the Fall, or at least was restored by the atonement of Christ, then grace is not irresistible. He writes, "the power to reject or accept offered grace remains with all the descendants of Adam through

---

[37]Translation by Coggins, *John Smyth's Congregation*, 173. *voluit enim spiritus sanctus Christi beneficium, Adami inoboedientiam dignitate et amplitudine superare: Si Christus quosdam homines solummodo redemit, non fregit caput serpentis, sed caudam: nam summa potestas adhuc manet quam nec voluit nec potuit Christus retundere: ideoque Christi gratia infirmior est peccato Adami cum hoc omnes homines perdidit, illa perpaucos admodum ab interitu vindicavit.* Smyth, *Works* 2:686-67.

[38]*gratia creationis* and *gratia redemptionis* Smyth, *Works* 2:687; Coggins, *John Smyth's Congregation*, 173.

[39]Translation by Coggins, *John Smyth's Congregation*, 175. *hoc autem dico respectu gratiae sive intelligendae sive expetendae: nos enervatam et diminutam dicimus naturalem illam potentiam et sive divino auxilio inanem et inefficacem: vos respectu gratiae penitus exstinctam defenditis.* Smyth, *Works* 2:689.

grace. . . . This is that general benefit which the human race obtained through the redemption of Christ."⁴⁰ Because each person retains the power of choice, he is personally responsible for his choice. God has not made the choice for anyone.

According to Smyth, predestination would limit human free will. If God predestined some people to condemnation then He has taken away their free will and forced them to choose sin. Smyth indicates that this would detract from the goodness of God. He asserts, "He is the origin and root of evil if He forces men by ordained necessity into sin. . . . If He makes the will of man to be inclined to evil through unavoidable and effectual decree, He effectively brings about evil itself."⁴¹ Predestining someone to destruction is completely against the nature of God according to Smyth. God is Creator and has created all humankind for salvation. Smyth says, "He does not create, does not ordain, does not predestine to destruction, unless someone wants to ascribe contradictory works and intentions to God."⁴²

Smyth holds that his rejection of predestination does not mandate a rejection of divine election or foreknowledge. He defines the elect as "Whoever is in Christ and perseveres."⁴³ He claims that God has known from the foundation of the world who would persevere and be saved and who would choose unfaithfulness. Although God has this knowledge, Smyth states, "This eternal foreknowledge of God occasions no necessity . . . but left untouched the free ability of doing and willing."⁴⁴

---

⁴⁰Translation by Coggins, *John Smyth's Congregation*, 175. *vires gratiam oblatam rejiciendi et assumendi per Adae posteros ex gratia re[man]sisse . . . hoc est generale illud beneficium quod humanum genus per Christi redemptionem adeptum est.* Smyth, *Works* 2:689.

⁴¹Translation by Coggins, *John Smyth's Congregation*, 179. *est autem origo et radix mali, si homines fatali necessitate in peccatum trudit . . . Si hominis voluntatem in malum propendere facit per ipsius inevitabile et efficax decretum, ipsum malum agit efficaciter.* Smyth, *Works* 2:693.

⁴²Translation by Coggins, *John Smyth's Congregation*, 179-80. *si non creat non ordinat nec predestinat ad interitum: nisi quis velit deo opera et proposita contradictoria ascribere.* Smyth, *Works* 2:693-94.

⁴³Translation by Coggins, *John Smyth's Congregation*, 180. *qui in Christo est et perseverat ille electus est.* Smyth, *Works* 2:695.

⁴⁴Translation by Coggins, *John Smyth's Congregation*, 181. *Haec dei*

Smyth's work, *Propositions and Conclusions*, is of special interest. Its purpose is to demonstrate Smyth's Mennonite doctrine to the English, i.e., the Puritans and Separatists. Because his audience would be mostly Reformed, Smyth states his new beliefs in fuller form. Articles 14 and 17 relate Smyth's view on the freedom of men to choose or reject God, opposing the doctrine of irresistible grace. In article 14 he says, "That god created man with freedome of will, so that he had habilitie to chuse the good, and eschew the evil, or to chuse the evil, and refuse the good, and that this freedome of will was a naturall faculty or power, created by god in the soule of man."[45] In article 17 he continues by saying, "That Adam being fallen did not loose anie naturall power or facultie which god created in his soul . . . and therfor being fallen he still retained freedome of will."[46] There are two reasons that the free will is retained in Adam's descendants. First, Smyth says that sin, which is a "worke of the devill" does not destroy God's work. In each person, including Adam, God's creation of the "freedome of will" is maintained. Second, Smyth says that no effect of original sin such as the loss of free will passes to Adam's descendants because "Christs death, which was effectuall before Caine and Abells birth he being the lambe slaine from the begininge of the world, stopped the issue and passage therof."[47]

Article 18 manifests Smyth's refusal to accept the idea of original sin. He says, "That original sin is an idle terme, and that ther is no such thing as men intend by the word."[48] In article 19 he adds further assurance that original sin does not bring judgment on all generations. If the guilt of original sin did exist, then the death of Christ overcame it and kept it from being passed to Adam's descendants.[49]

While Smyth held that Christ's death delivered humans from the effects of original sin, he did not hold a universalist position that Christ's death brought salvation to everyone. He rejects this view clearly in article 35 when he says, "the efficacie of Christ[s] death is only deriued

---

prescientia eterna nullam necessitatem infert . . . sed liberam agendi et volendi potestatem reliquit. Smyth, *Works* 2:695.

[45]Smyth, *Works* 2:734-35.
[46]Smyth, *Works* 2:735.
[47]Smyth, *Works* 2:735.
[48]Smyth, *Works* 2:735.
[49]Smyth, *Works* 2:735.

to them, which do mortifie ther sinnes, which are grafted with him to the similitude of his death."[50] He continues in article 41:

> That these that are grafted with Christ to the similitude of his death and buriall shall also be to the similitude of his resurrection . . . for he doth quicken or give life vnto them, together with himself . . . for that is their salvation, and it is by grace.[51]

Christ's death protects free will and cancels original sin for all humanity. However, salvation comes by grace only to those who mortify their sins through repentance and faith. God's desire for a human to exercise repentance and faith can be thwarted because every "man hath power to receive or reiect" Him.[52]

Smyth also rejected predestination, while affirming the foreknowledge of God. In article 25 he says, "god doth not create or predestinate anie man to destruction."[53] Though in article 26, he does allow for God to have known before the foundation of the world who would choose salvation and who would reject it.[54] Smyth made similar statements in *Defence of Ries's Confession*. There he added the comment that God's foreknowledge contained no obligation. God's foreknowledge in no way restricts the freedom of humans to choose or reject salvation.

Because Christ's general atonement had stopped the passing of original sin, Smyth believed that infants were universally redeemed. In *The Character of the Beast*, Smyth had suggested that either all infants are saved or that the eternal position of infants is one of the Lord's secrets.[55] At that time, he concluded that their eternal position is one of the Lord's secrets, so their eternal status is unknown to humankind. However, when Smyth moves to a position of rejecting original sin, he reverses his decision. No longer are infants of unknown status; he now claims that all infants who die are granted eternal life through the grace of God. In article 20 of *Propositions and Conclusions*, Smyth states that

---

[50]Smyth, *Works* 2:738.
[51]Smyth, *Works* 2:739.
[52]Smyth, *Works* 2:743.
[53]Smyth, *Works* 2:736.
[54]Smyth, *Works* 2:736.
[55]Smyth, *Works* 2:634.

"infants are conceiued and borne in innocencie without sinne, and that so dyinge are undoubtedly saued, and that this is to be vnderstoode of all infants vnder heauen."[56]

Source of Smyth's Views

As Smyth's theological career is traced, it becomes apparent that late in his career he rejected Reformed ideas. While scholars agree on this point, there are varied opinions on how Smyth developed his new views. The root of this question concerns the source from which Smyth drew his anti-Reformed views. A. C. Underwood has suggested four possibilities. First, Smyth could have drawn these ideas from his own study of the Bible. Second, Peter Baro of Cambridge could have influenced Smyth. Third, the Arminian debate in Amsterdam could have influenced him. Fourth, the Mennonites could have influenced Smyth. B. R. White asserts that the last three suggestions are viable options.[57]

Stephen Brachlow traces the idea of mutual or conditional covenant through the theology of the Separatists and the English Puritans. He shows the development of the Separatist ecclesiology being based on a covenant. He insists that there was a movement within Puritanism to interpret God's covenant as based on the condition of obedience.[58] Brachlow holds that this idea of a conditional covenant was at the heart of Separatist covenant ecclesiology. He also insists that this idea of a conditional covenant was what eventually led to Smyth's acceptance of believers' baptism and a view of general atonement.[59] While Brachlow's tracing of the idea of a conditional covenant has merit, his conclusions for Smyth are tenuous.

It is possible that Smyth could have shifted from his Separatist ideal of a mutual covenant to the idea of believers' baptism as being a part of that covenant. This is the focus of Brachlow's argument. He states:

There is sufficient evidence of a shared perspective concerning theology

---

[56]Smyth, *Works* 2:735. "Infants" and "heauen" have been emended.
[57]Underwood, *A History of the English Baptists*, 41; White, "The English Baptists of the Seventeenth Century," 19.
[58]Brachlow, "Puritan Theology and General Baptist Origins," 181-83.
[59]Brachlow, "Puritan Theology and General Baptist Origins," 180.

and ecclesiology between Smyth and his co-religionists within radical Puritanism and Separatism to warrant the conclusion that the logic of Smyth's Baptist convictions was rooted in English nonconformity.[60]

While this may be true, it does not mean that Smyth's movement to general atonement is also clearly connected to the idea of a conditional covenant found in some Puritan and Separatist thought.

In the defense of his views to the Separatists, Smyth does not use the argument of a conditional covenant to persuade them of his new truth. Instead, by the time Smyth rejects His Reformed ideas, covenant has moved from the forefront of his mind. In *Defence of Ries's Confession* where Smyth defends an anti-Reformed position, his mention of covenant has an unconditional not a conditional nature. He says that just as Cain has participated in the sin of Adam, so he also participates in the benefit of Christ. Smyth adds, "this covenant was made with Adam and all his children."[61] It is the redemption of Christ, which is part of God's unconditional covenant that removes the guilt of original sin. Therefore, the two thoughts of conditional covenant and general atonement do not seem to be connected in Smyth's writings. Smyth's belief in a conditional covenant relates to his understanding of the human obligation for faithfulness. Smyth's acceptance of general atonement, however, relates to his understanding of the efficacy of Christ's work and is not based on the condition of human faithfulness.[62]

Lonnie Kliever says that Smyth accepted the Mennonite view of the freedom of the will and rejected his Reformed views after becoming a Mennonite.[63] Kliever attempts to demonstrate that, as Baptists, Smyth and Thomas Helwys held to Reformed views. After Smyth began discussions with the Mennonites, Helwys broke away and produced *Synopsis Fidei* to demonstrate the views of his group in contrast to Smyth's. Kliever uses

---

[60]Brachlow, "Puritan Theology and General Baptist Origins," 189.

[61]Translation by Coggins, *John Smyth's Congregation*, 172. hoc foedus factum est cum Adamo ipsiusque liberis omnibus. Smyth, *Works* 2:685. See chap. 4, above.

[62]See the section on "Unconditional Covenant" in chap, 4 for more discussion.

[63]Lonnie D. Kliever, "General Baptist Origins: The Question of Anabaptist Influence," *Mennonite Quarterly Review* 36 (October 1962): 313.

this confession of Helwys's group as representative of Smyth's beliefs before Mennonite contact. He then compares *Synopsis Fidei* with Smyth's Mennonite works to determine his shift.

The main weakness of Kliever's argument is his use of *Synopsis Fidei* as the representative of Smyth's views before Mennonite influence. There are two significant difficulties with this approach. The first difficulty is that there is a major work of Smyth's available that comes during his Baptist stage before any notable Mennonite influence, *The Character of the Beast*. In this work, Smyth is clear in his support of the doctrines of predestination and original sin. With this work available, Helwys's work is not the best source to determine what Smyth believed before Mennonite influence. While Kliever is correct in pointing out that Smyth does make several theological changes as a result of Mennonite influence, it is insufficient to use *Synopsis Fidei* as his sole source of argument.

The second difficulty is that *Synopsis Fidei* was produced after Smyth's *Corde Credimus*, which was produced as a portion of the dialogue with the Waterlanders. Helwys relied on Smyth's *Corde Credimus* for the structure of his confession and for much of the doctrine espoused in *Synopsis Fidei*.[64] Also, Helwys's confession is not free of direct Mennonite influence. Helwys says in his letters to the Mennonites, which came immediately before and after his production of the confession, that he appreciates the teaching he received from them.[65] He also relays this sentiment in his conclusion to *Synopsis Fidei*:

> And thus through God's mercy, we learned about Christ, in accordance with His word. Therefore, recognizing that we are uneducated and ignorant; and always prepared with all reverence and humility to be

---

[64]Saito gives a detailed comparison of these two confessions to demonstrate Helwys's dependence at this stage on Smyth's Mennonite theology. Goki Saito, "An Investigation into the Relationship between the Early English General Baptists and the Dutch Anabaptists" (Th.D. diss., Southern Baptist Theological Seminary, 1974) 102-109; Pater, *Karlstadt as the Father of the Baptist Movements*, 266-69; Whitley, "Notes" in *Works of John Smyth*, 772; Estep, *The Anabaptist Story*, 291-92; Coggins, *John Smyth's Congregation*, 76, 137.

[65]Burrage, *The Early English Dissenters*, 181, 185-87; Coggins, *John Smyth's Congregation*, 171.

taught by God through instruments of this kind, which our Lord has stirred up for our greater formation in the truth, and blessing God for the excellent means of this kind, which was supplied to us by you; humbly calling upon our Lord Jesus Christ, that he may direct you and us into all truth through His Spirit.[66]

So, for Kliever to present Helwys's view in *Synopsis Fidei* as not being influenced by the Mennonites is a flawed conclusion. Actually, Helwys had been affected by the Mennonites directly through their teaching and indirectly through Smyth.

Michael Watts does not give much detail as to his reasons behind suggesting that the Mennonites had a direct influence on Smyth in this area. He states that the timing of Smyth's rejection of Reformed views is sufficient evidence of Mennonite influence.[67] While Watts is correct in stating that the timing of Smyth's rejection is the most obvious argument for Mennonite influence, there is more evidence that needs analyzing. The timing does not require Mennonite influence. The Arminian controversy in the Netherlands at the time would have brought the arguments for and against the Reformed position to the forefront of every mind. So, it is possible that Smyth had ruminated for years on Peter Baro's ideas, and that the current debate had caused him to rethink his position. Also, it is possible that Smyth became involved in discussions with the Remonstrant debate that was raging around him and was somehow convinced by their argument.

Other scholars do not give a detailed analysis of Smyth's reasons for moving to a view of general atonement. B. R. White says that there is no indication in Smyth's writings or otherwise that indicates why he rejected Reformed beliefs. Yet, he does suggest that Smyth was forced into

---

[66]*Et Sic per dei misericordiam, Christum, secundum eius verbum didicimus: agnoscentes tamen nosipsos simplices et ignaros; et semper paratos cum omni reverentia et humilitate a deo instrui per huiusmodi instrumenta, quae dominus noster excitaverit pro nostra, in veritate, ampliore informatione: et deo benedicentes pro huiusmodi optimis medijs quae a vobis nobis suppeditata sunt: dominum nostrum Iesum Christum suppliciter invocantes, ut vos et nos per spiritum suum in omnem dirigat veritatem.* Burrage, *The Early English Dissenters* 2:184.

[67]Watts, *The Dissenters* 1:46.

choosing sides by the contemporary Arminian debate.[68] Addressing the issue of timing, White notes that Richard Clyfton mentioned in his work, *The Plea for Infants*, that Smyth had just circulated a work that presented two positions: "1. Christs Redemption strecheth to all men. 2. Man hath not lost the facultie of willing any good thing that is shewed him. And with all added thereunto his Reasons in defence thereof."[69] This work was published in 1610, contemporary with Smyth's application to the Mennonites. Most scholars agree that Smyth accepted general atonement sometime after contacting the Mennonites, but before he petitioned them for acceptance into their congregation.[70]

Another argument for Mennonite influence on Smyth's rejection of Reformed beliefs is given by James Coggins. He takes into account several factors. He agrees with Watts that timing is a convincing argument. However, he does not rely on this as the only evidence. He also indicates that the similarities between Smyth's beliefs and the Mennonites' beliefs found in the "Short Confession" of Hans de Ries show some dependence by Smyth. Some similarities that Coggins mentions are the responsibility of humans for their own fate, the relationship of the atonement to prevenient grace, the denial of original sin, and the ability of humans to reject grace.[71]

Coggins also gives reasons why other source theories of Smyth's view of general atonement are not sufficient. The main reason for Baro's not being the source was the considerable time lapse of almost twenty years between Smyth's possible interaction with Baro's ideas and his acceptance of general atonement. Another point that could be added to

---

[68]White, *The English Baptists of the Seventeenth Century*, 19-20; White, *The English Separatist Tradition*, 139.

[69]Clyfton, "An Answer to Mr Smith's Epistle to the Reader," in *The Plea for Infants and Elder People*, n.p.; White, *The English Separatist Tradition Separatist*, 139.

[70]Estep, *The Anabaptist Story*, 291; and Pater, *Karlstadt as the Father of the Baptist Movements*, 263, 267-68. In *A History of the English Baptists*, 40-41, Underwood insists that it does not become clear until Smyth produces *Propositions and Conclusions*.

[71]Coggins, *John Smyth's Congregation*, 140-41. Coggins gives several examples of statements in Smyth's *Corde Credimus* that reflect the thoughts of Ries in his "A Short Confession of Faith."

Coggins's argument is that while at Cambridge, Smyth seems to have been more influenced by William Perkins and Reformed views than by Baro or others who spoke against these views.[72]

Coggins's case against Arminian-Remonstrant influence is that there are significant differences in the way that Smyth's statements against Reformed views are made. He maintains that Smyth and the Remonstrants held different opinions on election, universal atonement, total depravity, resistible grace, and perseverance of the saints.[73] Also, he notes that there is no known historical link between the Remonstrants and John Smyth's group, while the links with the Mennonites are substantial. However, it must be recognized that, had Smyth desired to do so, there were plenty of Arminian publications for him to consult in Amsterdam. Coggins is correct in pointing out that Smyth does not mention making such a consultation.

While the basic line of Coggins's argument seems to be sound, the differences that he notes between Smyth and the Remonstrants may not be as extreme as he proposes. He says that the Remonstrants supported predestination whereas Smyth did not. The Remonstrant position should not be called one of supporting predestination. Arminius had rejected the Reformed idea of predestination. His doctrine of predestination was that God predestined that those who believed in Christ would be justified. Arminius writes in his *Examination of Perkins's Pamphlet on the Order and Mode of Predestination*:

> You confound the two kinds of predestination, and join into one two diverse acts. The predestination by which God decreed to justify and adopt as sons believers in Christ, is not the same with that by which He decreed to bestow faith by certain means upon these and not upon those. For in the latter case the decree is concerning the bestowal of faith; in the former, respecting the justification and adoption of believers.[74]

---

[72]See the earlier section of this chapter, which demonstrates Smyth's Puritan views.

[73]Coggins, *John Smyth's Congregation*, 138-40. Coggins compares Smyth's theology with the "Five Articles of the Remonstrance" (1610), which were produced by Arminius's followers.

[74]*The Works of James Arminius*, vol. 3, ed. and trans. by William Nichols (London: Thomas Baker, 1875) 3:298.

The Remonstrants continued the teaching that God ordained that all who continued in the faith would be saved and those who did not would be damned. This is not significantly different from Smyth's statement in *Propositions and Conclusions* that God had determined the way to salvation to be in Christ and He knew from the foundation of the world who would accept or reject it.[75]

Smyth was also similar to Arminius in that he rejected predestination because he believed that this would make God ultimately responsible for sin. Arminius put it in these terms, "Adam did not fall through the decree of God, neither through being ordained to fall nor through desertion, but through the mere permission of God, which is placed in subordination to no predestination either to salvation or to death, but which belongs to providence so far as it is distinguished in opposition to predestination."[76] Smyth gives the same idea in article 15 of *Propositions and Conclusions* where he says that "Adam sinninge was not moved or inclined therto by god, or by anie decree of god."[77] Smyth and Arminius are in agreement on their rejection of predestination.

In his argument, Coggins says the Remonstrants supported total depravity, while Smyth did not. Although this is roughly the case, it is not that well defined. The Remonstrants said that humans are incapable of drawing themselves to God and therefore need the work of the Holy Spirit.[78] Smyth's statement has a similar tone. When he speaks of regeneration he says, "the father, the word and the holy ghost, immediately worketh that worke in the soule, wher the free will of men cann doe nothing."[79]

On the subject of general atonement, Smyth and the Remonstrants are also closer than Coggins affirms. He contends that the Remonstrant view of general atonement differs in that it maintained that only those who

---

[75]Smyth, *Works* 2:736, 738.

[76]Arminius, *The Works of James Arminius*, vols. 1 and 2, ed. and trans. by James Nichols (London: Longman, Hurst, Rees, Orme, Brown, and Green, 1825–1828) 2:716.

[77]Smyth, *Works* 2:735.

[78]*The Creeds of the Evangelical Protestant Churches*, 3 vols., ed. Philip Schaff (London: Hodder & Stoughton, 1877) 3:546-47.

[79]Smyth, *Works* 2:743.

believed received forgiveness of sins. It is true that Smyth held that Christ's work affected all people, as His death stopped the passage of original sin. However, Smyth's statements do not end there. He states in article 35 of *Propositions and Conclusions*, "the efficacie of Christ[s] death is only deriued to them, which do mortifie ther sinnes."[80] While Christ's work may remove original sin from all, only those who repent of their sins will receive salvation. So, actually Smyth's thought contained some of the same arguments that were used by Arminius. Arminius had argued that Christ had paid the penalty for all sinners, which enabled all to be called to salvation. Even though someone was called, he might not accept the calling, which means that Christ's sacrifice would not be effectual for him. Arminius states, "The lutron or 'price' of the death of Christ is affirmed to be universal in its sufficiency, but particular in its efficacy; that is, sufficient for the redemption of the whole world, and for the expiation of all sins; but that its efficacy does not appertain to all universally; which efficacy consists in its actual application by faith."[81]

Coggins also suggests that there was some ambiguity among the Remonstrants on whether grace was actually resistible or just appeared to be so. Their support of resistible grace may not be stated as extremely as Smyth's, but it is hardly ambiguous. The Remonstrant statement on grace has been summed up in these words, "grace does not force the man to act against his inclination, but may be resisted and rendered ineffectual by the perverse will of the impenitent sinner."[82] The Contra-Remonstrants at the Synod of Dort did not think that the Remonstrants were ambiguous. At the Synod, the Reformed delegates rejected the Remonstrants and their affirmation of resistible grace. The Synod disagreed with the idea that "man nevertheless can so resist God and the Spirit . . . thus it remains in his own power, whether he will be regenerated or not."[83] Earlier Arminius had addressed the subject of free will in his "Certain Articles." There he states:

---

[80]Smyth, *Works* 2:738.
[81]Arminius, *The Works of James Arminius* 3:324.
[82]*The Articles of the Synod of Dort*, ed. Thomas Scott (Harrisonburg VA: Sprinkle Publications, 1993) 160n.
[83]*The Articles of the Synod of Dort*, 312.

> All unregenerate persons have freedom of will, and a capability of resisting the Holy Spirit, of rejecting the proffered grace of God, of despising the counsel of God against themselves, of refusing to accept the Gospel of grace, and of not opening to Him who knocks at the door of the heart.[84]

The Arminian-Remonstrant view of resistible grace is very similar to Smyth who says that God "created man with freedome of will, so that he had habilitie to chuse the good, and eschew the evil, or to chuse the evil, and refuse the good."[85]

There are several similarities between Smyth's views and Arminian-Remonstrant views. However, this does not hold true in their respective views of original sin. Arminius is clear in his support of the passage of some measure of original sin. He does not support the Reformed view of original sin, but instead refers to original sin as the "absence of original righteousness."[86] In his reaction to Perkins's work, Arminius says that infants whose ancestors have rejected grace, have participated in the rejection of their predecessors. In this discussion, he affirms "all his posterity have sinned in Adam, and thereby have merited punishment and desertion."[87] Smyth rejects any view that supports the passage of original sin, no matter the description of original sin. He states plainly, "That original sin is an idle terme, and that ther is no such thing as men intend by the word."[88] He argues that no one is condemned because of someone else's sin. This includes infants not being condemned on account of the sins of their parents.[89]

Though Coggins may have overestimated the distance between several of Smyth's views and the Remonstrants' views, it is still correct to say that the Remonstrants are not the most likely source for Smyth's view of general atonement. The main reason for this is the significant difference between the Arminian- Remonstrant position and Smyth's position on original sin. Arminius devotes his effort to debating the

---

[84] Arminius, *The Works of James Arminius* 2:721.
[85] Smyth, *Works* 2:734.
[86] Arminius, *The Works of James Arminius* 2:375, 717.
[87] Arminius, *The Works of James Arminius* 3:344-45.
[88] Smyth, *Works* 2:735, 725.
[89] Smyth, *Works* 2:725, 728.

Reformed views of election, predestination, and limited atonement. When he does mention original sin, he supports the idea. Conversely, Smyth discusses his complete rejection of original sin in several works. He indicates his rejection of original sin in *Defence of Ries's Confession*, and focuses on this rejection in portions of *Corde Credimus, Argumenta Contra Baptismum Infantum,* and *Propositions and Conclusions*. This significant difference, along with other slight variations, is sufficient to cast doubt on Arminian influence on Smyth.[90] This is especially true when Smyth's similarities with the Mennonites are noted.

There is some further evidence that can be added to what scholars have given to support the theory of Mennonite influence on Smyth in this area of thought. The evidence that has been given by Coggins lies in the doctrinal similarities between Mennonite doctrine and Smyth's *Corde Credimus*. Since Smyth is presenting *Corde Credimus* to gain Mennonite approval for his application for union, he may have purposely used their terms in presenting his ideas. If Mennonite doctrine could be found in Smyth's other writings such as *Propositions and Conclusions*, then the case for Mennonite influence would be enhanced. The later work is his attempt to explain his beliefs to an English audience, therefore, he would most likely use phrases that would be familiar to that audience. Any similarity in language between Smyth and the Mennonites in this confession could verify his dependence on the latter for the development of his ideas.

There is one similarity that apparently Coggins overlooks between the doctrine of Ries and that of Smyth's congregation expressed in this English confession. When he is describing the similarities of Ries's "Short Confession" with those of Smyth's doctrine, Coggins says that Ries's confession "upheld the foreknowledge of God, which was not mentioned in the Smyth congregation's confessions."[91] Actually, Smyth's congregation did support the foreknowledge of God. In article 26 of *Propositions and Conclusions*, Smyth writes, "That god before the foundation of the world, hath determined the way of life and saluation to

---

[90]Another possible argument is that Smyth does not seem to have any connections with the merchant class of Amsterdam, with whom Arminian thought was most prevalent.

[91]Coggins, *John Smyth's Congregation*, 140.

consist in Christ, and that he hath foreseen who would follow it."[92] However, Smyth's beliefs were that this foreknowledge did not impose necessity on humans.[93] In the article immediately preceding, Smyth had affirmed that God does not predestine anyone to destruction. In article 7 of his confession, Ries relates the two thoughts. In that article he says that while God has not predestined anyone, he has known from the foundation of the world who would follow his appointed plan of salvation in Christ.[94]

Other similarities between Ries's confession and Smyth's English confession, *Propositions and Conclusions*, which have not been appreciated by other scholars, are their arguments for general atonement. Both Smyth and Ries believed that God's goodness in his redemption would be as great and as far reaching as his goodness in creation.[95] If God had created all humans good and in His image, surely His redemption would reach all humans. As God created humans in innocence, His redemption would place them back in that position. So, all people are in a state of innocence until they choose to sin.

Both confessions give straightforward statements on the free will of humans. Smyth says, "That god created man with freedome of will."[96] Humans can choose good or evil. Ries likewise makes the statement that "Man being created good" would have the "free powre to the choise of evill" and the "free powre to the choise of good."[97] It is noticeable how Smyth used similar phrasing to express his ideas. There is enough similarity between Smyth's *Propositions and Conclusions*, published in 1612, and Ries's confession, published in 1610, to conclude that his doctrine could have come from the Mennonites. However, the strongest substantiation still lies in Smyth's *Corde Credimus*, presented in 1610,

---

[92]Smyth, *Works* 2:736. "Foundation" has been emended.

[93]Smyth, *Works* 2:695, 736.

[94]Burrage, *The Early English Dissenters* 2:189. Quotations from the "A Short Confession of Faith" in this section are taken from Smyth's translation of the original thirty-eight articles version found in Burrage, *The Early English Dissenters* 2:188-99, not the later version of forty articles, which has been translated by Cornelius J. Dyck.

[95]Smyth, *Works* 2:736 and Burrage, *The Early English Dissenters* 2:188.

[96]Smyth, *Works* 2:734.

[97]Burrage, *The Early English Dissenters* 2:188-89.

compared with Ries's "Short Confession."

In Coggins's attempt to prove Mennonite influence, he offers several similarities in the way that Smyth phrases his rejection of Reformed views and the way the Mennonite doctrine is expressed in Hans de Ries's "A Short Confession of Faith." After briefly stating some of the similarities between Smyth's *Corde Credimus* and Ries's confession, Coggins states, "Such similarity cannot be an accident. The Smyth congregation clearly derived their 'Arminian' position from the Mennonites."[98] While Coggins is correct in this statement, he does not give any explanation of how Smyth was influenced to accept the Mennonite position. Also, we can see that there are possibly even stronger connections than Coggins or others indicate between the views that Smyth expresses in his *Corde Credimus* and the views of Ries's confession. It is likely that Smyth had his translated version of Ries's confession in mind as he expressed the views of his congregation in *Corde Credimus*. In fact, Smyth used Ries's confession as a pattern for his congregation's confession.

The purpose of Smyth drawing up his *Corde Credimus* was to offer an official expression of the doctrine of his congregation. This would facilitate their application for membership being approved by the Waterlanders and the other members of *Bevredigde Broederschap*. Smyth had been convinced of general atonement in the interaction that he had with the Mennonites. In trying to demonstrate to the Mennonite brotherhood his similarity with them, it could be that he purposely chose to use the language and structure of Ries's confession. Perhaps, Smyth was convinced by Ries's confession of some doctrines that he had been considering. Whatever his reasons, Smyth held the confession in high regard. This is evidenced by him and his congregation signing it, and by his detailed defense of it in his *Defence of Ries's Confession*.

The similarity of doctrine between Smyth's confession and Ries's confession could be illustrative of the direct connection between the two works, though the most convincing argument is the structure of Smyth's confession. The events could have happened in this order. After receiving some instruction from the Mennonites, Smyth was convinced of the impropriety of his self-baptism and submitted an application for

---

[98]Coggins, *John Smyth's Congregation*, 141.

membership in the Mennonite congregation that was signed by thirty-two members of his congregation.[99] To help explain Mennonite doctrine further and to give the groups a common document on which to agree, Ries, with Lubbert assistance, produced the "Short Confession" in thirty-eight articles. Smyth translated this confession into English for his congregation's use. To demonstrate their acceptance of Mennonite doctrine, Smyth's group produced *Corde Credimus* using the "Short Confession" as a guideline. Once this was presented to the Mennonites, negotiations resumed. Then, Ries edited his confession, adding articles 19 and 22 bringing the total to forty. As negotiations were stalled by the other Mennonite congregations, a Reformed critic attacked Ries's confession. Smyth, who supported Ries's document, wrote a defense of the confession including comments on the two added articles.

Both his *Corde Credimus* and his *Defence of Ries's Confession* substantiate the claim that Smyth's rejection of Reformed views comes through Mennonite influence. More specifically, Smyth's expression of this doctrine in *Corde Credimus* comes from the direct influence of Hans de Ries through his "Short Confession." The structure of Smyth's *Corde Credimus* and Ries's "Short Confession" are strikingly similar. Like many confessions, both of these documents begin with statements referring to the Trinity. After affirming the Trinity, both confessions state that God created all humans for salvation and through his redemption all humans are given the opportunity to obtain salvation.[100]

The next six ideas vary slightly in order in the two works, but are still remarkably similar. Smyth presents the idea that God does not force sin on anyone, but all humans "by Satanic instigation" choose it. Next, he states that Christ has come and replaced the law, which was impossible to fulfill. Third, he denies original sin. Fourth, Smyth makes a statement on incarnation declaring that, "Jesus Christ is true God and true man . . . the Son of God." Fifth, he describes Jesus' earthly ministry as leading toward him being declared King, Priest, and Prophet of the Church. Finally, Smyth declares that through the grace of God all humans

---

[99]Smyth, *Works* 2:681 and Burrage, *The Early English Dissenters* 2:178.
[100]Evans, *The Early English Baptists* 1:253, Burrage, *The Early English Dissenters* 2:188.

may either accept or reject God.[101]

In Ries's confession, the same six ideas are expressed together, but in a slightly different order. First, Ries addresses the idea that the grace of God has preserved the choice of humans to accept or reject God.[102] Second, he says that God does not cause sin to happen, but evil humans with "the spiritt of wickedness" within them choose it.[103] Third, he rejects predestination and original sin.[104] Fourth, Ries gives his statement on the incarnation describing Christ as "true god, & man . . . sonne of the living god." Fifth, he declares that Christ came to earth and should be honored as "Mediator, prophet, priest, and king, a lawgiver and teacher." Finally, Ries states that Jesus came and fulfilled figures of the Old Testament, removing the "intollerable burthen of the law of Moses."[105]

After Ries's further description of Christ's work as King, Priest, and Prophet, the two confessions return to a similar order. Smyth offers article 10 as an explanation of faith and justification. Ries includes two articles describing saving faith and justification, respectively.[106] Both confessions then include statements of the nature of good works and faith followed by statements that the true church consists of the faithful only.[107] In the next section both confessions include a proper definition of ministry and a description of the work of ministers including the sacraments.[108] Baptism and the Lord's Supper are described in both confessions as being "outward" or "external" signs of inner events. Continuing the idea of the church's ministry, both confessions then include statements on excommunication and avoidance. [109]Finally, both confes-

---

[101]Translation by Evans, *The Early English Baptists* 1:253. *Jesum Christum esse verum Deum et verum hominem . . . filio dei.* Smyth, *Works* 2:682-83.
[102]Burrage, *The Early English Dissenters* 2:188-89.
[103]Burrage, *The Early English Dissenters* 2:189.
[104]Burrage, *The Early English Dissenters* 2:189-90.
[105]Burrage, *The Early English Dissenters* 2:190.
[106]Evans, *The Early English Baptists* 1:253, and Burrage, *The Early English Dissenters* 2:193, respectively.
[107]Evans, *The Early English Baptists* 1:253-54, Burrage, *The Early English Dissenters* 2:193-94.
[108]Evans, *The Early English Baptists* 1:254, Burrage, *The Early English Dissenters* 2:194-96.
[109]Evans, *The Early English Baptists* 1:254, Burrage, *The Early English*

sions end with descriptions of eschatological events such as bodily resurrection and the judgment of Christ.[110]

The similarity in language and structure, along with the doctrinal commonalty that Coggins points out, are strong evidence that Smyth owed much of the development of his view of a general atonement to Ries. With Ries as his source for this doctrine, he would have had no qualms about using Ries's confession to help him express his ideas. Although many of the General Baptists that would succeed him may have adjusted their doctrines because of other influences, Smyth developed his belief in a general atonement from the direct influence of Hans de Ries and other Mennonites.

Reason for Smyth's Views

Another issue of interest in Smyth's Mennonite views is whether his acceptance of some doctrine precipitated his rejection of Reformed views. As we have seen, Stephen Brachlow suggests that it was Smyth's belief in a conditional covenant that moved him in the direction of rejecting Reformed views. The major problem with this supposition is that the ideas do not appear to be related in Smyth's thought. He does not use the conditional covenant as the basis of his arguments against the Reformed position.

James Coggins suggests another possible connection between two aspects of Smyth's theology. Coggins relates Smyth's rejection of Reformed beliefs to the despotism of the English Stuart monarchy. Coggins states, "the driving force behind the Smyth congregation's movement to a free-will position may thus have been mainly emotional and experiential."[111] The main experiential force that Coggins cites is the rejection of the godly prince myth by the Puritans and other Englishmen. He says that the connection between an unjust king who rules with arbitrary authority and a God who chooses people indiscriminately for damnation was too much for Smyth. Coggins suggests that Smyth's rejection of a Christian magistracy motivates his rejection of Reformed

---

Dissenters 2:195, 197.

[110]Evans, *The Early English Baptists* 1:254, Burrage, *The Early English Dissenters* 2:199.

[111]Coggins, *John Smyth's Congregation*, 144.

views, as if, the rejection of God's predestination and the rejection of the ecclesiastical authority of magistrates were two results of the same experience of an oppressive magistrate.[112] However, rejecting Reformed views is more fundamental than the rejection of a Christian magistracy for Smyth. His explanation of anti-Reformed views receives much more attention than his description of the relationship between church and state.

To gain more insight into Smyth's reason for rejecting his Reformed views, his articles in *Corde Credimus* must be reviewed thoroughly. Chronologically, this confession comes before his other Mennonite works, which give fuller descriptions of these views. Also, it appears from the rudimentary nature of these statements that Smyth's ideas are still in the embryonic stages of development. In this confession, which comes early in Smyth's Mennonite stage, there is no mention of church and state relations. In fact, the article on government is the most notable omission from *Corde Credimus* in comparison with Ries's confession. Therefore, Smyth had probably not come to full agreement with Ries and the other Mennonites on the rejection of the Christian magistracy. In which case this doctrine could not be the basis of Smyth's rejection of Reformed views, which does appear in *Corde Credimus*.[113]

With the noted shortcomings in the views of Brachlow and Coggins, an alternative view of Smyth's reasoning for accepting general atonement is needed. In *Corde Credimus*, Smyth states in article 2 "That God has created and redeemed the human race to his own image, and has ordained all men (no one being reprobated) to life."[114] Smyth was convinced that God's goodness and mercy shown in redemption were equal to that shown in his creation. Just as God had created humans in innocence, the "redemption of Christ" by God's "good pleasure" would restore that innocence and make salvation available to all. Humans could forsake this offer of salvation, and turn away from their restored innocence.[115] The restoration of innocence and preservation of free will through Christ's

---

[112]Coggins, *John Smyth's Congregation*, 142-44.
[113]See chap. 7 for more discussion of Smyth's Mennonite views of church and state.
[114]Translation by Evans, *The Early English Baptists* 1:253. *Deum creasse et redemisse genus humanum ad imaginem suam, omnesque homines (nemine reprobato) ad vitam predestinasse*. Smyth, *Works* 2:682.
[115]Articles 3, 4, and 5, Smyth, *Works* 2:682.

general atonement then becomes a common theme for Smyth throughout his Mennonite stage.

In his *Defence of Ries's Confession*, Smyth claims that, if the atonement of Christ is limited, then his work of redemption is severely marred. He says that Christ's redemption surpasses Adam's sin in "dignitate et amplitudine."[116] One significant benefit of this general redemption is that the free will of every human is preserved.[117] In his *Argumenta Contra Baptismum Infantum*, Smyth continues this idea of Christ's redemption being as universal as his creation. However, in this work, the central benefit of general atonement that he focuses on is the cessation of original sin. Smyth concentrates on this benefit because it is a major argument for Smyth as a Mennonite against infant baptism. He contends that the guilt of original sin does not exist because of the precedence of Christ's death. He states, "Christ's death forestalled original sin, so it is not passed on to Adam's posterity."[118] In other places in this work, Smyth argues that if the guilt of original sin existed, Christ's atonement stopped the "cursus" and "fluxus" of original sin.[119]

In *Propositions and Conclusions*, Smyth reiterates the primacy of Christ's redemption. Again, he demonstrates how Christ's death thwarts original sin. He states, "That if original sinne might haue passed from Adam to his posteritie, Christs death, which was effectuall before Caine and Abells birth he being the lambe slaine from the begininge of the world, stopped the issue and passage therof."[120] Smyth also continues his parallel between creation and redemption. He adds, "That as god created all men according to his image, so hath he redeemed all that fall by actuall sinne, to the same end: and that God in his redemption hath not swerved from his mercie, which he manifested in his creation."[121] Smyth indicates that redemption is not simply the restoration of original innocence but a return to the image of God. He says that even those that have participated in sin are in God's image. Creation and redemption

---

[116] Smyth, *Works* 2:686.

[117] Smyth, *Works* 2:689.

[118] *mors Christi prevenit peccatum originale ne transiret per traducem ad posteros Adae.* Smyth, *Works* 2:715.

[119] Smyth, *Works* 2:728.

[120] Smyth, *Works* 2:735.

[121] Smyth, *Works* 2:736. "Redemption" has been emended.

have the same result: humans who are in God's image.

So, what is the catalyst for Smyth's acceptance of general atonement and consequently for his rejection of Reformed views? Because of Hans de Ries's influence, Smyth became convinced that Reformed doctrine wrongly placed the responsibility for sin upon God through His predestination. Smyth was convinced that God had made it so that all responsibility for sin was down to human choice. Through Christ's atonement, each individual has the free choice to accept or reject God and His goodness. Therefore, all who are eternally condemned are in that state because of their personal decision.

Smyth makes several statements to demonstrate God's gracious retention of humans' personal responsibility. In *Corde Credimus*, he says, "That God imposes no necessity of sinning on any one; but man freely . . . departs from God." He adds:

> That men, of the grace of God through the redemption of Christ, are able . . . to repent . . . and to attain to eternal life; so on the other hand, they are able themselves to resist the Holy Spirit, to depart from God, and to perish for ever.[122]

In *Argumenta Contra Baptismum Infantum*, Smyth shows this responsibility by saying, "Christ does not save infants from their own sins, but impedes and restrains from infants the sin of someone else."[123]

God should not be connected in any way with humans' choice to sin. This idea becomes a major theme in Smyth's *Propositions and Conclusions* and in his *Defence of Ries's Confession*. In the former, Smyth states plainly, "That god is not the Author or worker of sinne . . . but that god only did foresee . . . what euil the free will of men and angels would doe: but he gave no influence, instinct, motion or inclination to the least sinne."[124] This thought is carried throughout the confession. Smyth's other

---

[122]Translation by Evans, *The Early English Baptists* 1:253. *Deum, nullam peccandi necessitatem cuiquam imponere, sed hominem libere . . . a deo deficere.* Smyth, *Works* 2:682. *Homines ex dei gratia per Christi redemptionem posse . . . resipiscere . . . et vitam eternam adipisci: sicut e contrâ, posse ipsos spiritui sancto resistere, á deo deficere, et in eternum perire.*" Smyth, *Works* 2:683.

[123]*Christus non servat infantes a peccatis suis, sed impedit et prohibet ab infantibus peccatum unum alterius.* Smyth, *Works* 2:728.

[124]Smyth, *Works* 2:734.

statements include that God created humans' free will and that Adam's sin was not the result of any design or decree of God. After his sin, Adam still retained his free will because his sin could not undermine the creation of God.[125] Through the work of Christ, God stopped the passage of original sin. Therefore, God does not reject anyone unless they remain unrepentant in their sins.

In *Defence of Ries's Confession*, Smyth makes his strongest statements to exonerate God from any involvement in human sin. He argues that if God had predestined some humans to damnation, then He has imposed the necessity of choosing evil. Smyth said if this was the case, then those who were condemned could say

> [God] deceived us; He said He was willing for us to be saved; the truth was not there in His heart; He hates us from eternity; God through His predestination placed us lower than the stork, the swallow, the dove [and] the crane; therefore, God cannot lament concerning us but mocks us wretched puppets.[126]

In his defense of another article, Smyth adds:

> If He makes the will of man to be inclined to evil through unavoidable and effectual decree, He effectively brings about evil itself. This is so wicked and blasphemous that the soul shudders to think [it].[127]

Smyth argues that the Reformed doctrine sets up a God who is spiteful and vindictive. He says that the Reformed position makes God to be a "most savage murderer who destines countless still innocent creatures to eternal torture."[128] A few paragraphs later, Smyth gives an elaborate

---

[125]Smyth, *Works* 2:734. Articles 14, 15, and 17, respectively.

[126]Translation by Coggins, *John Smyth's Congregation*, 178. *decepit nos deus, dixit se velle nos salvos fore, verum non erat illi in animo, ab eterno odit nos: deus nos per ipsius predestinationem ciconiae, hirundini, palumbi, grui postposuit, non ergo potest deus de nobis conqueri, sed irridet nos miseros homunciones.* Smyth, *Works* 2:691.

[127]Translation by Coggins, *John Smyth's Congregation*, 179. *Si hominis voluntatem in malum propendere facit per ipsius inevitabile et efficax decretum, ipsum malum agit efficaciter.* Smyth, *Works* 2:693.

[128]Translation by Coggins, *John Smyth's Congregation*, 180. *crudelissimum homicidam qui creaturas innumeras etiam innocentissimas eternis cruciatibus*

comparison between the Reformed portrayal of God and the Mennonite portrayal. He writes:

> The former is primarily a judge, never a father to the damned; ours is primarily a father, secondarily a judge. The former first pronounces a sentence of death against the innocent, then mocks the accused and tries his case for sport; ours first longs from the heart to benefit the criminal, treats the matter seriously [and] at last reluctantly punishes the [one who] perseveres in sins. The former is the god of the Reformed; the latter is ours.[129]

In all of Smyth's Mennonite works, his rejection of Reformed views is driven by his desire to portray a God who loves all humans and longs to grant salvation to each person. The atonement of Christ brings all humanity the "universal benefit imparted to everyone, in that they can receive offered grace."[130] So, the catalyst for Smyth's change is a new understanding of the extensiveness of God's love.

Debate with the Separatists

Smyth's acceptance of general atonement sparked a debate between him and his followers and the Separatists. Richard Clyfton seems to be the first Separatist to put his reaction to Smyth's attacks on Reformed views in print. In 1610, he says that even though Smyth may not be guilty of accepting the Mennonite incarnational theory, he has accepted the erroneous Mennonite doctrines of general redemption and free will. Clyfton also writes that Smyth had just produced a defense of general

---

destinavit. Smyth, *Works* 2:694.

[129] Translation by Coggins, *John Smyth's Congregation*, 180. *ille primo judex est, nusquam pater reproborum: noster primo pater est, post judex: ille primo contra innocentem sententiam mortis pronuntiat, deinde reum deridet ejusque caussam ludicro inquirit: noster primo (sonti) ex animo cupit benefacere, serio rem tractat: tandem in peccatis perseverantem tardus punit. Ille deus est reformatorum, his noster deus est.* Smyth, *Works* 2:694.

[130] Translation by Coggins, *John Smyth's Congregation*, 181. *universale . . . beneficium unicuique communicatum quo possunt gratiam oblatam recipere.* Smyth, *Works* 2:695.

atonement in two positions.[131]

Francis Johnson also responded to Smyth's anti-Reformed position in 1617 in *A Christian Plea*. Johnson addresses his response to any who advocate the beliefs of general atonement or free will. He promotes a view of limited atonement. He writes:

> Christ by his death hath redemed those only, for whom the Lords pleasure prospereth in his hand: whom also he maketh to be his seed. . . . Otherwise also we should extend the redemption of Christ, further then God himself (who gave him to death for us) intended it: and contrarie to the Scriptures, which apply it onely to some, and not to all and everie one in the world whosover.[132]

Johnson also argues that Smyth was in error in holding to a position of free will. He declares that Adam and Eve had been created in innocence, but this innocence was lost after they chose sin. He says: "They, before they fell, had freedome of will and abilitie unto good. But when once they had transgressed, al pronenes to evil was found in them: but free will and power unto good, now they had not."[133] Not only did Adam and Eve lose their ability to choose good, but their sin also caused this faculty to be absent from all their descendants.

John Robinson was another Separatist who opposed the anti-Reformed views of Smyth. In 1613, he published his *On Religious Communion, Private and Public*, which was a collection of essays on different subjects. The final essay in this publication was Robinson's detailed dispute of the doctrine propounded by Smyth in his *Propositions and Conclusions*. Robinson's style was either to summarize or to quote Smyth's article and then to present his arguments against its position.

Smyth had argued in article 10 of *Propositions and Conclusions* that God "did foresee and determine what euil the free will of men and angels would doe: but he gave no influence, instinct, motion or inclination to the least sinne."[134] Robinson said this portion of the article was "derogatory

---

[131]Clyfton, "An Answer to Mr Smith's Epistle to the Reader" in *The Plea for Infants and Elder People*, n.p.
[132]Johnson, *A Christian* Plea, 231.
[133]Johnson, *A Christian Plea*, 234.
[134]Smyth, *Works* 2:734.

to the infiniteness of God's power, and wisdom."[135] God had permitted human sin and used it to bring about His purpose. Therefore, Robinson writes:

> And thus sin, though it be always against the decrees of the commanding, approving, and effecting will of God, yet is not at all against his permitting will, or against that decree of manifestation of that one in itself, and simple will of God: neither is it wrought, he absolutely nilling it. For he being in heaven doth whatsoever he pleaseth.[136]

It was this type of seemingly arbitrary commanding by God that Smyth saw as contrary to his view of a loving Creator.

Robinson continues in his critique of Smyth's confession by saying that the freedom of the will that Smyth defends in article 17 is "untrue." He says that there is some freedom of the will that remained in Adam because without this essential characteristic he would have ceased to be human. However, Robinson argues that the free will, which was able to choose good before Adam's fall, was corrupted so that it could not desire the good. He tries to reverse Smyth's logic of sin not destroying God's creation by saying, "It is true then, that sin destroyeth not the natural powers, or parts of soul, or body, but only corrupteth, infecteth, and disordereth them."[137]

Articles 18 and 19 of Smyth's confession drew extensive comments from Robinson. Smyth's comments were that "original sin is an idle terme" and God had threatened death only to Adam "not to his posterite and bicause god created the soule Heb. 12. 9." The latter article includes the statement that if original sin could have been passed, then Christ's death "stopped the issue and passage therof."[138] Robinson's attack begins with his rebuttal of the immediate creation of every soul. He contends that an individual's soul comes as a natural result of the procreative process. When Adam had children in his image, they did not just receive their bodies from their father, but their souls as well. Robinson also gives numerous proof texts to demonstrate the presence of original sin in

---

[135] Robinson, *The Works of John Robinson* 3:239.
[136] Robinson, *The Works of John Robinson* 3:241.
[137] Robinson, *The Works of John Robinson* 3:245-46.
[138] Smyth, *Works* 2:735.

humans. He also gives his solution to the dilemma pointed out by Smyth. Robinson states:

> And if these two positions cannot stand together, that God createth the soul immediately; and that there is original sin: where these men conclude, that there is therefore no original sin, I conclude, contrariwise, that therefore, the soul is not immediately created, nor the place in the Hebrews, so to be expounded; since the proofs for original sin are so certain, and evident.[139]

Robinson's evidence for the presence of original sin then moves to a more practical level. He says that experience confirms that children do not have to be taught to lie or to be selfish. These behaviors develop naturally as the result of original sin.[140] He goes on to conclude that none of Adam's "naturally conceived posterity bear the image of his innocency."[141]

There is no hesitation on Robinson's part to uphold the doctrine of predestination. Smyth argued that God loves humans as a father does his children and therefore does not "create or predestinate anie man to destruction."[142] Robinson contradicts Smyth by saying that "God hath from eternity decreed the condemnation of some for sin, fore-purposed by him to be suffered." He also writes, "God's very doing a thing, in time, is an unanswerable proof that he purposed the same thing, before time and from eternity."[143] He held that other than scripture, the strongest proof that God designed some humans for condemnation was that he withheld from Adam the grace that would have removed the temptation to sin.

God not only has determined that Christ would be the path to salvation but also has foreseen who would follow it. Robinson adds that God "hath also determined, in particular, whom he would effectually call to the participation of that grace."[144] According to Robinson, God knows who will accept salvation, because He knows whom He will call through

---

[139]Robinson, *The Works of John Robinson* 3:248.
[140]Robinson, *The Works of John Robinson* 3:249-50.
[141]Robinson, *The Works of John Robinson* 3:253.
[142]Smyth, *Works* 2:736.
[143]Robinson, *The Works of John Robinson* 3:255-56.
[144]Robinson, *The Works of John Robinson* 3:257-58.

His grace. The whole matter of salvation rests on the good and gracious pleasure of God.

Robinson disagrees with Smyth's contention that if God has not removed original sin then his grace of redemption is less than His grace of creation. He remarks, "It is no swerving at all of God's goodness, if he extend not the grace of redemption to as many as he did the grace of creation."[145] He contends that if this was the case, then Christ should have redeemed the angels as well. Christ's redemption does not affect all creation. Robinson points out that even Smyth recognizes that only those who repent of their sins receive the full benefit of Christ's redemption. However, Robinson holds that Smyth does not go far enough; instead he holds that for "whomsoever Christ did indeed and effectually die, they should certainly be saved; and that, whomsoever God did reconcile by his death, he will much more save by his life."[146] This argument will resurface as Robinson discusses the doctrine of perseverance.

On the basis of his interpretation of Romans 5, Robinson makes two conclusions. They are: "1. That Christ did not effectually die for, or reconcile, by his death all men in particular: for then all should be saved by his life: and 2ndly, That whomsoever he so died for, and effectually reconciled, they shall be kept by the power of God, and of his grace, unto eternal life."[147] So, Robinson sees the limited atonement relating to the perseverance of the saints. Christ's death has its effect on those who are of the elect. This effect is to remove the guilt of their sins and to give them eternal life, which cannot be lost. Robinson ends the discussion of these articles of Smyth's confession by stating, "To conclude this point, they who either hold, that Christ effectually redeemed all from their natural corruption, or, that any truly justified and sanctified, may wholly fall away and perish, do divide Christ from himself."[148] Robinson believes that these divisions would leave Christ as only a partial Savior of people. He would have saved them from original sin, but not actual sin. Alternatively, he would have saved them from original sin and actual sin, but only until they turned from grace. Robinson holds that Christ's

---

[145]Robinson, *The Works of John Robinson* 3:258-59.
[146]Robinson, *The Works of John Robinson* 3:261.
[147]Robinson, *The Works of John Robinson* 3:262.
[148]Robinson, *The Works of John Robinson* 3:263.

salvation is more definite than this. He writes, "All who have any part in Christ, are in Christ, and so free from condemnation."[149]

Robinson intended for his comments to be a rebuke of not only Smyth's writings but also of any who held similar opinions.[150] Most of Smyth's followers had moved with him to his anti-Reformed beliefs. John Murton was a member of Smyth's congregation who had come with the group to Amsterdam from Gainsborough. He had been among the original group baptized by Smyth. However, he sided with Thomas Helwys when Smyth wavered on the validity of their baptism. Murton accompanied Helwys back to England in 1612 and succeeded him as pastor of the congregation upon Helwys's death. In 1620, Murton published *A Description of what God hath predestinated*, which defended general atonement and free will and which opposed predestination and original sin. Murton's views show close similarity with Smyth's in these areas.

Henry Ainsworth took Murton's publication as an opportunity to attack his views and the views that Smyth had defended in *Propositions and Conclusions*. Ainsworth published *A Censure of a Dialogue*, as his defense of a Reformed position. His style of argument was to take the points made by Murton in *A Description of what God hath predestined* and to debate them one by one. In the area of free will, Ainsworth argues on the same lines as Robinson does. He argues that human will is not destroyed completely, but it cannot choose good until it has been regenerated by Christ. He writes:

> As for will in man, we know it to be a natural facultie, still remaining, though corrupted by sin, as all other like faculties in us. We acknowledge it still to be free from compulsion or constreynt, for so will should be no will. But we confesse with greife that in respect of bondage to sinne . . . it may rather be called Bond-will then Free will: for it is not free to refuse sin, untill it be renued by Christ . . . freed by grace, and willeth things that are good.[151]

Ainsworth had written this in response to Murton's statements which

---

[149] Robinson, *The Works of John Robinson* 3:264.

[150] Timothy George, *John Robinson and the Separatist Tradition*, NABPR/DS 1 (Macon GA: Mercer University Press, 1982) 214.

[151] Henry Ainsworth, *A Censure upon a dialogue of the Anabaptists* (Amsterdam: Giles Thorp, 1623) 26.

echoed Smyth's idea that if human free will was lost through Adam's sin, then it was restored through Christ's atonement. Murton writes, "I say, that what Adam had in creation, and lost by transgression, for himselfe and his posterity, that is restored through Christ, yea and more too: for although of ourselves we can doe nothing as of ourselves that good is, yet through the strength of Christ we shall bee able to doe all things."[152]

Smyth held that infants were innocent because they had not yet willfully chosen sin. Ainsworth disagreed with Smyth on this point. He used a simple argument of nature to show that indeed infants were participants in a sinful nature. He believed that death was one resulting punishment for sin. He says, "And by infants death, we certainly conclude that they are sinners."[153]

This debate continued between Smyth's successors and their Reformed opponents for several decades. Even when a separate group of English Baptists arose in the mid-seventeenth century, the relationship was strained over this doctrine. Smyth's descendants, the General Baptists, continued their support of general atonement. The latter group, the Particular Baptists, held to the Reformed doctrine of their semi-Separatist origins.[154]

Conclusion

Smyth's acceptance of the Mennonite view of general atonement was a significant shift in his theology. This shift was due to the influence of the Waterlander Mennonites. More specifically, the "Short Confession" of Hans de Ries played a central role in Smyth's rejection of his Reformed roots. Through the influence of Ries and the Mennonites, Smyth became convinced that the Reformed doctrine of predestination put the responsibility on God for sin and eternal condemnation. Instead Smyth believed that through Christ's atonement human free will and original innocence

---

[152] John Murton, *A Description of what God hath Predestinated* (London: n.p., 1620) 107.

[153] Ainsworth, *A Censure upon a Dialogue of the Anabaptists*, 41.

[154] For more information on the relationships between these two Baptist groups see B. R. White, *The English Baptists of the Seventeenth Century*, 19-24. Also, see B. R. White, "Frontiers of Fellowship between English Baptists, 1609–1660," *Foundations* 11 (July-September 1968): 244-56.

was preserved. Humans could freely choose or reject God's offer of salvation. Smyth held that his view retained the goodness of God in His redemption as well as His creation.

Smyth's rejection of Reformed views put him at odds with the Separatist tradition from which he came. Many Separatists engaged him and his followers in debate over this doctrine. After some of Smyth's followers separated from his congregation and migrated back to England, they would be isolated even from other Baptists over this controversial issue.

Chapter 6
Smyth's View of Christ

John Smyth's Christology plays an important role in many areas of his thought. In the preceding chapters, we have seen the impact his view of Christ had on his typology, his view of the covenant, and his understanding of atonement and original sin. Smyth's understanding of authority in the church is also impacted by his Christological views.

As Smyth began discussions with the Mennonites, he began to answer charges that he had accepted their Christology. This had been a source of great disagreement between the Reformed and the Anabaptists since early in the sixteenth century. The unusual brand of Christology, with its peculiar incarnational view, traces back to Melchior Hofmann and Caspar Schwenckfeld. The Christology in question began with Hofmann and Schwenckfeld, and continued through Menno Simons and Dirk Philips. Smyth's contemporary, Hans de Ries, made concessions to this Christology. Also, Smyth's Christology experiences much transition from the views he held in his early career to his views once he came in contact with the Mennonites.

Mennonite Christology and the Incarnation

Melchior Hofmann's Christology was to leave a lasting impression on the Dutch Mennonite tradition. He developed some of his incarnational ideas under the influence of Caspar Schwenckfeld. Under the leadership of Menno Simons and Dirk Philips, his Christology became well-established among the Mennonites. Although not all of their descendants followed their lead, many such as Hans de Ries utilized aspects of this Christology in the doctrine of the later Mennonites.

The views of Melchior Hofmann and Caspar Schwenckfeld. At the center of the controversy over Melchior Hofmann's Christology is his incarnational view. He taught that Christ brought his flesh with him from heaven and is born of Mary without her playing any fundamental role in his birth.[1] Unless Christ's flesh is of a divine nature, then he cannot be

---

[1] Snyder, *Anabaptist History and Theology*, 357.

the perfect sacrifice required for forgiveness.² Christ does not take his flesh from Mary because her flesh carries the guilt of original sin.

Caspar Schwenckfeld holds similar views in regard to Christ's flesh originating in heaven. Schwenckfeld differs from Hofmann in that he contends that Mary did give nourishment to the flesh. Her nourishment gives evidence of Christ's humanity. However, his emphasis on the spiritual nature of Christ's flesh led many to believe that he was indeed denying Christ's humanity. Schwenckfeld answers these charges of Docetism by saying that he had no intention of denying this essential characteristic of Christ.³

The views of Menno Simons and Dirk Philips. The incarnational view taught by Hofmann and Schwenckfeld was transferred to the later Dutch Anabaptists through their two main leaders in the mid-sixteenth century, Menno Simons and Dirk Philips. Simons agrees with Hofmann and Schwenckfeld that the Word became flesh, but did not take flesh from Mary. He said that Christ "did not become flesh of Mary, but in Mary."⁴ Simons holds that the heavenly flesh theory is important because Christ could not be tainted with Adam's sinful flesh. He argues that if Christ receives His flesh in the natural manner then, "Not the first-born and only-begotten Son of God, but the fatherless son of Mary of the accursed sinful flesh of Adam died for us."⁵ He does not accept traditional descriptions of the unity of the divine and human natures of Christ. He says that these descriptions establish two Christs, one of the pre-existent Word and one of human flesh.

Dirk Philips also accepts the heavenly flesh theory of the incarnation. His emphasis in the theory is on the idea of preserving the perfect sacrifice of Christ. If Christ has taken his flesh from Mary, then there is not a sufficient sacrifice. He asks:

> If the flesh of Christ is from the earth and earthy, yes, from Adam and his seed, which after all is of a sinful nature and subject to corruption.

---

²Williams, *The Radical Reformation*, 530.
³Schwenckfeld, *An Answer to Luther's Malediction*, 179-80.
⁴Simons, *The Complete Writings of Menno Simons*, 431-32.
⁵Simons, *The Complete Writings of Menno Simons*, 825.

... How then could Christ make eternal satisfaction and pay for our sins, John 1:14, 3:16?[6]

As the mantle of leadership passes from Simons and Philips to the later Mennonites, there are different degrees of acceptance of the Melchiorite Christology. One leader who addresses the doctrine, Hans de Ries, has significant influence in the Netherlands during the time of John Smyth's group.

The views of Hans de Ries. According to Keeney, the incarnation is the "cornerstone" of the Christology of Menno Simons and Dirk Philips.[7] However, the incarnation does not have such prominence in the Christology of the Waterlander Mennonite, Hans de Ries. In fact, Ries's early confessions make only a brief reference to the incarnation of Christ. In "The First Waterlandian Confession of Faith," Ries makes a statement on the incarnation that sounds traditional but vague. He asserts, "Therefore we confess Christ Jesus to be true God and Son of God from all eternity; that in the fulness of time He became completely man, and that He thus has both a divine and a human nature."[8] The confession does not give a description of the details of the incarnation but surmises that Christ was "born in an inexpressible and incomprehensible manner."[9] Because of this ambiguity, Ries and the others who prepared the confession refused to be dogmatic on their stance on the incarnation. Instead, their phrasing makes both a traditional and a Melchiorite Christology acceptable to the Waterlanders.

In 1578 in "The Middelburg Confession of Hans de Ries," Ries makes it clear why he does not use precise language to describe the incarnation. He affirms his earlier statement in that he sees the details of Christ's incarnation as "inexpressible."[10] He continues by asserting that Christ is the seed of Abraham and David according to the flesh. Christ has both a human and a divine nature. Ries then argues that declaring Christ as truly God and man is all that is necessary for true doctrine. He states, "Scriptures do not tie salvation to a knowledge of the origin of the

---

[6]Philips, *The Writings of Dirk Philips*, 147.
[7]Keeney, "Dirk Philips, a Biography," 98.
[8]Ries, "First Waterlandian Confession," 9.
[9]Ries, "First Waterlandian Confession," 9.
[10]Ries, "Middelburg Confession," 152.

212 / The Theology of John Smyth

flesh of Christ."[11] Therefore, Ries will not refuse fellowship with someone over differences in their incarnational views. He says that he will continue "brotherly relations" with others even if they have a different opinion on "the origin of the flesh of Christ."[12] So, a detailed incarnational statement is not necessary for Ries's Christology.

In the "Short Confession," which was written in the context of the Mennonite negotiations with John Smyth's group, Ries still gives only one article that discusses the incarnation. However, he gives several articles on the work of Christ and his role for the church. These additional articles on Christology are a new feature for Ries's confessions. Why is this a big issue for this confession? There are two possible explanations. First, James Coggins suggests that the doctrine had become a chief concern for Ries and the other Mennonites since his earlier confessions in the 1580s.[13] It can be seen from the writings of Menno Simons and Dirk Philips that Christology had been a point of concern since the mid-sixteenth century. Incarnational questions and the Socinian challenge of antitrinitarianism caused Ries to address his Christology in several tracts.[14] So, it is possible that during the ebb and flow of the debate the controversy had raged especially high, causing Ries to give it more attention.

While this is possible, the more likely explanation has to do with the specific occasion for the confession. Ries states in his introduction to the confession that it is written "at the request of several Englishmen [who had] fled from England for conscience sake."[15] So, if the confession is to answer the questions of Smyth's group, it is likely that Ries spends so much time on Christology because it is a chief area of concern for Smyth's group. Evidence for this can be seen in the emphasis on Christ as King, Priest, and Prophet in the confession. Christ's work in these roles had long been important to Smyth's understanding of the church. There is no reference in Ries's earlier confessions to Christ's fulfilling these three roles, but here they are discussed in six articles. Why is

---

[11]Ries, "Middelburg Confession," 152.
[12]Ries, "Middelburg Confession," 152.
[13]Coggins, *John Smyth's Congregation*, 86-88.
[14]See Dyck, for more background on Ries's publications on Christology, especially his reply to anti-Trinitarian thought.
[15]Ries, "A Short Confession of Faith," 8.

incarnation mentioned only in one article but the roles of Christ in six? Besides the fact that Ries did not see the logistics of the incarnation as essential doctrine, there could be another reason. Ries's purpose is to state the Mennonite doctrine in terms that would be familiar and appealing to the English. Therefore, he stresses the roles of Christ because they would offer important common ground for the merger of Smyth's group and the Mennonites.

Ries's incarnational statement in the "Short Confession" says that Christ was born of Mary through the work of the Holy Spirit. Twice Ries mentions Christ's being born of Mary. He does not mention anything about Christ's flesh coming from heaven, but simply states that he is "one Person true God and man born of Mary."[16] In common with his earlier confessions, Ries asserts that the details of the incarnation are not central to true doctrine. For Ries and the Waterlanders the spiritual knowledge of Christ is more important than having knowledge of Christ according to the flesh. That is why the details of the incarnation are unimportant. Ries stresses this spiritual knowledge of Christ by saying:

> From what has thus been said concerning the ascension, glorification, office, and service of Christ in glory we believe and confess that he must not only be known according to the flesh, or confessed literally according to historical knowledge, or only in his incarnation, birth, manifestation in the flesh, his life, miracles, suffering, death, cross, and other events. Rather we must rise higher and confess Christ also according to the Spirit, in his exaltation and glory, according to his glorious office and, as the Scriptures teach, receive this knowledge with a believing heart.[17]

Ries makes it clear that without a spiritual knowledge of Christ, being correct on the details of Christ's life is not a sufficient Christology.[18] This

---

[16]Ries, "A Short Confession of Faith," 12.

[17]Ries, "A Short Confession of Faith," 14. This article is not found in Smyth's translation of the confession, which seems to indicate that Ries added it a short time later before the confession was published later in 1610. Coggins holds that it was added as a result of the deliberations with Smyth's group. Coggins, *John Smyth's Congregation*, 90-93.

[18]Ries, "A Short Confession of Faith," 15. The discussion of this topic continues under Smyth's views of the natural and spiritual flesh of Christ.

idea is important in the interaction between Ries and Smyth. However, before the results of this interaction are demonstrated, Smyth's early views should be understood.

Smyth's Early Christology

Many aspects of John Smyth's theology underwent change throughout his career. His Christology is no exception. Early in Smyth's career, he seems to have held Christological views that were similar to those of other Puritans. Even during his Separatist stage, he maintained much of the same thought. However, during his Baptist and Mennonite stages, Smyth began to deal with charges that he had abandoned a more traditional Christology for Melchiorite Christology. There are two major parts of Smyth's early Christology that undergo change once he becomes a Mennonite. They are his views on the typology of Christ and on Christ as the King, Priest, and Prophet of the church. Identifying the changes in these two important aspects of Smyth's Christology is helpful in determining his level of acceptance of the Mennonite doctrine of Christ.

Smyth's typology of Christ. One idea that is fundamental to Smyth's early Christology is that Christ is the full revelation of God and therefore fulfils all types. The idea drives his view that the Old Testament foreshadows the New Testament. He held that the New Testament is the truth and the Old Testament is the type, because Christ is fully revealed in the New Testament whereas he is veiled in the Old. Smyth uses similar thinking in his discussion of the nature of the covenant relationship between God and his people. God's covenant with Abraham had Christ in mind; it was through the faithful that the spiritual covenant was passed. After Christ, the carnal covenant is eliminated, and only the spiritual covenant remains. Understanding Smyth's view of the relationship of the testaments and his view of the covenant is crucial for interpreting Smyth's thought. However, neither of these essential thoughts can be complete without a comprehension of his Christology.

Smyth believes that the Old Testament points to Christ and is fulfilled in him in regards to its ceremonies and personalities. An obvious example of this is his earliest published work, *The Bright Morning Starre*. It is an exposition of Psalm 22 in which he interprets the psalm typologically. Smyth states that this is the proper way of understanding the psalm:

The Prophet Dauid is here to be considered. 1. in his owne person. 2. sustaining the person of a godly man. 3. as a type of Christ, whose sufferings and glorie, whose priesthood in his sacrifice and intercession, with his propheticall office in teaching, and kingdome in gathering and guiding his Church in all ages, places, and times, are here not obscurely figured . . . and of the doctrine of the Gospell in the offices of Christ.[19]

Smyth's tendency is to use typology to see depictions of Christ in the Old Testament. The quotation also shows that from an early stage Smyth is concerned with Christ's work in the church as King, Priest, and Prophet.

As Smyth moves into his Separatist period, he still holds to the view that Christ is the full revelation of God and is typed in the Old Testament. This is evident in his interpretation of certain aspects of the Old Testament. He gives an example of the Old Testament ceremonies typing Christ in *The Differences of the Churches*. As Smyth is discussing proper worship, he interprets typologically the shewbread with incense on the golden altar found in Leviticus, chapter twenty-four. He says that the incense demonstrates that the faithful are accepted by God "through Christs perfume" and the shewbread indicates they are "fed with Christ Iesus the true bread of life."[20] Smyth demonstrates this type of thinking consistently in reference to Christ's fulfillment of the Old Testament.

The coming of Christ is the most important event of history to Smyth. He believes that all doctrine has to understand properly the impact of Christ's coming. In the introduction to his work, *Principles and Inferences*, Smyth states:

Remember that there be alwaies a difference put betwixt the covenant of grace; and the manner of dispensing it, which is twofold: the forme of administring the covenant before the death of Christ, which is called the old testament; and the forme of administring the covenant since the death of Christ which is called the new Testament or the kingdome of heaven. In this litle treatise the ordinances of Christ for the dispensing of the covenant since his death are described.[21]

---

[19]Smyth, *Works* 1:15.
[20]Smyth, *Works* 1:305.
[21]Smyth, *Works* 1:250.

He later reiterates this belief that Christ's coming was the introduction of the New Testament by stating that the Old Testament is abolished by Christ on the cross and that the New Testament is established by the blood of Christ.[22]

Smyth believes that one purpose of the Old Testament is to teach Christ through its types.[23] The Jews were to learn about Christ through the Old Testament, even though He was veiled there.[24] One way that the Jews were to learn about Christ was through certain persons of the Old Testament who were types of Christ. An example of this belief is the earlier quotation from *The Bright Morning Starre*, where Smyth describes David as a type of Christ.[25]

Two more examples of persons in the Old Testament typing Christ are the High Priest and Moses. As Smyth is arguing that there is only one type of elder, he states that in the Old Testament there was only one type of priest, excluding the High Priest which typed Christ.[26] Smyth's use of typology to find Old Testament representations of Christ was not uncommon in the Puritans or Separatists, or in the Reformation in general. However, as Smyth accepted Baptist views, he started using a typological comparison of Christ with Moses which would not be common in the Reformed tradition.

Smyth interprets Moses as a type of Christ, which was a customary practice in the seventeenth century. As a type of Christ, Moses taught the constitution of the Old Testament church, just as Christ taught the constitution of the New Testament church.[27] As in the rest of the Old Testament, Christ is veiled in Moses and therefore is not fully revealed. Christ must be looked to as the one who established the New Testament ordinances, as Moses had done for the Old Testament.

In his debate with Richard Clifton, Smyth says that Christ as the mediator of the New Testament will be at least as clear as Moses was as mediator. Having said this, Smyth argues that there is no clear instruction

---

[22]Smyth, *Works* 2:556.
[23]Smyth, *Works* 2:598.
[24]Smyth, *Works* 2:609, 631-33.
[25]Smyth, *Works* 1:15. This quotation appears above, at n. 19.
[26]Smyth, *Works* 1:308.
[27]Smyth, *Works* 2:667.

in the New Testament for infant baptism, like there was for circumcision in the Old. There are clear instructions for believers' baptism in the New Testament, according to Smyth. He holds that the New Testament identifies proper candidates for baptism as

> persons confessing their sinnes, Mat. 3.6. . . . Persons beleeving. Act. 8. 12. 13. & vs. 36-38. persons that had receaved the holy Ghost, & expressed the same by prophecying, Act. 10. 46-48 persons penitent, Act. 2. 38. persons that are by teaching made Disciples, Mat. 28. 19. Ioh. 4. 1. persons borne againe. Ioh. 3. 3.[28]

Smyth argues that if anyone other than these are to be baptized, "then is not the New Testament so cleer as the Old, nor Christ as Faithful as Moses."[29]

Christ as King, Priest, and Prophet of the Church. Smyth's references to Christ's role as King, Priest, and Prophet appear early in his career. In introducing his first work, *The Bright Morning Starre*, he mentions the importance of Christ in these roles. Later in the work, he discusses Christ's role in the church as Prophet and Priest, demonstrating the connection of these two roles. He says, "for the propheticall office of Christ principally reuealeth vnto vs the redemption of Christ which is the principall worke of his preisthood."[30] He also states that "the propheticall office of Christ is a fruit of his preisthood, of his redemption, sacrifice and intercession: for if Christ had not died for vs, he had neuer reuealed his fathers will vnto vs."[31]

When he became a Separatist, Smyth charged that the Puritans of the Church of England had not allowed Christ to fulfil His threefold role properly.[32] The hierarchy of the Church of England was not allowing Christ to be the King of the church. Smyth found this unacceptable because he believed that to have Christ as Priest and Prophet, but not King, leads to a false church, for it denies an essential aspect of the work of Christ.[33] Smyth held that it is an improper Christology if someone has

---

[28]Smyth, *Works* 2:612-13.
[29]Smyth, *Works* 2:613.
[30]Smyth, *Works* 1:59.
[31]Smyth, *Works* 1:59.
[32]Smyth, *Works* 2:458, 468.
[33]Smyth, *Works* 2:553-56.

the correct knowledge about the person of Christ, but denies him as King or Priest or Prophet. In *Paralleles, Censures, Observations*, he charges Richard Bernard and other Puritans by saying that

> the summe of the gospel is this, that Iesus Christ the Sonne of God, & the Sonne of Mary, is the only King, Preist, & Prophet of his Church, governing, Sacrificing, making intercession, & prophecying after that holy manner & according to those rules which he hath prescribed in his Testament: Now to beleeve truly concerning the person of Christ, & to beleeve falsely concerning his office as you doe, is not to beleeve the whole gospel, but only a peece of it.[34]

According to Smyth, a proper recognition of Christ in these roles is an essential part of the true gospel. Smyth reaffirms his stance later in *Paralleles, Censures, Observations* where he states that if someone does not claim Christ as King, Priest, and Prophet, then his faith is false. It does not matter that the person may have proper beliefs about Christ's person.[35]

Smyth said that the Puritans within the Church of England had a false church because they held to a false faith concerning Christ. A true church can result only if its members properly acknowledge Christ as King, Priest, and Prophet. A mixed congregation cannot do this properly, because only saints can give true recognition to Christ's roles.[36] In a true church, as each saint recognizes Christ, all power and authority come through Christ and are given to each member.[37] The church is then enabled to carry out its duties as a true church. So, acknowledging Christ in His roles is fundamental to the church and is the medium for Christ to grant it His authority.

---

[34]Smyth, *Works* 2:471. In Smyth's Separatist stage, he often repeats the formula of King, Priest, and Prophet. As a Puritan, he held to these three offices but was looser in the order in which he presents them. See 1:15, 60. The reason for this could be that as a Separatist he stresses the kingship of Christ because he feels that his Puritan opponents are denying this office. Therefore he develops a formula that mentions that office first.

[35]Smyth, *Works* 2:499.
[36]Smyth, *Works* 2:383.
[37]Smyth, *Works* 2:394-95.

Douglas Shantz uses the idea of Christ's roles in the church to show that Smyth's Christology is central to his covenant ecclesiology.[38] Christ is the King, Priest, and Prophet of the church that enters into covenant with Him. Smyth believes that covenanting to be a church is the proper recognition of Christ's lordship. Because Christ is being recognized, He then grants His power and authority to the covenanted community.

Smyth's emphasis on Christ's roles as an essential element of the church becomes evident in his Separatist work, *Principles and Inferences*. There he writes, "Private persons separating from al synne, and joyning together to obey Christ their king, priest and prophet, as they are bound, are a true visible Church."[39] Smyth's emphasis on the covenant is obvious throughout his Separatist works. However, in this description of a church the term "covenant" does not appear, even though the idea does. As a Separatist, Smyth defines the church as a group of the faithful who covenant together to be obedient to Christ. Christ being acknowledged in His roles is a crucial part of this formula.

He declares that once these people recognize Christ in His roles, then the true church is the kingdom of Christ.[40] Christ grants the church certain authority and establishes it in His covenant. In his book, *Paralleles, Censures, Observations*, Smyth defines the true visible church as a covenanted community who have been given the things of God including Christ as King, Priest, and Prophet. He says, "But a true visible church, that is a communion of Saynts, joyned together in the true covenant, is that only communion of men wherto God hath given his covenant, his promises, his holy things, Christ for King, Preist & Prophet."[41] Having Christ as King, Priest, and Prophet is inseparable from the covenant of the church. This becomes clearer in Smyth's discussion of the power of the elders within a congregation. Smyth argues that the authority in the church has been given to the entire congregation. As a congregation elects elders, it does not transfer its authority to them. Smyth says that this would be impossible because Christ gives the authority to the whole church on the basis of its covenant with God.

---

[38]Shantz, "The Place of the Resurrected Christ in the Writings of John Smyth," 199-200.
[39]Smyth, *Works* 1:267.
[40]Smyth, *Works* 2:357.
[41]Smyth, *Works* 2:350. "Men" has been emended.

God's gift to the church through the covenant is Christ as King, Priest, and Prophet.[42]

Smyth's Christology as a Mennonite

It seems that for the major part of his career, Smyth held to a traditional view of the incarnation. It does not surface as an issue of debate early in his career. He makes only brief comments on the subject, including that the union of the two natures never dissolved, so that the godhead was not severed from Christ.[43] On a few occasions Smyth comments that Christ was the Son of God and Mary and the only Savior.[44] This is the basic summary of his belief on the subject as a Puritan and Separatist.

Because it was not an area of dispute, Smyth does not mention often the incarnation in much detail as either a Puritan or a Separatist. However, one exception to this is in his Puritan work, *The Bright Morning Starre*. As he relays his exposition of Psalm 22:9, he says, "The Lord preserued Christ in his conception from the contagion of sinne, he beeing framed of the substance of the virgin by the power of the holy ghost without the helpe of man, by reason whereof the course of originall sinne was stayed which is deriued to vs in generation: wherefore in this sence Christ had no father."[45] His description of the incarnation is a traditional view. Smyth affirms that Christ is made of Mary's substance. Also, he supports the traditional defense of Christ's perfection being maintained by the absence of the seed of a man. At this point, Smyth's opponents see no reason to question his Christology. However, in his Baptist and Mennonite stages, Smyth is challenged frequently on his incarnational views.

Answering two charges. In his "Epistle to the Reader," which was attached to his Baptist work, *The Character of the Beast*, Smyth denies Richard Clyfton's charge that he had accepted the Melchiorite incarnational view. He says that it is a slanderous error to say that he and his

---

[42]Smyth, *Works* 2:437.
[43]Smyth, *Works* 1:20-21.
[44]Smyth, *Works* 2:407, 471, and 486.
[45]Smyth, *Works* 1:33. "Sence" has been emended.

followers are "Heretiques in denying the humanity of Christ."[46] Smyth addresses this charge by saying:

> Finally, concerning the Flesh of Chr. we do beleve that Chr. is the seed of Abrah. Isaac, & Iacob, & of David, according to the Prophecyes of the Scriptures, & that he is the Sonne of Mary his Mother, made of her substance, the holy Ghost overshadowing her: So have other children ther bodyly substance from their parents: also that Chr. is one person in two distinct natures, the God-head & manhood, & we detest the contrary errors.[47]

At this stage of his career, Smyth does not support the Melchiorite view of the incarnation. He confirms that Christ received His flesh in the natural process from Mary. He states that Christ is "made of her substance." So, in giving this statement, Smyth not only confirms that he and his group hold to the traditional view of the incarnation, but also makes clear that they are intolerant of alternative views.

Later a similar charge is levelled at Smyth from a more intimate source. After separating from his group, Thomas Helwys makes a charge that Smyth is denying the flesh of Christ. Again, Smyth is being charged with accepting the Melchiorite incarnational theory. In a letter that is attached to his *A Declaration of Faith*, Helwys charges Smyth with six errors. The charge that is pertinent here is "That CHRIST concerning the first matter off his Flesh, he affirmed, that all the Scriptures would not prove that he had it of the virgine Marie, but his second matter which he said was his nourishment that the Scriptures proved he had of Marie, thus making CHRIST to have two matters of his Flesh."[48] Smyth responds to the charge in *The Last Booke*. He argues that separating the first and second flesh of Christ agrees with biblical testimony and contemporary medical theory. He writes:

---

[46]Smyth, *Works* 2:571.
[47]Smyth, *Works* 2:572. "Contrary" has been emended.
[48]Helwys, *A Declaration of Faith*, in Burgess, *John Smyth, the Se-Baptist*, 180. McGlothlin revises the word "matter" to "mother" in his reproduction of the work: William J. McGlothlin, ed., *Baptist Confessions of Faith* (Philadephia: American Baptist Publication Society, 1911) 92-93. The term is more likely to be "matter" as this is the term Smyth uses in his response to Helwys' charge: Smyth, *Works* 2:759.

> Another imputation of Mr. Hel. is concerninge the flesh of Christ: wherto I say: that he that knoweth not, that the first and second flesh of an Infant in the mothers wombe are to be distinguished, knoweth not yet the groundes of Nature and naturall resaon. I affirmed concerning Christ that his second flesh, that is his nourishment he had from his mother, and that the scriptures are plain for yt: but concerninge the first matter of Christ[s] flesh whence it was I said thus much: That although I yeeld it to be a truth in nature that he had it of his mother Mary, yet I dare not make itt such an Article of faith as that if anie man will not consent vnto it I should therfore refuse brotherhood with him, and that the Scriptures do not lead vs (as farr as I conceiue) to the searchinge of that point, whereof Christ[s] naturell flesh was made.[49]

Therefore, Smyth believes that anyone who holds to the Melchiorite incarnational theory is not denying the humanity of Christ. He contends that his belief concerning the first flesh of Christ is not essentially different from that of Helwys. The only difference is that he does not think that the first flesh is a matter that demands a dogmatic stance.[50]

In the body of his *A Declaration of Faith*, Helwys gives a description of the incarnation that relies heavily on Smyth's comments in his "Epistle to the Reader." Helwys's statement declares that Christ is "the Sonne off Marie the Virgine, made of hir substance, Gal. 4-4. By the power off the HOLIE GHOST overshadowing hir."[51] In Smyth's response to Helwys's charges, he says that he agrees with Helwys on the source of Christ's flesh, but he refuses to make it a test of fellowship. Smyth contends that the main difference between him and Helwys is in their level of tolerance of other views.[52]

Smyth's new tolerance did not please Helwys. Helwys writes his "An Advertisement" to Ries and the other Mennonites to contradict Smyth's views. He says, "You have amongst you that deny Christ to have taken flesh of Mary, some holding that he brought it from heaven and some not

---

[49]Smyth, *Works* 2:758-59. "And" has been emended.
[50]Smyth, *Works* 2:759-60.
[51]Helwys, *A Declaration of Faith*, in Burgess, *John Smyth, the Se-Baptist*, 214; Lumpkin, *Baptist Confessions of Faith*, 119; McGlothlin, *Baptist Confessions of Faith*, 89.
[52]Smyth, *Works* 2:759.

knowing whence he brought it, both which destroy the faith of Christ."[53] Helwys is maintaining the strict view that he and Smyth held during their early Baptist days. The difference between him and Smyth is caused by Smyth's move to toleration of varying incarnational views.

Smyth and the Melchiorite incarnational theory. As Smyth's relationship with the Mennonites grew, his statements about the incarnation became more numerous. Smyth had some medical training while at Cambridge, and this training was to play a part in his Christological conversations with the Mennonites. One contemporary medical theory was used by Smyth and the Mennonites in their discussions of the flesh of Christ. This theory is that the father provided the first flesh or seed of a child and that the mother provided the second flesh or nourishment. The nourishment would be essential, but otherwise the mother does not provide any material to the child.[54]

Menno Simons refers to this theory in defense of his Christology. He believes that the substance and origin of the child is from the father and not from the mother. In his *Reply to Micron*, Menno says that three rules apply to the procreative process of any child. They are: "(1) that no procreation can take place without a father; (2) that procreative seed is not found with woman, and (3) that nevertheless the woman in no less necessary in procreation."[55] Smyth also refers to this theory in *The Last Booke* in his response to Helwys's charge. He said that anyone who does not know, "that the first and second flesh of an Infant in the mothers wombe are to be distinguished," does not understand nature or natural reason.[56]

Although Smyth does make similar references to the medical theory, he does not fully accept the Melchiorite incarnational view. James Coggins argues that Smyth does indeed accept this view. He says of Smyth, "In any case, like most Mennonites, he accepted that Christ's

---

[53]Helwys, *An Advertisement or Admonition, unto the Congregations* (N.p., 1611) 8.

[54]Joyce Irwin, "Embryology and the Incarnation: A Sixteenth-Century Debate," *Sixteenth Century Journal* 9 (1978): 95-98.

[55]Simons, *The Complete Writings of Menno Simons*, 897. See also 806-807 for more on Menno's view that the woman does not provide the seed for a child.

[56]Smyth, *Works* 2:758.

flesh was not derived from Mary."[57] However, this is a direct contradiction of Smyth's statement that the first flesh and second flesh were from Mary. He affirms that the scriptures are very clear in that Christ received his second flesh from Mary. He also says that the scriptures are not concerned with the source of Christ's first flesh, but that he agrees with Helwys that it comes from Mary.[58] Coggins attempts to dismiss this statement by saying it is just a product of Smyth's "later tentativeness."[59] Actually, this is Smyth's way of affirming the view that he held in common with Helwys at the beginning of their relationship with the Mennonites.

In his "Epistle to the Reader" Smyth made clear the beliefs of himself, Helwys, and his other followers concerning the incarnation. Smyth affirms the traditional descriptions of the incarnation. He indicates that Christ is "made of her substance," which contradicts the heavenly flesh theory of Hofmann and many of the Mennonites.[60] In Smyth's later statement in *The Last Booke*, he demonstrates that his view of the incarnation has not changed significantly since the beginning of the negotiations. However, he had followed the example of Hans de Ries and several other Mennonites and had become tolerant of other views.

Additionally, Coggins misinterprets Smyth's use of medical theory. Smyth is not trying to convince Helwys of Melchiorite Christology. Instead, he is trying to demonstrate to Helwys that the Melchiorite view does not deny the humanity of Christ because it acknowledges that Christ received his second flesh from Mary. Smyth tells Helwys that although he agrees with him concerning the first flesh of Christ, he refuses to make it a test of fellowship. He writes, "That although I yeeld it to be a truth in nature that he had it of his mother Mary, yet I dare not make itt such an Article of faith as that if anie man will not consent vnto it I should therfore refuse brotherhood with him."[61] So, Smyth is not trying to show a difference in his belief in the incarnation from that of Helwys;

---

[57]Coggins, *John Smyth's Congregation*, 124.
[58]Smyth, *Works* 2:758-59.
[59]Coggins, *John Smyth's Congregation*, 125.
[60]Smyth, *Works* 2:572.
[61]Smyth, *Works* 2:759.

instead he intends to explain why he believes that he can fellowship with those who hold the Melchiorite view despite their differences.

1. *Smyth's statements in Defence of Ries's Confession.* According to Coggins, Smyth gives his strongest support to the Melchiorite incarnational view in his *Defence of Ries's Confession.* In this work, Smyth makes two statements that give some indication to his view of the incarnation. The first statement deals with the uncertainty of Christ's flesh. The second statement is an analogy that compares regeneration to the incarnation.

a. *The uncertainty of Christ's flesh.* In the first statement, Smyth says that the evidence about Christ's flesh is inconclusive; though Mary did not generate Christ. He writes, "We believe whatever the sacred Scripture says. As yet we do not perceive any phrase that indicates the material of Christ's flesh. We hear your deductions and conclusions; we do not see any clear words."[62]

However, he continues a few lines later, "And nothing is in Christ which was not generated by God; for we assert that God the Father generated the whole Christ. We deny that Mary generated Christ."[63] It is possible that Smyth referred to this statement in *The Last Booke.* As Smyth is answering the charge made against him by Helwys, he says, "That this was my speech and the somme of my assertion concerning this point I call the lord and all that hard, as witnesses: wherby appeareth Mr. Helwis his partiality in reporting this particular."[64] To which assertion is he referring? Probably the assertion was the verbal form of what he had written in *Defence of Ries's Confession.*

In the quotation from *Defence of Ries's Confession,* he argues that scripture does not indicate, with any certainty, what the substance of Christ's flesh was. Then he says that, because of the absence of scriptural information, the substance of Christ's flesh is better left uncertain. Smyth

---

[62]Translation by Coggins, *John Smyth's Congregation,* 182. *credimus quaecumque loquitur sacra scriptura; phrasin ullam materiam carnis Christi indicantem non adhuc percipimus, sequelas et consequentias vestras audimus, verba diserta non videmus.* Smyth, *Works* 2:696.

[63]Translation by Coggins, *John Smyth's Congregation,* 182. *neque quicquam esse in Christo quod a Deo non est genitum: nam affirmamus deum patrem totum Christum genuisse, mariam negamus Christum genuisse.* Smyth, *Works* 2:696.

[64]Smyth, *Works* 2:759. "And" has been emended.

proposes, "Therefore, I prefer to leave it undecided rather than to argue about trifles."[65] Instead one needs to seek the spiritual flesh of Christ that is described in Ephesians 5:30, as it speaks of being members of His body, of His flesh, and of His bones. In *The Last Booke*, he says that his summary of this argument is that the scriptures do not lead to a searching of the nature of Christ's flesh, but that believers should "searche into Christs spirituall flesh, to be made flesh of that his flesh and bone of his bone."[66] Smyth reaffirms his view of the uncertainty of the nature of Christ's flesh that he made in *Defence of Ries's Confession* by making this statement in *The Last Booke*.

With this fact in mind, Smyth's statement in *Defence of Ries's Confession* can be seen in a new way. As Smyth is dealing with the Reformed critic's comments about Ries's article on the incarnation, he separates his response into three parts. The first part deals with possible contradictions with other beliefs stated in the confession. Smyth quickly dismisses the critic's comments as being insignificant. The second part is the main section of Smyth's response where he clearly states that uncertainty is the best solution on the nature of Christ's flesh. This part contains the statements that he later summarized to Helwys.

The third part has some confusing comments in it. It is on this third part that Coggins bases his theory of Smyth's acceptance of the Melchiorite view of the incarnation. However, this would be in direct contradiction of Smyth's statement in the second part which later, in *The Last Booke*, he describes as the summary of his argument. So, the third part of this response must be interpreted in the light of Smyth's later summary of his argument. One particular statement stands out in this part as demanding special attention. This statement is, "*mariam negamus Christum genuisse: conceptum et natum ex muliere fatemur, genitum negamus: pater siquidem eum genuit.*"[67] There are two keys to interpreting this statement and relating it to Coggins's theory.

The first key is Coggins's use of the first-person singular in his translation. He translates the phrase, "We deny that Mary generated

---

[65]Translation by Coggins, *John Smyth's Congregation*, 182. *mallem ergo in dubio relinquere quam de lana caprina contendere.* Smyth, *Works* 2:696.
[66]Smyth, *Works* 2:759.
[67]Smyth, *Works* 2:696.

Christ. I confess that He was conceived in and born from the woman; we deny that He was generated by her, since in fact the Father generated Him."[68] The term *fatemur* that Coggins translates as "I confess" should more properly be "we confess" which would fit better with the surrounding phrases and the purpose of this part. Smyth is attempting to defend the beliefs of the Mennonites that are expressed in Ries's confession. He is not simply stating his own view.

The second key is an understanding of the term *genitum* meaning "begotten or generated." The question that Smyth deals with is the ultimate origin, not the material of Christ's flesh. He said in the previous part that the material of Christ's flesh cannot be determined. However, it is completely clear to Smyth that Christ has His ultimate source in the Father, not Mary. Smyth makes the distinction between the process of conception and birth and the original source. While conception is in and birth is out of Mary, Christ is "begotten" (*genitus*) of God. The context of this statement and the use of specific terms by Smyth indicate clearly that he was not an advocate of Melchiorite incarnational theory, but agreed that Christ found His origin in God and that His spiritual flesh was to be the focus of attention. This interpretation of this section would be in agreement with what he relates to Thomas Helwys during *The Last Booke*.[69] It would also be in agreement with the aspect of Ries's theology, which Smyth is defending. Ries was not an advocate of the heavenly flesh theory, but did make the same distinction as Smyth makes between Christ's conception in Mary and his ultimate source being from God.[70]

b. *Regeneration and the incarnation.* Smyth's second statement in *Defence of Ries's Confession* that must be taken into consideration is that Christ's incarnation pictures our regeneration. He describes the incarnation, "Just as in the generation or conception of Christ in His mother's womb the Father generated the Son through the Holy Spirit . . . the Father generates us as His sons through the Holy Spirit."[71] In this

---

[68]Coggins, *John Smyth's Congregation*, 182.
[69]Smyth, *Works* 2:759.
[70]Ries, "A Short Confession of Faith," 12, Dyck, "Hans de Ries: Theologian and Churchman," 220-21.
[71]Translation by Coggins, *John Smyth's Congregation*, 186. *Quemadmodum in Christi generatione sive conceptione in utero materno pater filium genuit per spiritum sanctum . . . pater nos gignit filios suos per spiritum sanctum.* Smyth,

analogy, Smyth goes on to compare the hearts of believers with the womb of Mary. He says that the heart receives the seed like fertile ground and the seed grows by the power of the Holy Spirit. The heart, like the womb of Mary, fosters the seed. Because this statement is an analogy, it should not be pushed too far in an attempt to discover Smyth's incarnational view. He is discussing regeneration, not the incarnation. His argument is that as Christ has God as His ultimate source, so does a person's regeneration. Nothing else can be said about the incarnation from the analogy.

Smyth's confessional statements. The incarnational statements found in the two confessions published during Smyth's Mennonite phase were not significantly different from the statements that he made in *The Last Booke.* In *Corde Credimus,* Smyth relates that Jesus is "true God and true man" and that he has taken on "the true and pure nature of man" and exists in a "true human body."[72] When Smyth addresses the incarnation, his language is intentionally vague. He states, "Jesus Christ, who concerning the flesh, was conceived by the Holy Spirit in the womb of the Virgin Mary."[73] Smyth's statements about the incarnation are similar to the incarnational statements of Hans de Ries's "Short Confession."[74] Ries refers to Jesus as "true God and man" and that he was born from Mary due to the work of the Holy Spirit.[75] Smyth's vagueness could be a result of his attempt to copy Ries's tendency to present the incarnation in broad terms which would be acceptable to people who held either the Melchiorite or the traditional view of the incarnation.

In *Propositions and Conclusions,* Smyth declares in article 31 that "the word became flesh John 1. 14, wonderfully by the power of God in the wombe of the virgin Marie: he was of the seed of David according to the flesh Phil. 2. 7: Hebre 10: Rom. 1. 3."[76] Again, Smyth's language

---

Works 2:701.

[72]*verum Deum et verum hominem,"* "*hominis veram et puram naturam, vero corpore humano,* Smyth, *Works* 2:682.

[73]*Jesum Christum, quod ad carnem attinet, per spiritum sanctum in utero virginis Mariae conceptum fuisse.* Smyth, *Works* 2:682.

[74]See chap. 5 for a more detailed comparison of Smyth's confession with Ries's confession.

[75]Ries, "A Short Confession of Faith," 12.

[76]Smyth, *Works* 2:737.

could be acceptable to either side of the incarnational debate. Also, neither of the incarnational statements in these confessions gives any allusion to Smyth's overt acceptance or complete rejection of Melchiorite incarnational theory.

Natural flesh and spiritual flesh of Christ. While Smyth's acceptance of the heavenly flesh theory is questionable at best, there is one aspect of Mennonite Christology that Smyth fully accepts from Ries. Smyth holds that Christ has both a natural flesh and a spiritual flesh. This dichotomy is apparent in several aspects of his Mennonite understanding of Christ. In *Defence of Ries's Confession*, Smyth lists several aspects of Christ's humanity that have both natural and spiritual characteristics. He says that Christ's body, his bones, his afflictions, his conception, his birth, and his miracles all have natural and spiritual traits.[77] Though Smyth mentions several aspects of Christ as having both natural and spiritual characteristics, it is the flesh of Christ that he describes in detail. In his defense of article 34 of Ries's confession, Smyth attempts to explain what he means by the natural and spiritual flesh of Christ. He writes:

> The natural flesh of Christ is that which [was] conceived in the virgin's womb, which was later exhausted hanging on the cross and pierced through by the soldiers. On the other hand, the spiritual flesh of Christ is that which the faithful eat every day. . . . He is Christ's brother who does the will of His heavenly Father; for he who has this in common with Christ that he keeps God's commands is Christ's brother. Consequently, the spiritual flesh of Christ is either true obedience or something similar.[78]

This quotation gives some clarification of Smyth's thoughts. However, as Smyth continues, his thought loses this clarity. He says, "This spirit is the spiritual flesh of Christ, not the Holy Spirit Himself but

---

[77]Smyth, *Works* 2:698-99, Coggins, *John Smyth's Congregation*, 183-84.

[78]Translation by Coggins, *John Smyth's Congregation*, 191. *Caro Christi naturalis est ea quae in utero virginis concepta, quae postea cruce pendens exanimata est et transfixa a militibus. Caro autem Christi spiritualis est ea quam fideles quotidie comedunt . . . is est frater Christi qui facit voluntatem patris sui coelestis: qui enim hoc cum Christo commune habet ut dei mandata observet, is frater est Christi, caro igitur spiritualis Christi est vel oboedientia vera vel aliquid simile.* Smyth, *Works* 2:706.

the heavenly gifts of the Holy Spirit which are poured out into the hearts of the faithful. This flesh of Christ is the spiritual food and drink of our souls."[79] So, it seems that Smyth says two different things about the spiritual flesh of Christ. In one phrase he refers to "obedience" as the spiritual flesh, but just a few sentences later the spiritual flesh is the "heavenly gifts of the Holy Spirit poured out into the hearts of the faithful." Whatever the spiritual flesh is, it is what gives life to the faithful.[80] Smyth's vagueness produces some uncertainty as to what exactly is meant by his use of the phrase, the spiritual flesh of Christ.

For Smyth, partaking of Christ's spiritual flesh brings about a spiritual union between the faithful and Christ. The biblical text that Smyth cites most often when discussing the spiritual flesh is Ephesians 5:30. Sometimes he simply includes the reference and other times he adds the phrase to become "flesh of His flesh" and "bone of His bones."[81] His use of Ephesians 5:30 gives some indication as to Smyth's understanding of the spiritual flesh. The emphasis of the verse is the spiritual union that the faithful are to have with Christ.

The spiritual flesh seems to have more to do with the inward aspect of humanity than with the Holy Spirit. This may be difficult to ascertain because even early in his career, Smyth used the term "spirit" with fluidity. In his Separatist work, *The Differences of the Churches*, he describes what he means by the term. He writes:

> The Fountayne . . . whence spirituall worship proceedeth is the spirit. . . . The spirit signifieth 2. things. 1. the spirit of God. 2. the spirit of man: that is the regenerate part of the soule. . . . The work of the holy spirit is to suggest matter & to move the regenerate part of the soule. . . . Finally the work of the Regenerat part of the soule is an Eccho

---

[79]Translation by Coggins, *John Smyth's Congregation*, 191-92. Coggins's "This Spirit" has been changed to "This spirit" for the same reason explained below in n. 88. The term "spirit" relates to the inward, regenerated soul of humans rather than the Holy Spirit, so for clarity the capitalization has been changed. *Hic spiritus est caro spiritualis Christi, non ipse spiritus sanctus, sed spiritus sancti dona celestia quae in corda fidelium effunduntur; haec caro Christi cibus et potus est spiritualis animarum nostrarum.* Smyth, *Works* 2:707.

[80]Smyth, *Works* 2:707; Coggins, *John Smyth's Congregation*, 192.

[81]Smyth, *Works* 2:696, 698, 699, 706, 708, 746, 759, 760.

correspondent to the work of the holy spirit & the condition of the word of God which in tyme of spirituall worship is administred.[82]

As a Mennonite, the discussion changes from spiritual worship to spiritual flesh. However, Smyth still uses "spirit" for both meanings, often in close connection with one another.

Smyth's emphasis on the spirit meaning inward becomes apparent when noticing his arrangement of his longest discussions of the spiritual flesh. In *Defence of Ries's Confession*, Smyth includes his most detailed discussion of spiritual flesh in defending Ries's position on the inward significance of the Lord's Supper, not in his comments about how the Holy Spirit was at work in Christ.[83]

This pattern holds true in Smyth's own confession, *Propositions and Conclusions*. His reference to being flesh of Christ's flesh occurs when he points to the inward meaning of the sacraments, not in his article of the Holy Spirit's work in the faithful. In the previous quotation from *Defence of Ries's Confession*, Smyth says that the spiritual flesh is the spirit which anoints the faithful. This spirit is not the Holy Spirit specifically, but is the gifts that the Holy Spirit gives to the faithful through which they have a sustaining union with Christ. Just as in his Separatist discussion of worship, the Holy Spirit's work is closely associated, but not synonymous, with the "spirit" of the spiritual flesh.

A close union with Christ results when humans partake in His spiritual flesh. Therefore, the spiritual flesh becomes the essential Christological issue to Smyth. He does not want to seem to deny the validity of Christ's natural flesh, so he states the general benefit of the natural flesh. Smyth says that all people benefit from Christ's natural flesh, because it was through the suffering of the natural flesh that atonement was provided for sins. The benefit is a "general grace" because its privileges extend to everyone. Because of the suffering of Christ's natural flesh, all humans have had the guilt of original sin removed.[84] There is no response needed, so this is not where Smyth puts his plea. Smyth desires for people to partake in the spiritual flesh of Christ so they can experience the "particular grace" of "true life." He states:

---

[82]Smyth, *Works* 1:276.
[83]Smyth, *Works* 2:689-90.
[84]See chap. 5 for Smyth's views of a general atonement.

232 / The Theology of John Smyth

> Not that that natural flesh is of no benefit at all, but inasmuch as that flesh does nothing in this respect; for it was a sacrifice in humility for our sins and not for ours only but for the sins of the whole world. This is the general grace and common benefit. The particular grace and benefit peculiar to the church or body of Christ is this spiritual flesh which supplies true life to those who eat.[85]

This quotation is another demonstration of Smyth's acceptance of Mennonite views of the atonement. His acceptance of their views had caused him to write about the universal aspect of the covenant, the universal application of Christ's atonement, and now the universal benefit of the natural flesh. All of these things result in the removal of the guilt of original sin.

Smyth continues his discussion of the spiritual flesh by saying that the new creation is nourished by the spiritual flesh and that "the faithful may be made genuine brothers of Christ through the koinonian . . . for those two, that is, Christ and the church, are of one flesh through this great sacrament of this spiritual union: Eph. 5:31, 32, 30."[86] It is this union that is strengthened by obedience and the faithful's exercising of the spiritual gifts. The union, or the spiritual flesh is also what gives life to the believer.

Smyth's views have obvious similarities with statements from Ries's confession. Ries uses the phrase to "know Christ according to the spirit" instead of Smyth's phrase of "spiritual flesh."[87] Ries stresses the need to

---

[85]Translation by Coggins, *John Smyth's Congregation*, 192. *non quod illa caro naturalis nihil omnino prodest, sed nihil respective agit siquidem illa caro, erat enim victima pro peccatis nostris in humilitate neque pro nostris solum, sed pro peccatis totius mundi: haec erat generalis gratia et beneficium commune: specialis gratia, et beneficium, ecclesia sive corporis Christi peculiare est caro haec spiritualis, quae veram vitam prebet eam comedentibus.* Smyth, *Works* 2:707.

[86]Translation by Coggins, *John Smyth's Congregation*, 192-93. *fideles Christi fratres germani, per ejusdem spiritualis carnis koin_nian . . . sunt enim duo illi, id est Christus et ecclesia in carnem unam per magnum hoc sacramentum spiritualis hujus coniugis. Eph. 5: 31. 32. 30.* Smyth, *Works* 2:708.

[87]Smyth does use similar language to Ries's in article 50 of *Propositions and Conclusions*, Smyth 2:741.

have a spiritual knowledge of Christ, so that "his image and likeness may be born within us." He goes to explain that this image would allow the believer to participate in the spiritual work of Christ. Ries also urges, "We must know Christ according to the spirit that he may baptize us with the Holy Spirit and with fire, feed us with heavenly food and drink, making us partakers of the divine nature."[88] Ries identifies "knowing Christ according to the spirit" as the catalyst for allowing the believer to have a union with the divine. Once the believer partakes in the divine nature then he is to live according to this "new life."

Ries's reliance on Schwenckfeld for his understanding of the spiritual flesh becomes apparent in the similar phrases used by both to describe how this flesh leads to participation in the divine nature. Paul Maier also indicates that although Schwenckfeld discusses the topic often, still he is imprecise in his description of how one partakes of the spiritual flesh of Christ.[89] This imprecision carries over into the writings of Ries and Smyth. Even though neither Ries nor Smyth is completely clear on how the believer is to partake in the spiritual flesh of Christ, this does not diminish its importance to them. After his discussion of spiritual knowledge, Ries declares, "This we call a knowledge of Christ according to the spirit, without which the knowledge of Christ according to the flesh is not sufficient for salvation."[90]

In Smyth's Mennonite works he takes a stance that is similar to that of Ries. Smyth's defining stance on the issue of Christology is that the natural flesh of Christ is not the primary concern, but the spiritual flesh is. He writes in *The Last Booke*:
True, this I did affirm, and this I defend as the most excellent and comfortable truth in the scriptures: for who knoweth not that to knowe and be made conformable to the similitude of Christs death, buriall and

---

[88]Ries, "A Short Confession of Faith," 15. I have chosen to use "according to the spirit" instead of Dyck's "according to the Spirit" for clarity. This use of the term "spirit" relates to the inward, not the Holy Spirit. See also above, n. 79, for further comment.

[89]Paul L. Maier, *Caspar Schwenckfeld on the Person and Work of Christ* (Assen: Royal VanGorcum Ltd., 1959) 22. Maier includes some of Schwenckfeld's phrases for describing communion with the spiritual flesh.

[90]Ries, "A Short Confession of Faith," 15. I have replaced "Spirit" with "spirit." See nn. 79 and 88 above for the reason.

resurrection in the mortification of synne and the new creature, to be made flesh of his flesh, and bone of his bone, spiritually in the fellowship of one holy anoynting, which is Christs spiritual flesh, who knoweth not I say that this, is better then the knowledge of Christs naturall flesh.[91]

In article 50 of *Propositions and Conclusions*, Smyth does not use the terms natural and spiritual flesh. Instead, he uses the terms flesh and spirit to present the same idea. A spiritual knowledge of Christ leads to salvation. He says:

> That the knowledge of Christ according to the flesh is of small profit . . . but the knowledge of Christ according to the spirit is effectual to saluation which is spiritually to be grafted to the similitude of Christs birth, life, miracles, doings, sufferings, death burial, resurrection ascension, and exaltation.[92]

Knowing Christ according to the spirit brings an union between Christ and the believer; it is synonymous with partaking of the spiritual flesh.

Smyth's Revisions to His Christology

Two areas of Smyth's Christology demonstrate his changes as a Mennonite. In his typology, he shifts to the position that, just as the Old Testament gives only a glimpse of Christ compared with the New Testament, so His work on earth is equally only a partial view of His glorified status. Secondly, in his understanding of Christ as King, Priest, and Prophet, he highlights the fulfillment of Christ in these roles only after His return to heaven. For Smyth, no longer is Christ's earthly ministry the full revelation of these roles. On the contrary, Christ's earthly work in these roles serves as an indicator of what He does spiritually as the risen King, Priest, and Prophet.

Revisions to the typology of Christ. As a Mennonite, Smyth continues to support the idea that Christ fulfills the Old Testament types. In his *Defence of Ries's Confession*, he declares that the letter or type is found in the Old Testament, but that Christ is the truth. He indicates that many of the Old Testament practices were ceremonial. Then, he writes, "For the

---

[91]Smyth, *Works* 2:759-60. A similar sentiment is expressed in *Defence of Ries's Confession* 2:696.

[92]Smyth, *Works* 2:741. "Ascension" has been emended.

letter has already perished; the shadow has passed by; the body and the truth is Christ."[93] This quotation is similar to Smyth's way of relating the testaments early in his career where Christ is the truth typed in the Old Testament. Also, in *Argumenta Contra Baptismum Infantum*, Smyth refers to Moses being a type of Christ just as he had done in *The Character of the Beast*. His argument as a Mennonite reflects a similar use of typology as he had as a Baptist. He says:

> [B]ut we respond, the sacraments of the New Testament should be so clearly revealed by Christ who is the Son and most faithful in the whole house of God, because he held to all the circumstances, and also by Moses it was done concerning the sacraments of the Old Testament: nor can we flee to circumcision in order that from it we may bring light to baptism. For who expounds the New Testament through the Old? . . . Who interprets Christ through Moses?[94]

Although some aspects of his typology of Christ remain the same at this stage of his career, Smyth also makes a notable adjustment. In addition to the things of the Old Testament typing Christ, the natural things of Christ type the spiritual. His human actions shadow the divine. Smyth demonstrates this concept by saying, "For, as all the figures and ceremonies of the Old Testament foreshadow the person of Christ and His attributes, so the same person of Christ, His actions and His sufferings borne in humility were a certain shadow of His own self already exalted in glory at the right hand of the Father."[95]

---

[93]Translation by Coggins, *John Smyth's Congregation*, 189. *Litera enim jam obiit, umbra preteriit, corpus et veritas est Christus.* Smyth, *Works* 2:704.

[94]*sed nos respondemus debere sacramenta novi testamenti a Christo qui filius est et fidelissimus in tota domo dei tam dilucide explicari, quod attinet ad omnes circumstantias, atque a Mose factum est de sacramentis veteris testamenti: neque posse nos confugere ad circumcisionem ut inde lucem afferamus baptismati. quis enim exponeret testamentum novum per vetus? . . . quis Christum per Mosen interpretaretur?* Smyth, *Works* 2:729-30.

[95]Translation by Coggins, *John Smyth's Congregation*, 183. *Quemadmodum enim omnes figurae et ceremonia veteris testamenti Christi personam ejusque accidentia adumbrarunt: sic ipsa Christi persona, actiones et perpessiones in humilitate gesta, umbra quaedam fuerunt suiipsius jam gloria exaltati ad dextram dei pa[tris].* Smyth, *Works* 2:698.

236 / The Theology of John Smyth

Smyth later reaffirms this thought in *Propositions and Conclusions*. In article 51 of that confession, he says that the things Christ did on earth, He now does from heaven in the lives of believers. He writes:

> That Christ Jesus according to the flesh and history in his doings and suffering, is a great misterie, and diuine sacrament of himself, and of his ministerie, in the spirit, and of those spirituall things, which he worketh in those which are to be heires of saluation Rom. 6.3.6: Eph. 2.5.6 and that spiritually he performeth all those miracles in the regenerate, which he wrought in his flesh.[96]

With this comment Smyth is not denying the historicity of Christ's earthly ministry, but wants to emphasize that the contemporary spiritual work of Christ has greater importance for eternity. His use of the term "sacrament" indicates that he sees the earthly work pointing to a higher significance of the ongoing, spiritual work. Christ's physical nature types the hidden, spiritual nature.

Revisions to Christ as King, Priest, and Prophet. Another repercussion of Smyth's emphasis on Christ's spiritual work over His physical work is the change in his views of Christ as King, Priest, and Prophet of the church. Smyth says that it was upon His resurrection and ascension that Christ fully assumed these roles. A slight indication of this can be seen in article 7 of Smyth's *Corde Credimus*. Here he discusses the person of Christ, including the statement that He "was conceived by the Holy Spirit in the womb of the Virgin Mary, afterwards was born, circumcised, baptized, tempted . . . at last was crucified, dead buried, he rose again, ascended into heaven; and that to himself as only King, Priest, and Prophet of the church, all power both in Heaven and earth is given."[97] It appears that Smyth is stating these events in chronological order. If this remains consistent then Christ's assumption of the roles of King, Priest, and Prophet comes only after His ascension.

---

[96]Smyth, *Works* 2:741-42.

[97]Translation by Evans, *The Early English Baptists* 1:253. *per spiritum sanctum in utero virginis Mariae conceptum fuisse, posteanatum, circumcisum, baptisatum, tentatum fuisse . . . denique crucifixum, mortuum, sepultum fuisse, resurrexisse, in coelum ascendisse: ipsique, utpote soli Regi, Pontifici, et Prophetae Ecclesiae, omnem tum coelo tum in terra potestatem commissam esse.* Smyth, *Works* 2:682-83.

As Smyth proceeds further into Mennonite theology, this thought becomes more evident. He holds that Christ's earthly ministry prepares the way for His ultimate fulfilment of these three roles in His glorified state. Smyth writes in *Defence of Ries's Confession*, "For Christ's services and His works, or His accomplishments in glory, are much brighter and more excellent than those which He performed in humility. Christ received His kingdom, priesthood and prophecy after His glorification, however much He erected certain outward beginnings and foundations of it in humility."[98] In his earlier writings, Smyth emphasized the work of Christ on earth as King, Priest, and Prophet, as well as His work after His glorification. Now in this Mennonite stage, he accentuates Christ's fulfillment of these roles after His ascension. This belief complements his stress on the spiritual flesh of Christ. Just like all the other things that Christ did in his physical life are limited in comparison with their fulfillment in his spiritual acts, his roles as the Head of the church become fully realized upon His ascension and glorification.

In his "Short Confession," Hans de Ries demonstrates a similar belief. Articles 11, 12, and 14 of that confession explain what Christ did in His work on earth as a result of the three roles.[99] Then after mentioning the resurrection and ascension, Ries describes Christ's work in these roles after His death. Articles 17 and 18 of Ries's confession explain how the risen Christ continues to serve the church as Priest and King. After describing Christ in His roles on earth and after His glorification, Ries asserts that people must seek Christ in His glorified roles. Christ in His glorified status is fully able to allow them to fellowship with Him and to be victorious in spiritual warfare. As the glorified King, Priest, and Prophet, Christ strengthens His people.[100]

In *Defence of Ries's Confession*, after Smyth discusses the idea that Christ's earthly actions shadowed His glorified state, he says of this glorified state, "Here He begins His kingdom, His priesthood, His

---

[98]Translation by Coggins, *John Smyth's Congregation*, 184. *nam Christi munera eorumque opera sive effectus in gloria, multo illustriora et nobiliora sunt quam quae in humilitate transegit: regnum suum nactus est Christus, sacerdotium et prophetiam post glorificationem, quamvis externa quaedam rudimenta eorundem et fundamenta fecit in humiliatione.* Smyth, *Works* 2:699.
[99]Ries, "A Short Confession of Faith," 13.
[100]Ries, "A Short Confession of Faith," 14.

prophecy. Not that the former had no relevance to His kingdom, priesthood and prophecy, but that they are briefer in time and of less importance."[101] This quotation shows the shift in Smyth's thinking on the roles of Christ. In contrast to his earlier statements about Christ's roles, Christ's actions on earth in these roles of King, Priest, and Prophet are secondary to His actions after glorification. Because of the earthly nature of the former things, they cannot have the significance of the latter. Christ as the glorified King, Priest, and Prophet can work in the lives of all believers, which is the ultimate fulfillment of Christ's roles.

Smyth also stresses that the faithful are to take part in Christ's work in these roles. As the faithful partake of the spiritual flesh of Christ, then His reign as King, Priest, and Prophet becomes apparent in their lives. Smyth demonstrates their empowerment in article 30 of *Propositions and Conclusions* by saying, "he is become the mediatour of the new Testament (to wit) the kinge, Priest, and Prophet of the Church, and that the faithfull through him, are thus made spiritual kings, Priests, and Prophets."[102] The faithful have been granted authority in the church by Christ. This quotation also reinforces the centrality of Christ's role in the church for the faithful.

Smyth's Acceptance of Mennonite Christology

Smyth's level of acceptance of Mennonite Christology is difficult to ascertain. In his discussion of the subject, James Coggins states, "there is no doubt that in 1610 Smyth had definitely become an advocate of Mennonite Christology."[103] Unfortunately, in this statement, Coggins makes a significant oversight. Smyth never became an advocate of the heavenly flesh theory that was common in Mennonite Christology. However, he did accept the Mennonite idea of a natural and spiritual flesh of Christ. Coggins does not differentiate these ideas.

---

[101]Translation by Coggins, *John Smyth's Congregation*, 183. *Hic incipit, ipsius regnum, sacerdotium, prophetia. Non quod illa priora nihil ad regnum, sacerdotium, prophetiam pertinent, sed quod respectu horum minora sunt et minoris momenti.* Smyth, *Works* 2:698-99.

[102]Smyth, *Works* 2:737.

[103]Coggins, *John Smyth's Congregation*, 125.

The main document that Coggins uses to substantiate his theory is Smyth's *Defence of Ries's Confession*. He mentions the specific date of 1610, because that is the date of this work. This date is also mentioned because in *The Last Booke*, which is published in 1612, Smyth makes a statement against the Melchiorite incarnational view. Therefore, Coggins puts himself in a strange predicament when he says that Smyth was an advocate of Mennonite Christology, because Smyth's later statement was against it. Coggins solves the problem by saying that by 1610, Smyth accepted Mennonite Christology, but later became tentative on the subject.[104] However, two problems remain with this position.

First, Coggins's description of Smyth as an advocate of Mennonite Christology is based primarily on his statements in *Defence of Ries's Confession*, even though statements from Smyth's other works do not indicate a clear support for the incarnational theory. It is precarious to base such a strong statement on a work whose authorship is disputed over against works such as *The Last Booke* that are definitely Smyth's.[105] Even if Smyth's authorship of *Defence of Ries's Confession* is conceded, there is still a second, more fundamental problem.

The second problem is that Coggins apparently has merged two aspects of Mennonite Christology. One aspect of this Christology that Smyth accepts is the theory of the natural and spiritual flesh of Christ. However, he does not fully accept the Melchiorite theory of the incarnation. Smyth's statement that is used by Coggins as the strongest argument for Smyth's acceptance of the Melchiorite view of the incarnation is preceded by the statement, "As yet we do not perceive any phrase that indicates the material of Christ's flesh. We hear your deductions and conclusions; we do not see any clear words. Therefore, I prefer to leave it undecided rather than to argue about trifles."[106] Someone who is undecided on a particular doctrine could hardly be called an advocate of it. The rest of the statements in *Defence of Ries's Confession* that refer

---

[104]Coggins, *John Smyth's Congregation*, 125.
[105]See chap. 2 above, "Smyth's Life, Debates, and Writings," for the debate on Smyth's authorship of *Defence of Ries's Confession*.
[106]Translation by Coggins, *John Smyth's Congregation*, 182; *phrasi nullam materiam carnis Christi indicantem non adhuc percipimus, sequelas et consequentias vestras audimus, verba diserta non videmus: mallem ergo in dubio relinquere quam de lana caprina contendere*. Smyth, *Works* 2:696.

to Christology show Smyth's support of the natural and spiritual flesh of Christ, but not the Melchiorite heavenly flesh theory.

Smyth does emphasize the spiritual knowledge of Christ over the physical knowledge, which was common to Mennonite Christology. For example, Caspar Schwenckfeld argues that the only knowledge of Christ that is effectual for salvation is a spiritual one. He writes:

> The Lord Jesus Christ wishes to be known and believed by us not only according to the flesh and in a historical manner, that is . . . how he was born, died, taught and lived, what he suffered for us, what he earned and accomplished for us through his suffering; but he wishes much rather to be understood and pondered after the spirit and his new, glorified, entirely heavenly being, as a reigning Lord and king of heaven and earth.[107]

Schwenckfeld stresses that through the spiritual knowledge of Christ a believer can truly experience union with Christ. He explains, "To know Christ after the spirit is to know and feel in the heart the power and the wisdom of God (which is Christ); it is to taste in the inner recesses of the heart the heavenly gifts and powers of the world to come, yea, how sweet and pleasant the Lord is."[108] Hans de Ries continues the ideas of Schwenckfeld in arguing that Christ must not only be known "according to the flesh, or confessed literally according to historical knowledge." Instead Ries states, "Rather we must rise higher and confess Christ also according to the spirit, in his exaltation and glory."[109]

Smyth's own statements echo this characteristic of Mennonite Christology. His comments on Christ's assuming the full roles of King, Priest, and Prophet after his ascension stem from this belief. The work that Christ did in those roles on earth cannot have the same significance as the work he now does in the spirit of believers. Smyth's argument that the details of the incarnation are not essential to the faith also comes as a result of his Mennonite emphasis on the spiritual aspects of Christ. An

---

[107]*Corpus Schwenckfeldianorum*, 3:888; in Paul L. Maier, *Caspar Schwenckfeld on the Person and Work of Christ*, 70.

[108]*Corpus Schwenckfeldianorum* 14:258; in Schultz, *Caspar Schwenckfeld von Ossig*, 103.

[109]Ries, "A Short Confession of Faith," 14. I have replaced "Spirit" with "spirit," see above, nn. 79 and 88.

example of Smyth's use of this element of Mennonite Christology is in his confession, *Propositions and Conclusions*. In this confession, he stresses the spiritual aspects of Christ in several articles.

In article 49, Smyth says, "Christ Jesus, in his resurrection, ascention and exaltation, is more and rather lord and Christ, sauiour, anoynted, and kinge then in his humiliation sufferings and death."[110] He then describes Christ's suffering as the "meanes" which is lesser than the "end" which is His glorification. This idea is a result of Mennonite influence. Earlier in Smyth's career, he dedicates the entire work, *The Bright Morning Starre*, to describing the importance of Christ's death. In this work, he says,

> let vs further consider what afflictions befel him: they crucifie him, & mock him, they strip him naked . . . all which are so many sufferings of Christ for our good: he was crucified, & suffered the most accursed death of the crosse, to deliuer vs from the curse of the law . . . al these benefits we haue from all Christs sufferings.[111]

In Smyth's early works there is no downplaying of the importance of the earthly ministry of Christ. The crucifixion has more significance than as a passage into Christ's glorified state.

Smyth later puts the sufferings of Christ in vacuous terms. He asks, "For indeed what of the conception, birth, circumcision, baptism, temptation, preaching, miracles, death, burial, resurrection and ascension of Christ? Did these things happen for their own sakes or for the sake of certain others?"[112] Then he responds to his own question, "All of these things happened to Christ so that He would be able to enter into His glory and send the Holy Spirit to us from the Father."[113] Conspicuously absent from the reasons behind these earthly works of Christ are ideas

---

[110]Smyth, *Works* 2:741. "Ascention" has been emended.
[111]Smyth, *Works* 1:45. "From" has been emended.
[112]Translation by Coggins, *John Smyth's Congregation*, 183. *enim vero quid conceptio, nativitas, circumcisio, baptismus, tentatio, predicatio, miracula, mors, sepultura, resurrectio, ascensio Christi, numquid haec propter se ipsa, aut propter aliud quiddam potius contigerunt.* Smyth, *Works* 2:697-98.
[113]Translation by Coggins, *John Smyth's Congregation*, 183. *Christo contigerunt haec omnia ut possit in gloriam suam ingredi nobisque spiritum sanctum a Patre mittere.* Smyth, *Works* 2:698.

such as redemption or atonement.[114] His argument is that the ultimate achievement of Christ's life on earth is that His actions make possible His glorification. This downplays the inherent value of these earthly events and at the same time exalts the contemporary work of Christ through the spirit. Because knowledge of Christ's natural flesh does not bring salvation, Smyth argues that it is pardonable for a person to err "in the knowledge of Christs Historie."[115] He even implies that this was what Christ meant by saying it was forgivable to speak a word against the Son of Man.

It must be observed that Smyth downplays the earthly actions of Christ only in comparison to the spiritual aspects of Christ's continued work. Smyth, like Ries, stressed the inward, spiritual aspects of relating with Christ without discarding the outward aspects. Therefore, the crucifixion and other sufferings of Christ are important, but should not overshadow Christ's work in His glorified state. Also, outward ordinances such as baptism and the Lord's Supper are to be practiced, but they should always remind the faithful of the importance of the inner relationship with Christ.

A better description of Smyth's later Christology would be to say that in 1610 Smyth advocated Ries's and the other Mennonites' view of the natural and spiritual flesh of Christ and continued to do so for the rest of his career. At that time, he did not see a problem with allowing their theory of the incarnation. Later, he affirms a traditional view of the incarnation as seen by his statements in *The Last Booke*. Even though he avers the traditional view, he still refuses to make any incarnational theory a test of fellowship. Like Hans de Ries, Smyth did not believe that a definitive view on the nature of Christ's flesh was essential to salvation. This allowed him to accept the Mennonites despite any differences on the incarnation.

Conclusion

Smyth made some significant changes in his Christology once he became a Mennonite. The main aspects of his changes can be expressed in five points. First, Smyth is uncertain on the nature of Christ's flesh, so he

---

[114]Smyth's view of atonement is the subject of chap. 5.
[115]Smyth, *Works* 2:747.

does not make any definitive incarnational statements. Second, while Smyth does not support the Melchiorite incarnational view, he does become tolerant of those who hold differing views.

Third, Smyth does accept the views of Schwenckfeld and Ries on the natural and spiritual flesh of Christ. Through the spiritual flesh the believer can be unified with Christ. Although the natural flesh of Christ brings the benefit of general atonement to all, partaking of the spiritual flesh is what brings salvation to an individual. Fourth, Smyth sees the natural flesh typing the spiritual flesh as an extension of his earlier typology of Christ, where Christ is revealed more fully in the New Testament than the Old. Fifth, he understands that through the union made with the spiritual flesh, the risen Christ reigns in the spirit of believers.

Chapter 7
Smyth's View of Church and State

The General Baptists of the seventeenth century were catalysts in the religious tolerance movement in England. When Thomas Helwys came back to England after separating from John Smyth's church in Amsterdam, he pushed for the separation of church and state and religious tolerance. Scholars debate how much of this is due to Smyth's influence on Helwys, whether Smyth and Helwys developed their ideas from their Separatist ideals or whether they became advocates of religious tolerance because of Mennonite influence. There are significant differences between the church-state relations propounded by the Separatists and those taught by the Mennonites. Smyth defends these differing views in various stages of his career. Tracing the development can help to determine the influences on Smyth and how he in turn could have influenced Helwys.

The Background to Smyth's View of Church and State

The plea for religious tolerance and the separation of church and state increased in England and the Netherlands in the late sixteenth and early seventeenth centuries. While there were advocates of these views in several different groups, the views of the English Separatists and the Dutch Mennonites that could have influenced Smyth are of special interest to this study.

Separatist views of church and state. The Separatist tradition was a combination of Puritan theology and a radical separation of the righteous from the unrighteous. Because of the similarity of their theology, Separatists had many things in common with the Puritans. Their main area of difference was the proposed course of action to establish true churches among the English people. For the most part, the Puritans called for reform from within the Church of England. The Separatists moved beyond this mediating position. They held that for a true church to be instituted only those who professed faith and joined in covenant with God could be members. This view of strict separation affected their thinking on the relationship between church and state.

Most Puritans supported the ideal of a godly magistrate enacting the necessary reform for the church. For example, Thomas Cartwright, at the end of his *The Holy Exercise of a True Fast, Described Out of Gods*

Word says that Christian magistrates serve as "Fathers and Nurses to maintaine and cherish thy Church."[1] Puritans understood that the magistrate would be responsible for establishing true churches throughout the land. He would require all persons to be active in these churches, and would not permit slack observance of scriptural teaching. He would also stamp out all heresy and idolatry. In short, the magistrate was a tool in the hands of God both to establish true religion and to punish false religion.[2] Bishop Joseph Hall demonstrates the close connection that he sees between the civil and ecclesiastical powers by saying, "The Church and State, if they be two, yet they are twins; and that so, as either's evil proves mutual."[3]

Separatists agreed with the Puritans in that the magistrate's responsibility was to suppress idolatry and to encourage true religion. However, the Separatists claimed that the magistrate had no authority to establish churches. True religion could be encouraged by appointing city preachers or making laws that favored true religion. The magistrate could not form a church, or appoint ministers to serve a church. Neither was the church to be involved with the affairs of the magistrate. The Separatists supported some degree of separation of church and state. The Puritans, however, believed that the church and state were two distinct administrations, but that they were not "functionally unrelated."[4]

The Separatist, Robert Browne (*The Writings of Robert Harrison and Robert Browne*) deals at length with the relationship between the magistrate and the church in his *A Treatise of Reformation without Tarying for Anie*. His main concern is with ministers who acknowledge the need for reform in the Church of England but who are waiting for the magistrates to lead the reform. He says that these ministers have limited their own ability for ecclesiastical reform by deferring to the magistrates. Browne asks, "In deede can the Lordes spirituall governement be no waye exe-

---

[1]Thomas Cartwright, *Cartwrightiana*, ed. Albert Peel and Leland H. Carlson (London: George Allen & Unwin, 1951) 150.
[2]Wilbur K. Jordan, *The Development of Religious Toleration in England*, 4 vols. (London: George Allen & Unwin, 1936) 1:244-48.
[3]*The Works of . . . Joseph Hall* 9:468.
[4]Maclear, "The Birth of the Free Church Tradition," 100.

cuted but by the civill sworde?"[5] He calls for the ministers to lead the reform, even to the point of separating from the Church of England.

Browne holds that all Christian magistrates should be subject to the discipline of the church. Ministers should not have to worry about being displaced if they reprimand a magistrate. He writes, "They are in deede to keepe their Royal dignitie, yet keeping that they are to abase them selves unto God before the face of the Church."[6] Browne affirms the authority of the magistrates, but requires that their authority not be carried over into ecclesiastical matters. In discussing the ministers who tarry for the magistrates, he says, "But they put the Magistrates first which in a common wealth in deede are first, and above the Preachers, yet have they no ecclesiasticall authoritie at all, but onely as anie other Christians, if so be they be Christians."[7]

Part of Browne's problem with magistrates leading in reform was the relationship which the magistrate has with things of faith. Although he agrees that the magistrates are an ordinance of the Lord, he admonishes the ministers for waiting for the magistrates.[8] He says that these ministers are claiming that the kingdom of God can be established based on the authority of the magistrate's decree. On the contrary, he says that the kingdom of God comes from obedience to God's commands.[9] He states that just as a magistrate cannot establish God's kingdom, so also he cannot designate who should be a proper minister. Since the call to ministry is from the Lord, the magistrate should be excluded from being able to remove a minister.[10] This right of discipline belongs only to the church through Christ's authority.

Calling for a magistrate to enact reform is negligence by the minister, and it also goes against the apostolic example. If magistrates are the instruments of reform then people are forced into religion no matter what their beliefs. Browne objects, "The Lordes kingdome is not by force, neither by an armie or strength, as be the kingdomes of this worlde."[11]

---

[5]Browne, *The Writings of Robert Harrison and Robert Browne*, 153.
[6]Browne, *The Writings of Robert Harrison and Robert Browne*, 166.
[7]Browne, *The Writings of Robert Harrison and Robert Browne*, 155.
[8]Browne, *The Writings of Robert Harrison and Robert Browne*, 335.
[9]Browne, *The Writings of Robert Harrison and Robert Browne*, 156-57.
[10]Browne, *The Writings of Robert Harrison and Robert Browne*, 159.
[11]Browne, *The Writings of Robert Harrison and Robert Browne*, 161.

Here, Browne indicates what was at the heart of his concern in relating church and state. The covenant of God is a personal decision that should not be forced by a magistrate. If it was forced, then the purity of the covenant would be jeopardized.

The statement that most indicates the tendency of Browne and the other Separatists to call for at least a limited amount of separation between church and state is found in his *A Treatise of Reformation*. Here, Browne addresses the role of the magistrates by saying:

> Yet may they doo nothing concerning the Church, but onelie civillie and as civile Magistrates, that is, they have not that authoritie over the Church, as to be Prophetes or Priestes, or spiritual Kings, as they are Magistrates over the same: but onelie to rule the common wealth in all outwarde Justice, to maintaine the right, welfare, and honor thereof, with outward power, bodily punishment, & civil forcing of men. And therefore also because the church is in a commonwealth, it is of their charge: that is concerning the outward provision & outward justice, they are to look to it, but to compell religion, to plant churches by power, and to force a submission to Ecclesiastical governement by lawes & penalties belongeth not to them, as is proved before, neither yet to the Church.[12]

This quotation shows that Browne limited the magistrates' relationship to the church to a general obligation of "provision" and "justice." This is markedly different from the Puritan attitude that the magistrate was to lead in the reform of the church. While this statement does not go as far as promulgating religious tolerance, the statement "to compell religion . . . belongeth not to them" may at least be a precursor to the idea of tolerance. Browne was not an advocate of full religious tolerance, but he did want the magistrate to limit his rule to the commonwealth and allow the church to rule in spiritual matters.[13] For Browne this meant that the church would be responsible for church discipline and for appointing ecclesiastical authority. These would not fall under the responsibilities of the magistrate.

Robert Browne may have started the Separatist movement in the direction of the separation of church and state. However, Henry Barrow led the Separatists back toward a more Puritan view in these matters.

---

[12]Browne, *The Writings of Robert Harrison and Robert Browne*, 164.
[13]Browne, *The Writings of Robert Harrison and Robert Browne*, 167.

Barrow believed that it was the duty of the magistrate to lead in reform. In his fifth examination, he states that the magistrate ought to uphold the laws of God, and that they ought not to make laws that conflict with the laws of God. He says, "Yet I thinke it the dutie of every Christian, and principally of the prince, to enquire out and renue the lawes of God, and stir up al their subjectes to more diligent and careful keeping of the same."[14] Later, Barrow again upholds the right of the magistrates to be active in matters of religion. He says, "God hath incommended [intrusted] and injoyned the booke of his lawe to al princes, therbie to governe both the church and common wealth in al things."[15] His main concern was that the Christian magistrates would base their rule on the truth of God and not on the supplications of the ecclesiastical hierarchy.

Barrow held that once Queen Elizabeth I had been shown through scripture the many errors of the Church of England, it was her duty to God "to abolish and depose" it as a false church.[16] He believed that the magistrates have a twofold role in religion. They are responsible for the establishment of true religion and must remove all false worship within their dominions.[17] Barrow thought that a magistrate should fulfill this role not only as a magistrate, but also as a Christian. He writes:

> Espetially and above all, it is the office and dutie of princes and rulers to whom the word and sword of God is therefore committed, most carefully to advance and establish in their dominions the true worship and ministerie of God and to suppresse and roote out all contrary, as they tender their owne salvation at that day of all accompts and the salvation of that people under their charge.[18]

Both the Word of God and the sword of God are within the authority of the magistrate. Barrow commends the queen for her suppression of

---

[14]Barrow, *The Writings of Henry Barrow, 1587–1590*, 198.
[15]Barrow, *The Writings of Henry Barrow, 1590–1591*, 363.
[16]Barrow, *The Writings of Henry Barrow, 1587-1590*, 230.
[17]"That the prince ought to proclaime and publish the gospel of Christ, with the true preaching and sincere practise thereof in all things that God shal give knowledge of. And to forbid and exterminate all other religions, worship and ministeries within her dominions." Barrow, *The Writings of Henry Barrow, 1587-1590*, 227-28.
[18]Barrow, *The Writings of Henry Barrow, 1587-1590*, 228-29.

idolatry, but says that the priests should have taken care of that.[19] He says that the slack discipline within the Church of England has forced the magistrate to use the sword to repress some sins.[20] In Barrow's mind the correction of sins is the responsibility of the clergy, but since they are failing then the magistrate is to fulfill this role.

Barrow supports the idea of a Christian magistrate. However, he contends that such a magistrate is personally still under the authority of the church. If a prince or a magistrate refuses to be disciplined by the church, they cannot be members of the church. This would, nevertheless, have no effect on their authority as a civil magistrate.[21] Barrow says that it is dangerous to "exempt christian magistrates from subjection and obedience unto the scepter and government of Christ in his church."[22] This discipline could go as far as excommunication.[23]

Barrow holds that no magistrate has the right to require all the people of a nation to enter into the church. His Reformed doctrine comes into his reasoning. Since God has predestined some to salvation from the beginning, for a magistrate to force everyone to enter the church would be contrary to the plan of God.[24] Barrow holds that not even the kings of the Old Testament had this right. He says while it was true that these kings could plant religion and reform the state, they were not allowed to open the Temple to the heathen. The same was to be true of contemporary magistrates; they should not open the doors of the church to the unfaithful.[25] They could, however, force all to hear the truth.

Barrow called for the magistrate to end the persecution of the true church that the Separatists had discovered. He held that if the magistrate was to refuse to support the true religion, then a Christian must obey God over the prince.[26] Opposition from the magistrates is no reason to stop the

---

[19]Barrow, *The Writings of John Greenwood and Henry Barrow, 1591-1593*, 163.

[20]Barrow, *The Writings of Henry Barrow, 1590-1591*, 253.

[21]Barrow, *The Writings of Henry Barrow, 1587-1590*, 289.

[22]Barrow, *The Writings of Henry Barrow, 1587-1590*, 641.

[23]Barrow, *The Writings of Henry Barrow, 1587–1590*, 641-46; and Barrow, *The Writings of Henry Barrow, 1590–1591*, 354.

[24]Barrow, *The Writings of Henry Barrow, 1587–1590*, 287-88.

[25]Barrow, *The Writings of Henry Barrow, 1587–1590*, 289.

[26]Barrow, *The Writings of Henry Barrow, 1590–1591*, 355.

advancement of true religion. The necessity of obedience to true religion regardless of the actions of the magistrate became a common theme in Separatist writings.

Much of Henry Barrow's thought continues in "A True Confession." This Separatist confession was composed in 1596, mostly under the leadership of Henry Ainsworth and Francis Johnson.[27] In article 39, the Separatists asseverate:

> That it is the Office and duty of Princes and Magestrates, who by the ordinance of God are supreme Governers under him over all persons and causes within their Realmes and Dominions, to suppress and root out by their authoritie all false ministeries, voluntarie Relligions and counterfeyt worship of God, to abolish and destroy the Idoll Temples, Images, Altares, Vestments, and all other monuments of Idolatrie. . . . And on the other hand to establish & mayntein by their lawes every part of Gods word his pure Relligion and true ministerie to cherish and protect all such as are careful to worship God according to his word, and to leade a godly lyfe in all peace and loyalltie; yea to enforce al their Subjects whether Ecclesiasticall or civile, to do their dutyes to God and men, protecting & mainteyning the good, punishing and restreyning the evill according as God hath commanded, whose Lieutenants they are heer on earth.[28]

In this article several points are made. The magistrates are recognized as an ordinance of God. Also, their three main tasks are mentioned. First, they are to suppress all false religions within their realm. Second, they are to maintain the true religion. Third, as they are maintaining true religion, they are to force people to do "their dutyes to God and men." This means that they are to see that their subjects practise proper worship and observe civil justice. Noticeably absent from this article is any notion of religious tolerance toward any group but their own. The Separatists did not express any desire for complete religious tolerance.

The confession espouses other Barrowist positions on the relationship between church and state. In article 42, the Separatists affirm Barrow's statement that a Christian should obey God no matter what the decisions of the magistrate. At the risk of the loss of land, goods, or even life, a

---

[27]"A True Confession," in Lumpkin, *Baptist Confessions of Faith*, 79-97.
[28]Lumpkin, *Baptist Confessions of Faith*, 94-95.

Christian should "obey God rather then man."[29] However, the agreement of the magistrate "maketh it much more peaceable" for a person to obey God.[30] Occasionally, God graciously allows for the magistrates to protect the faithful, and these magistrates serve as "nourcing Fathers and nourcing Mothers to his Church."[31]

Twenty-one years after this confession, in 1617, Francis Johnson published *A Christian Plea*, where he reasserts many of the principles presented in the Separatist confession. His views on the magistrate seem to be relatively unchanged by twenty years of exile in Amsterdam. He says that Christian magistrates should "submit themselves and their scepters to the Lord Jesus Christ, who is Prince of the kings of the earth, and to see the truth of God mainteyned, and his ordinances observed, in all things."[32] Therefore, the magistrates can be used by God to further His will. However, while the magistrates do have a protective role for true religion, there are limits to their involvement. They must not "intrude themselves into the peculiar dueties of the Ministers."[33] Exercising ecclesiastical discipline and exerting authority in spiritual matters are not among the duties of the magistrates.

Johnson continues his discussion of the relationship between the church and the magistrate by adding that no action of the magistrate removes the church's obligation to obey God. The church is accountable to the magistrate, but it is ultimately accountable to God. Johnson echoes the sentiments of articles 40-42 of "A True Confession" when he writes:

> [N]o Princes, nor Prelates, Synodes, Churches, or any persons whosoever, can make that lawful, which God hath made unlawfull, nor that unlawfull which God makes lawfull. But Princes and Magistrates may graunt outward peace & help to the Church: for which (wheresover it be had) we are bound to be thankfull to God and them. And if they will not suffer us with peace to walk in the faith and way of Christ, according to the word of God: yet ought we notwithstanding so to doe, obeying God rather then man; and patiently to suffer what they shall lay

---

[29]Lumpkin, *Baptist Confessions of Faith*, 96.

[30]Lumpkin, *Baptist Confessions of Faith*, 95.

[31]Lumpkin, *Baptist Confessions of Faith*, 95. This quotation echoes the thought of the Puritan, Thomas Cartwright. See n. 1, above.

[32]Johnson, *A Christian Plea*, 322.

[33]Johnson, *A Christian Plea*, 322.

upon us, even to imprisonment, banishment, confiscation of goods, and death itself.[34]

Fred Powicke summarizes the Separatist position in six statements. First, the princes are to suppress all false religion. Second, they are to enforce attendance at the services of the true church. Third, they are to suppress evils contrary to the law of God inside and outside the church. However, fourth, the prince is to oversee only indirectly the fulfillment of the divine law in the church. Fifth, the prince is to be disobeyed if he attempts to force religion in a way contrary to God. Sixth, the prince's personal standing in the church is like that of every other Christian who is subject to church discipline.[35] Powicke describes the Separatist position as one that may have limited the powers of the magistrate in the church, but without denying the right of the magistrates to exercise some authority in matters of the church. He includes the comment that the Anabaptists did deny this right to the magistrate.[36]

A Mennonite view of church and state. Hans de Ries was responsible for at least three confessions for the Mennonites.[37] In two of the confessions he made statements that pertained to the relationship between church and state. In his "Middelburg Confession," which was published in 1578, he clarifies his stance on the separation of church and state. In article 11, he affirms the authority of magistrates to handle civil affairs. However, he also says, "This authority does not extend to the church of Christ, the heavenly city in which God himself is judge, for over spiritual things-faith and unbelief, matters concerning conscience and the Word of God- over these things we have a single head and ruler, our only king Christ Jesus."[38] The separation of church and state is based on two things: the difference of worldly and spiritual matters, and the necessity of Christ

---

[34]Johnson, *A Christian Plea*, 323.
[35]Powicke, *Henry Barrow, Separatist* 128-29.
[36]Powicke, *Henry Barrow, Separatist*, 210-11.
[37]See Cornelius J. Dyck's translations of these confessions: "The First Waterlandian Confession of Faith," *Mennonite Quarterly Review* 36 (January 1962): 5-13; "The Middelburg Confession of Hans de Ries," *Mennonite Quarterly Review* 36 (April 1962): 147-61; "A Short Confession of Faith by Hans de Ries," *Mennonite Quarterly Review* 38 (January 1964): 5-19.
[38]Ries, "Middelburg Confession," 153.

directing matters of conscience such as religion. The freedom of an individual's conscience is essential in true faith. Therefore, the magistrate should not force obedience in religious matters. Ries says, "Therefore, whenever the state with her sword and judgment interferes and seeks to control the spiritual things of God and the soul of man, that is in matters of faith, she usurps the office of the Lord."[39] This idea is furthered in article 15 where Ries urges that spiritual errors should be corrected by the spiritual weapons of the church, not by the authority of the magistrate.[40]

In his third confession, which was the "Short Confession" presented to Smyth's congregation in 1610, Ries opposes the idea of a Christian magistrate. He does support government in general by saying it is "ordained of God as necessary for the maintenance of public life, of orderly citizenship, for the protection of the good and punishment of evil."[41] This article restates the sentiment that he expressed earlier in the "Middelburg Confession" where he writes, "I have taught with the Apostle Paul that the state is of God, ordained as a servant of God to punish those who commit evil, to exercise authority in worldly, political affairs."[42] He states that Christians are to obey the government unless they command something that is contrary to God.[43] However, he is clear in his opposition to a Christian magistrate, he says:

> This office of secular powers has not been given by the Lord Jesus in his spiritual kingdom to the members of his church. He has not called his disciples to be secular kings, princes, dukes, or authorities, nor instructed them to seek and assume such office, nor to rule the world in a worldly manner.[44]

Ries opposes the idea of a Christian magistrate because he says that the magistracy contains elements that are contrary to Christian values. Because of the contradictions, Christians are to avoid these offices. Ries states, "All this then, together with the many other things which are attached to worldly office—the waging of war, the destroying of life and

---

[39] Ries, "Middelburg Confession," 153.
[40] Ries, "Middelburg Confession," 154.
[41] Ries, "A Short Confession of Faith," 18.
[42] Ries, "Middelburg Confession," 153.
[43] Ries, "A Short Confession of Faith," 18.
[44] Ries, "A Short Confession of Faith," 18.

property of the enemy, etc., which things do not harmonize with the new life in Christ—lead us to avoid these offices and services."[45] In 1578, Ries opposed the magistrate exerting any authority in the church. By 1610, he added his opposition of a Christian holding the office of a magistrate.

Smyth's Writings on Church and State

In his writings, Smyth demonstrates a kinship with the views of his predecessors. His views and influences changed as he progressed through his career.

Smyth's Puritan writings. As a Puritan, Smyth's view of the role of the magistrate in religion was similar to that of other Puritans. In his work, *A Paterne of True Prayer*, Smyth says that the king is responsible for matters in the church and state.[46] He states that next under Christ in the church, it is the king who is "the supreme Gouernor in all causes, and ouer all persons, aswell ecclesiasticall, as ciuill."[47] Because the magistrate is responsible for the religious state of his dominion, Smyth affirms that a "Prince hath authoritie to substitute ecclesiastical Magistrates according to the word, for the polity of the Church, in the exercising of iurisdiction, visitation of Churches, and ordination of Ministers."[48] All of this power has its responsibility. Smyth holds that magistrates are to be a major part of erecting the kingdom of God. He asserts that the kingdom of God is erected "when the Magistrate by law doth establish the worship of God according to the word."[49]

A godly magistrate is essential for establishing a true church according to Smyth. The magistrate was to be a catalyst for ecclesiastical reform. He says that magistrates are to "further the kingdome of Christ." Moreover, they are to "erect and maintaine the faith and true religion by the sword."[50] They are to promote this true religion by making godly or

---

[45]Ries, "A Short Confession of Faith," 19. Later in this chapter, Ries's ideas in their relationship with Smyth's are discussed further.
[46]Smyth, *Works* 1:234.
[47]Smyth, *Works* 1:158.
[48]Smyth, *Works* 1:158-59.
[49]Smyth, *Works* 1:159.
[50]Smyth, *Works* 1:161.

wholesome laws and by seeing "that both the tables of the Commandements be observed."[51]

In *A Paterne of True Prayer*, Smyth encourages Christians to pray for both magistrates and ministers. The reason for these prayers is that the magistrates and ministers are the two pillars of God's kingdom. The prayer should be that "God would vouchsafe to adde the operation of his spirit, to the outward meanes both of Magistracie and Ministerie."[52] He adds that abolishing the role of the magistrate in religion is "a thing that the diuell would wish . . . and therefore hee hath inspired that diuellish doctrine into the confused heads of the Anabaptists, who take away all rule and authoritie and all superioritie among men."[53]

Smyth also stresses that magistrates must not to give in to the pressure for religious tolerance because through the toleration of many religions, "the kingdom of God is shouldered out a doores by the diuels kingdome."[54] Instead of tolerating other religions, Smyth says, "Magistrates should cause all men to worship the true God, or else punish them with imprisonment, confiscation of goods, or death as the qualitie of the cause requireth."[55]

So, during his Puritan stage, Smyth supported the need for a Christian magistrate. He also defended a close relationship between church and state, which allowed the magistrate to lead in reform. Smyth also opposed any form of religious tolerance.

Smyth's Separatist writings. During Smyth's years as a Separatist, he continued his support of a positive role in reform by a Christian magistrate. In his work, *Principles and Inferences*, he declares that each church has the power to reform itself, but that the magistrates are still to help establish true churches and to "command all their subjects to enter into them."[56] While the magistrates make this command, individuals are "bound in conscience" to be members of these churches. It is not because of the magistrate's ordinance that a person is to join a church, but it is because "every man is bound to obey Christ in his kingdome and

---

[51] Smyth, *Works* 1:161, 203.
[52] Smyth, *Works* 1:163-64.
[53] Smyth, *Works* 1:165.
[54] Smyth, *Works* 1:166.
[55] Smyth, *Works* 1:166.
[56] Smyth, *Works* 1:267.

spirituall regiment and no other . . . and the true visib[l]e church is Christs kingdome and house."[57]

Smyth also makes a statement that demonstrates that he agreed with the Separatists' intolerance toward other religious groups. He argues that God has not ordained any monasteries, convents, nor Catholic or Anglican parish churches. A true church formed through a covenant is the only proper place to worship God. Smyth contends, "The true visible church is the narrow way that leadeth to life which few find. . . . Other religious communions are the broad way that leadeth to destruction which many find."[58] Smyth, as a Separatist, continued to support the need for Christian magistrates and gave no indication of a desire for religious tolerance. His agreement with the Separatists on these issues can be inferred from the fact that in his work, *The Differences of the Churches*, Smyth does not mention church-state relations as an area of debate between himself and the other Separatists.

In discussing limits on the relationship between church and state, Smyth dealt mainly with the magistrate's authority to appoint ministers. In *Paralleles, Censures, Observations*, he says that, while the princes were to encourage the preaching of the word, they were not to choose ministers. Only the church should select its ministers. Smyth supported the prince's authority to commission a person to preach to the people, but that person could not be considered the true minister of a true church.[59] He continues this thought in "A Lettre written to Mr. A. S.," which was published in conjunction with *Paralleles, Censures, Observations*, by arguing that the state cannot determine the positions of authority in a true church. When he asks A. S. where his authority is from, Smyth says, "if you say you have your authoritie from the civil State, I answere, the civil State can not give Ecclesiastical authoritie."[60]

In his letter to A. S., Smyth gives what he sees as the eleven fundamental principles of Separatism. Two of these principles demonstrate Smyth's understanding of how the true church is to relate to the state. He says about the members of the church, "If Kings and States forbid the

---

[57]Smyth, *Works* 1:267.
[58]Smyth, *Works* 1:252.
[59]Smyth, *Works* 2:507.
[60]Smyth, *Works* 2:554.

faithfull to vse any of these helps and meanes which God hath given and commaunded them to vse, they are to lose their lives rather then to forbeare, bicause they are bound to obey God rather then men."[61] Second, he states, "If Princes and States commaund the Church and faithfull to entertaine any other ordinances, then these before rehearsed, they are not to obey, but rather to leese their lives."[62] Both of the statements could be summarized by saying that no restriction of true religion or legislation for false religion by the magistrate is to be obeyed. Smyth says that in these matters the magistrates have overstepped their bounds by disobeying God. His comments echo the sentiments of the Separatist work, "A True Confession." The authors of that confession assert that if the magistrate tries to restrict true religion then the church is

> to walke in the obedience of Christ even through the middest of all tryalls and aflictions, not accompting their goods, Lands Wyves, Children, Fathers, Mothers, brethren, Sisters, no nor their own lyves dear unto them . . . [and] to obey god rather then man.[63]

This Separatist ideal caused Richard Bernard to make the accusation that Smyth and the other Separatists were undercutting the authority of the magistrates. Smyth responds to his indictment in *Paralleles, Censures, Observations*, where he discusses the idea of obedience to the magistrates. The same imputation had been levied against the Separatists before. Almost twenty years earlier, George Gifford made a similar accusation against Henry Barrow. Barrow answered the charge:

> And now let the christian reader judge what cause Mr. Giffard had to pronownce this mine answere to the bishopp's question Anabaptistical, when I therein acknowledged the whole lawe of God, the place, office, and whole power of princes that God hath given them, all which the Anabaptistes utterly denie. Or with what conscience he hath charged us as seduced by [Robert] Browne's writing. And [to accuse me] to hold that princes ought not to compel their subjects to the true worship of

---

[61]Smyth, *Works* 2:550.
[62]Smyth, *Works* 2:550.
[63]Lumpkin, *Baptist Confessions of Faith*, 96.

Smyth's View of Church and State \ 259

God. Neither ought to reforme the church. All which sclanders this my answere which he here endevoreth to confute, refuteth to his face.[64]

Barrow claims that he differed from Robert Browne and the Anabaptists in that he supports the idea of a Christian magistrate intervening in religious matters.

Smyth echoes much of Barrow's sentiment. He says, "You say we hold that princes have no more to do in ecclesiastical causes then one of vs in a particular congregacion: I say for myne owne part, & I think I may say it for al the brethren of our Church, that herin you do shamefully believe: I wil therfor manifest what we hold & teach concerning Princes Supremacy."[65] At this point, Smyth describes what he sees as the authority of the magistrates. He says that the magistrates are an ordinance of the Lord and are to be obeyed always. There is no excuse for a Christian to take part in a revolt.[66] Smyth supports the statements which he made as a Puritan by reaffirming that the magistrates are "to be the keeper of both the tables of the commaundements . . . also to commaund & cause al men within these Dominions to walk in the wayes of God."[67] In the sixth point in this discussion, Smyth makes a clear statement of the role of a Christian magistrate in the church. He writes, "That a Prince hath powre in a particular visible Church, to punish any wickednes any one committeth: and to cause that visible Church to assume & practise any truth Gods word teacheth."[68] So, magistrates can punish anyone within the church that is not following the commandments of God. However, they still must be members of a church and submit to its authority. They can be censured if they are unrepentant, but a censured magistrate is still to be prayed for and obeyed.[69]

During this stage of his career, Smyth upheld the idea of a godly magistracy. The magistrate would have supreme control in the state and would have some power in the church. He was to encourage the true church, but should not interfere in ecclesiastical matters such as the

---

[64]Barrow, *The Writings of Henry Barrow, 1590–1591*, 364.
[65]Smyth, *Works* 2:519. "Congregacion" has been emended.
[66]Smyth, *Works* 2:519.
[67]Smyth, *Works* 2:519. "Commaundements" has been emended.
[68]Smyth, *Works* 2:519-20.
[69]Smyth, *Works* 2:520.

choosing of ministers. In this point, Smyth held there should be limited separation between matters of church and state. However, he still held firm to the idea that there was no room for religious tolerance. Instead the magistrate should "abolish Idolatry & al false wayes."[70]

Smyth's Baptist writings. As a Baptist, Smyth again has to deal with the charge that he is denying the authority of the magistrates. Richard Clyfton, who makes the accusation, is attempting to associate Smyth with a common charge made against the Anabaptists. In fact, as a Puritan, Smyth had made the same charge against the Anabaptists.[71] However, in his attempt to show his orthodoxy on the matter of the magistrates, Smyth makes a statement in "The Epistle to the Reader," which was added to *The Character of the Beast*, that magistrates are an ordinance of the Lord and all should be subject to them. He mentions that magistrates "are the ministers of God to take vengeance on them that do evil."[72] The other statements, which Smyth includes in this response, demonstrate that his view of a Christian's responsibility to the magistrate has not changed much from his Separatist letter to "A. S." The Christian must pray for, pay tribute to, and respect the magistrate's position.

However, in the second half of Smyth's response to Clyfton's charge, he does question the validity of a Christian magistracy. He does not deny outright the possibility that a magistrate could become a Christian and still maintain his office. He does say that magistrates who became Christians were a problem for him. To indicate his uncertainty on the subject he says, "but of Magistrates converted to the Faith & admitted into the Chu. by baptisme, ther may many questions be made, which to answer neither wil we if we could, neither can we if we would."[73] He does not mention if it is permissible for a Christian to become a magistrate. This response did not satisfy Richard Clyfton. He says that Smyth should not leave the question of Christian magistrates open. Clyfton argues that Smyth is either denying that the New Testament teaches all things clearly, or denying Christian magistrates.[74]

---

[70]Smyth, *Works* 2:519.

[71]Smyth, *Works* 1:165. Smyth claims that Anabaptists wanted anarchy.

[72]Smyth, *Works* 2:572.

[73]Smyth, *Works* 2:572. It is likely that this statement is an early indication of Mennonite influence on Smyth.

[74]Richard Clyfton, "An Answer to M. Smyth's Epistle to the Reader" in *The*

Although Smyth seemed to be wavering on the issue of a Christian magistracy, his dogmatic rejection of the ideas of others shows that his views on tolerance remained unchanged. He does not address what the magistrate ought to do about religious tolerance, but he does display his personal intolerance for the Separatists, Anglicans, or Roman Catholics. His intolerance is demonstrated in "The Epistle to the Reader" where he says:

> Be it knowne therfor to all the Seperation that we account them in respect of their constitution to bee as very an harlot as either her Mother England, or her grandmother Rome is, out of whose loynes she came: & although once in our ignorance we have acknowledged her a true Chu. yet now being better informed we revoke that our erroneous judgment & protest against her, aswel for her false constitution, as for her false ministery, worship, & government.[75]

From the attitude of intolerance displayed throughout *The Character of the Beast*, one would not expect Smyth to advocate an official policy of religious tolerance.[76] He is silent on the relationship of church and state, but it is likely that he maintained the view from his Separatist writings of limited separation between the two. His comments in "The Epistle to the Reader" suggest that he is beginning to question the legitimacy of a Christian magistrate.

Smyth's Mennonite writings. In Smyth's later writings, his uneasiness about Christian governmental leaders becomes more negative. Smyth discusses the subject of a Christian magistracy in two works, *Defence of Ries's Confession* and *Propositions and Conclusions*. In these works, it becomes clear that Smyth opposes the idea of a Christian magistracy. A Christian magistracy is where the magistrate uses his civil position to coerce people to accept a certain faith or where he exerts his authority in the church to determine matters of faith. While Smyth opposes the Christian magistracy, he only questions if a magistrate should retain his

---

Plea for Infants and Elder People, n.p.
[75]Smyth, *Works* 2:565.
[76]It is possible that Smyth held to his personal intolerance for opposing views but allowed for liberty of conscience. However, the point is that this thought does not surface in Smyth's *The Character of the Beast*.

position if he becomes a Christian. He does not deny the permissibility of a magistrate being a Christian.

In *Defence of Ries's Confession* and *Propositions and Conclusions*, three reasons for Smyth's opposition to a Christian magistracy emerge. First, he sees Christian magistracy as the continuation of an Old Testament practice. He opposes this continuation because he believes that the godly kings in the Old Testament represented Christ who came as the true King of the Church. After Christ came and established himself as King of his Church, there was no need for a magistrate to legislate in matters of faith. Moreover, Christ did not establish the need for a magistrate in the New Testament church. Smyth's typological interpretation of the Old Testament led him to regard the Christian magistracy as an Old Testament type which should be discontinued.[77] Smyth makes the sardonic statement, "For, by the same reasoning by which you baptize infants and retain the authority of the magistrate in the church of Christ, we can restore the priesthood, altar and sacrifices of sheep and cattle."[78] In another section of *Defense of Ries's Confession*, Smyth argues that neither Christ nor the apostles called for the magistrate to have a role in the New Testament church. He writes, "Indeed neither Christ nor the apostles nor that first and pure church recognized the office of magistrate or the use of the civil sword. What about us? It remains that we should follow in their footsteps since we lack holier and sounder judgement."[79]

Second, also based on his typological theology, Smyth sees the magistracy as a position which is concerned with worldly matters, whereas Christians are to be concerned with spiritual matters. He says that the concept of a Christian magistracy is foreign to the thinking of Christ because He is concerned with a spiritual kingdom not an earthly

---

[77]Coggins, *John Smyth's Congregation*, 182-83, 190, 193; Smyth, *Works* 2:696-97, 705, 709.

[78]Translation by Coggins, *John Smyth's Congregation*, 190. *eadem enim ratione qua vos infantes baptizatis, et magistratus authoritatem in ecclesia Christi retinetis, possumus nos sacerdotium, altare et victimas ovium et boum reducere.* Smyth, *Works* 2:705.

[79]Translation by Coggins, *John Smyth's Congregation*, 193. *verum officium magistratus sive usum gladii civilis non agnovit sive Christus sive Apostoli, sive prima illa et pura ecclesia: quid nos? restat ut eorum vestigiis insistamus ne sanctiora et saniora sapimus.* Smyth, *Works* 2:709.

one. The church does not have the right to rule in civil matters because it belongs to Christ's spiritual kingdom. He writes:

> However, I assert that Christ is a spiritual king and His church is a spiritual kingdom, and all the servants of the church are spiritual servants; its weapons are spiritual, its laws spiritual, its punishments spiritual, its rewards spiritual, its soldiers spiritual, its warfare spiritual; and, therefore, I do not see how the church of Christ can administer that external and fleshly commonwealth.[80]

He asks why Christ decided to advance His spiritual kingdom through persecution and death if He saw the magistrate as a medium for promoting the faith. Christ's rule was among the persecuted and He did not try to win the magistrates to have them force everyone into the church.[81] Smyth concludes, "Therefore, either the office of magistrate is not proper for the church, or the primitive church was not [well] enough instructed regarding his maintenance and defense, or in these here times of ours a more auspicious age is to be seen for the church of Christ."[82]

Third, Smyth challenges the Christian magistracy because of the acts of revenge that must accompany the office of a magistrate. It is in this third reason that Smyth points out the inherent contradiction in a Christian serving as a magistrate. In *Defence of Ries's Confession*, he argues that a Christian magistrate would be in a predicament when forced to practice revenge, which was contrary to Christian values. He asks, "And finally, when Christ bade us to love our enemies, I wonder how the Christian magistrate can take revenge on his foes? I want all these to be

---

[80]Translation by Coggins, *John Smyth's Congregation*, 182. *ego autem affirmo Christum esse regem spiritualem ipsiusque ecclesiam esse regnum spirituale omnesque ecclesiae ministros esse ministros spirituales, arma esse spiritualia, leges spirituales, poenas spirituales, praemia spiritualia, milites spirituales, bellum spirituale: ideoque non video quomodo externa illa et carnalis politia ecclesiam Christi administrare possit.* Smyth, *Works* 2:696-97.

[81]Coggins, *John Smyth's Congregation*, 182-83; Smyth, *Works* 2:697.

[82]Translation by Coggins, *John Smyth's Congregation*, 183. *ergo aut magistratus officium non est ecclesiae idoneum, aut primitiva ecclesia non erat satis instructa ad ipsius tutelam et defensionem: aut hisce nostris temporibus feliciora secula visura est ecclesia Christi.* Smyth, *Works* 2:697.

explained to me from the New Testament."[83] This predicament is expressed again in his English confession, *Propositions and Conclusions*. Here, Smyth holds that a magistrate cannot do his job properly, and still express the Christian virtues of humility and submission to persecution. He states in article 85 that a Christian magistrate would have to submit to others as a Christian, which it is impossible to do and maintain control with the sword. Smyth says of the magistrate, "he must suffer persecution and affliction with Christ, and be slaundered, reviled, blasphemed, scourged, buffeted, spit vpon, imprisoned and killed with Christ: and that by the authoritie of magistrates, which things he cannot possiblie doe, and reteyne the reuendge of the sword."[84]

Statements like this one from *Propositions and Conclusions* and the previous one from *Defence of Ries's Confession* caused Smyth's opponents to charge him with denying that a magistrate could be a Christian. However, Smyth never states that a magistrate could not be a Christian. In his defense of Ries's article 37, Smyth writes, "We deign magistrates who now profess Christ [to be] of equal honor with the kings and elders of the people of Israel under the Old Testament, and we believe they can be just as pleasing to God as the magistrates of the Jewish church."[85]

In article 85 of his own confession, *Propositions and Conclusions*, Smyth gives a hypothetical situation to demonstrate the difficulties that face a magistrate who becomes a Christian. He says:

> That if the magistrate will follow Christ, and be His disciple, he must deny himself . . . he must loue his enemies and not kill them, he must pray for them, and not punishe them, he must feed them . . . not imprison them: banish them: dismember them: and spoyle their Goods.

---

[83]Translation by Coggins, *John Smyth's Congregation*, 182. *denique cum Christus jussit nos inimicos nostros deligere, miror quomodo magistratus Christianus possit vindictam exercere contra ipsius hostes? Haec omnia vellem mihi ex novo testamento exponi.* Smyth, *Works* 2:696.

[84]Smyth, *Works* 2:748.

[85]Translation by Coggins, *John Smyth's Congregation*, 193. *Nos magistratus qui jam Christum profitentur equali dignamur honore cum regibus et senioribus populi Israelitici sub vetere testamento eosque posse eque deo placere credimus atque magistratus ecclesiae judaicae.* Smyth, *Works* 2:709.

Not only must the magistrate refrain from these offences,

> he must suffer persecution and affliction with Christ, and be slaundered, reviled, blasphemed, scourged, buffeted, spit vpon, imprisoned and killed with Christ . . . which things he cannot possiblie doe, and reteyne the reuendge of the sword.[86]

Though he does not deny explicitly the possibility of a Christian magistrate, a question surfaces from Smyth about the feasibility of Christian magistrates. While Smyth agrees that it is possible for a magistrate to be a Christian, it is also inadvisable for a Christian to be a magistrate.

In article 83 of *Propositions and Conclusions*, Smyth says that magistrates are a permissive ordinance of God to keep order, for the good of mankind. Magistrates should bring honour to God through their position by doing what is just.[87] When we compare these statements with those that Smyth made in his Separatist and Baptist stages, there is a significant change.[88] In all three stages he claims that the position of a magistrate is an ordinance. In each case he affirms that the magistrate is to do what is good and just in the eyes of God. However, in this later statement on magistrates, he adds the word "permissive" to describe the ordinance of God for magistrates. He suggests that magistrates are only to preserve civil order. This is very different from the role that he urged for the magistrate as a Puritan or Separatist. John Robinson, *The Works of John Robinson*, the Separatist, challenged Smyth's inclusion of the phrase "permissive ordinance of God." He says that this phrase is a contradiction. If it is an ordinance of God then "it is confessed good." However, he adds, "Where it is made "permissive," it is condemned as evil: since only evil is permitted or suffered of God."[89]

In article 84, Smyth offers a statement concerning the separation of church and state. In this article, he not only renounces the need for a Christian magistrate by clearly defining the separation of civil and religious duties, but he also indicates a call for religious tolerance from the magistrate. He states, "That the magistrate is not by vertue of his

---

[86]Smyth, *Works* 2:748.
[87]Smyth, *Works* 2:748.
[88]Smyth, *Works* 2:519, 572.
[89]Robinson, *The Works of John Robinson*, 3:275-76.

office to meddle with religion, or matters of conscience, to force and compell men to this or that form of religion, or doctrine: but to leave Christian religion free, to every mans conscience, and to handle onely ciuil transgressions."[90] Unfortunately, Smyth does not elaborate on this idea. Therefore, it is impossible to determine if Smyth is advocating full religious liberty or simply calling for the magistrate not to legislate on any religious issue. The context is that Jesus is "the king, and lawgiuer of the church and conscience."[91] Full religious liberty seems unlikely because his plea seems simply to be for the magistrate not to be involved in religion, which would result in some measure of tolerance.

In *The Last Booke*, Smyth discusses the "grievous sins" of the Church of England hierarchy. In this discussion, he does not mention errors in church government or worship, or any of the other topics that he mentioned in his earlier works. His charge here is that Anglican hierarchy err when they force "ther subscription Canons, and Ceremonies vppon mens consciences, vppon payne of excomunication deposition, silence, imprisonment, banishment, and the like penalties."[92] Smyth states that when they do this, then they "sitte as Antichrist, in the temple of God, which is the conscience."[93] Smyth's desire for tolerance caused him to call for both the civil magistrates and the ecclesiastical hierarchy to leave each person to make his own decision about faith.

As a Mennonite, Smyth opposes the idea of a Christian magistracy. He also held to a complete separation of church and state. Since these were two different realms, the magistrate should not take part in religious affairs. The absence of magisterial involvement would allow for some amount of religious tolerance. Tolerance is important because it allows God to work freely in a person to lead him to a decision about true faith.

Source of Smyth's Thought

The source of Smyth's ideas on church-state relations is debated. There are basically two schools of thought on the subject. The first school holds that Smyth took the Separatist ideal of a limited separation between

---

[90]Smyth, *Works* 2:748.
[91]Smyth, *Works* 2:748.
[92]Smyth, *Works* 2:754. "Imprisonment" has been emended.
[93]Smyth, *Works* 2:754.

church and state to its logical conclusion. Scholars such as James Maclear, Thomas Lyon, and Slayden Yarbrough fall in this category. The other school of thought is that Smyth's later views were a result of the direct influence of the Mennonites. Timothy George, Leon McBeth, and Stephen Brachlow argue this.

The position of the first school. Representatives of the first school, Maclear and Lyon, present similar cases for Smyth's views to be a continuing development of ideas of church-state relations that had existed among Puritans and Separatists before him. Maclear says that the tendency to differentiate between the powers of church and state was inherent in Puritanism and Separatism. He says that the Puritans evolved "to make ever more radical the distinction between the civil and religious realms."[94] He adds that the Separatists furthered the Puritan ideas by progressing from "the separation of the powers of the two domains to a partial separation of ends as well."[95] Maclear argues that the idea of the separation of civil and religious realms, combined with their view that true religion was voluntary, drew the Separatists and Smyth to the concept of religious tolerance.

Maclear assesses the Separatist ideal of the role of the magistrate by saying, "Though proclaiming the liberty of the church from any bondage to earthly authority, they by no means excused the magistrate from his duties to true religion."[96] He also argues that the Separatists did not hold to religious tolerance. In their view, there could be only one true church and it must be obeyed by all.[97] If a true church such as that of the Separatists were in power, then it could properly enforce true religion through the magistracy. The current magistrates could not enforce true religion because they were being directed by the Church of England, not by a true church.[98] Maclear also observes that the intolerance that the different groups of Separatists had for each other indicates that they were not interested in religious tolerance.[99]

---

[94]Maclear, "The Birth of the Free Church Tradition," 102.
[95]Maclear, "The Birth of the Free Church Tradition," 106.
[96]Maclear, "The Birth of the Free Church Tradition," 106.
[97]Maclear, "The Birth of the Free Church Tradition," 105.
[98]McBeth, *The Baptist Heritage*, 16-17.
[99]Maclear, "The Birth of the Free Church Tradition," 108-109.

Lyon also draws attention to the idea of separation of church and state found in Separatist thought. He says that the Separatists held to a "strict separation" of spiritual and temporal powers.[100] Lyon says that though the Separatists maintained that the magistrate was responsible for defending true religion and persecuting error, there was a difference in the roles of church and state. The civil authorities were not to interfere "in certain religious actions," moreover the church's power of excommunication "should not interfere with the civil rights of the State or of its citizens."[101] Lyon holds that this Separatist idea made Smyth and other Baptists more open to the idea of religious tolerance.[102] In an attempt to strengthen his argument for Separatist influences on Smyth, Lyon indicates two subtle differences, which he perceives between Smyth's views and those of the Mennonites.[103] The first difference is that Smyth puts more emphasis on "the value of the magistrate in preserving civil good" and he holds that the magistrates may please God in their duties.[104] The second difference is that the "Short Confession" of the Mennonites denies Christian magistrates "explicitly" where Smyth is more "cautious."[105]

Yarbrough also holds that Smyth's views on religious tolerance are a development from his Separatist background. He argues that Smyth took the thoughts of Robert Browne and others Separatists to their logical conclusion. Yarbrough says that the Separatists had not fully developed the idea of the separation of church and state. He says, "They did not envision a society in which the church and the state were totally separate."[106] When it comes to religious tolerance, the Separatists desired

---

[100]Thomas Lyon, *The Theory of Religious Liberty in England 1603–1639* (Cambridge: Cambridge University Press, 1937; repr.: New York: Octagon Books, 1976) 107.
[101]Lyon, *The Theory of Religious Liberty in England*, 107.
[102]Lyon, *The Theory of Religious Liberty in England*, 108.
[103]Lyon, *The Theory of Religious Liberty in England*, 114-15.
[104]Lyon, *The Theory of Religious Liberty in England*, 114.
[105]Lyon, *The Theory of Religious Liberty in England*, 114-15.
[106]Slayden A. Yarbrough, "The English Separatist Influence on the Baptist Tradition of Church-State Issues," *Baptist History and Heritage* 20/3 (July 1985): 20.

toleration for their views only. The magistrate was to suppress false religion and conduct governmental affairs according to biblical principles.[107]

Yarbrough contends that two aspects of Separatism led to Smyth's belief in religious tolerance and the separation of church and state: theory and practice. Their theory was that the covenanted community, that is, the true visible church, was ultimately responsible to God and not to the magistrate. They also believed that membership in the true church must be voluntary, not coerced. The Separatist practice was significant because they acted on their belief that the church had the necessary powers for reform and did not need to wait for the magistrate's lead.[108] Yarbrough concludes his argument by saying, "On the foundation of Separatist thought and practice, the early Baptists constructed their views on church and state issues."[109]

There are two common weaknesses in the arguments of scholars from the first school. The first weakness is that the significant differences between the Separatist views and Smyth's Mennonite views are not recognized properly. For example, even though Barrow argued that the church could reform itself without direct action by the state, this did not lead him to a view of toleration. He writes that "the prince ought to proclaime and publish the gospel of Christ, with the true preaching and sincere practise thereof in all things that God shal give knowledge of. And to forbid and exterminate all other religions, worship and ministeries within her dominions."[110] This is in direct contradiction with Smyth's statement that the magistrate should not "meddle with religion" or "force and compell" a certain form of religion, but instead should leave "religion free, to every mans conscience."[111] In comparing Smyth's Mennonite views with a Separatist contemporary, John Robinson, significant differences again become apparent.

In his *On Religious Communion*, Robinson challenges Smyth's Mennonite position. Robinson argues that a godly magistrate may pray for his enemies and punish them also. He disagrees with Smyth's view

---

[107]Yarbrough, "The English Separatist Influence on the Baptist Tradition," 20.
[108]Yarbrough, "The English Separatist Influence on the Baptist Tradition," 20-21.
[109]Yarbrough, "The English Separatist Influence on the Baptist Tradition," 21.
[110]Barrow, *The Writings of Henry Barrow, 1587–1590*, 227-28.
[111]Smyth, *Works* 2:748.

that these duties are mutually exclusive. Smyth had also argued that, with Christ as the only King of the church, the magistrate should not interfere in matters of faith. Instead, he should leave "religion free" to each individual. Robinson objects by saying that Christ's role as King of the church means that the magistrate "may alter, devise, or establish nothing in religion otherwise than Christ hath appointed, but proves not that he may not use his lawful power lawfully for the furtherance of Christ's kingdom and laws."[112] Robinson and other Separatists desired only a limiting of the magistrate's role in the church. Smyth, however, argued for the magistrates not to have authority in religious matters and he ends his career with questioning the expediency of a magistrate retaining his position on becoming a Christian. With the recognition of these differences between Smyth and his Separatist predecessors and contemporaries, it is difficult to agree with the idea that the Separatist views were the "foundation" upon which Smyth built his ideas.[113]

In *The Last Booke*, Smyth himself recognized the significant difference in his appeal for tolerance and that of the Separatists. His view was that if someone had accepted the gospel, then that was all that was important. No outward matters should be a point of contention.[114] The toleration which Smyth called for in his work was not the limited tolerance pursued by the Separatists. Actually, Smyth draws a contrast with them by saying he is not a part of those that "peremptorily censure all men except those of their owne vnderstanding . . . of which sort are those of our English nation."[115] Smyth realized that the tolerance that he was advocating was more inclusive than the Separatist view. He said that the Separatists condemned all other churches "except those of their owne societie and fellowshipp." Where Smyth said that he would not "shutt my eares from hearinge anie instruction which others may affoord mee."[116] These comments, along with the fact he allowed the magistrate no role in arbitrating between true and false religion, separated Smyth's Mennonite views from his Separatist background.

---

[112] Robinson, *The Works of John Robinson*, 3:277.
[113] Yarbrough, "The English Separatist Influence on the Baptist Tradition," 20.
[114] Smyth, *Works* 2:752-55.
[115] Smyth, *Works* 2:752.
[116] Smyth, *Works* 2:752.

The second weakness in the first school of thought is that the obvious similarities between Smyth and other Mennonites are dismissed too easily. In Lyon's discussion, he suggests that Smyth differs from the Mennonites in that he has a more positive evaluation of the role of the magistrates for preserving good. Actually, Smyth's comments are similar to the statements in Hans de Ries's "Short Confession." Ries asserts, "Government, or secular authority, is ordained of God as necessary for the maintenance of public life, or orderly citizenship, for the protection of the good and punishment of the evil, Rom. 13:1f."[117] This has the same sentiment as Smyth's statement, "That the office of the magistrate, is a disposition or permissiue ordinance of God, for the Good of mankinde: that one man like the bruite beasts devoure not another Rom. 13. and that iustice and ciuilitie may be preserued amonge men."[118] Both of these statements confirm the magistrate's role in preserving civil order, but do not give any indication of the magistrate having any role in promoting religion.

Lyon also adds that Smyth differs from the Mennonites in that he does not deny Christian magistracy explicitly, while the Mennonites do. Again, Smyth's statements resemble Ries's statements in his "Short Confession." Ries says there is an inherent contention between being a Christian and being a magistrate. The role of a magistrate includes waging war, confiscating goods, and executing enemies. All of these contradict Christian values according to Ries.[119] Smyth observes the same discrepancies between Christianity and the magistracy. As a Christian, the magistrate must not kill his enemies, punish or imprison them, banish them or take their goods. However, Smyth says that avoiding these things is difficult for a magistrate to do.[120]

The position of the second school. Timothy George approaches Smyth's view from a different perspective. He says that there might be a case against Mennonite influence on Smyth in believers' baptism and general atonement, but "this case can hardly be made with reference to his view of church and state."[121] He notes that Smyth agrees with the

---

[117]Ries, "A Short Confession of Faith," 18.
[118]Smyth, *Works* 2:748. "Ordinance" has been emended.
[119]Ries, "A Short Confession of Faith, 19.
[120]Smyth, *Works* 2:748.
[121]Timothy George, "Between Pacifism and Coercion: The English Baptist

Mennonite tradition of relating church and state. George contends that Smyth believed that a Christian could not be a magistrate, a view similar to that of the early Anabaptists in the Schleitheim Confession and to the more recent "Short Confession" of Hans de Ries. George claims, "Smyth's view of religious toleration derived from his apolitical ethic and his essentially negative evaluation of magistracy."[122] George argues that Smyth's view was a radical departure from the Puritan-Separatist view of magistrates, and that Thomas Helwys's view serves as a mediating position between Smyth and the Separatists.

Leon McBeth also rejects the idea that the Separatists were interested in complete religious tolerance. His claim is that the Separatists desired for their persecution to end, but that they never envisioned tolerance for other groups.[123] He gives evidence of Separatist support for a godly magistrate enforcing true religion. McBeth holds that Separatists such as John Robinson and Henry Ainsworth did not oppose the right of the magistrate to strike out against false religion, but they did oppose the influence of a false church on the magistrate. McBeth summarizes his views on the Separatists and other groups by saying that, other than Smyth and the Baptists, "No other voices or pens had yet taken up the plea for complete religious liberty and separation of church and state."[124]

Brachlow fits loosely in the category of the second school. He does not discuss the Mennonite influence on Smyth, but he does indicate that Smyth does not belong to the "central separatist political ideals."[125] Brachlow traces the views of church-state relations through the thought of the Puritans and the Separatists. He differs from A. F. Scott Pearson, B. R. White, and Timothy George when he says that there was no significant difference between Separatist views and the Puritan ideal of religion as not being coerced.[126] Brachlow argues that, while Browne and

---

Doctrine of Religious Toleration," *Mennonite Quarterly Review* 58 (January 1984): 35.

[122]George, "Between Pacifism and Coercion," 36.

[123]H. Leon McBeth, *English Baptist Literature on Religious Liberty to 1689* (New York: Arno Press, 1980) 15.

[124]McBeth, *English Baptist Literature on Religious Liberty to 1689*, 19.

[125]Stephen Brachlow, *The Communion of Saints. Radical Puritan and Separatist Ecclesiology, 1570-1625* (Oxford: Oxford University Press, 1988) 254.

[126]Brachlow, *The Communion of Saints*, 249-50.

Barrow, among others, may differ in emphasis from the Puritans, their doctrine of church and state was basically the same. This doctrine is that the magistrate should not force entrance into the church but should ensure the protection of true religion. So, the magistrate maintains a custodial role for the true church. Brachlow submits that Smyth rejects the Puritan and Separatist traditions when he disallows any role for the magistrate in protecting true religion.[127]

The weakness with George's argument is that he says that Smyth's view of religious toleration "derived from . . . his negative evaluation of the magistracy."[128] Smyth did struggle with the notion of revenge, which he saw as inseparable from the magistracy. However, this is not the source from which Smyth "derived" his view. It is only the manner in which he defended it. It is much more likely that Smyth adopted his beliefs on church-state relations because of the typological nature of his theology. He saw church and state as two different realms. George does not recognize this aspect of Smyth's thought as the central factor in his acceptance of the separation of church and state. George acknowledges that the division of a civil or temporal realm from the spiritual realm is central to the arguments of Helwys and his succeeding Baptists.[129] The same tendency is apparent in Smyth and is the focus for his defense of the separation of civil and ecclesiastical matters. The reason behind Smyth's acceptance of the separation of church and state and religious toleration is that the magistrate has civil duties but should have nothing to do with religious matters. This dichotomy was carried on by Helwys and the General Baptists.

The weakness with Brachlow's position is that there is a difference of degree between the Puritan and Separatist view of the separation of church and state. If nothing else, the Separatists were willing to act out their belief that the state was not to be involved in ecclesiastical decisions. While Puritans may have had similar beliefs, they were not willing to pursue them to the length that the Separatists were.

The strength of the arguments of Brachlow and George is their indication of the break that Smyth had with the Puritan and Separatist ideas

---

[127]Brachlow, *The Communion of Saints*, 254.
[128]George, "Between Pacifism and Coercion," 36.
[129]George, "Between Pacifism and Coercion," 41.

of magistrates. Smyth the Separatist and Smyth the Mennonite have two different perspectives. As a Separatist, he drew on the views of his fellow Separatists. As a Mennonite, he rejected that tradition and accepted the views of Ries and the Waterlanders. There is a major difference in the Mennonite views of Smyth and those of the Separatists such as John Robinson.[130]

While McBeth does claim that Smyth was different from the Separatists in his views of religious tolerance, he still claims that there is some connection. He suggests that Smyth took the "Separatist doctrine of religious individualism to its logical conclusion in absolute religious liberty."[131] Strangely, he seems to contradict his own statement when discussing the possible sources of Smyth's belief in religious liberty. There he states, "That religious liberty is the logical conclusion of Separatism, and thus explains the Baptist position, is equally unsatisfying."[132] The reason for this apparent contradiction is that McBeth tries to acknowledge that Smyth's views do have some similarities with his Separatist predecessors. At the same time, McBeth contends that it was Mennonite influence that convinced Smyth in the area of church-state relations.[133] However, he does not include evidence to support this view but simply states that "Mennonite influence was clearly formative" for Smyth and his successors.[134] His failure to give clear evidence of Mennonite influence and his conflicting statements of the Separatists' influence on Smyth are the main weaknesses with his case.

A new argument for Mennonite influence. The quandary that McBeth puts himself in can be avoided if Smyth's views of church-state relations are separated into three categories: Christian magistracy, separation of church and state, and religious tolerance. The rejection of a Christian magistracy and the question of whether a magistrate could be a Christian appear only late in Smyth's writings and were the result of Mennonite influence. The same is true with religious tolerance. Smyth expresses

---

[130]George, *John Robinson and the Separatist Tradition*, 243; Walter H. Burgess, *John Robinson, Pastor of the Pilgrim Fathers* (London: Williams & Norgate, 1920) 153-54; Brachlow, *The Communion of Saints*, 264-65.

[131]McBeth, *English Baptist Literature on Religious Liberty to 1689*, 20.

[132]McBeth, *English Baptist Literature on Religious Liberty to 1689*, 281.

[133]McBeth, *English Baptist Literature on Religious Liberty to 1689*, 282.

[134]McBeth, *English Baptist Literature on Religious Liberty to 1689*, 283.

these views only after initiating talks with the Mennonites. However, the idea of a limited separation of church and state surfaces as early as Smyth's Separatist works.

The idea of limited church-state separation in Smyth's Separatist and Baptist writings seems to result from the Separatist teaching that the church is responsible to Christ, not to the magistrate. While they did support the idea of both the magistrate and the church enforcing true religion, most Separatists believed that the realms of authority were to be separate. The magistrate was not to exert authority in many matters of the church, nor was the church to be involved in civil matters. The main reasoning behind this idea in Separatist thinking was twofold. First, the Separatists did not trust the current magistrates to be able to reject the counsel of the established church and to support true religion. Second, each person is responsible for his or her response to God's covenant. Because of the individual nature of faith, any forced obedience cannot be seen as true faith. In his book on political philosophy, Desmond Clarke expresses the idea of voluntary obedience in these words:

> This basic moral obligation cannot be satisfied if the individual is coerced, either in favour of or against some religious beliefs, because the kind of free, voluntary acts which are characteristic of religious faith cannot properly be said to be performed if an agent is coerced. Since each man has a moral obligation . . . to seek the truth in this way, it would be unacceptable if civil authorities interfered with this most basic moral/religious obligation.[135]

Separatists held to the idea that the magistrates could encourage true religion, but should not exercise any authority in church matters. Therefore, there is a limited amount of separation between church and state. The separation is only limited because while each person has a moral obligation to pursue truth, it is not immoral for the magistrate to constrain those who hold to false beliefs. So, the magistrate still has some responsibility for true religion.

The idea of a limited separation of church and state was developed by Smyth to the point where he came to believe as a Mennonite that the

---

[135]Desmond M. Clarke, *Church and State: Essays in Political Philosophy* (Cork: Cork University Press, 1984) 99-100.

two were completely unrelated and mutually independent. The Separatists did not possess the tolerance necessary to allow for a complete separation of the two. If individuals are allowed to follow their own consciences even if they are in error, then the civil magistrates do not have the responsibility for promoting or even protecting the true church. The Separatists would not agree with this position because they held that the truth was of higher value than religious tolerance. Since they believed that they had exclusive ownership of the truth, the Separatists had a reason "to devalue the autonomy of others in favour of leading them, freely or otherwise, to the truth."[136] So, while true religion could not be accepted because of force, the magistrates were still to promote the spread of the truth and to eliminate false teachings.

Clarke gives this description, "Religious tolerance implies neither favouring or discriminating against individual citizens . . . solely because of their personal choice with respect to religious belief. It applies to non-religious citizens as much as to those who support a religious tradition."[137] Separatists had no intention of granting such freedom. Their desire was for everyone at least to know their teachings, if not accept them fully. J. D. Hughey differentiates between the type of tolerance that Separatists promulgated and the type that Smyth held. He describes the Baptists who followed Smyth as having insisted on tolerance for all religions, in contrast to those who advocate tolerance for "the true religion" only.[138] Smyth's Mennonite views were similar to Clarke's definition of religious tolerance. So, while Smyth's view of the separation of church and state was present to some extent in the Separatist tradition, his view of religious tolerance and the rejection of a Christian magistracy were drawn from the Mennonites.

Smyth's three reasons for rejecting a Christian magistracy were his view of the typological relationship between the Old Testament and the New Testament, his typological understanding of the spiritual and temporal realms, and his opposition to a Christian exacting revenge. These three reasons are the same as those given by Hans de Ries for

---

[136]Clarke, *Church and State*, 85.

[137]Clarke, *Church and State*, 84.

[138]John D. Hughey, "Baptists and Religious Freedom," *Baptist Quarterly* 17 (April 1958): 251.

rejecting a Christian magistracy. In article 35 of Smyth's version of Ries's confession these three ideas emerge. Ries says, "This office of the worldly Authority the Lord Jesus hath not ordeyned in his spiritual kingdom the church of the new testament. . . . Neyther hath he called his disciples or followers to be worldly kinges, Princes, Potentates, or magistrates."[139] This quotation mentions the first two reasons that Smyth uses in his rejection of a Christian magistracy. Later, in the article, Ries says the magistrate has "to hurt his enemiess in body or goodes."[140] Here, Ries demonstrates the same opposition to revenge that Smyth held. That Smyth not only held to a similar teaching on a Christian magistrate as Ries, but also used the same reasoning, is strong evidence that Smyth drew from him in this doctrine.[141]

There is another statement that Ries makes that is similar to a later one by Smyth. In his "Middelburg Confession" of 1578, Ries speaks of the magistrate's authority: "This authority does not extend to the church of Christ, the heavenly city in which God himself is judge, for over spiritual things- faith and unbelief, matters concerning conscience and the Word of God- over these things we have a single head and ruler, our only king Christ Jesus."[142] Ries's comments have the same purpose as Smyth's assertion in article 84 of *Propositions and Conclusions*. Smyth says, "the magistrate is not by vertue of his office to meddle with religion, or matters of conscience . . . for Christ onelie is the king, and lawgiuer of the church and conscience."[143] Matters of the spiritual realm dealing with faith and conscience are governed by Christ as the king of the spiritual realm. The magistrate's proper sphere of influence is only in civil or temporal matters.

Smyth's acceptance of the Mennonite views of religious tolerance causes questions of Socinian influence on Smyth's church-state views. Any similarities between Smyth's view of religious tolerance and those

---

[139]Burrage, *The Early English Dissenters* 2:197-98; In Dyck's version, "of the new testament" does not appear: "A Short Confession of Faith," 18-19.

[140]Burrage, *The Early English Dissenters* 2:198; Dyck's version ("A Short Confession of Faith," 19) has "destroying of life and property of the enemy."

[141]A discussion of the same three reasons in Smyth's writings appears earlier in this chapter.

[142]Ries, "Middelburg Confession," 153.

[143]Smyth, *Works* 2:748.

of the Socinians are due to the common link of the Mennonites, though the amount of influence the Socinians had on the Mennonites in this area is debatable.[144] There is a difference in the reasoning behind the Socinians' view and Smyth's reasoning. Religious tolerance in Socinianism was based on the fact that all things in religion must come from the New Testament and must be rational. Since the important matters were discernible by reason, anything that required something other than reason was to be rejected. Because these essentials were logical, all Christians would accept them. Discrimination based on any secondary matters would be illogical. Tolerance was based on the idea that all Christian groups held to some essential points. Other differences were to be overlooked.[145]

Smyth's view is similar in that he held that differences in secondary matters of religion should not incite intolerance. He states:

> The Articles of Relligion which are the ground of my salvation, are these, wherin I differ from no Good Christian: That Jesus Christ the sonne of God, and the sonne of Marie, is the Anointed king, Priest, and Prophett of the church, the onlie mediator of the new Testament, and that through true repentance and faith in him who alone is our saviour, wee receiue remission of sinnes, and the holie ghost in this lyfe, and there-with all the redemption of our bodies, and everlastinge life in the resurrection of the bodie: and whosoeuer walketh accordinge to this rule, I must needs acknowledge him my brother: yea, although he differ from me in diuers other particulars.[146]

However, Smyth was not Socinian in his view. His view has nothing to do with the truth being determined by reason. Smyth's plea for tolerance of other Christian traditions is based on the idea of the liberty of the conscience. Liberty of conscience allows for the idea that truth in central matters of the faith can be shared even though there may be a difference in peripheral matters.[147] Also, Smyth's plea for religious

---

[144]See Luigi Sturzo, *Church and State*, vol. 2 (South Bend: University of Notre Dame Press, 1962) 275-78.

[145]Sturzo, *Church and State* 2:276.

[146]Smyth, *Works* 2:752-53. "From" and "and" have been emended.

[147]See Blair Worden, "Toleration and the Cromwellian Protectorate" in W. J. Shiels, ed. *Persecution and Toleration* (Padstow: Basil Blackwell, 1984) 199-234. Worden gives a clear explanation of the differences between the Socinian call for

tolerance from the magistrate stems from his view that the magistrates are not to take part in religious affairs because of the difference in the realms of church and state. This lack of involvement will result in religious tolerance. Therefore, religious tolerance exists because matters of religion should not be forced by the magistrates, not because matters of faith can be determined by reason as the Socinians argued.

Relationship with Other Aspects of Smyth's Theology

An interesting question is how Smyth's view on church and state relates to the other aspects of his theology. Coggins holds that Smyth's understanding of the relationship between the magistrate and the church is directly related to his view of general atonement. He suggests that Smyth rejected an arbitrary electing God because of an arbitrary ruling king.[148] Though this relationship has already been questioned in the previous chapter, there could still be some connection between the two ideas. Instead of Smyth's view of government determining his theology of atonement, the roles might be reversed. Perhaps Smyth first came to the conclusion that through grace God protects the right of each individual to choose salvation, and afterwards came to realize that, if God allows each individual to choose or reject faith, then the magistrate should do no less. For Smyth, it is not logical to claim that God refuses to make the choice of religion for a person, but that the magistrate should.

There are two aspects of Smyth's theology that allowed him to accept the Mennonite view of the magistrate and religious tolerance. First, Smyth believed in the personal and voluntary nature of faith. Smyth's view of the covenant and salvation requires each person to be accountable for his or her response to God. Smyth's understanding of this accountability was more evident once he had rejected the idea of predestination. People had to choose individually how they would respond to God's offer of grace. Smyth accepted the idea that neither the magistrate nor any religious group should force acceptance in matters of faith. Tolerance does not result only from the fact that many groups hold to the essentials of salvation, but also from the fact that all people are personally accountable for their response to truth. So, it is not only inappropriate to

---

tolerance and the plea for liberty of the conscience (209).
[148]Coggins, *John Smyth's Congregation*, 143-44.

dictate direction in matters of faith, but also ineffectual. Only a voluntary, personal acceptance of the truth has any credence with God.

George Selement suggests that Separatists were convinced that the Church of England had claimed to be the contemporary covenant nation replacing Israel. Yet the Separatists believed that the Old Testament concept of a covenanted nation had been replaced by the New Testament concept of a personal covenant for the local church.[149] No longer could religion be dictated by the civil magistrate because Christ was now the ruler of these covenanted individuals. Although Selement may have exaggerated the implications of tolerance that the Separatists drew from the voluntary nature of the covenant, his argument does have value for Smyth.

Smyth did reject the idea of a national covenant. He held instead that God had established an eternal covenant with the faithful. It was through the special covenant relationship that power to govern the church was granted by Christ to each member of the congregation.[150] Christ governed his covenanted kingdom directly. There was no room for the interference of the civil magistrates.

Perhaps Smyth's time as an exile strengthened these views. From Amsterdam he wrote "A Lettre written to Mr. A. S." The idea of covenant dominates the letter. He insists that the covenant is not based on the desires of any magistrate. The king cannot set up a national covenant, because the covenant is not in his power. The covenant is given to the faithful by God directly. He does not need the assistance of "any State, Prince, Priest, Prelate whatsoever." The faithful must then commit themselves to the covenant "to obey God in every one of his precepts, even the least, though it cost them their lives."[151] The covenant extends beyond any king or kingdom, Smyth says, "whersoever two or thre faithful people arise in the world, in what countrie or nation soever, at what tyme soever, there & then, the covenant, promises, & Christ is theirs, & with them."[152]

---

[149]George Selement, "The Covenant Theology of English Separatism and the Separation of Church and State," *Journal of the American Academy of Religion* 41 (1973): 66-68.

[150]Smyth, *Works* 2:386-87.

[151]Smyth, *Works* 2:548.

[152]Smyth, *Works* 2:548.

Second, Smyth's typological theology led him to accept the Mennonite view of a radical break between spiritual matters and temporal matters. Smyth came to see the position of a magistrate as a temporal, carnal position, whereas religious faith was a spiritual matter. No one should attempt to blend the two into one office or responsibility. Christ governs in spiritual matters with the magistrate having authority only in civil duties. Smyth rejected the idea of a godly magistracy, because he saw parts of the magisterial office as inconsistent with Christian virtues. He pleaded for the freedom of religion from the magistrate's control, and confirmed the need for a complete separation of church and state, because matters of faith belonged in the spiritual realm not in the temporal realm of the state.

Selement maintains that the Separatists' typological understanding of scripture led them to replace the Old Testament's national covenant with the New Testament's individual covenant. He concludes, "Such an interpretation of the Scriptures led Separatists to the repudiation of national covenants, their own peculiar typological interpretation of Israel, and eventually to a denial of the magistrate's right to interfere in religious matters."[153] Indeed, this method of interpreting scripture may have played a part in the Separatist view of church-state relations. It certainly became a part of Smyth's discussions of the topic.

Smyth understood Christ and the New Testament as not teaching the need for the magistrates to further the kingdom of God. He held that the idea of the godly magistracy was an Old Testament one. He challenged his opponents by saying that if they were going to insist on a godly magistrate, then they must find someone from the house of David based on the Old Testament practice.[154] Smyth believed that the Old Testament godly prince had been replaced by the New Testament kingdom of saints with Christ as the Head.

In one section of *Defense of Ries's Confession* it is evident that typology was a factor in Smyth's rejection of magisterial authority in the church. He writes to his Reformed opponent, "For, by the same reasoning by which you baptize infants and retain the authority of the magistrate in the church of Christ, we can restore the priesthood, altar and sacrifices of

---

[153]Selement, "The Covenant Theology of English Separatism," 68.
[154]Smyth, *Works* 2:705; Coggins, *John Smyth's Congregation*, 190.

sheep and cattle. For that reason you expel these things and we the others."[155] Smyth's argument is that based on a typological interpretation of the Old Testament, the Reformed critic would have seen the priesthood, the altar, and the sacrifices as types which were not to be continued in the New Testament. Smyth asserts that he and the other Mennonites have rejected infant baptism and the godly magistracy also on the basis of typology.

Comparison of Smyth with Thomas Helwys

When Thomas Helwys separated from John Smyth's congregation, he primarily opposed the "successionism" of Smyth. It is through the small group of followers that accompanied Helwys back to England that the General Baptists developed. During the seventeenth century, the General Baptists were proponents of religious tolerance in England, with Helwys pioneering this stance. In his work, *A Short Declaration of the Mistery of Iniquity (1612)*, Helwys calls upon King James for religious tolerance for all.[156] How much of Helwys's thought was due to the influence of Smyth? Scholars suggest a variety of answers.

Estep argues that Helwys incorporated much of Smyth's thought into his doctrine. The disagreement between Smyth and Helwys was on the subject of the magistrate's ability to belong to the church.[157] George focuses on the differences between Smyth and Helwys on the magistrate. He uses this difference to claim that the two were a great distance from each other in the area of religious toleration. George claims that, while Smyth abandoned his Puritan and Separatist background for the Mennonite doctrine, Helwys "remained faithful to the Calvinist-Puritan-

---

[155]Translation by Coggins, *John Smyth's Congregation*, 190. *eadem enim ratione qua vos infantes baptizatis, et magistratus authoritatem in ecclesia Christi retinetis, possumus nos sacerdotium, altare et victimas ovium et boum reducere, qua vos ratione haec eijcitis eadem et nos reliqua.* Smyth, *Works* 2:705.

[156]Thomas Helwys, *A Short Declaration of the Mistery of Iniquity, 1612*, ed. H. Wheeler Robinson (London: Kingsgate Press, 1935) 69. Hereafter, the shortened title *Mistery of Iniquity* will be used.

[157]William R. Estep, "Thomas Helwys: Bold Architect of Baptist Policy on Church-State Relations," *Baptist History and Heritage* 20/3 (July 1985): 32.

Separatist tradition from which they had sprung."[158] This is a striking statement because, as will be shown, Helwys has much more in common with Smyth than with the intolerant Separatists.

Jordan states that Helwys's thought was an important advance on the views of the Separatists. He says that Helwys saw the hypocrisy of the Separatists' call for tolerance of their version of the truth only. He says, "Helwys stripped this philosophy of the religious phraseology in which it had always been clothed and exposed its hideous implications."[159] Jordan argues for a basic continuity between Smyth and Helwys. He says, "The tolerant sentiments which Smyth had expressed were considerably expanded by his contemporary, Thomas Helwys."[160] He adds that Helwys's contribution to the debate for religious tolerance lay in his clear division between affairs of the church and affairs of the state.[161] Jordan indicates that this division had surfaced in Smyth. He says that Smyth's view of this separation was based on his belief in "the intensely spiritual nature of religion."[162] This dichotomy also occurs in Helwys's arguments for tolerance.

A weakness in Jordan's comments occurs when he is discussing Smyth's view of religious tolerance. He argues that this tolerant nature existed in Smyth from an early stage and this is supported by Jordan's use of isolated statements from Smyth's earlier works. For example, he takes a comment from Smyth's Puritan work, *A Paterne of True Prayer*, saying that Smyth did not want the prince to persecute God's ministers or the members of God's church. This isolated statement against wrongful persecution is not in the same spirit as Smyth's later statements of tolerance. Moreover, in *A Paterne of True Prayer*, there is an expression of Smyth's intolerance during that stage of his career. He makes a statement that condemns wrongful persecution, but also discourages tolerance. He writes that the magistrates are evil where "persecution is raised against the true worshippers of God and true religion: or else when there is a Toleration of many Religions, whereby the kingdom of God is

---

[158]George, "Between Pacifism and Coercion," "Pacificism," 39.
[159]Jordan, *The Development of Religious Toleration in England* 2:277.
[160]Jordan, *The Development of Religious Toleration in England* 2:274.
[161]Jordan, *The Development of Religious Toleration in England* 2:274.
[162]Jordan, *The Development of Religious Toleration in England* 2:270.

shouldered out a doores by the diuels kingdome."[163] Here, Smyth classifies persecution of true religion and religious tolerance as equally wrong. A strength of Jordan's work is his demonstration of the continuance from Smyth to Helwys, even though the latter may have revised and expanded the former's views.

New insight can be added to this debate by using the paradigm that has been given for Smyth's thought. It has been mentioned in this chapter that Smyth's view of church-state relations should be divided into three categories. The use of the three categories will demonstrate the similarities between Smyth and Helwys. First, Helwys agrees with Smyth's rejection of the Christian magistracy, although he does not question a Christian being a magistrate. Second, the two men agree, with a slight difference in reasoning, on the complete separation of church and state. Third, they concur on the subject of religious tolerance, with Helwys being the more vocal advocate.

Though there was some debate between Helwys and Smyth on Christian magistrates, they were in agreement in their opposition to Christian magistracy. Neither man wanted the magistrate to play any part in encouraging true religion or in opposing false religion. Neither man gave the magistrate any authority in the church's decisions. Helwys said in *Mistery of Iniquity* that if Christ was alive in the flesh in England, then he would be subject to King James's civil authority. In the same manner, King James must be subject to Christ in His kingdom of the church. Helwys says that surely King James realizes that he should not "enter upon Christs kingdome, and appoint (or by his power suffer to be appointed) Lawes, Lords, Law makers over or in this kingdome of Christ."[164]

Helwys challenges Smyth's hesitancy on Christian magistrates. Helwys had no reservations in supporting the fact that the magistrate could be a Christian and maintain his office. In his *A Declaration of Faith*, he attempts to demonstrate the differences between his beliefs and those of Smyth. In article 24 of this confession, Helwys makes clear his support of a Christian magistrate. He says, "And therefore they may bee members off the Church of CHRIST, reteining their Magistracie, for no

---

[163]Smyth, *Works* 1:166.
[164]Helwys, *Mistery of Iniquity*, 41.

Holie Ordinance of GOD debarreth anie from being a member off CHRISTS Church."[165] Helwys supports a Christian being a magistrate as long as he is willing to be obedient to Christ. Helwys's view is similar to the Separatist view that the magistrate could be a Christian as long as he is willing to be under the discipline of the church. Helwys does not share Smyth's struggle with a Christian magistrate exacting revenge. In fact, he admits that the king has the right to take away all of his goods and even his life, if he disobeys the king's civil commands. He writes, "Thus doth God give our lord the King power to demaund and take what he will of his subjects, & it is to be yeilded him and to comaund what ordinance of man he will and wee are to obey it."[166] So, Helwys sees no problem with a Christian being a magistrate, but this position would give the magistrate no special authority in the church.

Helwys agrees with Smyth on the complete separation of church and state. Like Smyth, Helwys sees civil matters as a part of an earthly kingdom, where matters of faith are left for Christ and the spiritual kingdom. Helwys says, "Then let our lord the K. in all happines & prosperity sitt in his owne Princely throne of that mighty kingdome of Great Britanne. And let our lord Jesus Christ in power and Majesty sitt upon Davids throne, the throne of the kingdome of Israel."[167] While Smyth and Helwys both argue for a complete separation of the two realms, their arguments are put in different terms. Smyth defends the separation using the Mennonite idea that the two realms are of different natures. While Helwys alludes to the difference between the two realms, he also adds an argument incorporating the Christian magistrate. Though the king is supreme in temporal matters, if he is a Christian, he must be subservient to Christ in spiritual matters. Therefore, he cannot be both supreme and submissive in spiritual matters. Helwys writes:

[T]he kingdome of Christ, which is heavenly and endureth for ever: the sword of whose kingdome is spirituall, by the power of which sword onely, Christs subjects are to be ruled, and kept in obedience to namely

---

[165]Helwys, *A Declaration of Faith*, in Burgess, *John Smyth, the Se-Baptist*, 218; Lumpkin, *Baptist Confessions of Faith*, 123; McGlothlin, *Baptist Confessions of Faith*, 91-92.
[166]Helwys, *Mistery of Iniquity*, 40.
[167]Helwys, *Mistery of Iniquity*, 48.

the which sword our lord the K. must be kept in obedience himself, if he be a disciple of Christ, & a subject of Christs kingdome. And this takes away (without gainsaying) all the kingly power & authority of our Lord the K. in the kingdome of Christ, for he cannot be both a king & a subject, in one and the same kingdome: the kings understanding hart, will easily deserne this.[168]

Helwys concludes that even if a magistrate is a Christian, he should not exert authority in ecclesiastical matters. Practically, this means that Christ ordained each local church as his agents in matters of faith. Each church, not the magistrate, should be responsible for the appointment of ministers, administering the sacraments, and exercising church discipline. The magistrate should not attempt to make his subjects follow any particular faith.

Helwys and Smyth were also in basic agreement on religious tolerance. However, for Smyth, religious tolerance did not become the focus of discussion, with the possible exception of a few paragraphs of *The Last Booke*. He mentions religious tolerance in only a few articles of his English confession, while Helwys is willing to risk everything for it. Not only does Helwys write *Mistery of Iniquity* as a plea for religious tolerance, but he also tried to deliver it personally to King James. When this attempt failed, he included a handwritten note in the flyleaf asking for the king's attention to his work.

The idea that true religion could not be forced also found its way into Helwys's thinking. Smyth argued that all people must be responsible for their response to God's offer of the covenant. Helwys also argued that salvation was a personal matter for which the king was not accountable. This led to his argument that various religious groups were to be tolerated. He said, "For mens religion to God, is betwixt God and themselves; the King shall not answere for it, neither may the King be judg betwene God and man. Let them be heretikes, Turcks, Jewes, or whatsover it apperteynes not to the earthly power to punish them in the least measure."[169]

Helwys is more direct in calling for political religious tolerance than Smyth who called for liberty of conscience for all in the "Christian reli-

---

[168]Helwys, *Mistery of Iniquity*, 48.
[169]Helwys, *Mistery of Iniquity*, 69.

gion."[170] The difference can be seen when comparing the previous statement of Helwys with that of Smyth in an earlier article of *Propositions and Conclusions*.[171] There Smyth says, "That all penitent and faithful Christians are brethren in the communion of the outward church . . . be they Roman Catholics, Lutherans, Zwinglians, Calvinists, Brownists, Anabaptists, or any other pious Christians."[172] While his thought was progressive for his day, Smyth did not extend this toleration beyond Christianity nor did he appeal directly to a specific magistrate for a policy change as Helwys did.

Clearly, there are enough similarities in the areas of the separation of church and state and religious tolerance between these two men to conclude that Smyth could have influenced Helwys or that at least they both drew from the same source. However, it is also clear that Helwys did not agree with Smyth in the latter's questions about a magistrate being a Christian. Because of these questions, in a letter he attached to his *A Declaration of Faith*, Helwys charged Smyth with the error of denying the magistrate a place in the church. He saw this as a grave error on Smyth's part.[173]

Conclusion

As a Mennonite, Smyth advocated separation of church and state based on the conflict between the spiritual realm and the temporal realm. He also denied the Christian magistracy for the same reason.[174] Both of these, especially the former, indicate the influence on Smyth of Ries's statement in his "Short Confession." If the magistrate would not exert authority in matters of conscience then, according to Smyth, religious tolerance would result. Moreover, his tolerance of other expressions of the Christian faith

---

[170]Smyth, *Works* 2:748.

[171]The statement is absent from the published English version of the confession. However, a Dutch translation of this confession exists in the Mennonite archives in Amsterdam. Burgess refers to this translation as being made from an "earlier draft." The statement is found in that version of the confession; Burgess, *John Smyth, the Se-Baptist*, 252.

[172]Evans, *The Early English Baptists* 1:267.

[173]McGlothlin, *Baptist Confessions of Faith*, 92-93.

[174]Smyth, *Works* 2:696-97; Coggins, *John Smyth's Congregation*, 182-83.

also results from the idea that only a few things are essential to salvation. Other doctrines or practices are outward matters that do not disqualify another group from fellowship.[175] This idea also serves as evidence against Smyth's move to religious tolerance being a conclusion of his Separatist ideals. He understood the Separatists as being completely intolerant of other views and therefore exclusive in their fellowship.[176]

Helwys argued for the separation of church and state along the same lines as Smyth. He also opposed Christian magistracy. However, he supported a magistrate being a Christian, and also affirmed that a Christian magistrate could use the sword to punish evil. His position on religious tolerance was that all matters of religion should be left to the individual, not to the king. This tolerance should be available to all religious groups, including non-Christians.

Thomas Helwys carried on much of Smyth's views on church-state relations as well as other aspects of his thought. Through Helwys, and his successor John Murton, Smyth's legacy in church-state relations, as well as other aspects of his thought, continued in the General Baptists, even after they were back on English soil.

---

[175]Smyth, *Works* 2:752-53, 755-56.

[176]At this time, most of the English Reformed, whether Separatist or Puritan, did not distinguish between tolerance and liberty of conscience. During the mid-seventeenth century, this would change. Worden, "Toleration and the Cromwellian Protectorate," 202-10.

Conclusion

Both historical research and theological interpretation have been utilized to present a balanced analysis of the history and theology of John Smyth. Some of the insights gained from this study include the establishment of solid connections between Smyth and his Separatist predecessors and the definitive influence of the Mennonites on Smyth. The main elements of his thought developed in the context of his contemporary debates. Smyth's works often present these themes in combative tones due to the apologetic purpose of the works. The frequent shifts in Smyth's theology often angered his contemporaries and continue to fascinate modern scholars. A detailed discussion of Smyth's life and thought enables us to answer the questions about his purpose, his sources, and his influence on his successors.

Smyth's Pursuit of Truth

In observing Smyth's transitions from Puritan to Mennonite, one purpose becomes clear: a commitment to following his perception of the truth. Whatever the stage of his career, he had a tireless desire to pursue his concept of God's truth. When he perceived a truth Smyth followed it regardless of the consequences. For Smyth, faithful obedience was the only proper response to revealed truth. In his *Principles and Inferences*, Smyth invites his audience to determine truth and then for them to "let practise answerable to the truth follow thereupon."[1] This trait won him the admiration of his followers and the ridicule of his opponents.

In his preface to *Paralleles, Censures, Observations*, Smyth says that the book is addressed to "every one that seeketh after the truth in sincerity."[2] At the end of this work, in his letter to "A. S.," Smyth warns his readers that the truth brings dangerous results. He claims that the truth causes the true disciple to be a passenger as well as pilgrim. He writes:

---

[1] Smyth, *Works* 1:250.
[2] Smyth, *Works* 2:328. He makes similar statements in *Differences*, "To every true lover of the truth," and in "The Epistle to the Reader," "To every one that loveth the truth," 1:270 and 2:564, respectively.

> [W]e cal God to record to our soules that the evidence of the truth workinge uppon our consciences through the Lords unspeakeable mercie, even contrarie to our rebellious nature, hath mightelye convinced & violentlie caried us to this truth we professe & practise.[3]

Not only does this quotation provide a glimpse of Smyth's view of revelation, but also of his view of obedience as the proper response to revelation. Smyth says that God has led him to further truth in his doctrine ("professe") and in his actions ("practise").

These changes in belief and practice had led Smyth's opponents to charge him with inconsistency. In "The Epistle to the Reader" Smyth responds to these charges by commending theological consistency. He describes inconsistency in doctrine as a "folly or weaknes." However, he adds a pivotal statement:

> This must needs be true, (& we confesse it) if one condition be admitted, that the Religion which a man chandgeth be the truth: For otherwise to chandge a false Religion is commendable, & to retaine a false Religion is damnable.[4]

Smyth believed the transitions in his theology derived from further revelation. A contradiction of former positions inevitably results. In *The Differences of the Churches*, Smyth writes:

> And although in this writing somthing ther is which overtwharteth my former judgment in some treatises by mee formerly published: Yet I would intreat the reader not to impute that as a fault unto mee: rather it should be accounted a vertue to retract erroers.[5]

The willingness to accept and to act upon a new truth and to reject his former, incorrect position continued with Smyth even through his Mennonite stage. Smyth perceived that his Mennonite positions could also change. He does not give the impression that he had arrived at the culmination of his thought. In *The Last Booke*, Smyth says:

---

[3]Smyth, *Works* 2:547.
[4]Smyth, *Works* 2:564.
[5]Smyth, *Works* 1:271.

> Now I have in all my writings hithertoe, received instruction of others, and therfor have I so oftenn tyme beene accused of inconstancie: well, let them thinke of mee as they please, I professe I have changed, and shall be readie still to change, for the better.[6]

These remarkable words were spoken by Smyth from his deathbed. What was the reason for this intriguing characteristic of Smyth's thought? Why was he so willing to change? He gives the reason in his Separatist work, *The Differences of the Churches*, where he states:

> I do profese this . . . that I will every day as my erroers shalbe discovered confesse them > renounce them: For it is our covenant made with our God to forsake every evill way whither in opinion or practise that shalbe manifested unto us at any tyme.[7]

Obedience to God involved a willingness to accept changes in "opinion" (doctrine) and "practise." To this aspect of his covenant with God Smyth was faithful to his dying day.

Smyth's Mennonite Doctrine

Among the shifts that his pursuit of truth led Smyth to make, his acceptance of Mennonite doctrine was his greatest change. Smyth maintained many aspects of his theology when he moved from being a Puritan to a Separatist and from being a Separatist to a Baptist. However, when he became a Mennonite even the central aspects of his doctrine underwent radical change. He began to interpret the New Testament, as well as the Old Testament, typologically. Also, the theme of covenant, which had dominated many of his early writings, was rarely mentioned in his Mennonite works. His Christology took on many new spiritualist tendencies, even to the point of de-emphasizing the earthly life of Christ. While these areas of his doctrine experienced great change, his rejection of Reformed views and his acceptance of Mennonite views of church-state relations mark his most significant breaks with his early thought. Smyth

---

[6]Smyth, *Works* 2:752.
[7]Smyth, *Works* 1:271.

rejected the notion of original sin and also argued for religious tolerance. Both of these positions were in direct opposition to his early views.

There were certain facets of Smyth's theology before he became a Mennonite that might have made him more susceptible to accepting their views. However, his agreement with them was not caused by any existing aspect of his theology. He came to believe these views from the direct influence of Hans de Ries and the Waterlander Mennonites of Amsterdam. The influence of Hans de Ries on Smyth's theology has not been fully appreciated. Not only did Smyth accept Ries's views in the major areas of his thought, but he also used his English translation of Ries's "Short Confession" to explain Mennonite doctrine to his congregation. Smyth also used Ries's confession as a pattern for expressing his Mennonite views in *Corde Credimus*. Furthermore, Smyth later defended Ries's confession against the attacks of a Reformed critic. In his *Defence of Ries's Confession*, Smyth reveals his personal attachment to the confession by his use of the first person plural pronoun in several passages. His defense is often termed, "we confess," or that critic "objects against us."[8] To say that Smyth became a disciple of Hans de Ries is extreme, yet it may be the best way to capture the relationship between Smyth and Ries.

Smyth's Influence on the General Baptists

When Smyth petitioned the Waterlander Mennonites for union with their congregation, Thomas Helwys led a group to break away from Smyth's congregation. Although the historical connections between these two groups were cut by their schism and by the migration of Helwys's group back to England, the theological connections remained. It was Helwys, not Smyth, who eventually established the first General Baptist church on English soil. So, how could Smyth be considered the founder of the group? Through his theological legacy, Smyth continued to influence the English General Baptists for decades.

General Baptist John Murton's 1620 publication, *A Description of what God hath Predestinated* indicates Smyth's influence. In this work,

---

[8] *Fatemur*, Smyth, *Works* 2:696; *nobis objicit*, 2:706; see 2:696, 708, and 709 for other examples.

Conclusion \ 293

Murton presents a similar case to Smyth in defense of general atonement. In agreement with Smyth's statements, he writes, "I say, that what Adam had in creation, and lost by transgression, for himselfe and his posterity, that is restored through Christ, yea and more too."[9]

Another aspect of theology in which Smyth seems to have influenced future General Baptists is in his Baptist argument for the carnal and spiritual covenants. Murton again exemplifies this by using different terms, but the same argument. He says:

> The olde covenant, the Law, was made with the children of Abraham after the Flesh, & had circumcision in their flesh for a signe thereof. The new covenant the Gospell, is not made with both these seeds; but with one seed . . . they that are of the Faith of Abraham.[10]

Murton's argument about the old and new covenants echo Smyth's arguments about the carnal and spiritual covenants. Modern scholars, Underwood and Whitley, demonstrate the continuity of Smyth's thoughts of spiritual worship into late seventeenth-century General Baptist thought.[11] Underwood suggests that the General Baptists' views on Christology and their reluctance concerning military service could also be holdovers of Smyth's influence.[12]

Smyth's deep impact on the General Baptist tradition surfaced in his debate with Thomas Helwys. As Helwys urged Smyth to accept that their baptism was valid, he charged Smyth with a serious error. Smyth had moved forward to a new truth in their baptism, and Helwys saw his petition to the Mennonites as a return to an old position of successionism. Helwys and his group refused to take this backward step. Smyth had instilled in them the belief that they were to pursue truth relentlessly. After the revelation of truth, radical obedience was the only proper response to truth. In doing this, the General Baptists indeed carried on the spirit of their pioneer, John Smyth.

---

[9]Murton, *A Description of what God hath Predestinated*, 107.
[10]Murton, *A Description of what God hath Predestinated*, 146.
[11]Underwood, *A History of the English Baptists*, 53-54; Whitley, "Biography" 1:lxxxvii-lxxxviii.
[12]Underwood, *A History of the English Baptists*, 54-55.

Bibliography

Primary Sources

Ainsworth, Henry. *The communion of saincts.* Amsterdam: n.p., 1607.
_____. *Counterpoyson. A Reply to Four Books.* Amsterdam: n.p., 1608.
_____. *A defense of the Holy Scriptures, worship, and ministerie used in the Christian churches separated from Antichrist: against the challenges, cavils, and Contradicton of M. Smyth, in his book intituled The differences of the churches of the separation.* . . . Amsterdam: Giles Thorp, 1609.
_____. *An animadversion to Mr. Richard Clyftons Advertisement who under pretense of answering Chr. Lawnes book, hath published an other mans private letter, with Mr. Francis Iohnsons answer thereto: which letter is here justified; the answer thereto refuted; and the true causes of the lamentable breach that hath lately fallen out in the English exiled church at Amsterdam, manifested.* Amsterdam: Giles Thorp, 1613.
_____. *A Censure upon a dialogue of the Anabaptists.* Amsterdam: Giles Thorp, 1623.
_____, and Francis Johnson. *An Apologie or Defence of Brownists.* Amsterdam: n.p., 1604. Reprint: New York: Da Capo Press; Amsterdam: Theatrum Orbis Terrarum Ltd., 1970.
Arminius, James. *The Works of James Arminius.* Volumes 1 and 2, edited and translated by James Nichols. London: Longman, Hurst, Rees, Orme, Brown, and Green, 1825, 1828. Volume 3, edited and translated by William Nichols. London: Thomas Baker, 1875.
Baptist Confessions of Faith. See under William Lumpkin and William McGlothlin.
Barrow, Henry. *The Writings of Henry Barrow, 1587–1590.* Edited by Leland H. Carlson. London: George Allen & Unwin, 1962.
_____. *The Writings of Henry Barrow, 1590–1591.* Edited by Leland H. Carlson. London: George Allen & Unwin, 1966.
_____. *The Writings of John Greenwood and Henry Barrow, 1591–1593.* Edited by Leland H. Carlson. London: George Allen & Unwin, 1970.
Bernard, Richard. *Christian Advertisements and Counsels of Peace: Also dissuasions from the Separatists Schisme, commonly called Brownisme.* London: Felix Kyngston, 1608.

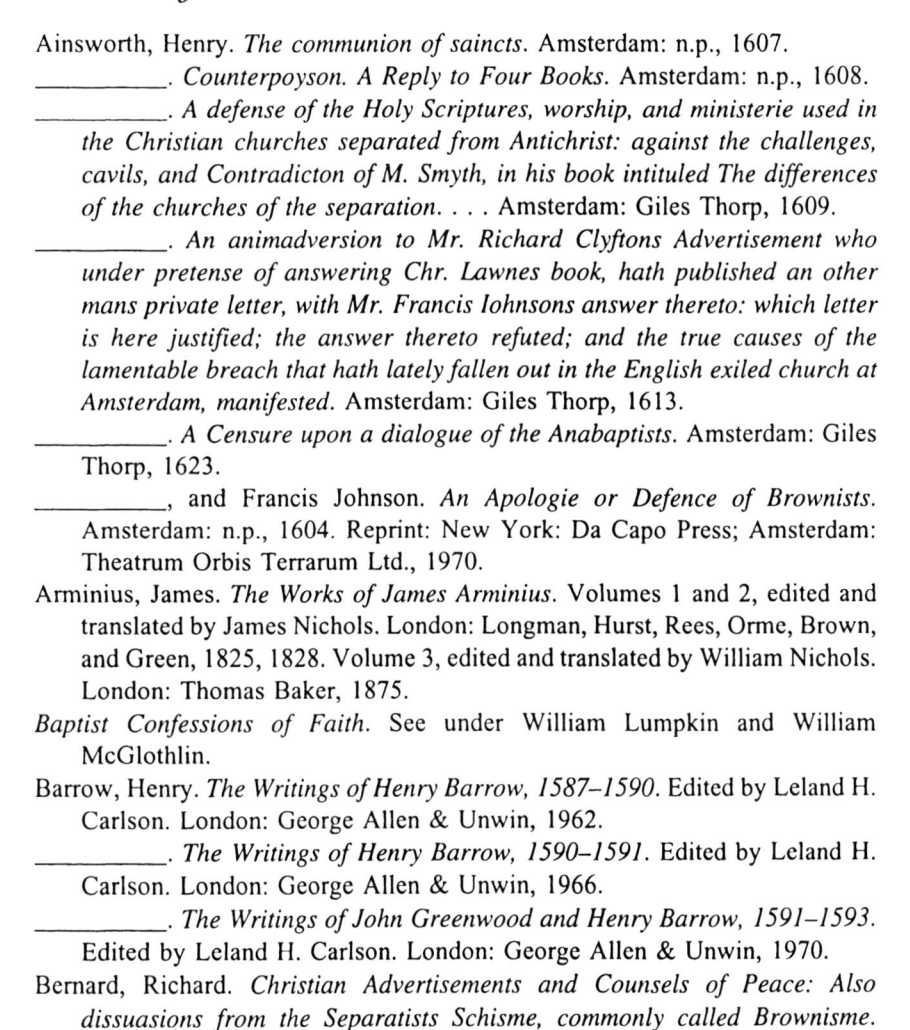

_____. *Plaine Evidences: The Church of England Is Apostolicall, the Separation Schismaticall.* London: printed by T. Snodman for Edward Weaver and William Welby, 1610.

The Boke of Common Prayer and Adminstracion of the Sacramentes, and Other Rites and Ceremonies in the Churche of England. London: Edwarde Whytchurche, 1552. Also see in *The First and Second Prayer-Books of King Edward the Sixth.* London: J. M. Dent & Sons, 1910.

Bradford, William. *Of Plymouth Plantation, 1620–1647.* New Edition. Edited by Samuel Eliot Morison. New York: Alfred A. Knopf, 1952. First edition published in 1856 under the title *History of Plimouth Plantation.*

Bromhead, Hughe, and Anne Bromhead. *A Letter.* N.p., 1609.

Browne, Robert. *The Writings of Robert Harrison and Robert Browne.* Edited by Albert Peel and Leland H. Carlson. London: George Allen & Unwin, 1953.

Burrage, Champlin. *The Early English Dissenters in the Light of Recent Research.* Two volumes. Cambridge: Cambridge University Press, 1912.

Busher, Leonard. *Religious Peace; or a Plea for Liberty of Conscience.* N.p., 1614.

Cartwright, Thomas. *Cartwrightiana.* Edited by Albert Peel and Leland H. Carlson. London: George Allen & Unwin, 1951.

Cheyney, Edward P. *Readings in English History Drawn from the Original Sources.* New York: Ginn & Co., 1922.

Clyfton, Richard. *The Plea for Infants and Elder People, concerning Their Baptisme.* Amsterdam: Gyles Thorp, 1610.

Documents of the Christian Church. Selected and edited by Henry Bettenson. London and New York: Oxford University Press, repr. 1957 of [1]1943. Second edition. London/Oxford/New York: Oxford University Press, 1963.

Foxe, John. *Acts and Monuments with a Life of the Martyrologist and Vindication of the Work.* Eight volumes. Edited by George Townsend. London: Seeley, Burnside, and Seeley, 1843–1849. Especially volume 8 (1849). Original: London: Seeley, Burnside, and Seeley, (2-8) 1837–1839, (1) 1841. Popularly known of course as *The Book of Martyrs,* and now *Foxe's Book of Martyrs.*

Greenwood, John. *The Writings of John Greenwood, 1587–1590,* edited by Leland H. Carlson. London: George Allen and Unwin, 1962.

_____. See also above, under Henry Barrow.

Hall, Joseph. *The Works of the Right Reverend Father in God, Joseph Hall.* Ten volumes. Edited by Josiah Pratt. London: C. Whittingham, 1808.

Harrison, Robert. See above, under Robert Browne.

Helwys, Thomas. *A Declaration of Faith of People Remaining at Amsterdam in Holland.* Amsterdam: n.p., 1611. Reprinted in Walter H. Burgess, *John*

Smyth, the Se-Baptist, Thomas Helwys and the First Baptist Church in England. London: James Clarke & Co., 1911.
_____. *An Advertisement or Admonition, unto the Congregations.* N.p., 1611.
_____. *A Short Declaration of the Mistery of Iniquity, 1612.* Edited by H. Wheeler Robinson. London: Kingsgate Press, 1935. Also see *A Short Declaration of the Mystery of Iniquity (1611/1612).* Edited and introduced by Richard Groves. Classics of Religious Liberty 1. Macon GA: Mercer University Press, 1998.
_____. and John Murton. *Objections Answered.* London: n.p., 1615. Reprint: New York: Da Capo Press; Amsterdam: Theatrum Orbis Terrarum, 1973.
Hetherington, John. *A Description of the Church of Christ, with her peculiar priuiledges, and also of her commons, and entercommoners with some oppositions and answers of defence, for the maintenance of the truth which shee prossesseth . . . Against Certaine Anabaptisticall and Erronious Opinons . . . Maintained and Practised By one Master John Smith. . . .* London: printed for Nathaniel Fosbrooke, 1610.
Hofmann, Melchior. *The Ordinance of God.* Edited and translated by George H. Williams. In *Spiritual and Anabaptist Writers.* Edited by George H. Williams and Angel M. Mergal. London: SCM Press, 1957.
Johnson, Francis. *An Answer to Maister H.[enry] Jacob His Defence of the Churches and Ministery of England.* Middelburgh, Holland: n.p., 1600.
_____. *A brief treatise . . . against two errours of the Anabaptists.* Amsterdam: n.p., 1609.
_____. *A short treatise concerning the words of Christ, Tell the Church.* Amsterdam: n.p., 1611.
_____. *A Christian Plea Conteyning three Treatises: The first, touching the Anabaptists, & others mainteyning some like errours with them. The second, touching such Christians, as now are here, commonly called Remonstrants or Arminians. The third, touching the Reformed Churches, with whom my self agree in the faith of the Gospel of our Lord Jesus Christ.* Amsterdam: n.p., 1617.
Johnson, George. *A discourse of some troubles in the banished English Church at Amsterdam.* Amsterdam: n.p., 1603.
Lumpkin, William Latane, editor. *Baptist Confessions of Faith.* Revised Edition. Valley Forge PA: Judson Press, 1969. First edition, 1959.
McGlothlin, William Joseph, editor. *Baptist Confessions of Faith.* Philadelphia and Boston: American Baptist Publication Society, 1911.
Murton, John. *A Description of what God hath predestinated.* London: n.p., 1620.

Peel, Albert, editor. *The seconde parte of a register: being a calendar of manuscripts under that title intended for publication by the Puritans about 1593, and now in Dr. Williams's Library, London.* Two volumes. Cambridge: Cambridge University Press, 1915.

Philips, Dirk. *The Writings of Dirk Philips.* Edited by William E. Keeney and others. Scottdale PA: Herald Press, 1992.

Philips, Obbe. *A Confession.* Translated by Christiaan T. Lievestro. In *Spiritual and Anabaptist Writers.* Edited by George H. Williams and Angel M. Mergal. London: SCM Press, 1957.

Piggott, Thomas. *The Life and Death of John Smyth.* N.p., 1613.

Plymouth church records 1620–1859. Volume 22. Boston: Publications of the Colonial Society of Massachusetts, 1920.

Ries, Hans de. "The First Waterlandian Confession of Faith." Translated by Cornelius J. Dyck. *Mennonite Quarterly Review* 36 (January 1962): 5-13.

_____. "The Middelburg Confession of Hans de Ries." Translated by Cornelius J. Dyck. *Mennonite Quarterly Review* 36 (April 1962): 147-61.

_____. "A Short Confession of Faith by Hans de Ries." Translated by Cornelius J. Dyck. *Mennonite Quarterly Review* 38 (January 1964): 5-19.

Robinson, John. *The Works of John Robinson, Pastor of the Pilgrim Fathers.* Three volumes. Edited by Robert Ashton. London: J. Snow, 1851.

Schaff, Philip, editor. *The Creeds of the Evangelical Protestant Churches.* Three volumes. London: Hodder & Stoughton, 1877.

Schwenckfeld, Caspar. *Corpus Schwenckfeldianorum.* Nineteen volumes. Edited by Chester David Hartranft et al. Leipzig: Breitkopf & Hartel, 1907-1965.

_____. *An Answer to Luther's Malediction.* Translated by George H. Williams and Selina Gerhard Schultz. In *Spiritual and Anabaptist Writers.* Edited by George H. Williams and Angel M. Mergal. London: SCM Press, 1957.

Scott, Thomas, ed. *The Articles of the Synod of Dort.* Harrisonburg VA: Sprinkle Publications, 1993.

Simons, Menno. *The Complete Writings of Menno Simons.* Edited by John Wenger. Scottdale PA: Herald Press, 1956.

Smyth, John. *The Works of John Smyth, Fellow of Christ's College, 1594–1598.* Two volumes. Tercentenary edition for the Baptist Historical Society. Edited with notes and biography by William Thomas Whitley. London: Cambridge University Press, 1915.

Underhill, Edward Bean, editor. *Tracts on Liberty of Conscience, 1614–1661.* London: J. Haddon, 1848.

_____. *Confessions of Faith and Other Public Documents Illustrative of the History of the Baptist Churches of England in the 17th Century.* London: Haddon, Brothers, and Company, 1854.

Williams, George Huntston, and Angel M. Mergal, editors. *Spiritual and Anabaptist Writers. Documents Illustrative of the Radical Reformation.* Library of Christian Classics 25. London: SCM Press, 1957. Philadelphia: Westminster Press, 1957.

Secondary Sources

Acheson, R. J. *Radical Puritans in England, 1550–1660.* London and New York: Longman Group, 1990.
Armitage, Thomas. *A History of the Baptists.* Revised Edition. New York: Bryan, Taylor, & Co., 1886.
Bangs, Carl. *Arminius: A Study in the Dutch Reformation.* Nashville and New York: Abingdon Press, 1971.
Blomberg, Craig, William W. Klein, and Robert L. Hubbard. *Introduction to Biblical Interpretation.* Edited by Kermit A. Ecklebarger. Dallas: Word Books, 1993.
Bogue, David, and James Bennett. *History of Dissenters, from the Revolution in 1688, to the Year 1808.* Four volumes. London: printed for the authors and sold by Williams and Smith, 1808–1812.
Brachlow, Stephen. "John Smyth and the Ghost of Anabaptism: A Rejoinder." *Baptist Quarterly* 30 (July 1984): 296-300.
_____. "The Elizabethan Roots of Henry Jacob's Churchmanship: Refocusing the Historiographical Lens." *Journal of Ecclesiastical History* 36 (April 1985): 228-54.
_____. "Puritan Theology and General Baptist Origins." *Baptist Quarterly* 31 (October 1985): 179-94.
_____. *The Communion of Saints. Radical Puritan and Separatist Ecclesiology, 1570–1625.* Oxford: Oxford University Press, 1988.
Brackney, William H. *The Baptists.* New York: Greenwood Press, 1988.
Burgess, Walter Herbert. *John Smyth, the Se-Baptist, Thomas Helwys and the First Baptist Church in England with Fresh Light upon the Pilgrim Fathers' Church.* London: James Clarke & Co., 1911.
_____. *John Robinson, Pastor of the Pilgrim Fathers. A Study of His Life and Times.* London: Williams & Norgate; New York: Harcourt, Brace & Howe, 1920. Alternate title: *The Pastor of the Pilgrims. A Biography of John Robinson.*
Carter, Alice Clare. *The English Reformed Church in Amsterdam in the Seventeenth Century.* Amsterdam: Scheltema & Holkema NV, 1964.
Christian, John T. *A History of the Baptists.* Nashville: Sunday School Board of the Southern Baptist Convention, 1922.

Clarke, Desmond M. *Church and State: Essays in Political Philosophy.* Cork: Cork University Press, 1984.
Clasen, Claus-Peter. *Anabaptism: A Social History, 1525–1618.* Ithaca NY: Cornell University Press, 1972.
_____. *The Anabaptists in South and Central Germany, Switzerland, and Austria.* Goshen: Mennonite Quarterly Review, 1978.
Coggins, James R. "The Theological Positions of John Smyth." *Baptist Quarterly* 30 (April 1984): 247-64.
_____. "A Short Confession of Hans de Ries: Union and Separation in Early Seventeenth-Century Holland." *Mennonite Quarterly Review* 60 (1986): 128-38.
_____. *John Smyth's Congregation: English Separatism, Mennonite Influence, and the Elect Nation.* Scottdale PA: Herald Press, 1991.
Collinson, Patrick. *The Elizabethan Puritan Movement.* London: Jonathan Cape, 1967. Berkeley: University of California Press, 1967.
Coolidge, John S. *The Pauline Renaissance in England.* Oxford: Clarendon Press, 1970.
Cramp, J. M. *Baptist History.* London: E. Stock, 1871.
Crosby, Thomas. *The History of the English Baptists from the Reformation to the Beginning of the Reign of King George I.* Four volumes. London: printed for and sold by the editor, 1738–1740. Facsimile reprint: Lafayette TN: Church History Research & Archives, 1979.
Daniélou, Jean, A. H. Couratin, and John Kent. *Historical Theology.* Harmondsworth: Penguin, 1969.
Davies, Horton. *Worship and Theology in England from Andrews to Baxter and Fox, 1603–1690.* Princeton NJ: Princeton University Press; London: Oxford University Press, 1975.
Deppermann, Klaus. "Melchior Hofmann: Contradictions between Lutheran Loyalty to Government and Apocalyptic Dreams." In *Profiles of Radical Reformers*, edited by Hans-Jürgen Goertz, 178-90. Scottdale PA: Herald Press, 1982.
_____. *Melchior Hofmann.* Translated by Malcolm Wren and edited by Benjamin Drewery. Edinburgh: T. & T. Clark, 1987.
Dosker, H. E. *The Dutch Anabaptists.* Philadelphia: Judson Press, 1921.
Dowley, T. "Baptists and Discipline in the 17th Century." *Baptist Quarterly* 24 (October 1971): 157-66.
Durnbaugh, Donald F. "Baptists and Quakers: Left-wing Puritans?" *Quaker History* 62 (Autumn 1973): 67-82.
Dyck, Cornelius J. "Hans de Ries: Theologian and Churchman: A Study in Second Generation Dutch Anabaptism." Ph.D. dissertation, University of Chicago Divinity School, 1962.

Ellis, Edward Earle. *The Old Testament in Early Christianity*. Tübingen: J. C. B. Mohr, 1991.
Estep, William R. *Anabaptist Beginnings*. Nieuwkoop: B. de Graaf, 1976.
_____. "Thomas Helwys: Bold Architect of Baptist Policy on Church-State Relations." *Baptist History and Heritage* 20/3 (July 1985): 24-34.
_____. *The Anabaptist Story*. Third Edition. Grand Rapids MI and Cambridge: Eerdmans, 1996.
Evans, Benjamin. *The Early English Baptists*. Volume 1. London: J. Heaton & Son, 1862. Facsimile repr.: Greenwood: Attic Press, 1977.
France, Richard T. *The Gospel according to Matthew. An Introduction and Commentary*. Tyndale New Testament Commentaries 1. Leon Morris, general editor. Grand Rapids MI: Eerdmans, 1985.
Friedmann, Robert. *The Theology of Anabaptism: An Interpretation*. Scottdale PA: Herald Press, 1973.
George, Timothy. *John Robinson and the Separatist Tradition*. National Association of Baptist Professors of Religion Dissertation Series 1. Macon GA: Mercer University Press, 1982.
_____. "Between Pacifism and Coercion: The English Baptist Doctrine of Religious Toleration." *Mennonite Quarterly Review* 58 (January 1984): 30-49.
_____. "Predestination in a Separatist Context: The Case of John Robinson." *Sixteenth Century Journal* 15 (1984): 73-85.
Goertz, Hans-Jürgen, editor. *Profiles of Radical Reformers*. Scottdale PA: Herald Press, 1982.
_____. *The Anabaptists*. Translated by Trevor Johnson. London and New York: Routledge, 1996.
Goldingay, John. *Models for Interpretation of Scripture*. Grand Rapids MI: Eerdmans, 1995.
Goppelt, Leonhard. *Typos. The Typological Interpretation of the Old Testament in the New*. Translated by Donald H. Madvig. Foreword by E. Earle Ellis. Grand Rapids MI: Eerdmans, 1982.
Grant, R. M. *The Letter and the Spirit*. London: SPCK, 1957.
Grant, Robert, with David Tracy. *A Short History of the Interpretation of the Bible*. London: SCM Press, 1984.
Greaves, Richard L., and Robert Zaller, editors. *Biographical Dictionary of British Radicals in the Seventeenth Century*. Three volumes. Brighton: Harvester Press, 1984.
Hawthorne, G. F. *Tradition and Interpretation in the New Testament*. Grand Rapids MI: Eerdmans, 1987.
Haykin, Michael A. G. *Kiffin, Knollys, and Keach*. Leeds: Reformation Today Trust, 1996.

Hillerbrand, Hans J. *Anabaptist Bibliography 1520–1630*. St. Louis: Center for Reformation Research, 1991.
Horst, Irvin B. *The Radical Brethren: Anabaptism and the English Reformation to 1558*. Nieuwkoop: B. De Graaf, 1972.
_____. "Menno Simons: The New Man in Community." In *Profiles of Radical Reformers*, edited by Hans-Jürgen Goertz, 203-13. Scottdale PA: Herald Press, 1982.
Hudson, Winthrop. "Who Were the Baptists?" *Baptist Quarterly* 16 (July 1956): 303-12.
Hudson, Winthrop and Gunnar Westin. "Who Were the Baptists?" (a reply). *Baptist Quarterly* 17 (April 1957): 53-55.
Hughey, John D. "Baptists and Religious Freedom." *Baptist Quarterly* 17 (April 1958): 249-55.
Hylson-Smith, Kenneth. *The Churches in England from Elizabeth I to Elizabeth II. Volume I. 1558–1688*. London: SCM Press, 1996.
Irwin, Joyce. "Embryology and the Incarnation: A Sixteenth-Century Debate." *Sixteenth Century Journal* 9 (1978): 93-104.
Ivimey, Joseph. *History of the English Baptists*. Four volumes. London: 1811-30.
Jones, Rufus M. *Mysticism and Democracy in the English Commonwealth*. New York: Octagon Books, 1965.
Jordan, Wilbur K. *The Development of Religious Toleration in England*. Four volumes. London: George Allen & Unwin, 1936.
Keeney, William E. *The Development of Dutch Anabaptist Thought and Practice from 1539 to 1564*. Nieuwkoop: B. de Graaf, 1968.
_____. "Dirk Philips, a Biography." In *The Writings of Dirk Philips*. Edited by William E. Keeney et al. Scottdale PA: Herald Press, 1992.
Kendall, R. T. *Calvinism and English Calvinism to 1649*. New Edition. Carlisle, Cumbria UK: Paternoster Press, 1997.
Klaassen, Walter, editor. *Anabaptism Revisited*. Scottdale PA: Herald Press, 1992.
Kliever, Lonnie D. "General Baptist Origins: The Question of Anabaptist Influence." *Mennonite Quarterly Review* 36 (October 1962): 291-321.
Knappen, Marshall M. *Tudor Puritanism*. Gloucester MA: Peter Smith, 1963.
Krahn, Cornelius. *Dutch Anabaptism: Origin, Spread, Life, and Thought (1450–1600)*. The Hague: Martinus Nijhoff, 1968.
Kraus, C. Norman. "Anabaptist Influence on English Separatists as seen in Robert Browne." *Mennonite Quarterly Review* 34 (January 1960): 5-19.
Lake, Peter. "Dilemma of the Establishment Puritan: The Case of Francis Johnson." *Journal of Ecclesiastical History* 29 (January 1978): 23-35.
Lamont, William M. *Godly Rule: Politics and Religion, 1603–1660*. London: Macmillan, 1969.

Lienhard, Marc. *The Origins and Characteristics of Anabaptism*. The Hague: Martinus Nijhoff, 1977.
Littell, Franklin H. *The Origins of Sectarian Protestantism*. New York: Macmillan Company, 1964.
Lyon, Thomas. *The Theory of Religious Liberty in England 1603–1639*. Cambridge: Cambridge University Press, 1937. Reprint: New York: Octagon Books, 1976.
McBeth, H. Leon. *English Baptist Literature on Religious Liberty to 1689*. New York: Arno Press, 1980.
_____. "Baptist Beginnings." *Baptist History and Heritage* 15/4 (October 1980): 36-41.
_____. *The Baptist Heritage*. Nashville: Broadman Press, 1987.
McCoy, Charles S. and J. Wayne Baker, *Fountainhead of Federalism: Heinrich Bullinger and the Covenantal Tradition*. Louisville: Westminster/John Knox Press, 1991.
McLaughlin, R. Emmet. *Caspar Schwenckfeld, Reluctant Radical*. New Haven CT and London: Yale University Press, 1986.
Maclear, James F. "The Birth of the Free Church Tradition." *Church History* 26 (June 1957): 99-131.
Maier, Paul L. *Caspar Schwenckfeld on the Person and Work of Christ*. Assen: Royal VanGorcum Ltd., 1959.
Manley, K. R. "John Rippon and Baptist Historiography." *Baptist Quarterly* 28 (July 1979): 109-24.
The Mennonite Encyclopedia. Volumes 1–4. Edited by Harold S. Bender and C. Henry Smith. Scottdale PA: Mennonite Publishing House; Hillsboro KS: Mennonite Brethren Publishing House; Newton KS: Mennonite Publishing Office, 1955–1959. Volume 5. Edited by Cornelius J. Dyck and Dennis D. Martin. Scottdale PA: Herald Press, 1990.
Mills, Susan J. "Sources for the Study of Baptist History." *Baptist Quarterly* 34 (April 1992): 282-96.
Mullet, Michael A. *Radical Religious Movements in Early Modern Europe*. London: George Allen & Unwin, 1980.
Nettles, Tom. "Smyth and Helwys: the Key to Anabaptist-Baptist Relations." *Southwestern Journal of Theology* 19 (Fall 1976): 101-104.
Nuttall, G. F. "Dissenting Churches in Kent before 1700." *Journal of Ecclesiastical History* 14 (October 1963): 175-89.
_____. "The English Separatist Tradition." *Baptist Quarterly* 24 (January 1972): 200-204.
Ozment, Steven E. *Mysticism and Dissent*. London: Yale University Press, 1973.
_____. *Reformation Europe: A Guide to Research*. St. Louis: Center for Reformation Research, 1982.

Pater, Calvin A. *Karlstadt as the Father of the Baptist Movements.* Toronto, Buffalo, London: University of Toronto Press, 1984.
Payne, Ernest A., editor. *Studies in History and Religion.* London: Lutterworth Press, 1942.
_____. *The Anabaptists of the Sixteenth Century and Their Influence in the Modern World.* London: Carey Kingsgate Press, 1949.
_____. "The Anabaptist Impact on Western Christendom." In *The Recovery of the Anabaptist Vision.* Edited by Guy F. Hershberger. Scottdale PA: Herald Press, 1957.
_____. *Radical Reformation Reader.* Concern Pamphlet Series 18. Scottdale PA: Concern, 1971.
Pearse, Meic. *The Great Restoration.* Carlisle, Cumbria UK: Paternoster Press, 1998.
Powicke, Fred J. *Henry Barrow, Separatist, and the Exiled Church of Amsterdam.* London: James Clarke & Co., 1900.
Ramm, Bernard L. *Protestant Biblical Interpretation. A Textbook of Hermeneutics.* Third revised edition. Grand Rapids MI: Baker Book House, 1970.
Rankin, Richard A. "The Use of Aristotelian Logic and Metaphysical Principles in the Ecclesiology of John Smyth." Ph.D. dissertation, Southwestern Baptist Theological Seminary, 1994.
Saito, Goki. "An Investigation into the Relationship between the Early English General Baptist and the Dutch Anabaptists." Th.D. dissertation, Southern Baptist Theological Seminary, 1974.
Schultz, Selina Gerhard. *Caspar Schwenckfeld von Ossig.* Norriston PA: Board of Publication of the Schwenckfelder Church, 1947.
Selement, George. "The Covenant Theology of English Separatism and the Separation of Church and State." *Journal of the American Academy of Religion* 41 (1973): 66-74.
Sellers, Ian. "Edwardians, Anabaptists, and the Problem of Baptist Origins." *Baptist Quarterly* 29 (July 1981): 97-112.
Shantz, Douglas. "The Place of the Resurrected Christ in the Writings of John Smyth." *Baptist Quarterly* 30 (January 1984): 199-203.
Snyder, C. A. *Anabaptist History and Theology.* Kitchener ON: Pandora Press, 1995.
Sprunger, Keith L. *The Learned Doctor William Ames.* Urbana, Chicago, London: University of Illinois Press, 1972.
_____. "English Puritans and Anabaptists in the Early 17th Century." *Mennonite Quarterly Review* 46 (April 1972): 113-28.
_____. *Dutch Puritanism.* Leiden: E. J. Brill, 1982.

_____. "Jan Theunisz of Amsterdam (1569-1638): Mennonite Printer, Pamphleteer, Renaissance Man." *Mennonite Quarterly Review* 68 (October 1994): 437-60.
Stassen, Glen H. "Anabaptist Influence in the Origin of Particular Baptists." *Mennonite Quarterly Review* 36 (October 1962): 322-48.
Sturzo, Luigi. *Church and State*. Volume 2. South Bend IN: University of Notre Dame Press, 1962.
Tennant, D.F. "Anabaptist Theologies of Childhood and Education, part 1, The Repudiation of Infant Baptism." *Baptist Quarterly* 29 (July 1982): 293-307.
_____. "Anabaptist Theologies of Childhood and Education, part 2." *Baptist Quarterly* 29 (October 1982): 356-73.
Tolmie, Murray. *The Triumph of the Saints: The Separate Churches of London 1616-1649*. Cambridge: Cambridge University Press, 1977.
Torbet, Robert G. *A History of the Baptists*. Revised Edition. Valley Forge: Judson Press, 1963.
Trueman, Carl R. *Luther's Legacy: Salvation and English Reformers*. Oxford: Clarendon Press, 1994.
Underwood, A. C. *A History of the English Baptists*. London: Baptist Union Publication Department, 1947.
Vedder, Henry C. *A Short History of the Baptists*. Revised Edition. Philadelphia: American Baptist Publication Society, 1907.
Venn, John and J. A. Venn. *The Book of Matriculations and Degrees*. Cambridge: University Press, 1913.
_____. *Alumni Cantabrigienses*. Four volumes. Cambridge: University Press, 1927.
Verheyden, A. L. E. *Anabaptism in Flanders, 1530-1650*. Translated by John Howard Yoder, Meintje Kuitse, and Jan Matthijssen. Scottdale PA: Herald Press, 1961.
Voolstra, Sjouke. "The Word Has Become Flesh. The Melchiorite-Mennonite Teaching on the Incarnation." *Mennonite Quarterly Review* 57 (1983): 155-60.
_____. "The Path to Conversion." *Anabaptism Revisited*. Edited by Walter Klaassen. Scottdale PA: Herald Press, 1992.
Walker, Michael J. "Relation of Infants to Church, Baptism, and the Gospel in 17th Century Baptist Theology." *Baptist Quarterly* 21 (April 1966): 242-62.
Watson, John H. "Baptists and the Bible." *Foundations* 16 (July-September 1973): 239-54.
Watts, Michael R. *The Dissenters*. Volume 1. *From the Reformation to the French Revolution*. Oxford: Clarendon Press, 1978.

Weigelt, Horst. "Caspar von Schwenckfeld: Proclaimer of the Middle Way." In *Profiles of Radical Reformers*, edited by Hans-Jürgen Goertz, 214-25. Scottdale PA: Herald Press, 1982.

White, Barrie (Barrington) Raymond. "A Puritan Work by Robert Browne." *Baptist Quarterly* 18 (July 1959): 109-17.

_____. "Frontiers of Fellowship between English Baptists, 1609-1660." *Foundations* 11 (July-September 1968): 244-56.

_____. *The English Separatist Tradition*. London: Oxford University Press, 1971.

_____. "Early Baptist Letters." *Baptist Quarterly* 27 (October 1977): 142-49.

_____. "The English Separatists and John Smyth Revisited." *Baptist Quarterly* 30 (October 1984): 344-47.

_____. *The English Baptists of the Seventeenth Century*. Revised Edition. Didcot Oxfordshire UK: Baptist Historical Society, 1996.

Whiteley, J. B. "Loughwood Baptists in the 17th Century." *Baptist Quarterly* 31 (October 1985): 148-58.

Whitley, William Thomas. "Biography." In volume 1 of *The Works of John Smyth, Fellow of Christ's College, 1594-1598*. London: Cambridge University Press, 1915.

_____. *A Baptist Bibliography, Volume 1 1526-1776*. London: Kingsgate Press, 1916.

Whittock, Martyn. "Baptist Roots: The Use of Models in Tracing Baptist Origins." *Evangelical Quarterly* 57 (1985): 317-26.

Williams, George H. *The Radical Reformation*. Third Edition. Kirksville MO: Sixteenth Century Journal Publishers, 1992.

Wood, A. S. *The Principles of Biblical Interpretation*. Grand Rapids Mi: Zondervan,1967.

Worden, Blair. "Toleration and the Cromwellian Protectorate." In *Persecution and Toleration*, edited by W. J. Shiels, 199-234. Padstow: Basil Blackwell, 1984.

Yarbrough, Slayden A. "The English Separatist Influence on the Baptist Tradition of Church-State Issues." *Baptist History and Heritage* 20/3 (July 1985): 14-23.

Index

Ainsworth, Henry, 15, 16, 18, 19, 52, 53, 54, 55, 57, 58, 59, 61, 64, 67, 68, 69, 72, 75, 76, 78, 81, 93, 206, 207, 251, 272
Amsterdam, 17, 18, 19, 33, 35, 37, 38, 42, 48, 49, 50, 51, 52, 53, 54, 56, 60, 66, 68, 69, 72, 75, 77, 84, 85, 89, 94, 95, 124, 128, 182, 187, 191, 206, 245, 252, 280, 287, 292
Anabaptist, 2, 3, 19, 20, 21, 22, 24, 25, 26, 31, 35, 43, 85, 100, 164, 184
Anabaptists, 1, 2, 3, 4, 18, 19, 20, 21, 22, 24, 27, 28, 29, 31, 40, 80, 84, 100, 123, 152, 184, 207, 209, 210, 253, 256, 259, 260, 272, 287
Ancient Church (Separatist), 18, 52, 53, 54, 57, 69, 71
Argumenta Contra Baptismum Infantum, 86, 90, 109, 122, 123, 152, 153, 155, 174, 175, 177, 191, 198, 199, 235
Arminius, Jacob, 42, 187, 188, 189, 190
atonement, limited, 36, 91, 167, 168, 169, 178, 191, 202, 205
Baro, Peter, 42, 88, 182, 185, 186
Barrow, Henry, 5, 13, 14, 15, 17, 18, 46, 56, 61, 64, 68, 78, 128, 131, 132, 133, 134, 135, 137, 142, 151, 248, 249, 250, 251, 258, 259, 269, 273
Bernard, Richard, 18, 42, 46, 59, 60, 61, 62, 63, 64, 65, 66, 67, 68, 78, 81, 93, 101, 114, 116, 118, 119, 121, 139, 142, 145, 161, 169, 170, 218, 258

Bevredigde Broederschap, 34, 37, 38, 193
Brachlow, Stephen, 89, 158, 161, 162, 163, 164, 182, 183, 196, 197, 267, 272, 273
Bradford, William, 4, 18, 46, 48, 49, 50, 51, 69, 136
Bright Morning Starre, The, 44, 99, 167, 168, 214, 216, 217, 220, 241
Browne, Robert, 4, 5, 9, 10, 11, 12, 13, 14, 15, 20, 56, 64, 112, 128, 129, 130, 131, 135, 137, 141, 160, 246, 247, 248, 258, 259, 268, 272
Calvinism, 21, 168
Calvinist. *See* Reformed
Cambridge University, 3, 4, 6, 7, 10, 13, 15, 18, 19, 41, 42, 43, 49, 60, 88, 168, 182, 187, 223, 268
Cartwright, Thomas, 10, 12, 18, 57, 140, 245, 246, 252
Character of the Beast, The, 76, 77, 78, 79, 80, 81, 85, 86, 90, 111, 149, 152, 153, 157, 160, 164, 165, 171, 172, 173, 174, 176, 181, 184, 220, 235, 260, 261
Christ's College, 6, 15, 16, 41, 42, 43, 168
Christian magistracy, 21, 38, 197, 260, 261, 262, 263, 266, 271, 274, 276, 277, 284, 287, 288
Christian magistrate, 82, 250, 254, 256, 259, 261, 263, 264, 265, 277, 284, 285, 288
Christology: King, Priest, and Prophet, 195, 212, 214, 215, 217, 218, 219, 220, 236, 237, 238, 241

church and state, 197, 245, 246, 248, 251, 253, 255, 256, 257, 260, 261, 265, 266, 267, 268, 269, 271, 272, 273, 274, 275, 276, 279, 281, 284, 285, 287, 288
Church of England. *See* England, Church of
Clyfton, Richard, 46, 48, 56, 58, 64, 67, 73, 75, 77, 78, 79, 81, 82, 83, 85, 100, 102, 117, 118, 119, 127, 145, 146, 148, 153, 156, 160, 162, 171, 172, 173, 186, 202, 220, 260
Coggins, James, 1, 19, 34, 36, 37, 38, 41, 47, 53, 60, 71, 83, 85, 89, 90, 98, 103, 112, 113, 120, 141, 153, 154, 158, 159, 160, 161, 162, 163, 178, 179, 183, 184, 186, 187, 188, 189, 191, 193, 196, 197, 200, 201, 212, 213, 223, 224, 225, 226, 227, 229, 230, 232, 235, 237, 238, 239, 241, 262, 263, 264, 279, 281, 282, 287
Corde Credimus, 87, 88, 91, 174, 175, 184, 186, 191, 193, 194, 197, 199, 228, 236, 292
covenant, 1, 5, 8, 9, 11, 12, 13, 16, 17, 18, 21, 26, 30, 46, 47, 57, 59, 62, 67, 68, 73, 75, 76, 78, 79, 80, 81, 82, 89, 90, 92, 99, 102, 106, 107, 111, 113, 114, 115, 118, 123, 126, 127, 128, 129, 130, 131, 132, 133, 134, 135, 136, 137, 138, 139, 140, 141, 142, 143, 144, 145, 146, 147, 148, 149, 150, 151, 152, 153, 154, 155, 156, 157, 158, 159, 160, 161, 162, 163, 164, 165, 172, 173, 182, 183, 196, 209, 214, 215, 219, 220, 232, 245, 248, 257, 275, 279, 280, 281, 286, 291, 293

conditional, 131, 133, 139, 142, 156, 158, 162, 164, 182, 183, 196
local church, 21, 47, 127, 128, 130, 133, 134, 135, 137, 138, 140, 144, 145, 151, 152, 158, 160, 165
covenant ecclesiology, 1, 139, 140, 141, 143, 144, 157, 159, 164, 182, 219
Defence of Ries' Confession, 89, 90, 102, 112, 113, 153, 154, 155, 177, 181, 183, 191, 194, 198, 200, 225, 226, 227, 229, 231, 234, 237, 238, 239, 240, 261, 262, 263, 264, 292
Differences of the Churches, The, 50, 52, 53, 54, 55, 56, 57, 58, 76, 102, 103, 108, 115, 169, 215, 230, 257, 290, 291
Dyck, Cornelius, 24, 34, 35, 36, 37, 38, 39, 40, 124, 192, 212, 227, 233, 253, 277
England, Church of, 5, 6, 7, 12, 13, 14, 15, 16, 44, 45, 47, 51, 52, 55, 59, 60, 61, 65, 67, 72, 74, 75, 76, 78, 79, 80, 102, 127, 128, 130, 131, 136, 137, 139, 142, 169, 170, 217, 218, 245, 246, 247, 249, 250, 266, 267, 280
First Waterlandian Confession, 36, 211, 253
Fitz, Richard, 7, 8, 9
Gainsborough, England, 45, 46, 48, 49, 56, 61, 136, 206
Gerrits, Lubbert, 26, 31, 33, 34, 37, 40, 87
Greenwood, John, 13, 14, 15, 17, 61, 64, 133, 250
Hall, Joseph, 51, 52, 63, 65, 74, 75, 76, 246
Harrison, Robert, 5, 10, 11, 12, 128

Index \ 309

Helwys, Thomas, 42, 46, 49, 60, 67, 72, 73, 81, 87, 93, 94, 95, 160, 167, 184, 185, 206, 221, 222, 223, 224, 225, 226, 227, 245, 272, 273, 282, 283, 284, 285, 286, 287, 288, 292, 293
Hofmann, Melchior, 22, 24, 25, 26, 27, 28, 33, 37, 209, 210, 224
John Smyth's congregation, 26, 34, 37, 38, 46, 49, 51, 52, 53, 54, 60, 77, 83, 87, 160, 193, 206, 254, 282, 292
Johnson, Francis, 5, 15, 16, 17, 18, 19, 42, 46, 47, 51, 52, 53, 54, 55, 56, 57, 58, 61, 64, 66, 69, 74, 75, 78, 103, 137, 169, 202, 251, 252
Last Booke, The, 67, 92, 93, 94, 156, 221, 223, 224, 225, 226, 227, 228, 233, 239, 242, 266, 270, 286, 290
Lincoln, England, 41, 43, 44, 45
Mennonite Christology, 209, 239
Melchiorite incarnational theory, 21, 27, 31, 33, 36, 92, 211, 214, 220, 221, 222, 223, 224, 225, 226, 227, 228, 229, 239, 240, 243
Mennonites, 1, 19, 20, 21, 25, 26, 27, 31, 33, 35, 37, 38, 40, 77, 78, 81, 83, 84, 85, 86, 87, 88, 89, 90, 104, 123, 124, 127, 167, 174, 182, 184, 185, 186, 187, 191, 193, 194, 196, 197, 207, 209, 211, 212, 222, 223, 224, 227, 242, 245, 253, 267, 268, 271, 275, 276, 278, 281, 282, 289, 291, 292, 293
"Middelburg Confession," 37, 253, 254, 277
Munter, Jan, 83, 95
Murton, John, 206, 207, 288, 292, 293
original sin, 16, 28, 33, 37, 44, 88, 91, 153, 154, 155, 156, 157, 162, 165, 167, 169, 170, 171, 172, 173, 174, 175, 176, 177, 180, 181, 183, 184, 186, 189, 190, 191, 195, 198, 200, 203, 204, 205, 209, 210, 232, 292
Paralleles, Censures, Observations, 59, 60, 61, 66, 67, 70, 76, 81, 93, 100, 101, 108, 110, 114, 116, 121, 139, 142, 158, 161, 164, 169, 218, 219, 257, 258, 289
Paterne of True Prayer, A, 44, 45, 66, 167, 168, 255, 256, 283
Philips, Dirk, 25, 26, 30, 31, 32, 33, 34, 209, 210, 211, 212
Plumbers' Hall congregation, 7, 13
predestination, 16, 37, 38, 42, 44, 88, 91, 139, 147, 148, 167, 168, 174, 179, 181, 184, 187, 188, 191, 195, 197, 199, 200, 204, 206, 207, 279
Principles and Inferences, 46, 47, 50, 52, 56, 117, 136, 137, 140, 144, 158, 169, 215, 219, 256, 289
Propositions and Conclusions, 91, 153, 154, 159, 180, 181, 186, 188, 189, 191, 192, 198, 199, 202, 206, 228, 231, 232, 234, 236, 238, 241, 261, 262, 264, 265, 277, 287
Puritans, 1, 2, 3, 6, 10, 18, 40, 55, 59, 61, 70, 89, 92, 127, 133, 139, 161, 162, 164, 168, 169, 180, 182, 196, 214, 216, 217, 218, 245, 246, 255, 267, 272, 273
Reformed, 16, 35, 36, 38, 42, 86, 88, 89, 91, 92, 103, 139, 147, 153, 154, 167, 168, 169, 170, 173, 174, 175, 177, 178, 180, 182, 183, 185, 186, 187, 190, 191, 193, 194, 196, 197, 199, 201, 202, 206, 207, 208, 209, 216, 226, 250, 281, 282, 291, 292
religious tolerance, 245, 248, 251, 256, 260, 261, 265, 266, 267, 268, 269,

272, 274, 276, 277, 279, 282, 283, 284, 286, 287, 288, 292
Ries, Hans de, 26, 33, 34, 35, 36, 37, 38, 39, 40, 87, 89, 123, 124, 125, 126, 167, 186, 192, 193, 194, 195, 196, 197, 199, 200, 207, 209, 211, 212, 213, 214, 222, 224, 226, 227, 228, 229, 231, 232, 233, 234, 237, 239, 240, 242, 243, 253, 254, 255, 264, 271, 272, 274, 276, 277, 281, 287, 292
Robinson, John, 12, 18, 46, 48, 49, 51, 52, 55, 57, 62, 64, 67, 68, 69, 70, 71, 73, 78, 81, 83, 202, 203, 204, 205, 206, 265, 269, 270, 272, 274
Schwenckfeld, Caspar, 22, 23, 24, 26, 27, 33, 38, 39, 209, 210, 233, 240, 243
Scrooby, England, 48, 49, 61, 71
Separatists, 1, 2, 3, 4, 5, 6, 7, 8, 9, 12, 14, 15, 16, 17, 18, 19, 20, 40, 42, 45, 46, 51, 52, 53, 55, 56, 59, 60, 61, 62, 63, 64, 65, 68, 71, 73, 74, 75, 76, 78, 79, 80, 83, 85, 89, 92, 102, 120, 127, 128, 129, 130, 131, 133, 134, 135, 136, 137, 139, 140, 145, 146, 147, 148, 151, 152, 160, 161, 162, 164, 180, 182, 183, 202, 208, 216, 245, 246, 248, 250, 251, 257, 258, 261, 267, 268, 270, 272, 273, 274, 275, 276, 280, 281, 283, 288
Shantz, Douglas, 158, 162, 163, 164, 219
"Short Confession" of Hans de Ries, 37, 38, 87, 89, 90, 124, 186, 192, 194, 207, 212, 213, 237, 254, 268, 272, 287, 292
Simons, Menno, 25, 26, 27, 28, 29, 30, 31, 32, 33, 34, 37, 86, 209, 210, 211, 212, 223

Smyth's baptism, 69, 72, 74, 77, 85
Socinian, 212, 277, 278
spiritual flesh, 107, 126, 213, 226, 227, 229, 230, 231, 232, 233, 234, 237, 238, 239, 242, 243
"True Confession, A," 16, 17, 134, 251, 252
Waterlander Mennonites, 21, 26, 33, 34, 35, 36, 37, 40, 84, 87, 90, 95, 124, 174, 207, 211, 292
White, B. R., 1, 3, 4, 6, 9, 12, 13, 18, 19, 41, 43, 46, 47, 49, 53, 73, 76, 77, 78, 84, 88, 93, 95, 130, 131, 137, 141, 157, 158, 159, 160, 162, 163, 164, 182, 186, 207, 272